Legal Executions in Delaware, the District of Columbia, Maryland, Virginia and West Virginia

AF776588

Also by Daniel Allen Hearn
and from McFarland

Legal Executions in New England: A Comprehensive Reference, 1623–1960 (1999; paperback 2008)

Legal Executions in Georgia: A Comprehensive Registry, 1866–1964 (2015)

Legal Executions in Illinois, Indiana, Iowa, Kentucky and Missouri: A Comprehensive Registry, 1866–1965 (2015)

Legal Executions in North Carolina and South Carolina: A Comprehensive Registry, 1866–1962 (2015)

Legal Executions in Delaware, the District of Columbia, Maryland, Virginia and West Virginia

A Comprehensive Registry, 1866–1962

Daniel Allen Hearn

McFarland & Company, Inc., Publishers
Jefferson, North Carolina

LIBRARY OF CONGRESS CATALOGUING-IN-PUBLICATION DATA

Hearn, Daniel Allen, 1958–
Legal executions in Delaware, the District of Columbia, Maryland, Virginia and West Virginia : a comprehensive registry, 1866–1962 / Daniel Allen Hearn.
p. cm
Includes index.

ISBN 978-0-7864-9540-5 (softcover : acid free paper) ♾
ISBN 978-1-4766-1825-8 (ebook)

1. Executions and executioners—Middle Atlantic States—History—Chronology. 2. Executions and executioners—Middle Atlantic States—Registers. I. Title.

HV8699.U6M5544 2015
364.660975'09041—dc23 2015019563

BRITISH LIBRARY CATALOGUING DATA ARE AVAILABLE

© 2015 Daniel Allen Hearn. All rights reserved

No part of this book may be reproduced or transmitted in any form or by any means, electronic or mechanical, including photocopying or recording, or by any information storage and retrieval system, without permission in writing from the publisher.

On the cover: John Hardy (center, facing camera) on gallows prior to his hanging on January 19, 1894 (West Virginia State Archives)

Printed in the United States of America

McFarland & Company, Inc., Publishers
Box 611, Jefferson, North Carolina 28640
www.mcfarlandpub.com

Contents

Cowardice wears many masks.
Failure to enforce the law is one of them.

Introduction

This book does not require a lengthy opening. It follows close upon the previously released *Legal Executions in North Carolina and South Carolina: A Comprehensive Registry, 1866–1962* (2015) and adheres to the same basic plan. The only real difference here is the addition of an appendix containing tentative lists of pre–1866 executions that I hope to explore more fully in a future volume. Even after a quarter-century of research, I only feel confident enough at this point to go to press with the post–Civil War era. Further investigation and additional years will be needed to ferret out what still awaits discovery.

One thing that I can state with certainty is that America's experience with capital punishment is more extensive than anyone previously imagined. The states of Maryland and Virginia in particular offer good examples of this. Neither state was squeamish about executing criminals (as their high body counts attest), but purported inventories thereof (most notably the so-called Espy File) have grossly underreported the actual tallies. Indeed, while the Espy File notes 309 legal executions in Maryland, my own research indicates more than 700 there. The disparity is even more pronounced in Virginia, where Espy reports 1,283 legal executions compared to more than 2,000 by my count. More than 80 legal executions in Virginia were missed by Espy during the post–Civil War period alone. Furthermore, it bears mentioning that so much of Virginia's recorded history has been lost to the ravages of time (especially for the colonial period) that if the full extent of the number of legal executions there were known, that total would probably be closer to 3,000.

As high as these numbers sound, they are also deceptive. This is because they represent only a small minority of the overall number of convicts who were sentenced to death. It was easy to receive a death sentence in a Maryland or Virginia court of law, since at one time virtually every felony known to jurisprudence was at least nominally a capital offense. It was, however, an entirely different matter for that sentence to be carried out. Pardons and commutations saved perhaps as many as 80 percent of those condemned to die. The gallows and the electric chair were mostly reserved for those deemed beyond reclamation. Nineteenth-century anti–death penalty activists called this "blessed executive clemency," but in reality it often masked something far grimmer. Those who were young and physically fit fared the worst of all, the premise being a simple one in the minds of so-called Progressives: *What will it profit the state to hang them when it can work them to death instead?* Hence as early as the 1770s and 1780s one finds the governors of Maryland and Virginia (among them Thomas Jefferson) commuting death sentences right and left in favor of involuntary servitude. White offenders and free persons of color who dodged the gallows through this means were made to break their backs digging the James River Canal. Untold numbers ultimately perished from work-related injuries like spinal damage, ruptures, hernias or "broken bellies," to use the vernacular of that time. Others were forced into front-line military service. It will never be known how many of them died in the fusillades and the shelling instead of with ropes around their necks, as originally intended.

The origin of this hypocrisy can be traced back even further to the year 1718, when an Act of Parliament virtually forced the colonies of Maryland and Virginia to accept entire shiploads of English jailbirds. A significant number of these "transport felons" had originally been sentenced to death for crimes committed in England but had had their sentences commuted to what was called "transportation to His Majesty's plantations," where they were worked like animals amid conditions akin to slavery. Many of them promptly reverted to their criminal ways upon reaching America. The result was an ever-worsening crime wave in the colonies as the eighteenth century wore on and the number of transport felons steadily increased. Benjamin Franklin complained bitterly about this "Tyburn Trash" being dumped on American shores. It was a contributing factor to the American Revolution, but one that history books seldom mention.

The next level was reached when Maryland and Virginia (and to a lesser extent Delaware) began to routinely commute the death sentences of condemned slaves. Execution was again reserved for the worst, but those attainted for crimes against property (such as burglary, robbery and horse stealing) mostly wound up in the hands of slave traders. There was nothing humanitarian about it. The motive was purely mercenary, since a healthy slave (unlike a free person) was regarded as a valuable head of livestock, especially if he or she had a certified skill like carpentry, smithing or weaving. The price for such a slave could range anywhere from $300 to $1,000 in gold, depending on their health and skill level. This was close to a fortune in those days, when a common laborer was lucky to earn $10 or $12 per month. The law mandated that the owner of a slave legally hanged for a capital crime was entitled to monetary compensation for the loss of such livestock (albeit human livestock), payable from the state or county treasury. This policy became increasingly burdensome to the government as the slave population rose, and more and more of them were held accountable for felonies in the County Courts of Oyer & Terminer. So from the 1770s onward it became more of an economy measure on the part of state government, rather than any purported humanitarian one, that resulted in the lessening of the law's severity in the cases of condemned slaves. Commutations surpassed executions at a steadily increasing ratio, not because of what Northern Liberals had to say, but because of that ubiquitous root of all evil called "money."

Critics of capital punishment naively hailed this change as "the enlightened alternative to the gallows," but it meant earthbound damnation for those actually affected by it. What happened to the recipients of this "mercy" is one of the true horror stories of American history. Many "reprieved" slaves were herded overland like cattle to places like North Georgia, where they were worked to death in the mines and quarries. Others were packed into squalid transport ships and sent to Louisiana, where a living death awaited them in the cane fields, with overwork, stifling humidity, poisonous snakes and yellow fever.

Fast-forward to the post–Civil War era and one sees the continued evolution of this twisted liberalism. Its cover name was the "Convict Lease System"—a quasi-legal form of slavery in which state Departments of Corrections leased prisoners to private and/or public contractors as a source of cheap labor. The cruelty, corruption and abuses of this "enlightened alternative to the gallows" comprise another American horror story that goes beyond the scope of this book, but those same evils were also direct and indirect results of Reformist pipe dreams that created more problems than they solved.

Governor Robert Lowry of Mississippi (during the 1880s) was an ardent proponent of this practice. He commuted eight out of every ten death sentences that came to his attention in order to maximize the labor pool on convict farms. Northern liberals adored Lowry for his disuse of capital punishment when in reality he was one of the most cynical men of the Jim Crow era.

Another fallacy recently brought to light concerns executions for crimes other than murder or rape. I had first begun to think about this as a high school student, when I noticed that almost every book and scholarly article that I read on the subject of capital punishment was written with an abolitionist slant. I got tired of reading political propaganda instead of history. I began to wonder if the propagandists who published such works were to at least some degree mountebanks who were overstating their case. Revisionist accounts had a lot of denunciatory things to say about executions for so-called "lesser offenses" or "Class B Felonies," as they are nowadays called. The sheer tone of their moralizing caused me to suspect that there was more to the story. Sure, a lot of criminals—both white and non-white—were executed for felonies other than murder and rape, but were they really punished in that way for being "lesser offenders" so much as they were for being *habitual* offenders? My subsequent research found that many of these "unfortunate victims of the *Bloody Code*" were in fact hardened criminals with records traceable all the way back to England. A disconcerting number of them (as already stated) had even been sentenced to death on one or more occasions only to push their luck beyond the limits of jurisprudential endurance. Recidivism, I found, had been a long-standing problem, and the only guaranteed way to prevent it was through meaningful law enforcement.

A good example of this soft-on-crime futility is the case of George Crowder. He made his first known appearance at the Old Bailey on October 18, 1769, telling their Lordships that he had recently come thence from Greenland. The charge against him was burglary, in that during the early morning hours of September 1, 1769, he and two co-defendants had broken into the house of a Hoxton victualer named John Risbrough and carried off clothing belonging to the daughter of that man: four linen shifts, two muslin aprons, two pairs of muslin ruffles and a black silk handkerchief. The thieves sold these items to a used clothing dealer who later testified against them. Sentence of the court: death by hanging. Crowder then spent the next six months sweating it out in the infamous "Condemned Hold" at Newgate Prison. He saw the dreaded Tyburn death wagon carry off no less than *eighteen* of his fellow prisoners during that time. Then, on April 25, 1770, something unexpected happened: the governor of Newgate announced to Crowder that "His Majesty has been graciously pleased to spare your life." The death sentence hanging over him had been commuted to fourteen years of transportation beyond the seas. Crowder resurfaced in the spring of 1776 at Perth Amboy in the soon-to-be State of New Jersey. It was there, during the last session of the New Jersey Supreme Court held under the old colonial system, that George Crowder once again stood convicted of burglary and had "the solemn sentence of death" passed upon him for a second time. However, Crowder had not yet run out of luck. He got free somehow and headed south. He turned up next at Baltimore in the spring of 1778 as a condemned convict for a third time. Crowder had robbed the storehouse of a Baltimore County merchant named Cumberland Dugan. He got caught and stood trial at the Baltimore Assizes. The verdict was "guilty" and the sentence was death by hanging. The governor of Maryland pardoned Crowder, possibly because he had no knowledge of his previous record. This slippery convict had wiggled free yet again. Next stop: Pennsylvania, where Crowder reportedly fell in with the notorious Doane Gang of Bucks County. This was a troublesome group of *banditti* who throughout the years of the American Revolution became the bane of Patriots and Loyalists alike. They thrived on the civil upheaval of that era, robbing, stealing and plundering their way in a wide geographical swath from the Raritan to the Susquehanna rivers. The full extent of Crowder's involvement is incalculable based on surviving records, but it was apparently substantial. The fall of 1781 saw him pop up again as a prisoner facing prosecution for a capital offense. This time the place was Philadelphia. The indictment charged that Crowder was one of a team of burglars who looted the mercantile firm of Mifflin, Butler & Company. The evidence in Crowder's case was not deemed sufficient and he squeaked free with a verdict of acquittal. The close call, however, did nothing to reform him. Crowder finally overplayed his hand in 1784, when he burglarized the house of a Mr. Turner in the Southwark District of Philadelphia. He was once again hauled before a court of law and made to answer for what he had done. This time the jury said "guilty as charged." A presiding judge put on the black cap and sentenced George Crowder to die on the gallows—for the *fourth* time. This death sentence stuck because the authorities could take no more. It then fell to the municipal hangman for the City and County of Philadelphia to mete out his own brand of permanent rehabilitation to the likes of George Crowder. He did so very effectively on October 16, 1784. Three prior death sentences had been pronounced only to be set aside by Reformist influence. The fourth time was a tough sell even for the Reformers. Nor was Crowder unique. There are many such examples of this failed liberalism.

The information in this book was obtainable for me because experience had taught me where to look. The first rule was to never take second-hand accounts at their word because they are prone to error. The same holds true for Internet resources, because computers are only as good as the people who program them. For me, there were no acceptable substitutes for original archival materials. I scoured court records, newspapers, prison records, death certificates, gubernatorial records, and financial records to either confirm or disprove the occurrence of legal executions. I also checked foreign sources for snippets culled from lost issues of certain American newspapers like the *Virginia Gazette*. I even hunted through cemeteries to find names and dates on gravestones. Research for this book was done in the following places: the Delaware State Archives, the Delaware Historical Society in Wilmington and the University of Delaware Microfilm Collection, as well as the Maryland

State Archives, the Baltimore Public Library Newspaper Collection, the Library of the United States Naval Academy and the University of Maryland Historical Collections. In addition, the West Virginia University Library in Morgantown proved indispensible for information regarding that state, as did the Virginia State Archives in Richmond for the pre–1866 years. Visits to numerous county courthouse records rooms were also necessary in both of the Virginias. The "Library of Virginia" (both new and old buildings) was where I spent many a day poring over archival material. The Alderman Library at the University of Virginia became my hideaway for weeks at a time and was where I developed a need for reading glasses after hundreds of hours studying old newspapers on microfilm. Research for the District of Columbia proved the easiest, since its newspaper coverage is extensive. The Microform Department at Yale University's Sterling Memorial Library filled that need (and also took a toll on my vision). The staff of these institutions were and are dedicated professionals, without whom it would have been impossible to complete this fact-finding task. I owe them all a gigantic debt of gratitude and will always hold them in the highest regard.

Delaware

(in chronological order)

1866

William Manluff (black, age 25). *Aggravated Burglary.* The crime was committed on 3/29/1866 in New Castle County. Executed for a nocturnal break-in at the house of 71-year-old Hannah Febiger Jones (white, a widow), during which he assaulted the homeowner's maidservant (Lizzie Griffith, white, age about 20) with intent to commit rape, slashing her about the head and neck with a knife. He was hanged for this crime at New Castle on July 20, 1866. Source: *Delaware Gazette*, 4/3/66 (2:3) and 7/24/66 (2:3); *Delaware State Journal & Statesman*, 3/30/66 (2:4), 4/3/66 (2:3) and 7/24/66 (2:3).

1867

Andrew Armstrong (white, age 46). *Murder.* The crime was committed on 5/19/1866 in New Castle County. Uxoricide. Executed for the hatchet killing of 36-year-old Caroline Douglass Armstrong (white), her body having also been illegally buried in a pig pen. Motive: domestic row. The homicidal husband was hanged at New Castle on February 8, 1867. Source: *Smyrna (DE) Times*, 5/30/66 (2:2) and 6/6/66 (2:4); *Delaware Republican*, 2/11/67 (2:5); *Delaware Tribune*, 2/14/67 (4:3). See also 1860 U.S. Census (New Castle Co., DE), which notes both parties.

1870

Joshua Jones (black, age 17) and **Louis Carpenter** (black, age 21). *Rape.* Their crime was committed on 9/17/1869 in New Castle County. Indecent assault on the person of 43-year-old Mary "Molly" Meredith (white), she having been attacked in her own home and in the presence of her children. The rapists were hanged at New Castle on February 4, 1870. Source: *Baltimore Sun*, 2/5/70 (1:5); *Delaware Tribune*, 2/10/70 (1:6); *New York Herald*, 2/5/70 (5:5); *The World* (NYC), 2/5/70 (1:6).

Edward Darnell Young (black, age 19). *Murder.* The crime was committed on 3/16/1870 in Kent County. Executed for the murder of roughly 50-year-old Thomas Hogan (white), who had been knocked unconscious with a fence rail, dragged into a pond and there forcibly held with his face submerged until he drowned. Motive: highway robbery. The killer was hanged at Dover on June 24, 1870. Source: *Delaware Tribune*, 3/31/70 (2:6) and 6/30/70 (3:2); *Baltimore Sun*, 6/25/70 (1:5); *The World* (NYC), 6/25/70 (5:4).

Benjamin Johnson (black, age 33). *Rape.* The crime was committed on 7/5/1870 in Sussex County. Serial rapist. Specifically executed for an indecent assault on the person of 28-year-old Charlotte Fletcher (white). He was hanged at Georgetown on December 16, 1870. Source: *Middletown (DE) Transcript*, 7/16/70 (2:4) and 12/24/70 (2:3); *Delaware Tribune*, 12/22/70 (3:2). See also 1870 U.S. Census (Sussex Co., DE), which notes both parties.

1872

Andrew Clark (black, age 41). *Rape.* The crime was committed on 12/30/1871 in New Castle County. Serial rapist. Specifically executed for an indecent assault on the person of 14-year-old Martha Rakes (black). He was hanged at New Castle on July 12, 1872. Baltimore and Philadelphia newspapers erroneously reported that the sexual assault victim in this case was a white girl. Source: *Wilmington (DE) Every Evening*, 1/4/72 (3:1) and 7/12/72 (3:2). See also 1870 U.S. Census (New Castle Co., DE), which notes the miscreant.

1873

William Dennis (black, age 20). *Rape.* The crime was committed on 3/27/1872 in New Castle County. Indecent assault and physical mutilation of 26-year-old Mary Thompson (white), she having barely survived. The rapist was legally hanged at New Castle on January 24, 1873. Source: *New York Times*, 1/25/73 (1:3); *Wilmington (DE) Every Evening*, 3/28/72 (3:3), 6/8/72 (3:2) and 1/24/73 (3:2). See also 1870 U.S. Census (New Castle Co., DE), which notes the female party.

Joseph Burton (black, age 23). *Rape.* The crime was committed on 3/24/1873 in Sussex County. Executed for indecently assaulting 14-year-old Hannah Lank (white). The rapist was legally hanged at Georgetown on June 20, 1873. Source: *Middletown (DE) Transcript*, 3/29/73 (2:2) and 6/28/73 (2:4); *Wilmington (DE) Every Evening*, 6/20/73 (4:3); *New York Herald*, 6/21/73 (8:1).

1877

John Rhodes (black, age 24). *Murder.* The crime was committed on 4/21/1877 in New Castle County. Executed for the murder of James Temple (black, age not recorded), who had been bludgeoned with a stick and his throat cut to make sure that he was dead. Motive: rivalry for a female. The killer was hanged at New Castle on September 21, 1877. Source: *Wilmington (DE) Every Evening*, 4/23/77 (1:4) and 9/21/77 (1:4).

1878

Samuel Chambers (black, age 34) and **George Collins** (black, age 19). *Rape.* Their crime was committed on 8/15/1877 in New Castle County. Indecent assault on the person of 32-year-old Mary Catherine Smith (white), known to some as "Kate O'Toole," under circumstances that were deemed sufficiently aggravated to warrant their execution. They were hanged at New Castle on March 22, 1878. Source: *Wilmington (DE) Every Evening*, 11/26/77 (4:1) and 3/22/78 (1:3); *New York Herald*, 3/22/78 (6:1).

1882

James Redden, alias "James R. Loat" (black, age 19). *Rape.* The crime was committed on 2/23/1882 in New Castle County. Indecent assault on the person of 14-year-old Sarah Jane Purse (white). The rapist was legally hanged at New Castle on August 25, 1882. Source: *Wilmington (DE) Every Evening*, 2/25/82 (3:3) and 8/25/82 (1:3); *Baltimore Sun*, 8/26/82 (5:7). See also 1880 U.S. Census (New Castle Co., DE), which notes the ages and the name variations of both parties.

1886

Charles Robinson (black, age 33). *Rape.* The crime was committed on 10/3/1885 in New Castle County. Executed for an indecent assault on the person of 21-year-old Ella F. Gardner (white), the wife of Orson Gardner. Further details are withheld out of deference to the victim's descendants. The rapist was hanged at New Castle on April 16, 1886. Source: *Wilmington (DE) Every Evening*, 10/5/85 (3:2) and 4/16/86 (3:1); *Smyrna (DE) Times*, 10/7/85 (2:5). See also Black Bird Hundred (New Castle Co.), birth cert. no. 34 (dated 5/24/83), which notes Mrs. Gardner as a young mother.

1888

Charles Henry Riedel (white, age 36). *Murder.* The crime was committed on 9/17/1887 in New Castle County. Executed for the handgun slayings of 37-year-old Lena Riedel and 7-year-old Wilhelm Riedel (both white), his wife and son, respectively. Motive: despondency. He was hanged at New Castle on August 10, 1888. Source: *Wilmington (DE) Every Evening*, 9/17/87 (3:1), 9/19/87 (4:3) and 8/10/88 (3:1); *Baltimore Sun*, 8/11/88 (5:7).

1891

Jesse Proctor (black, age 35) and **Frederick Young** (black, age 17). *Murder.* Their crime was committed on 8/28/1890 in Kent County. Both executed for the murder of 82-year-old Stephen Lindsay (black), who was bludgeoned with a stick, beaten, kicked and stomped to death. Motive: mugging. The killers were hanged at Dover on February 13, 1891. Source: *Wilmington (DE) Every Evening*, 8/30/90 (3:1) and 2/13/91 (3:1).

Shakespeare Reeves, alias "Jacob Storker" (black, age 32). *Rape.* The crime was committed on 9/28/1890 in New Castle County. Executed for indecently assaulting 10-year-old Grace Clark (white), a felony that was further aggravated by the fact that he was a knowing spreader of venereal disease. This rapist was hanged at New Castle on March 6, 1891. Source: *Wilmington (DE) Every Evening*, 10/3/90 (4:1) and 3/6/91 (3:1).

James Thoroughgood (black, age 22). *Rape.* The crime was committed on 1/25/1891 in Kent County. Indecent assault on the person of 8-year-old Louisa Gertrude Huffington (black), the victim having been left permanently disabled. This rapist was hanged at Dover on August 7, 1891. Source: *Wilmington (DE) Evening Journal*, 8/7/91 (3:1).

1897

Edward Wright (black, age 19). *Murder.* The crime was committed on 7/30/1896 in New Castle County. Executed for the handgun slaying of 23-year-old Ida Crummell (black). Motive: jilted lover. He was hanged at New Castle on January 1, 1897. Source: *Wilmington (DE) Evening Journal*, 7/31/96 (1:5) and 1/1/97 (1:5). See also 1880 U.S. Census (New Castle Co., DE), which notes the victim, plus the census for King and Queen Co., VA, which notes the killer's correct age and origin.

Thomas Willis (black, age 23). *Murder.* The crime was committed on 5/4/1896 in New Castle County. Baby killer. Executed for the deliberate drowning of 1-year-old Callie Willis (black, his infant daughter), whose tiny body was subsequently torn apart by dogs. Motive: unwanted paternity. He was hanged at New Castle on February 19, 1897. Source: *Wilmington (DE) Evening Journal*, 5/25/96 (1:2), 5/28/96 (1:5) and 2/19/97 (1:3).

James M. Gordy (white, age 29). *Murder.* The crime was committed on 3/10/1897 in Sussex County. Uxoricide. Executed for the murder of 33-year-old Mary Estelle Gordy (née Lewis), she having been pushed out of a rowboat and then battered to death with a wooden oar. Motive: bunco. Gordy was also the prime suspect in the untimely deaths of his father (Peter B. Gordy), his first wife and their infant child, all of whom reportedly died after swallowing drinks that he had prepared for them. He was hanged at Georgetown on June 11, 1897. Source: *Wilmington (DE) Evening Journal*, 3/13/97 (1:2), 3/15/97 (1:4), 3/16/97 (1:6) and 6/11/97 (1:3).

1904

John Joiner (black, age 26). *Murder.* The crime was committed on 1/4/1904 in New Castle County. Executed for the murder of 23-year-old John R. Taylor (black), who was battered to death with an iron bar. Motive: robbery. The killer was hanged at New Castle on September 2, 1904. Source: *Wilmington (DE) Evening Journal*, 1/4/04 (1:3), 1/9/04 (7:4), 2/22/04 (1:5) and 9/2/04 (1:4). See also State of Delaware death cert. nos. 66830 and 69639, plus New Castle County Register of Deaths (1904), pgs. 126 and 249.

1907

William Archer (black, age 22). *Murder.* The crime was committed on 9/17/1906 in New Castle County. Executed for the handgun slaying of 28-year-old Ida Elizabeth Spires (black). Motive: lovers' quarrel. The killer was hanged at New Castle on January 11, 1907. Source: *Wilmington (DE) Evening Journal*, 9/18/06 (1:1) and 1/11/07 (1:7).

Lewis Johns (black, age 28). *Murder.* The crime was committed on 7/17/1906 in New Castle County. Executed for the murder of 24-year-old Arameda "Minnie" Jones (black), she having been battered to death with a wrought iron stove leg. Motive: jealous lover. Johns was hanged at New Castle on January 25, 1907. Source: *Wilmington (DE) Evening Journal*, 7/18/06 (1:5) and 1/25/07 (1:7).

1911

Reese Roberts (black, age 36). *Murder.* The crime was committed on 8/20/1910 in New Castle County. Executed for the murders of 71-year-old Robert Casey, Jr. and 65-year-old Ann Cloud Casey (white, a married couple), who were clubbed to death in their beds. Motive: burglary. The killer was hanged at New Castle on July 14, 1911. Source: *Wilmington (DE) Evening Journal*, 8/20/10 (1:1), 8/22/10 (1:1), 8/24/10 (1:1), 8/30/10 (1:1) and 7/14/11 (1:7). See also 1910 U.S. Census (New Castle Co., DE), which notes all parties.

1915

Peter Krakus (white, age 24). *Murder.* The crime was committed on 3/6/1915 in New Castle County. Specifically executed for the handgun slaying of 31-year-old Francis Xavier Tierney (white), a Wilmington police officer. Motive: resisting arrest. Additionally confirmed to have been a fugitive from Connecticut at that time and to have also been an active participant in a sensational double murder that had been committed there on 2/8/1915 during the course of a home invasion. The victims in that case were 54-year-old the Rev. Joseph Zebris (white, a Roman Catholic priest) and 36-year-old Iva Gilmanaitis (white, his female housekeeper) under circumstances of extreme atrocity. Krakus was hanged at New Castle on May 14, 1915. His accomplice, Bernard Montvid (white, age 23), met an identical fate in Connecticut on August 6, 1915. Source: *Wilmington (DE) Evening Journal*, 3/6/15 (1:6), 3/8/15 (1:7) and 5/14/15 (1:3); *Front Page Detective*, 10/43. See also Daniel Allen Hearn, *Legal Executions in New England* (McFarland, 1999), 332–33.

1917

Adam Argust (black, age 33), **William Prettyman** (black, age 28) and **Webster Purnell** (black, age 35). *Murder.* Their crime was committed on 9/23/1916 in Sussex County. All three were executed for the murder of 38-year-old Zadoc B. Parker, also known as "Harry Parker" (black), who was severely beaten before being slashed to death with a razor; his body was later dumped in a canal. Motive: whorehouse brawl. The killers were tried in Sussex County but then sent to the New Castle Workhouse, where they were hanged on September 28, 1917. Source: *Wilmington (DE) Every Evening*, 9/28/17 (1:1); *Wilmington (DE) Evening Journal*, 9/29/16 (11:3), 3/10/17 (2:5) and 9/28/17 (1:3). See also 1910 U.S. Census (Sussex Co., DE), which notes the victim as "Harry Parker."

1918

Samuel Gangas (white, age 23). *Murder.* The crime was committed on 7/22/1916 in New Castle County. Executed for the killing of 20-year-old Catherine Bodiska (white; surname also given as "Bodjeska"), she having been shot with a handgun and then mutilated with a butcher knife. Motive: thwarted lover gone berserk. Gangas was hanged at New Castle on January 11, 1918. Source: *Wilmington (DE) Evening Journal*, 7/24/16 (1:1), 7/25/16 (15:2), 7/26/16 (1:4) and 1/11/18 (1:1).

1920

Ernest Thomas (black, age 21). *Rape.* The crime was committed on 7/22/1920 in New Castle County. Indecent assault on the person of 58-year-old Emma Talley (white), she having also been beaten unconscious. This rapist was hanged at New Castle on November 26, 1920.

Source: *Wilmington (DE) Evening Journal*, 7/23/20 (1:1) and 11/26/20 (1:6).

Lemuel Price (black, age 28). *Murder.* The crime was committed on 11/13/1919 in New Castle County. Cop killer. Executed for the handgun slaying of 41-year-old Thomas L. Zebley (white). Motive: resisting arrest. Price died on the gallows at New Castle on December 3, 1920. Source: *Wilmington (DE) Evening Journal*, 11/13/19 (1:6), 11/14/19 (1:6) and 12/3/20 (1:8).

1926

Harry Butler (black, age 21). *Rape.* The crime was committed on 1/21/1926 in Sussex County. Indecent assault on the person of 12-year-old Eleanor Steinmetz (white), she having suffered a fractured skull in addition to vulvovaginitis. The rapist was hanged at Georgetown on February 26, 1926. Source: *Wilmington (DE) Evening Journal*, 1/22/26 (1:7) and 2/26/26 (1:1).

1927

Carl Asbury Skinner (black, age 27). *Rape.* The crime was committed on 4/4/1927 in Sussex County. Indecent assault on the person of 85-year-old Julia A. Bennett (white), she having been attacked in her own home. The rapist was hanged at Georgetown on May 27, 1927. Source: *Wilmington (DE) Evening Journal*, 4/5/27 (1:6) and 5/27/27 (1:1).

1930

Louis Galvano (white, age 21). *Murder.* The crime was committed on 12/24/1929 in New Castle County. Executed for the handgun slaying of 24-year-old Arthur C. Cline (white). Motive: highway robbery. The killer was hanged at New Castle on March 28, 1930. Source: *Wilmington (DE) Evening Journal*, 12/27/29 (1:7) and 3/28/30 (1:8).

Theodore Russ (black, age 24). *Rape.* The crime was committed on 2/23/1930 in New Castle County. Indecent assault on the person of 21-year-old Mary Kemp Reed (white), she having been attacked in her own home. The trial was held in Kent County, but Russ was hanged at the New Castle Workhouse on August 22, 1930. Source: *Wilmington (DE) Evening Journal*, 2/24/30 (1:7) and 8/22/30 (1:1).

1935

John C. Morgan (white, age 53). *Murder.* The crime was committed on 12/15/1934 in Kent County. Executed for the murder of 61-year-old Dominique J. Pierre (white male), the victim having been beaten to death with an automobile crank. Motive: land acquisition. Morgan also confessed to a second murder: that of 57-year-old Frank Foster (white), a man of the same vicinity who had vanished in July 1933. Foster's remains were located on December 21, 1934, when Morgan told authorities where to look. He was hanged at Dover on April 12, 1935. Source: *Journal Every Evening* (Wilmington, DE), 12/18/34 (1:1) and 4/12/35 (1:1); *Master Detective*, 7/46.

May Hitchens Carey (white, age 45) and **Howard Carey** (white, age 20)—mother and son. *Murder.* Their crime was committed on 11/7/1927 in Sussex County. Both were hanged for the murder of 55-year-old Robert H. Hitchens (white), who had been battered with a club and a sledgehammer before being finished off with a handgun. Motive: insurance fraud. The killers were executed at Georgetown on June 7, 1935. Many published accounts of this case incorrectly said that May Carey was the only white woman to be legally hanged in Delaware. Actually, she was just the first in living memory. Several others had met their ends that way during the eighteenth century. Source: *Sussex Countian* (Georgetown, DE), 12/14/34 (1:1) and 6/7/35 (1:6); *Real Detective*, 9/35; *Daring Detective*, 10/35; *Master Detective*, 2/46; *Front Page Detective*, 2/54.

1936

George Scott (black, age 26). *Murder.* The crime was committed on 7/12/1936 in New Castle County. Executed for the handgun slaying of 23-year-old Elbert Paul, also known as "Edward Paul" (black). Motive: rivalry for a female. The killer was hanged at New Castle on November 20, 1936. Source: *Journal Every Evening* (Wilmington, DE), 7/13/36 (13:5) and 11/20/36 (1:4).

1937

Isaiah Opher (black, age 36). *Murder.* The crime was committed on 8/10/1936 in New Castle County. Child killer. Executed for the handgun slaying of 13-year-old Isabelle Robinson (black). Motive: attempted sexual assault. The killer was hanged at New Castle on January 8, 1937. Source: *Journal Every Evening* (Wilmington, DE), 8/11/36 (1:2) and 1/8/37 (1:3).

Joseph Nelson (black, age 36). *Murder.* The crime was committed on 3/28/1937 in Sussex County. Executed for the ax murder of 51-year-old Carrie Lethel (black female). Motive: drunken row. Nelson was hanged at Georgetown on June 4, 1937. Source: *Journal Every Evening* (Wilmington, DE), 3/30/37 (6:5); *Sussex Countian* (Georgetown, DE), 4/22/37 (1:8) and 6/4/37 (1:8). See also 1937 State of Delaware death cert. no. 1234, which erroneously gives the victim's name as "Carrie Nelson" due to the mistaken perception that the parties were a married couple instead of common-law co-habitators.

1941

Curnel Robinson (black, age 34). *Rape.* The crime was committed on 8/21/1940 in New Castle County. Serial rapist. Specifically executed for an indecent assault on the person of a 15-year-old white female (name withheld), whom he knowingly infected with syphilis. Robinson had a long record of similar offenses (and deliberate infections) committed against girls of his own ethnicity. He was hanged at New Castle on January 14, 1941. Source: *Journal Every Evening* (Wilmington, DE), 8/22/40 (1:1) and 1/14/41 (1:4). See also Delaware Governors Papers (1940), record group 1302.7, File R, Inmate File No. 31465 (New Castle Workhouse), Delaware State Archives, plus F.B.I. file no. 506376.

1942

Ralph Ernest (white, age 32). *Rape.* The crime was committed on 6/24/1941 in New Castle County. Executed for an indecent assault on the person of a 6-year-old white female (name withheld) under circumstances that made clemency unthinkable. This rapist was hanged at New Castle on January 9, 1942. Source: *Journal Every Evening* (Wilmington, DE), 6/25/41 (3:3), 11/18/41 (18:1) and 1/9/42 (1:3).

1945

Anderson Butler (black, age 22). *Rape.* The crime was committed on 7/29/1945 in New Castle County. Indecent assault on the person of a 12-year-old white female (name withheld), whom he knowingly infected with syphilis. This rapist was hanged at New Castle on December 7, 1945. Source: *Journal Every Evening* (Wilmington, DE), 7/30/45 (11:1), 10/2/45 (13:1) and 12/7/45 (1:2). See also Inmate File no. 67020 (New Castle Workhouse), Delaware State Archives, plus F.B.I. file no. 4408396.

1946

Forest Sturdivant (black, age 34). *Murder.* The crime was committed on 11/17/1945 in Sussex County. Executed for the handgun slaying of 65-year-old George Leslie Polk (black). Motive: heated argument. The killer was hanged at Georgetown on May 10, 1946. Source: *Sussex Countian* (Georgetown, DE), 11/22/45 (1:3) and 5/16/46 (4:1).

District of Columbia

(in chronological order)

Note: Most previously published execution lists for this jurisdiction contain erroneous entries in the years 1864, 1889 and 1933. They comprise the names of five men (Hendricks, Pollard, Gordon, Green and Lowry) whose death sentences were commuted.

1871

James Grady (white, age 32). *Murder.* The crime was committed on 10/6/1870. Executed for the murder of 75-year-old Fanny Faulkner (white), she having been literally raped to death. Motive: burglary and sexual assault. The killer was hanged on March 24, 1871. Source: *Evening Star* (Washington, D.C.), 3/24/71 (4:2).

1872

George Jenkins (black, age 24). *Murder.* The crime was committed on 5/14/1872. Uxoricide. Executed for the murder of 20-year-old Lavinia Boston Jenkins (black), she having been hacked to death with a meat cleaver. Motive: marital discord. The killer was hanged on October 31, 1872. Source: *Evening Star* (Washington, D.C.), 10/31/72 (4:2).

Barney Woods (white, age 37). *Murder.* The crime was committed on 8/12/1872. Executed for the shotgun slaying of 47-year-old Samuel M. Cheeseman (white). Motive: disgruntled employee. The killer was hanged on December 6, 1872. Source: *Evening Star* (Washington, D.C.), 12/6/72 (4:2). See also 1870 U.S. Census (Orange Co., NY), which notes the murdered man.

Charles Johnson (black, age 32). *Murder.* The crime was committed on 9/28/1872. Uxoricide. Executed for the murder of 28-year-old Jane Eliza Johnson (black), she having been slashed to death with a razor. Motive: a heated argument about their home furnishings. The killer was hanged on December 10, 1872. Source: *Evening Star* (Washington, D.C.), 12/10/72 (4:2).

1873

Thomas Wright (black, age 21). *Murder.* The crime was committed on 12/24/1872. Executed for the murder of 40-year-old Samuel Rogerski (a Polish Jew), who was battered beyond recognition with a spade. Motive: robbery. The killer was hanged on June 6, 1873. Source: *Evening Star* (Washington, D.C.), 6/6/73 (1:4).

Henry Young, alias "Charles Williams" (black, age 27). *Murder.* The crime was committed on 3/29/1873. Executed for the murder of 24-year-old Amos Franklin Hahn (white), the victim having been blackjacked (slung shot) and otherwise clubbed to death. Motive: mugging. The killer was hanged on November 28, 1873. Source: *Evening Star* (Washington, D.C.), 11/28/73 (4:4). See also *Marriages of Shenandoah County, Virginia, 1850–1882*, compiled by Duane Borden and Jeannette Ritenour (privately published), 29, which notes Hahn's correct name and age.

1880

James Madison Wyatt Stone (black, age 33). *Murder.* The crime was committed on 10/5/1878. Uxoricide. Executed for the murder of 29-year-old Alberta Pitcher Stone (black), she having been slashed to death with a razor. Motive: marital estrangement. The drop tore the killer's head off at the gallows of the District of Columbia Jail on April 2, 1880. Source: *Evening Star* (Washington, D.C.), 10/7/78 (4:2) and 4/2/80 (1:4); *Washington Post*, 10/7/78 (1:1) and 4/3/80 (3:1). See also DC death cert. no. 17655.

Joseph Bedford, alias "Joe Neverson," alias "Babe Bedford" (black, age 19) and **Edward Queenan** (black, age 18). *Murder.* Their crime was committed on 1/7/1880. Both were executed for the murder of 22-year-old George Philip Hirth (white), the victim having been blackjacked by means of a stone wrapped in a handkerchief and his face kicked in almost beyond recognition. Motive: mugging. The killers were hanged on November 19, 1880. Source: *The Agitator* (Wellsboro, PA), 1/20/80 (2:2); *Evening Star* (Washington, D.C.), 11/19/80 (1:1). See also 1880 U.S. Census (Washington, D.C.), which notes the culprits.

1882

Charles Guiteau (white, age 39). *Murder.* The crime was committed on 7/2/1881. Presidential assassin. Executed for the fatal wounding of 49-year-old James Abram Garfield (white, the twentieth president of the United States), who succumbed to his injuries on September 19, 1881. Motive: probably deranged. Guiteau was hanged on June 30, 1882. Source: *Evening Star* (Washington, D.C.), 6/30/82 (1:1).

1883

Charles Shaw (black, age 19). *Murder.* The crime was committed on 1/16/1881. Sororicide. Executed for the murder of 22-year-old Susannah Shaw Carter (black), she having been bludgeoned with a rock. Motive: he resented her for implying that he had told a lie. Shaw was hanged on January 19, 1883. Source: *Evening Star* (Washington, D.C.), 1/17/81 (1:4), 1/21/81 (4:3), 1/28/81 (4:4) and 1/19/83 (1:3). See also 1880 U.S. Census (Washington, D.C.), which notes the victim.

1885

John Langster (black, age 20). *Murder.* The crime was committed on 9/9/1884. Cop killer. Executed for the handgun slaying of 42-year-old John H. Fowler (white). Motive: attempt to escape from custody. Langster was hanged on May 15, 1885. Source: *Daily Gazette* (Fort Wayne, IN), 9/10/84 (1:2); *Evening Star* (Washington, D.C.), 5/15/85 (1:5). See also 1880 U.S. Census (Washington, D.C.), which notes the murdered officer.

1886

Richard Lee (black, age 32). *Murder.* The crime was committed on 11/23/1885. Uxoricide. Executed for the handgun slaying of 30-year-old Mary Powell Lee (black). Motive: marital estrangement. The killer was hanged on April 30, 1886. Source: *Washington Post*, 11/24/85 (4:2); *Evening Star* (Washington, D.C.), 11/24/85 (3:6) and 4/30/86 (1:5).

Louis Sommerfield (white, age 49). *Murder.* The crime was committed on 11/20/1885. Executed for the handgun slayings of 52-year-old Christina Sommerfield and 43-year-old Gottlieb Eisenbaum (both whites), his wife and son-in-law, respectively. Motive: family problems. The killer was hanged on April 30, 1886. Source: *Evening Star* (Washington, D.C.), 4/30/86 (1:5). See also 1880 U.S. Census (Washington, D.C.), which notes all parties.

Antonio Nardello (white, age 22). *Murder.* The crime was committed on 7/28/1885. Executed for the murder of 50+-year-old Carmine Rotunno (white male), who was slashed to death with a razor. Motive: robbery. Nardello also confessed to two other murders: the December 19, 1884, handgun slaying of Antonio Baldo (white, age not recorded) in Cecil County, MD, and the fatal stabbing of another white man known only as "the Italian Blacksmith" (age not recorded) at Baltimore in April of that same year, both for the purpose of robbery. Nardello was hanged for the DC homicide on May 28, 1886. Source: *Washington Post*, 8/2/85 (2:1) and 8/3/85 (1:6); *Evening Star* (Washington, D.C.), 8/3/85 (4:2), 5/27/86 (4:2) and 5/28/86 (3:7).

1889

Nelson Colbert (black, age 22). *Murder.* The crime was committed on 10/3/1888. Executed for the handgun slaying of 74-year-old Philip Wentzell (white). Motive: obnoxious drunk. The killer was hanged on May 17, 1889. Source: *Evening Star* (Washington, D.C.), 5/17/89 (3:4). See also 1880 U.S. Census (Westmoreland Co., PA), which notes Wentzell.

1890

Benjamin Hawkins (black, age 28). *Murder.* The crime was committed on 3/14/1889. Uxoricide. Executed for the fatal stabbing of 26-year-old Cora Hawkins (black). Motive: infidelity on her part. The cuckold was hanged on May 29, 1890—possibly to show that "the unwritten law" regarding a husband's right to kill a cheating wife, was a myth. Source: *Washington Post*, 3/15/89 (1:5) and 5/30/90 (8:2); *Evening Star* (Washington, D.C.), 5/29/90 (5:5).

1893

Howard Schneider (white, age 24). *Murder.* The crime was committed on 1/31/1892. Executed for the handgun slayings of 22-year-old Amanda Hamlink Schneider and 21-year-old Frank Hamlink (both white), his wife and brother-in-law, respectively. Motive: family problems. The killer was hanged on March 17, 1893. Source: *Evening Star* (Washington, D.C.), 3/17/93 (1:1). See also 1880 U.S. Census (Washington, D.C.), which notes the gunman.

1894

Thomas Crumpton (black, age 42). *Murder.* The crime was committed on 6/9/1893. Executed for the handgun slaying of 24-year-old David Shanklin (black). Motive: feud between neighbors. The killer was hanged on April 27, 1894. Source: *Evening Star* (Washington, D.C.), 4/27/94 (8:2).

1895

James Travers (black, age 28). *Murder.* The crime was committed on 11/19/1894. Executed for the murder of 20-year-old Lena Gross (black), she having been slashed to death with a razor. Motive: lovers' quarrel. The killer was hanged on July 19, 1895. Source: *Evening Star* (Washington, D.C.), 11/20/94 (2:3) and 7/19/95 (1:7); *Washington Post*, 7/20/95 (3:1). See also 1880 U.S. Census (Washington, D.C.), which notes Lena Gross and her progeny.

Joseph Beam (white, age 44). *Murder.* The crime was committed on 12/22/1894. Executed for the handgun slaying of 35-year-old Annie Goetz Leahy (white—his stepdaughter), she having also been viciously stomped on as she lay dying. Motive: obnoxious drunk. The killer was hanged on July 26, 1895. Source: *Washington Post*, 12/23/94 (1:3) and 7/27/95 (2:2); *Evening Star* (Washington, D.C.), 7/26/95 (1:7). See also 1880 U.S. Census (Washington, D.C.), which notes Beam.

1896

John Harris (black, age 23). *Murder.* The crime was committed on 7/4/1895. Executed for the handgun slaying of 35-year-old Matthew Spruell (black). Motive: the killer suspected that the decedent had been ogling his wife. Harris was hanged on February 14, 1896. Source: *Evening Star* (Washington, D.C.), 7/5/95 (12:4) and 2/14/96 (1:7); *Washington Post*, 7/5/95 (2:2) and 2/15/96 (2:2).

Irvin Ford (black, age 30). *Murder.* The crime was committed on 5/4/1896. Executed for the fatal stabbing of 16-year-old Elsie A. Kreglo (white). Motive: attempted sexual assault. The killer was hanged on June 26, 1896. Source: *Evening Star* (Washington, D.C.), 6/26/96 (1:3); *Ft. Wayne (IN) News*, 6/26/96 (1:3); *Washington Post*, 6/27/96 (2:2). See also 1880 U.S. Census (Adams Co., PA), which notes Miss Kreglo as a baby.

1899

William Strathers (black, age 24). *Murder.* The crime was committed on 10/15/1897. Executed for the hatchet killing of 26-year-old Rosa Talbot (black). Motive: lovers' quarrel. The killer was hanged on May 5, 1899. Source: *Evening Star* (Washington, D.C.), 10/15/97 (16:2) and 5/5/99 (1:5); *Washington Post*, 5/6/99 (2:2).

Charles Winston (black, age 27). *Murder.* The crime was committed on 12/13/1897. Uxoricide. Executed for the handgun slaying of 31-year-old Emma Winston (black). Motive: suspected infidelity. The killer was hanged on May 5, 1899. Source: *Evening Star* (Washington, D.C.), 12/13/97 (2:3) and 5/5/99 (1:5); *Washington Post*, 12/14/97 (3:1) and 5/6/99 (2:2).

Edward Smith (black, age 46). *Murder.* The crime was committed on 11/15/1897. Executed for the hatchet murder of 32-year-old Edmonia Jackson (black). Motive: she would not be lured away from her husband. This killer was hanged on May 12, 1899. Source: *Washington Post,* 11/20/97 (1:6) and 5/13/99 (9:1); *Evening Star* (Washington, D.C.), 5/12/99 (1:5). See also 1899 DC death cert. no. 124957.

George William Horton (white, age 49). *Murder.* The crime was committed on 6/24/1898. Executed for the murder of 31-year-old Jane Nicholson (white), she having been slashed to death with a pocket knife. Motive: lovers' quarrel. The killer was hanged on December 8, 1899. Source: *Evening Star* (Washington, D.C.), 6/25/98 (11:2) and 12/8/99 (1:5); *Washington Post,* 6/25/98 (1:6) and 12/9/99 (2:2).

1900

Benjamin Snell (white, age 57). *Murder.* The crime was committed on 8/6/1899. Child killer. Executed for the murder of 13-year-old Lizzie Weisenberger (white), she having been slashed to death with a razor. Motive: she had reported the killer for sexually molesting her. Snell was hanged on June 29, 1900. Source: *Evening Star* (Washington, D.C.), 8/7/99 (3:1); *Washington Post,* 8/7/99 (1:1) and 6/30/00 (2:1).

Nelson Vale (black, age 69). *Murder.* The crime was committed on 1/14/1900. Executed for the handgun slaying of 29-year-old Alexander Jackson (black). Motive: rivalry for a female. The killer was hanged on July 6, 1900. Source: *Washington Post,* 1/15/00 (2:1) and 7/7/00 (11:1). See also 1900 U.S. Census (Washington, D.C.), which notes Vale, and 1880 U.S. Census (Baltimore, MD), which notes the victim as a minor.

Frank William Funk (white, age 22). *Murder.* The crime was committed on 6/23/1898. Executed for the hatchet murder of 73-year-old William H. Brooks (white). Motive: robbery and home invasion. Funk was hanged on November 9, 1900. Source: *Washington Post,* 6/24/98 (1:4), 6/25/98 (3:3), 8/17/99 (1:5) and 11/10/00 (2:1).

1902

Elijah Chapman (black, age 30). *Murder.* The crime was committed on 1/1/1902. Executed for the fatal stabbing of 25-year-old Ida Simms (black). Motive: lovers' quarrel. The killer was hanged on May 23, 1902. Source: *Washington Post,* 1/2/02 (2:3) and 5/24/02 (10:1).

1903

John St. Clair (black, age 35). *Murder.* The crime was committed on 4/16/1902. Executed for the handgun slaying of 24-year-old Daisy Madre (black). Motive: lovers' quarrel. The killer was hanged on January 30, 1903. Source: *Evening Star* (Washington, D.C.), 4/16/02 (11:3); *Washington Post,* 4/17/02 (12:1) and 1/31/03 (10:3).

Benjamin Hill (white, age 58). *Murder.* The crime was committed on 11/8/1902. Uxoricide. Executed for the handgun slaying of 41-year-old Carrie Marsden Hill (white). Motive: feelings of inadequacy. Hill was hanged on July 24, 1903. Source: *Washington Post,* 11/9/02 (2:1), 11/13/02 (2:2) and 7/25/03 (2:1). See also 1900 U.S. Census (Washington, D.C.), which notes both parties.

1904

John Wesley Burley (black, age 45). *Rape.* The crime was committed on 7/14/1903. Indecent assault on the person of 4-year-old Adeline Taylor (black) under circumstances that prompted President Theodore Roosevelt to call this case and others like it the reason why lynching had become so common in that era. Burley was known to have also committed two similar offenses. He was hanged on August 26, 1904. Source: *Washington Post,* 7/15/03 (4:7) and 8/27/04 (2:5); *Baltimore Sun*, 8/9/04 (4:1) and 8/27/04 (2:7).

1905

Augustus Shaffer (white, age 39). *Murder.* The crime was committed on 8/22/1903. Uxoricide. Executed for the murder of 31-year-old Katherine Ivey Shaffer (white), she having been slashed to death with a razor. Motive: acrimonious divorce. The killer was hanged on February 10, 1905. Source: *Washington Post,* 8/23/03 (2:4) and 2/11/05 (2:5). See also 1900 U.S. Census (Washington, D.C.), which notes the female party.

1906

William Walter Hamilton (black, age 28). *Murder.* The crime was committed on 6/20/1904. Executed for the strangulation killing of 27-year-old Mary Butler, known to some as "Lizzie Lyman" (black). Motive: lovers' quarrel. The strangler was hanged on February 2, 1906. Source: *Washington Post*, 6/22/04 (8:7) and 2/3/06 (12:4).

Charles Edward Grant (black, age 20). *Murder.* The crime was committed on 12/16/1905. Executed for the fatal stabbing of 20-year-old Eva Barnes (black), she having succumbed to her wound on 1/20/1906. Motive: lovers' quarrel. The killer was hanged on November 16, 1906. Source: *Washington Post*, 4/3/06 (2:4) and 11/17/06 (13:1); *Evening Star* (Washington, D.C.), 11/16/06 (10:2). See also 1906 DC death cert. no. 170412, as well as 1900 U.S. Census (Washington, D.C.), which notes the female party.

1907

William Burge (black, age 29). *Murder.* The crime was committed on 1/27/1905. Uxoricide. Executed for the handgun slaying of 19-year-old Daisy Jordan Burge (black). Motive: she had sought to leave him. Burge was hanged on April 23, 1907. Source: *Washington Post*, 1/28/05 (2:4) and 4/24/07 (13:3). See also 1900 U.S. Census (Dinwiddie Co., VA), which notes the killer.

1908

Joseph Paolucci (white, age 32). *Murder.* The crime was committed on 9/13/1906. Executed for the handgun slaying of 17-year-old Elizabeth V. Dodge (white). Motive: failed romance. The killer was hanged on March 23, 1908. Source: *Washington Post*, 9/14/06 (1:3) and 3/24/08 (16:4).

Albert Brown (black, age 23). *Murder.* The crime was committed on 11/4/1907. Fratricide. Executed for the handgun slaying of 24-year-old Harvey Brown (black). Motive: heated argument. The killer was hanged on June 29, 1908. Source: *Washington Post*, 11/5/07 (6:5) and 6/30/08 (10:1).

1909

Richard Gregory (black, age 36). *Murder.* The crime was committed on 8/31/1907. Executed for the murder of 32-year-old William A. Garner (black), who was clubbed to death. Motive: rivalry for a female. The killer was hanged on February 15, 1909. Source: *Washington Post,* 9/2/07 (2:4), 9/6/07 (2:5), 9/10/07 (14:3) and 2/16/09 (1:2).

1913

Samuel William Rauen (white, age 28). *Murder.* The crime was committed on 3/30/1912. Executed for the handgun slayings of 19-year-old Azalea Elizabeth Rauen (née Jones) and 23-year-old John M. Rauen (both white), his wife and his brother, respectively. Motive: despondency over personal failures and a simmering suspicion that the decedents were gravitating toward each other. The killer was hanged on February 14, 1913. Source: *Washington Post,* 3/31/12 (1:8) and 2/15/13 (5:3).

Nathaniel Green (black, age 22). *Rape.* The crime was committed on 12/25/1912. Indecent assault on the person of 37-year-old Adelaide E. Grant (white), she having been severely beaten and her jaw shattered on Christmas Day. The attacker was hanged on June 9, 1913. Source: *Washington Post,* 12/26/12 (1:4), 12/27/12 (1:3) and 6/10/13 (3:4).

1917

James T. Allen (black, age 35). *Murder.* The crime was committed on 11/11/1915. Uxoricide. Executed for the fatal stabbing of 36-year-old Flora Allen (black). Motive: family problems. The killer was hanged on September 12, 1917. Source: *Evening Star* (Washington, D.C.), 11/11/15 (15:4) and 9/12/17 (9:1); *Washington Post,* 9/13/17 (4:1).

1920

James Henry Jackson (black, age 26). *Murder.* The crime was committed on 1/24/1919. Executed for the handgun slaying of 22-year-old Lillian Hood (white), plus aggravated assaults upon the persons of 46-year-old Martha E. Geagan and 24-year-old Florence Fowler. Motive: sex maniac on a spree. Jackson was hanged on March 2, 1920. Source: *Washington Post,* 1/25/19 (1:8), 1/31/19 (1:7), 2/1/19 (1:8), 2/2/19 (18:5) and 3/3/20 (10:4).

Frank Bowman (black, age 35). *Murder.* The crime was committed on 7/7/1916. Executed for the handgun slaying of 26-year-old Clarence Keefer (white). Motive: anger at having had his privacy disturbed. This killer was hanged on October 22, 1920. Source: *Washington Post,* 7/8/16 (2:6), 7/9/16 (7:7) and 10/23/20 (2:5). Appeal: 50 DC 90–94.

1921

William Henry Campbell (black, age 20). *Murder.* The crime was committed on 3/11/1920. Executed for the murder of 46-year-old Gertrude Harrison Mann (white), she having been clubbed to death. Motive: purse snatching. The killer was hanged on March 11, 1921. Source: *Washington Post,* 3/14/20 (2:3), 3/15/20 (2:1), 8/5/20 (1:8) and 3/12/21 (4:4).

1922

John McHenry (white, age 19). *Murder.* The crime was committed on 12/14/1919. Executed for the handgun slayings of 27-year-old Wallace W. Mulcare and 41-year-old James E. Armstrong (both white), a storekeeper and a policeman, respectively. Motive: armed robbery and resisting arrest. The killer was hanged on March 17, 1922. Source: *Washington Post*, 12/15/19 (1:1), 12/16/19 (2:1), 12/17/19 (2:5), 12/21/19 (6:3) and 3/18/22 (2:3). See also 1910 U.S. Census (Washington, D.C.), which notes Mulcare.

1923

Ernest Shands (black, age 27). *Murder.* The crime was committed on 8/8/1922. Uxoricide. Executed for the hatchet killing of 28-year-old Catherine Spirggs Shands (black). Motive: marital disharmony. She lingered until September 16, 1922. Shands was hanged on March 9, 1923. Source: *Evening Star* (Washington, D.C.), 3/9/23 (5:1); *Washington Post*, 3/10/23 (2:4). See also 1922 DC death cert. no. 273560.

George Spencer Banton (black, age 18). *Murder.* The crime was committed on 8/19/1922. Executed for the handgun slaying of 39-year-old Samuel A. Frye (white). Motive: robbery. The killer was hanged on April 20, 1923. Source: *Washington Post*, 8/20/22 (1:4), 8/21/22 (2:5), 8/22/22 (10:5) and 4/21/23 (15:2). See also 1920 U.S. Census (Prince Geo. Co., MD), which notes Frye.

Charles Price (black, age 32). *Murder.* The crime was committed on 5/30/1918. Executed for the handgun slaying of 50-year-old Robert Smith (black). Motive: monetary dispute. The killer was hanged on May 3, 1923. Source: *Evening Star* (Washington, D.C.), 5/31/18 (3:1); *Washington Post*, 4/10/20 (2:1) and 5/4/23 (3:7). Appeal: 51 DC 106–109.

George Samuel Epps (black, age 31). *Murder.* The crime was committed on 12/28/1921. Uxoricide, etc. Executed for the handgun slayings of 31-year-old Katie Epps and 27-year-old Louise Hodges (both black). Motive: alienated husband. Epps suspected his wife of infidelity and the other woman of leading her astray. He was hanged for killing them on May 24, 1923. Source: *Washington Post*, 12/29/21 (11:5); *Evening Star* (Washington, D.C.), 5/24/23 (19:4). See also 1920 U.S. Census (Washington, D.C.), which notes George and Katie "Epse" [*sic*].

Rufus Gordon (black, age 35). *Murder.* The crime was committed on 9/12/1919. Executed for the handgun slaying of 30-year-old Simon Miller (white). Motive: robbery gone awry. The killer was hanged on June 23, 1923. Source: *Washington Post*, 9/13/19 (5:1) and 6/24/23 (8:3); *Evening Star* (Washington, D.C.), 6/23/23 (1:5).

1925

Ralph Thomas (black, age 40). *Murder.* The crime was committed on 8/1/1923. Uxoricide. Executed for the murder of 26-year-old Sadie Thomas (black), she having been slashed to death with a razor. Motive: marital breakdown. The killer was hanged on January 15, 1925. Source: *Evening Star* (Washington, D.C.), 1/15/25 (4:3); *Washington Post*, 1/16/25 (2:4). Appeal: 55 DC 89–91. See also 1920 U.S. Census (Washington, D.C.), which notes both parties.

Herbert Copeland (black, age 35). *Murder.* The crime was committed on

5/21/1918. Triple cop killer. Executed for the handgun slayings of 37-year-old John A. Conrad, 35-year-old Lawrence H. McParland and 63-year-old David T. Dunigan (whites), the last in a separate incident on the same day. Motive: resisting arrest. Copeland was tried only in the Dunigan case. He was also said to be a serial killer with nine prior victims but none of these can be fully substantiated based on available information. Copeland was hanged on January 22, 1925. Source: *Washington Post*, 5/21/18 (1:8), 5/22/18 (2:4) and 1/23/25 (5:1); *Evening Star* (Washington, D.C.), 1/22/25 (1:1). Appeal: 55 DC 106–109.

1928

Philip Jackson (black, age 30). *Rape.* The crime was committed on 2/18/1927. Indecent assault on the person of 35-year-old Daisy Welling (white), she having also been gravely wounded with a hatchet on the grounds of the U.S. Capitol. Her attacker was executed on May 29, 1928. Source: *Washington Post*, 2/19/27 (1:4), 2/20/27 (1:2) and 5/30/28 (18:1).

Lee Silverblatt, alias "Nicholas Lee Eagles" (white, age 34), **Samuel Marino** (white, age 19) and **John Cline Proctor** (white, age 18). *Murder.* Their crime was committed on 9/26/1926. Cop killers. Executed for the handgun slaying of 28-year-old Leo Busch (white). Motive: resisting arrest. They were all executed on June 22, 1928. Source: *Washington Post*, 9/27/26 (1:8) and 6/23/28 (1:2).

1930

Andrew Jackson Hawkins (black, age 29). *Murder.* The crime was committed on 12/22/1928. Executed for the handgun slaying of 21-year-old Ruth Watkins (black). Motive: lovers' quarrel. The killer was executed on June 5, 1930. Source: *Washington Post*, 12/23/28 (2:6) and 6/6/30 (3:5); *Baltimore Afro-American*, 6/14/30 (2:3).

1931

Cardoza Bell (black, age 23). *Murder.* The crime was committed on 8/16/1929. Executed for the shotgun slaying of 25-year-old Alice Metz (black). Motive: lovers' quarrel. The killer was executed on March 6, 1931. Source: *Washington Post*, 3/7/31 (3:6). Appeal: 60 DC 76–78.

1932

Alfred Scott Aldridge (black, age 20). *Murder.* The crime was committed on 7/6/1929. Cop killer. Executed for the handgun slaying of 30-year-old Harold J. McDonald (white). Motive: resisting arrest. The killer was executed on May 6, 1932. Source: *Washington Post*, 7/7/29 (1:3), 7/8/29 (1:8), 7/9/29 (20:1), 7/23/29 (1:2) and 5/7/32 (20:3); *Washington (DC) Afro-American*, 7/13/29 (4:4) and 5/14/32 (16:4).

John Borum (black, age 26) and **John Logan** (black, age 24). *Murder.* Their crime was committed on 4/12/1930. Cop killers. Executed for the handgun slaying of 36-year-old Lamar Watson York (white), a federal prohibition agent. Motive: resisting arrest. The killers were executed on June 29, 1932. Source: *Washington Post*, 4/12/30 (1:1), 4/13/30 (1:5), 4/14/30 (1:1) and 6/30/32 (12:1).

Charles Morris (black, age 32). *Murder.* The crime was committed on 7/26/1930. Executed for the handgun slaying of 32-year-old Maggie Landon (black). Motive: lovers' quarrel. The killer was executed on December 2, 1932. Source: *Baltimore Afro-American*, 8/9/30 (19:6); *Washington Afro-American*, 10/29/32 (1:8) and 12/10/32 (1:8).

1933

William C. Robinson (black, age 19). *Murder.* The crime was committed on 7/29/1931. Executed for the handgun slaying of 29-year-old Emanuel Solomon (white), a taxi driver. Motive: robbery. The killer was executed on October 27, 1933. Source: *Washington Post*, 7/30/31 (1:1), 7/31/31 (22:1), 8/3/31 (1:7), 11/20/31 (22:1) and 11/25/33 (26:3); *Washington Afro-American*, 11/4/33 (7:1) and 12/2/33 (10:8).

Charles Edward Washington (black, age 23). *Murder.* The crime was committed on 7/29/1931. Accomplice in the handgun slaying of 29-year-old Emanuel Solomon (white), a taxi driver. Motive: robbery. This offender was executed on November 24, 1933. Source: see **William Robinson** (executed 10/27/33).

Benjamin Montague (black, age 29). *Murder.* The crime was committed on 6/8/1932. Executed for the handgun slaying of 36-year-old Clara Williams (black). Motive: lovers' quarrel. The killer was executed on December 1, 1933. Source: *Evening Star* (Washington, D.C.), 6/9/32 (3:3); *Washington Afro-American*, 1/28/33 (20:4) and 12/9/33 (23:6); *Washington Post*, 12/2/33 (4:6). See also 1932 DC death cert. no. 344026.

1934

Ralph Edward Holmes (black, age 25), **Joseph James Jackson** (black, age 20) and **Irving Murray** (black, age 26). *Murder.* Their crime was committed on 8/7/1932. Cop killers. All three were executed for the murder of 28-year-old Milo J. Kennedy (white), who was felled by a brick and then fatally beaten with his own billystick. Motive: gang assault. The electric chair settled accounts with this trio on January 12, 1934. Source: *Washington Post*, 8/8/32 (1:4), 8/9/32 (14:4) and 1/13/34 (15:5); *Washington Afro-American*, 8/13/32 (1:3) and 1/20/34 (1:1).

Ernest Bolden (black, age 25). *Murder.* The crime was committed on 7/16/1932. Executed for the handgun slayings of 20-year-old Elsie Plummer Bolden and 54-year-old Janie Plummer (both black), his wife and mother-in-law, respectively. Motive: family problems. The killer was executed on April 27, 1934. Source: *Washington Post*, 4/28/34 (3:7); *Washington Afro-American* (2nd Edition), 5/5/34 (1:7). Appeal: 63 DC 45–47. See also 1930 U.S. Census (Washington, D.C.), which notes the female parties.

Joseph Goodman (black, age 38) and **George McKinley Pitmond** (black, age 33). *Murder.* Their crime was committed on 1/22/1933. Both were executed for the murder of 65-year-old William Simms (black), the victim having been mauled with a hatchet and then shot in the groin with his own handgun. Motive: burglary. The killers went to the electric chair on June 1, 1934. Source: *Washington Post*, 1/23/33 (1:1); *Washington Afro-American*, 3/31/34 (1:1) and 6/9/34 (10:6).

1936

Albert Preston (black, age 38). *Murder.* The crime was committed on 2/2/1935. Executed for the handgun slaying of 29-year-old Clarence E. Yancey (black). Motive: gambling dispute. The killer was executed on March 20, 1936. Source: *Washington Afro-American,* 4/13/35 (1:1); *Washington Post,* 3/21/36 (3:3).

1937

John Homer Cummings (black, age 27) and **Willett Marcus** (black, age 21). *Murder.* Their crime was committed on 1/4/1935. Both were executed for the handgun slaying of 42-year-old Joseph R. Wushnak (white). Motive: robbery. The killers were executed on April 23, 1937. Source: *Washington Post,* 1/9/35 (26:1) and 4/24/37 (3:1); *Washington Afro-American,* 1/19/35 (4:5) and 4/6/35 (9:4); *Baltimore Afro-American,* 5/1/37 (13:6).

1938

Norman Wesley Robinson (black, age 24). *Murder.* The crime was committed on 9/18/1936. Executed for the murder of 34-year-old Florence Daugherty Goodwin (white), she having been beaten, strangled and fatally bludgeoned with a heavy iron furnace shaker. Motive: sexual assault. Robinson paid for this crime in the DC electric chair on March 18, 1938. Source: *Washington Post,* 9/19/36 (1:1), 9/20/36 (1:4), 9/22/36 (15:5) and 3/19/38 (3:5); *Official Detective,* 12/1/36; *Master Detective,* 7/37.

1939

Will Kinard (black, age 36). *Murder.* The crime was committed on 11/6/1936. Uxoricide. Executed for the handgun slaying of 27-year-old Laura Kinard (black). Motive: domestic squabble. The killer was executed on February 3, 1939. Source: *Washington Afro-American,* 3/12/38 (24:2) and 2/11/39 (3:7); *Washington Post,* 2/4/39 (3:5).

1942

Heinrich Heinck (white, age 35), **Richard Quirin** (white, age 34), **Edward John Kerling** (white, age 33), **Herbert Hans Haupt** (white, age 22), **Herman Otto Neubauer** (white, age 32) and **Werner Thiel** (white, age 35). *Espionage and Conspiracy to Commit Wartime Sabotage.* Their crimes were committed throughout the week of 6/13/1942. These men were enemy combatants who were caught on American soil out of uniform for the purpose of intelligence gathering and vandalism. A state of war was then in existence between the foreign government that sent them (Nazi Germany) and the United States of America. They were found to have maps, money and explosives with which to implement their hostile mission. All six were executed in the DC electric chair on August 8, 1942, in accordance with the Rules of War. Source: *Washington Post,* 8/9/42 (1:1); *Front Page Detective,* 9/42; *Official Detective,* 9/42, 10/42 and 11/42. See also Michael Dobbs, *Saboteurs: The Nazi Raid on America* (Vintage Books, 2005).

William Isaac Robinson (black, age 34). *Rape.* The crime was committed on 8/6/1941. Indecent assault on the person of a 15-year-old white female (name withheld), she having been accosted in a public park and left tied up with her own clothes. Robinson was a repeat offender. He had previously served ten years in the West Virginia State Penitentiary for a similar crime. Released in 1939, he was re-arrested for the same thing in 1940 but released when the prosecutrix failed to appear in court. He was probably a serial rapist. The DC electric chair put a permanent end to his depredations on October 9, 1942. Source: *Washington Post*, 8/11/41 (1:4) and 10/10/42 (B:1:2).

William Thomas Mumford (black, age 20). *Murder.* The crime was committed on 2/15/1941. Executed for the handgun slaying of 56-year-old Fannie Cohen (white). Motive: robbery gone awry. The killer was executed on December 18, 1942. Source: *Washington Post*, 2/16/41 (1:2), 3/24/41 (13:6) and 12/19/42 (B:1:5); *Washington Afro-American*, 4/5/41 (5:1).

1943

Jarvis Roosevelt Catoe, known to all as "the DC Strangler" (black, age 36). *Serial Killer.* Specifically executed for the 3/8/1941 murder of 25-year-old Rose Simons Abramowitz (white), whom he strangled with his bare hands. Motive: sexual assault. Catoe was also confirmed to have murdered six other women under similar circumstances and to have raped an indeterminate number of others. The additional homicide victims were Josephine Robinson (black, age 34) in Washington, D.C., on 12/1/1939; Lucy Kidwell (black, age 57) in Washington, D.C., on 9/27/1940; Mattie Steward (black, age 48) in Washington, D.C., on 11/28/1940; Ada Puller (black, age 21) in Washington, D.C., on 1/22/1941; Jessie Elizabeth Strieff (white, age 23) in Washington, D.C., on 6/15/1941; and Evelyn D. Anderson (white, age 26) in Bronx, NY, on 8/4/1941. Catoe also confessed to an eighth murder—that of Florence Dancy (black, age 65) in Washington, D.C., in 1935, for which another man was convicted—but his story could not be entirely substantiated. All of the victims were strangled and raped. People of all races applauded when Jarvis Catoe was put to death on January 15, 1943. Source: *Washington Post*, 3/9/41 (1:1), 6/17/41 (1:8), 8/29/41 (1:4), 8/30/41 (1:8) and 1/16/43 (B:1:2); *New York Times*, 8/5/41 (22:3), 8/6/41 (38:1), 8/30/41 (6:2), 8/31/41 (17:1) and 9/2/41 (19:5); *Actual Detective*, 9/41, 10/41 and 11/41; *Front Page Detective*, 11/41; *True* (magazine) 12/41; *Crime Detective*, 2/42; *Master Detective*, 4/42.

1945

Monroe D. Neely (black, age 34). *Murder.* The crime was committed on 5/8/1943. Cop killer. Executed for the handgun slaying of 24-year-old Charles Riley Johnston (white). Motive: resisting arrest. Neely was executed on December 14, 1945. Source: *Washington Post*, 5/9/43 (10:3), 5/10/43 (B:6:6) and 12/15/45 (B:1:7).

1946

Earl McFarland (white, age 21). *Murder.* The crime was committed on 10/6/1944. Executed for the strangulation and traumatic tearing of 17-year-old Dorothy Berrum (white). Motive: sexual assault. McFarland was also the prime suspect in the sex slaying of a second Washington, D.C., woman: 63-year-old Margaret Fitzwater (white) on 9/26/1944. He went to his death in the electric chair on July 19, 1946. Source: *Washington Post*, 10/7/44 (1:1), 10/8/44 (1:2) and 7/20/46 (B:1:1);

Master Detective, 10/55; *Crime Detective*, 6/63.

William Copeland (black, age 41). *Murder.* The crime was committed on 2/4/1944. Executed for the handgun slaying of 34-year-old Dora Johnson (black), his sister-in-law. Motive: temper tantrum because he had been exposed as a bigamist. He was executed on December 20, 1946. Source: *Washington Post,* 2/10/44 (12:3) and 12/21/46 (1:1); *Washington Afro-American*, 2/19/44 (11:6).

Julius Fisher (black, age 34). *Murder.* The crime was committed on 3/1/1944. Executed for the murder of 37-year-old Catherine Cooper Reardon (white), she having been bludgeoned with a fireplace log. Motive: revenge. (She had reported Fisher for an allegedly poor job performance.) He died in the electric chair on December 20, 1946. Source: *Washington Post*, 3/3/44 (1:7) and 12/21/46 (1:1).

Joseph Medley (white, age 43). *Murder.* The crime was committed on 3/6/1945. Serial killer. Specifically executed for the handgun slaying of 50-year-old Nancy Boyer (white). Motive: bunco, robbery and despoliation. Two other known victims: 28-year-old Laura Fisher (white), who was forcibly drowned in a hotel bathtub at New Orleans on 12/24/1944, and 38-year-old Blanche Zimmerman (white), who was likewise slain in a Chicago hotel on 2/27/1945. The DC electric chair ended the deadly career of Joseph Medley on December 20, 1946. Source: *Washington Post*, 3/9/45 (1:1), 3/10/45 (1:2), 3/11/45 (1:4), 3/12/45 (1:2), 3/18/45 (1:1), 3/19/45 (1:1), 3/20/45 (1:6) and 12/21/46 (1:1); *Official Detective*, 7/45; *Master Detective*, 2/62 and 11/74; *Crime Detective*, 8/63.

1947

Alfred L. Hawkins (black, age 22). *Murder.* The crime was committed on 4/13/1946. Executed for the handgun slaying of 34-year-old John Paul Knight (white). Motive: robbery. The killer was executed on October 31, 1947. Source: *Washington Post*, 4/14/46 (1:2), 4/15/46 (1:8), 5/20/46 (1:1) and 11/1/47 (B:1:6).

1948

Jesse James Patton (black, age 21) and **Reginald Joseph Wheeler** (black, age 26). *Murder.* Their crime was committed on 6/5/1946. Both were executed for the handgun slaying of 52-year-old Maurice L. Bernstein (white). Motive: robbery. The killers were executed on December 10, 1948. Source: *Washington Post*, 6/6/46 (1:2), 6/7/46 (B:1:8), 3/12/47 (1:3) and 12/11/48 (B:1:4).

1949

Shirley Harris (black male, age 23). *Murder.* The crime was committed on 3/11/1947. Executed for the handgun slaying of 56-year-old Frank C. Kelly (white). Motive: mugging. The killer was executed on January 14, 1949. Source: *Washington Post*, 3/13/47 (1:1), 3/14/47 (1:2), 3/17/47 (1:1) and 1/15/49 (B:1:8); *Official Detective*, 7/47.

John H. Hall (black, age 31). *Rape.* The crime was committed on 10/5/1946. Indecent assault on the person of an 8-year-old black female (name withheld). This child rapist was put to death on February 25, 1949. Source: *Washington Post*, 11/20/47 (B:1:8) and 2/26/49 (B:1:6).

Theodore Martin Holmes (black, age 22). *Rape.* The crime was committed on 3/18/1948. Indecent assault on the person of a 9-year-old white female (name withheld), who was beaten into a coma. This child rapist was put to death on March 15, 1949. Source: *Washington Post*, 3/19/48 (1:3), 3/20/48 (1:2), 3/31/48 (B:1:7) and 3/16/49 (B:1:6); *Washington Afro-American*, 3/19/49 (11:6).

George Alfred Garner (black, age 25) and **Lawrence Joseph Garner** (black, age 23). *Murder.* Their crimes were committed on 2/27/1948 and 2/28/1948. Both were executed for the beating and handgun killings of 32-year-old James A. Hardy and 37-year-old Howard Jones (both black cab drivers), who were murdered eight hours apart. Motive: robbery. These killers were put to death on July 29, 1949. Source: *Washington Post*, 2/28/48 (1:3), 2/29/48 (1:2), 3/4/48 (1:3) and 7/30/49 (B:1:3).

1952

Fred Swanson Pritchett (white, age 38). *Murder.* The crime was committed on 7/10/1949. Executed for the handgun slaying of 50-year-old Clyde L. King (white). Motive: personal vindictiveness. Pritchett was a repeat killer. He had previously served 12 years (1934–1946) in the Virginia State Penitentiary for fatally shooting a Charlottesville man in an argument over a nickel. He died in the DC electric chair on February 15, 1952. Source: *Washington Post*, 7/11/49 (B:1:8), 7/12/49 (9:2) and 2/16/52 (B:1:2); *Real Detective*, 7/50, 5/70 and 5/75; *Master Detective*, 7/54.

William Andrew Tyler (black, age 18). *Murder.* The crime was committed on 4/7/1950. Executed for the fatal stabbings of 66-year-old John C. Carpenter and 56-year-old Oliver R. Hess (both white). Motive: burglary. This double killer was himself executed on July 25, 1952. Source: *Washington Post*, 4/8/50 (1:8), 5/6/50 (1:6), 5/7/50 (1:1) and 7/26/52 (13:8).

1953

Albert Allen (black, age 23). *Murder.* The crime was committed on 12/30/1950. Executed for the murder of 39-year-old George Schomber (white), the victim having been bludgeoned with a heavy industrial broom. Motive: robbery and ingratitude. Allen died in the electric chair on March 20, 1953. Source: *Washington Post*, 1/1/51 (1:2), 1/2/51 (1:6), 1/3/51 (1:4), 1/4/51 (1:5) and 3/21/53 (1:3).

1957

Robert Eugene Carter (black, age 24). *Murder.* The crime was committed on 7/11/1953. Cop killer. This offender had been a construction worker with no prior criminal record. He seemed an unlikely candidate for what befell him. He had no willful disinclination toward earning a living through honest means. Carter was neat in his personal habits and a devoted family man. The summer of 1953 saw him married with two children, plus a third on the way. Then came trouble; a slowdown in the local construction industry caused Carter to get furloughed from his job. Money became scarce and the situation showed no signs of improving, at least in the short term. Carter realized that he was getting close to the edge of financial ruin. He had to do something to make ends meet—with or without a paycheck.

Carter's home address was no. 1523 P Street NW. He knew of a certain dry cleaners less than two blocks away—at no. 1637 P Street NW, to be precise. Desperation induced him to rob that place on the above date. He armed himself with a German luger, and then entered the dry cleaning shop in an affable manner and asked to redeem some clothing. However, when the shop's proprietor—Irvin L. Kozak—went to check his inventory for the items, Carter stealthily followed him to a spot behind some clothing racks and struck Kozak with a pistol on the back of his head. Kozak fell to the floor, whereupon Carter grabbed money from a cash drawer and ran outside. Kozak rallied enough to totter into the street, hollering that he had been robbed. This was observed by two off-duty police officers named Joseph A. Berti and George W. Cassels, both of whom were unarmed and out of uniform at the time. Cassels immediately chased the fleeing bandit while Berti did what he could to help Kozak. The pursuit continued across 16th Street and then into an alley between Church Street and P Street NW. However, when Cassels (white, age 27) emerged from the other end of the alley, Carter was waiting for him. The latter fired two shots. One of these ejected harmlessly onto the ground, but the other one entered the officer's chest between two ribs, traveled downward and literally shredded his innards. Cassels died a few hours later despite frantic efforts to save him.

Carter escaped from the scene only to be hunted down in the following way: A 7-year-old boy who had been playing on a sidewalk in the 1500 block of P Street NW at the time of the shooting told police that "the bad man" had run past him and entered a private residence there. Carter had actually doubled back to his own home instead of continuing his flight in the opposite direction. Questioned closely, the suspect's wife (who was found together with her children at no. 1523 P Street NW) divulged important information—namely, that Carter had hurriedly stuffed money (later determined to have been most of the robbery loot) in a child's piggy bank, and that he had hidden a gun in his backyard garden before fleeing again. She had, in the meantime, retrieved the weapon and brought it back inside her house. The gun was then confiscated. It proved to be the murder weapon.

Fearful for the continued safety of her offspring, Mrs. Carter also told police of several places where her husband might go. One of these was his mother's house in Linden, Maryland. The latter lady, being questioned in turn, said that her son had been there for a short time earlier that day. He was accompanied by a second man whom she knew only as "Lowery," and that they had arrived in a light green Dodge automobile. Robert Carter did not own such a vehicle himself, so speculation turned to "Lowery." A check of all automobile registrations in Washington, D.C., and the surrounding area turned up a Thomas Levi Lowery at no. 748 Varnum Street as a possibility. Lawmen hurried to that address and there arrested Carter without further ado. Neither Mrs. Carter nor Lowery were charged with any offense.

Robert Carter admitted his guilt and seemed genuinely sorry for what he had done. Appeals kept him alive until April 26, 1957. Then "he walked calmly to his death" in the electric chair at the District of Columbia Jail, the last person to be legally executed in that jurisdiction to date. Source: *Washington Post*, 7/12/53 (1:1), 7/13/53 (1:1) and 4/27/57 (D:1:8); *Official Detective*, 10/53.

Maryland

(in chronological order)

1866

Thomas Davis (black, age 19), **William Henry Jones** (black, age 26), **Henry Luckett** (black, age 23) and **William Plater** (black, age 28). *Murder.* Their crime was committed on 7/14/1866 in Prince George's County. Executed for the handgun slaying of 57-year-old William Lyles (white), who was shot in the face at point-blank range. Motive: robbery and home invasion. The culprits ransacked the victim's house, taking a ham, a hat, blankets, bedspreads, articles of intimate apparel, a clock and money totaling approximately $2,000, the proceeds of harvest sales. They were all hanged at Upper Marlboro on November 2, 1866. Source: *Alexandria (VA) Gazette*, 7/18/66 (3:3); *Evening Star* (Washington, D.C.), 7/18/66 (3:1) and 11/2/66 (1:5); *Baltimore Sun*, 11/3/66 (1:3); *The World* (NYC), 11/6/66 (2:3).

1868

Lucy Purnell (black female, age not recorded). *Murder.* The crime was committed in Worcester County sometime in the year 1866. Executed for the murder of Hanson Robbins (black male, age not recorded), who had been knocked unconscious and then buried alive. Motive: she reportedly could not tolerate his snoring. The court papers for this case have not survived. Lucy Purnell was hanged at Snow Hill on February 28, 1868. Source: *Baltimore Sun*, 3/3/68 (1:5); *New York Times*, 3/3/68 (5:3); *Savannah (GA) Morning News*, 3/11/68 (1:1).

1869

George Bailey, alias "George W. Bryan" (black, age 26), **Frank Rounds**, alias "Frank Anderson" (black, age 27), **William Wells**, alias "Lindsay C. Wells" (black, age 19) and **William Wilson**, alias "Charles Wilson" (black, age 19). *Murder.* Their crime was committed on 3/30/1868 in Somerset County. Executed for the murders of 25-year-old Benjamin F. Johnson and 21-year-old Henry Cannon (both white—the skipper and mate of a Chesapeake Bay oyster schooner), who were attacked with axes and thrown overboard while still alive. Motive: piracy. These four killers were hanged at Princess Anne on March 5, 1869. Source: *Baltimore Sun*, 3/6/69 (1:3); *The World* (NYC), 3/6/69 (1:6).

George Truman (black, age 20). *Murder.* The crime was committed on 1/30/1869 in Frederick County. Executed for the murder of a wayfaring white man whose name and age were never ascertained, he having been bludgeoned with a stone and finished off with a shotgun blast (his body was later devoured by dogs). Motive: robbery. The killer was hanged at Frederick on May 28, 1869. Source: *Baltimore Sun*, 5/29/69 (4:1); *New York Herald*, 5/29/69 (3:7); *The World* (NYC), 5/29/69 (1:1).

1870

Nimrod Richards (black, age 24). *Murder.* The crime was committed on 7/14/1866 in Prince George's County. Accomplice in the handgun slaying of 57-year-old William Lyles (white) during the course of a violent home invasion. Richards was hanged at Upper Marlboro on August 12, 1870. Source: *Evening Star* (Washington, D.C.), 8/12/70 (1:6); *Baltimore Sun*, 8/13/70 (1:3); *New York Herald*, 8/13/70 (5:4). See **Thomas Davis et al.** (executed 11/2/66).

John Rice (black, age 19). *Rape.* The crime was committed in Calvert County sometime in the year 1870. Indecent assault on the person of 63-year-old Sarah Crandall (white). Court papers and local newspaper coverage used to exist for this case, but none have survived. Rice was legally hanged at Prince Frederick on September 16, 1870. Source: *Baltimore Sun*, 9/21/70 (1:7). See also 1860 U.S. Census (Anne Arundel Co., MD), which notes the female party, then residing at Bristol near the Calvert County line.

1871

John Howard (white, age 28). *Murder.* The crime was committed on 8/17/1870 in Allegany County. Executed for the murder of Henry Miller (white, a barge skipper, age not recorded), who was beaten to death with a wooden tow rope implement (similar to a cricket bat). Motive: disgruntled employee, with robbery as an afterthought. The killer was hanged at Cumberland on February 10, 1871. Source: *Cumberland (MD) Alleganian*, 8/24/70 (3:1) and 2/15/71 (3:2).

John Martin (black, age 20). *Rape.* The crime was committed on 4/6/1870 in Frederick County. Indecent assault on the person of 82-year-old Mary Butcher (white), while her enfeebled 103-year-old husband was forced to watch. This rapist was hanged at Frederick on February 10, 1871. Source: *Baltimore Sun*, 2/11/71 (4:4); *New York Herald*, 2/11/71 (6:2).

Mary Wallis (black female, age 17). *Murder.* The crime was committed on 7/2/1870 in Prince George's County. Baby killer. Executed for the fatal poisoning of 9-month-old Albert H. Reed (white). Motive: spitefulness. She was hanged at Upper Marlboro on February 10, 1871. Source: *Evening Star* (Washington, D.C.), 2/10/71 (4:2); *Baltimore Sun*, 2/11/71 (4:4); *New York Herald*, 2/11/71 (6:1). See also 1870 U.S. Census (Washington, D.C.), which notes the victim's correct name and gender concomitant with listings for his parents: Albert M. Reed and Celia M. Reed.

Frederick Lawrence (black, age 41). *Murder.* The crime was committed on 10/2/1870 in Talbot County. Executed for the ax murder of 29-year-old Emeline Handy (black). Motive: common-law relationship gone sour. The killer was tried in Caroline County but hanged at Easton on July 14, 1871. Source: *Easton (MD) Star*, 10/4/70 (3:1) and 7/18/71 (2:2); *New York Herald*, 7/16/71 (5:1); *Baltimore Sun*, 7/17/71 (4:2). See also 1870 U.S. Census (Talbot Co., MD), which notes the victim as a domestic in the house of Mr. Frank Wright, but erroneously records her surname as "Eaton" instead of "Handy."

William Henry Pritchard (black, age 17). *Rape.* The crime was committed on 8/3/1870 in Baltimore County. Indecent assault on the person of 19-year-old Mary Sendel (white), her male escort having been beaten "nearly to death" with brass knuckles. This attacker was tried at Baltimore City but hanged at Towson on September 29, 1871. Source: *Baltimore Sun*, 9/30/71 (4:2); *New York Herald*, 9/30/71 (10:1). See **Levin Palmer** (executed 8/22/73).

1873

William Craig (black, age 23). *Rape.* The crime was committed on 8/25/1872 in Allegany County. Indecent assault on the person of 73-year-old Lottie Dayton (white). The rapist was hanged at Cumberland on January 10, 1873. Source: *Baltimore Sun*, 1/11/73 (4:3). See also 1870 U.S. Census (Mineral Co., WV), which notes the culprit by his nickname, "Ben Craig," instead of his actual name.

Thomas Jackson (black, age 49). *Murder.* The crime was committed on 4/3/1873 in St. Mary's County. Executed for the killing and cremation of 48-year-old James Scofield (white, a storekeeper), who had his head knocked in and his place of business burned down around him. Motive: burglary. The killer was hanged at Leonardtown on July 11, 1873. Source: *Baltimore Sun*, 7/12/73 (1:3); *New York Herald*, 7/12/73 (5:4). See also 1870 U.S. Census (St. Mary's Co., MD), which notes Mr. Scofield.

Albert Sanders (black, age 22). *Murder.* The crime was committed on 12/21/1872 in Calvert County. Executed for the murder of Eugene Archie Burdell (white, an itinerant clockwright, age not recorded), he having been clubbed to death. Motive: highway robbery. Court papers and local newspaper coverage used to exist for this case, but none have survived. The killer was hanged at Prince Frederick on July 11, 1873. Source: *Baltimore Sun*, 7/12/73 (1:4); *Evening Star* (Washington, D.C.), 7/12/73 (1:6); *New York Herald*, 7/12/73 (5:3).

Joshua Nicholson (white, age 25) and **Thomas Hollahan**, alias "Thurman R. Whalen" (white, age 29). *Murder.* Their crime was committed on 1/2/1873 in Baltimore City. Executed for the beating and strangulation of 71-year-old Mary Ann Lampley (white—the grandmother of Nicholson's wife). Motive: robbery and ingratitude. The killers were hanged at Baltimore on August 1, 1873. Source: *Herald & Torchlight* (Hagerstown, MD), 5/14/73 (2:3) and 8/6/73 (2:4); *Baltimore Sun*, 8/1/73 (1:3) and 8/2/73 (1:4).

Levin Palmer (black, age 29). *Rape.* The crime was committed on 8/3/1870 in Baltimore County. Indecent assault on the person of 19-year-old Mary Sendel (white), her male escort having been beaten "nearly to death" with brass knuckles. This rapist was hanged at Towson on August 22, 1873. Source: *Baltimore Sun*, 8/22/73 (1:3) and 8/23/73 (1:3). See also **William Henry Pritchard** (executed 9/29/71).

James West (black, age 22). *Murder.* The crime was committed on 3/13/1873 in Baltimore City. Executed for the hatchet murder of 23-year-old Annie Gibson (black). Motive: lovers' quarrel. This killer was hanged at Baltimore on August 22, 1873. Source: *Baltimore Sun,* 8/22/73 (1:3) and 8/23/73 (1:2). See also 1870 U.S. Census (Baltimore, MD), which notes the female party.

1874

Joseph Wheeling Davis (white, age 22). *Murder.* The crime was committed on 4/5/1872 in Carroll County. Executed for the murder of 27-year-old Abraham L. Lynn (white), who was hacked to death by means of an adze. Motive: temper tantrum, with robbery as an afterthought. Davis was hanged at Westminster on February 6, 1874. Source: *Baltimore Sun,* 2/6/74 (1:2) and 2/7/74 (1:5); *New York Herald,* 2/7/74 (10:1).

William McCotter (white, age 23). *Murder.* The crime was committed on 9/7/1873 in Dorchester County. Executed for the murder of 52-year-old Robert Insley (white, his father-in-law), who was ambushed and clubbed to death. Motive: family strife. The killer was hanged at Cambridge on February 6, 1874. Source: *Baltimore Sun,* 2/6/74 (1:4) and 2/7/74 (1:4).

Ernest Smith (black, age 17). *Rape.* The crime was committed on 4/19/1874 in Talbot County. Indecent assault on the person of 17-year-old Kate E. Bartlett (white), she having been violated in the middle of a public road. The rapist was hanged at Easton on August 7, 1874. Source: *Baltimore Sun,* 8/8/74 (1:4); *New York Herald,* 8/8/74 (2:3). See also 1870 U.S. Census (Talbot Co., MD), which notes both parties.

1875

Joshua Griffin (black, age 22). *Murder.* The crime was committed on 10/12/1874 in Harford County. Executed for the murder of 47-year-old Susan R. Taylor (white), she having been clubbed to death. Motive: vindictiveness, with robbery as an afterthought. The killer was hanged at Bel Air on March 12, 1875. Source: *Baltimore Sun,* 3/12/75 (1:6) and 3/13/75 (1:4); *New York Herald,* 3/13/75 (6:1). See also 1870 U.S. Census (Harford Co., MD), which notes both parties.

George Wheeler (black, age 27). *Murder.* The crime was committed on 7/8/1874 in Talbot County. Executed for the murder of 72-year-old Margaret B. Wittman (white), she having been bludgeoned with a wagon axle. Motive: personal umbrage (she had finked on him for calling in sick to his job when he was not really ill). This killer was hanged at Easton on March 12, 1875. Source: *Baltimore Sun,* 3/12/75 (1:6) and 3/13/75 (1:5); *New York Herald,* 3/13/75 (6:1). See also 1870 U.S. Census (Talbot Co., MD), which notes both parties.

1876

Jenkins Showell (black, age 25). *Rape.* The crime was committed on 11/26/1875 in Worcester County. Serial rapist. Specifically executed for indecently assaulting pregnant 20-year-old Sally Mary Hadder (née Holloway), a young white woman. This rapist was hanged at Snow Hill on August 11, 1876. Source: *Baltimore Sun,* 8/11/76 (1:6) and 8/12/76 (1:5);

New York Herald, 8/12/76 (10:1). See also 1880 and 1900 U.S. Census (Worcester Co., MD), which note the continued presence of the female party in the same place under two name variations: "Sarah M. Hadder" and "Sallie M. Hadder."

1877

Martin Henry (black, age about 35) and **Charles Henry Simpson** (black, age about 35). *Murder.* Their crime was committed on 7/10/1876 in Charles County. Both were executed for the murder of 28-year-old John W. Everett (white), who was clubbed to death in his own bed. Motive: burglary. These killers were hanged at Port Tobacco on February 9, 1877. Source: *Evening Star* (Washington, D.C.), 2/9/77 (1:7); *Baltimore Sun*, 2/10/77 (4:1). See also 1870 U.S. Census (Charles Co., MD), which notes Everett.

James Rosebury Hawkins (black, age 19). *Rape.* The crime was committed on 4/23/1877 in Baltimore County. Indecent assault on the person of 13-year-old Ida Schaeffer (white), she having also been temporarily blinded with tobacco juice and tied upright to a tree. The rapist was hanged at Towson on November 23, 1877. Source: *Baltimore Sun*, 11/23/77 (4:3) and 11/24/77.

Richard Henry Norfolk (white, age 25). *Murder.* The crime was committed on 5/29/1877 in Anne Arundel County. Uxoricide. Executed for the murder of 24-year-old Sally Johnson Norfolk (white), she having been bludgeoned with a "heavy stick." Motive: the killer wanted to be free to pursue the victim's younger sister. He was hanged at Annapolis on December 21, 1877. Source: *Baltimore Bee*, 12/22/77 (4:1); *Baltimore Sun*, 12/22/77 (4:2). See also A. A. County Marriages, 1851–1875 (MD State Archives), which notes the correct names of both parties.

1878

Edward Costley (black, age 26). *Murder.* The crime was committed on 4/4/1877 in Frederick County. Executed for the shotgun slaying of 70-year-old Solomon Costley (black, his cousin), who was deliberately blasted from behind. Motive: robbery and ingratitude. The killer was hanged at Frederick on June 21, 1878. Source: *Baltimore Sun*, 6/22/78 (4:4); *New York Herald*, 6/22/78 (2:5). See also 1870 U.S. Census (Frederick Co., MD), which notes the victim.

Hiram Fooks (black, age 47). *Murder.* The crime was committed on 10/22/1877 in Somerset County. Executed for the murder of 18-year-old Jack Tyler (black), the victim having been beaten to death. Motive: bullying. The killer was hanged at Princess Anne on July 11, 1878. Source: *Baltimore Sun*, 7/13/78 (1:7); *Sedalia (MO) Daily Democrat*, 7/13/78 (1:3). See also 1870 U.S. Census (Somerset Co., MD), which notes Fooks.

1879

Medford Waters (black, age 16). *Murder.* The crime was committed on 11/13/1878 in Cecil County. Executed for the handgun slaying of 20-year-old Jenkins Whaley (black). Motive: workplace dispute. The killer was hanged at Elkton on December 5, 1879. (He had been born in Kent County on March 17, 1862.) Source: *Cecil County Whig*, 11/16/78 (3:4) and 12/6/79 (3:3); *Baltimore Sun*, 12/5/79 (4:5) and 12/6/79 (4:3); *Morning Herald* (Baltimore), 12/6/79 (1:5).

1881

John Gothard (black, age 49). *Murder.* The crime was committed on 12/2/1880 in Baltimore County. Executed for the murder of 47-year-old Joseph Woods (white), who was attacked with an axe and a club. Motive: disgruntled employee. The killer was hanged at Towson on April 29, 1881. Source: *Baltimore Sun*, 4/29/81 (4:1) and 4/30/81 (4:2). See also 1880 U.S. Census (Carroll Co., MD), which notes Mr. Woods.

Felix Munshour (white, age 28). *Murder.* The crime was committed on 8/5/1879 in Frederick County. Executed for the handgun slaying of 45-year-old James L. Wetzel (white). Motive: robbery and ingratitude. The killer was hanged at Frederick on November 11, 1881. Source: *Baltimore Sun*, 11/12/81 (1:6). See also 1880 U.S. Census (Frederick Co., MD), which notes the gunman.

1883

Arthur Preston (black, age 24). *Murder.* The crime was committed on 4/12/1882 in Harford County. Executed for the ax murder of 25-year-old Mary Dorsey (black). Motive: lovers' quarrel. The killer was hanged at Bel Air on January 19, 1883. Source: *Aegis and Intelligencer* (Bel Air, MD), 4/14/82 (2:4) and 1/26/83 (2:2); *New York Times*, 4/14/82 (5:2) and 1/20/83 (3:3); *New York Herald*, 1/20/83 (10:1). See also 1880 U.S. Census (Harford Co., MD), which notes Preston.

George Lake (black, age 34). *Rape.* The crime was committed on 4/15/1883 in Dorchester County. Indecent assault on the person of 41-year-old Clara Simmons (white). The rapist was hanged at Cambridge on June 29, 1883. Source: *Democrat & News* (Cambridge, MD), 4/21/83 (3:2) and 6/30/83 (3:4); *Baltimore Sun*, 6/30/83 (5:8). See also 1870 and 1880 U.S. Census (Dorchester Co., MD), which respectively note the culprit and the female party.

John Smith (black, age 32). *Murder.* The crime was committed on 5/15/1883 in Garrett County. Executed for the handgun slaying of 54-year-old Josiah Harden (white) and indecent assault on the person of Mrs. Harriet Harden, that man's wife. Motive: home invasion. Smith was hanged at Oakland on November 16, 1883. Source: *The Republican* (Oakland, MD), 5/19/83 (5:2) and 11/24/83 (5:2); *Morning Herald* (Baltimore), 11/17/83 (1:4). See also 1850 U.S. Census (Allegany Co., MD), which notes Mr. Harden as a young man.

1884

Frederick Cephas (black, age 35). *Murder.* The crime was committed on 4/7/1884 in Dorchester County. Executed for the murder of 68-year-old Celia Bush Murphy (white), she having been clubbed to death and mutilated with a knife. Motive: robbery. The killer was hanged at Cambridge on August 1, 1884. Source: *Democrat & News* (Cambridge, MD), 4/19/84 (3:2) and 8/2/84 (3:4); *Denton (MD) Journal*, 4/19/84 (2:1) and 5/10/84 (2:1). See also 1880 U.S. Census (Dorchester Co., MD), which notes the victim.

1886

Charles Williams (black, age 21). *Rape.* The crime was committed on 5/16/1885 in Dorchester County. Indecent assault on the person of 35-year-old Eliza J. Keene (white). The rapist was hanged at Cambridge on January 8, 1886. Source: *Baltimore Sun*, 1/9/86 (7:2); *Democrat & News* (Cambridge, MD), 1/9/86 (3:4). See also 1880 U.S. Census (Dorchester Co., MD), which notes the female party.

1887

Jim Stevens (black, age 44). *Rape.* The crime was committed on 7/11/1886 in Somerset County. Indecent assault on the person of 83-year-old Mary Trehearn (white). The rapist was hanged at Princess Anne on February 25, 1887. Source: *The News* (Frederick, MD), 7/13/86 (1:4); *Baltimore Sun,* 2/25/87 (6:4) and 2/26/87 (1:7); *Morning Herald* (Baltimore), 2/26/87 (1:1).

John Thomas Ross (black, age 27). *Murder.* The crime was committed on 12/10/1886 at Baltimore. Executed for the murder of 60-year-old Emily Brown (white), she having been bludgeoned with a brick and then finished off with a dagger thrust. Motive: body snatching. Ross was hanged at Baltimore City on September 9, 1887. Source: *Baltimore Sun*, 12/13/86 (1:5), 12/14/86 (4:2) and 9/10/87 (6:3); *Master Detective*, 6/35. See also 1850 U.S. Census (Talbot Co., MD), which notes the victim as a young woman.

1888

John Benjamin Briscoe (black, age 21). *Murder.* The crime was committed on 8/29/1886 in St. Mary's County. Executed for the murder of 64-year-old Robert R. Dixon (white, a ship master), who was bludgeoned in his bunk; afterward, his body was dumped overboard. Motive: robbery. The killer was hanged at Leonardtown on April 27, 1888. Source: *Baltimore Sun*, 4/27/88 (4:5) and 4/28/88 (1:6). See also 1880 U.S. Census (Baltimore, MD), which notes the murdered skipper.

1889

Melvin Garlitz (white, age 26). *Murder.* The crime was committed on 3/26/1889 in Allegany County. Uxoricide. Executed for the handgun slaying of 21-year-old Leah White Garlitz (white). Motive: a shiftless husband who blamed his failed marriage on everyone except himself. He was hanged at Cumberland on August 30, 1889. Source: *Baltimore Sun*, 8/31/89 (5:7). See also 1870 and 1880 U.S. Census (Allegany Co., MD), which notes the victim's maiden name as "Ethel Lee White."

1891

Ernest Forbes (black, age 19). *Rape.* The crime was committed on 11/6/1890 in Anne Arundel County. Indecent assault on the person of 16-year-old Bertha Phipps (white). The trial was held at Baltimore, but the rapist was hanged at Annapolis on April 3, 1891. Source: *Evening Capitol* (Annapolis, MD), 4/3/91 (3:2); *Baltimore Sun*, 4/3/91 (4:3) and 4/4/91 (4:3).

William Blaney (white, age 25). *Murder.* The crime was committed on 5/2/1890 at Baltimore. Executed for the ax murders of 80-year-old Sarah Blaney and 56-year-old Caroline Blaney (both white), his grandmother and his aunt, respectively. Motive: he was desperate for money. William Blaney was hanged at the Baltimore City Jail on June 12, 1891. Source: *Baltimore Sun*, 5/5/90 (6:1), 6/12/91 (6:1) and 6/13/91 (6:2). See also 1880 U.S. Census (Baltimore, MD), which notes the murdered women.

1892

Thomas Thompson (black, age 22). *Murder.* The crime was committed on 8/22/1891 in Kent County. Executed for the fatal stabbing of 27-year-old William Adams (black). Motive: rivalry for a female. This killer was hanged at Chestertown on January 29, 1892. Source: *Chestertown (MD) Transcript*, 8/27/91 (3:5) and 2/4/92 (3:5); *Morning Herald* (Baltimore, MD), 1/30/92 (1:8). See also 1880 U.S. Census (Wicomico Co., MD), which notes Adams.

1893

Buck Brooks (black, age 26), **Moses Brown** (black, age 31), **Frisbie Comegys** (black, age 17) and **Fletcher Williams** (black, age 23). *Murder.* Their crime was committed on 4/23/1892 in Kent County. All four were executed for the murder of 30-year-old James Heighe Hill (white), who was hit on the head with a rock and stabbed multiple times. Motive: racial animosity. The killers were hanged at Chestertown on January 13, 1893. Source: *Baltimore Sun*, 1/13/93 (8:8) and 1/14/93 (6:3). See also 1880 U.S. Census (Kent Co., MD), which notes Brown, Comegys and Mr. Hill.

Alfred Stout (black, age 25). *Murder.* The crime was committed on 2/3/1891 in Cecil County. Executed for the murder of 73-year-old George Ditmore (white), who was clubbed to death in his own home. Motive: burglary. The killer was hanged at Elkton on January 27, 1893. Source: *Herald and Torchlight* (Hagerstown, MD), 2/5/91 (2:2); *Baltimore Sun*, 1/28/93 (6:5). See also 1880 U.S. Census (Cecil Co., MD), which notes both parties.

William Bond (black, age 23). *Murder.* The crime was committed on 11/22/1891 in Montgomery County. Executed for the strangulation of 30-year-old Margaret Cephas (black). Motive: sexual assault. The killer was hanged at Rockville on April 14, 1893. Source: *Evening Star* (Washington, D.C.), 4/14/93 (3:6); *Washington Post*, 4/14/93 (6:2) and 4/15/93 (6:1); *Morning Herald* (Baltimore), 4/15/93 (1:4).

Daniel Barber (black, age about 28) and **William Pinkney** (black, age 22). *Murder.* Their crime was committed on 3/26/1893 in Prince George's County. Executed for the murder of 43-year-old Francis M. Bowie (white), who was clubbed on the head and thrown down a well. Motive: witness elimination, with robbery as an afterthought. The killers were hanged at Upper Marlboro on June 30, 1893. Source: *Evening Star* (Washington, D.C.), 3/28/93 (8:4), 3/29/93 (8:1), 3/30/93 (7:1), 3/31/93 (2:1), 4/1/93 (3:1), 4/3/93 (5:6) and 6/30/93 (1:5).

Arthur Courtney (black, age 24) and **Henry Taylor** (black, age 19). *Murder.* Their crime was committed on 6/11/1893 in Somerset County. Both were executed for the murder of Capt. Frank Cooper (white, a ship master, age not recorded), who was beaten with a blackjack, a handspike, a lead weight, a cudgel and several other objects before being thrown overboard and then battered with crowbars until he drowned. Motive: robbery. The killers were hanged at Princess Anne on December 15, 1893. Source: *The News* (Frederick, MD), 6/20/93 (1:4); *Baltimore Sun*, 12/16/93 (6:1); *Morning Herald* (Baltimore), 12/16/93 (2:1).

1894

William Leonard (white, age 49). *Murder.* The crime was committed on 9/5/1893 in Frederick County. Executed for the musket slaying of 28-year-old Jesse T. Armstrong (white). Motive: retaliation against a perceived tattletale. The trial was held in Montgomery County, but the killer was hanged at Frederick on February 16, 1894. Source: *Daily News* (Frederick, MD), 2/16/94 (3:2); *Baltimore Sun*, 2/17/94 (6:5).

James Allen (black, age 21). *Rape.* The crime was committed on 2/13/1894 in Prince George's County. Recidivist sex offender. Executed for an indecent assault on the person of 11-year-old Cora Simpson (white). Allen was hanged at Upper Marlboro on July 6, 1894. Source: *Baltimore Sun*, 2/15/94 (6:7), 2/16/94 (2:6), 2/17/94 (6:5) and 7/7/94 (6:5); *Evening Star* (Washington, D.C.), 7/6/94 (8:5).

William Jackson (black, age 62). *Murder.* The crime was committed on 4/18/1894 in Queen Anne's County. Executed for the murder of 43-year-old George J. Leager (white), who was felled with a hatchet and then finished off with a handgun. Motive: the killer had dreaded the consequences of having sassed his employer's wife. A court-ordered noose ended his life at Centreville on July 6, 1894. Source: *Baltimore Sun*, 7/7/94 (6:5). See also 1870 U.S. Census (Kent Co., DE), which notes young Mr. Leager.

1895

Horace Cooper (black, age 32). *Murder.* The crime was committed on 11/18/1894 in Cecil County. Executed for the handgun slaying of 29-year-old Margaret Pitt (black). Motive: jilted lover. Cooper was hanged at Elkton on June 21, 1895. Source: *Cecil Democrat* (Elkton, MD), 11/24/94 (3:3) and 6/22/95 (3:3); *Baltimore Sun*, 6/22/95 (6:5); *Morning Herald* (Baltimore), 6/22/95 (1:4). See also 1880 U.S. Census (Harford Co., MD), which notes a young Margaret Pitt.

1896

James Harry Truss (white, age 37). *Murder.* The crime was committed on 1/2/1896 in Cecil County. Executed for the murder of 50-year-old Thomas Camp (white), whose head was smashed in with a sledgehammer. Motive: robbery. The killer was hanged at Elkton on June 26, 1896. Source: *Baltimore Sun*, 6/27/96 (2:1).

James T. Smith (black, age 29). *Murder.* The crime was committed on 7/28/1896 in Prince George's County. Executed for the murder of 24-year-old Marguerite Alexander Drown (white), who had her throat cut with a kitchen knife. Motive: attempted sexual assault. The killer was hanged at Upper Marlboro on December 18, 1896. Source: *Evening Star* (Washington, D.C.), 7/29/96 (1:7), 7/30/96 (1:3) and 12/18/96 (1:7); *Baltimore Sun*, 12/18/96 (10:1) and 12/19/96 (6:7).

1897

George Matthews (white, age 31). *Murder.* The crime was committed on

8/2/1896 in Charles County. Executed for the shotgun slaying of 30-year-old James J. Irwin (white). Motive: love triangle. The killer was hanged at Port Tobacco on March 12, 1897. Source: *Evening Star* (Washington, D.C.), 8/3/96 (1:1), 8/4/96 (1:5), 8/5/96 (3:2), 8/6/96 (3:2), 8/7/96 (2:5), 8/8/96 (3:3) and 3/12/97 (1:1); *Master Detective*, 5/31. See also 1880 U.S. Census (Charles Co., MD), which notes both parties.

Peter Monahan (white, age 61). *Murder.* The crime was committed on 5/25/1897 at Baltimore. Uxoricide. Executed for the ax murder of 55-year-old Bridget Monahan (white). Motive: obnoxious drunk. He was hanged at the Baltimore City Jail on August 13, 1897. Source: *Baltimore Sun*, 5/26/97 (10:3), 8/13/97 (8:1) and 8/14/97 (7:5).

1898

Sommerfield J. Dennis (black, age 17). *Murder.* The crime was committed on 1/24/1898 in Worcester County. Executed for the rifle slaying of 67-year-old America Holland (black, his stepfather). Motive: rebellious adolescent. The killer was hanged at Snow Hill on August 12, 1898. Source: *Baltimore Sun*, 8/13/98 (8:1). See also 1880 U.S. Census (Worcester, MD), which notes the victim.

Lewis Wesley Johnson, alias "Wesley Boyer" (black, age 38). *Rape.* The crime was committed on 7/8/1898 in Baltimore County. Indecent assault on the person of 40-year-old Ianthe Ensor Stevenson (white) in the course of a highway robbery. The culprit had been released from the Maryland State Penitentiary only 12 days earlier. He was hanged at Towson on November 11, 1898. Source: *Baltimore Sun*, 7/9/98 (12:1) and 11/12/98 (7:1). See also 1880 U.S. Census (Baltimore Co., MD), which notes the injured lady.

1899

Joseph Wright (black, age 21). *Murder.* The crime was committed on 11/4/1897 in Kent County. Executed for the handgun slaying of 60-year-old William Newcomb (black). Motive: obnoxious drunk. The killer was hanged at Chestertown on March 24, 1899. Source: *Trenton (NJ) Evening Times*, 3/24/99 (6:2); *Baltimore Sun*, 3/25/99 (8:4).

John Berry (black, age 16). *Murder.* The crime was committed on 3/18/1899 in Prince George's County. Executed for the murder of 52-year-old Mary Amanda Clarke (white), who was battered to death with a heavy metal potato masher. Motive: resentment for having been verbally scolded. The killer was hanged at Upper Marlboro on June 16, 1899. Source: *Evening Star* (Washington, D.C.), 3/20/99 (8:4) and 6/16/99 (1:5); *Baltimore Sun*, 6/17/99 (9:1).

Joseph Bryan (black, age 39). *Murder.* The crime was committed on 4/23/1899 at Baltimore. Executed for the murder of 35-year-old Mary Pack (black), whose throat was cut with a potato knife. Motive: lovers' quarrel. The killer was hanged at the Baltimore City Jail on July 28, 1899. Source: *Baltimore Sun*, 4/24/99 (7:3) and 7/29/99 (7:1).

Cornelius Gardner (black, age 23), **Charles James** (black, age 21) and **John Myers** (black, age 19). *Rape.* Their crime was committed on 5/8/1899 at Baltimore. All were executed for the gang rape of 15-year-old Anne Bailey (black), she having barely survived. Her three attackers were hanged at the Baltimore City Jail on July 28, 1899. Source: *Baltimore Sun*, 7/29/99 (7:1).

John Alfred Brown (black, age 43) and **Armstead Taylor** (black, age 27). *Murder.* Their crime was committed on 5/13/1899 in Montgomery County. Both were executed for the murders of 26-year-old Louis Rosenstein and pregnant 24-year-old Dora Rosenstein (both white—a married couple), who were bludgeoned with an iron bar. Motive: robbery and home invasion. The killers were tried in Frederick County but hanged at Rockville on August 18, 1899. Source: *Evening Star* (Washington, D.C.), 5/13/99 (1:5), 5/15/99 (1:7), 5/17/99 (1:7), 5/18/99 (1:7), 5/19/99 (1:7) and 8/18/99 (1:3); *Washington Post*, 5/14/99 (1:6) and 8/19/99 (4:1); *Morning Herald* (Baltimore), 5/19/99 (2:5).

Samuel Johnson (black, age 27). *Rape.* The crime was committed on 7/27/1899 in Washington County. Indecent assault on the person of 12-year-old Emma Kerfoot (white). The rapist was hanged at Hagerstown on December 8, 1899. Source: *Baltimore Sun*, 7/29/99 (9:3) and 12/9/99 (8:1); *Evening Times* (Cumberland, MD), 12/8/99 (1:2).

1900

Robert Wyatt (white, age 21). *Murder.* The crime was committed on 10/15/1899 in Anne Arundel County. Executed for the hatchet killing and cremation of 46-year-old Oliver M. Caulk (white, a ship master), as well as the concomitant murder of a Negro deckhand (name and age never determined) who was felled with a club and thrown overboard. Motive: robbery. Wyatt was tried in Howard County but hanged at Annapolis on July 27, 1900. Source: *Evening Capitol* (Annapolis, MD), 7/27/00 (1:4). See also 1880 U.S. Census (Talbot Co., MD), which notes Oliver Caulk.

Amos Smith (black, age 25). *Murder.* The crime was committed on 11/23/1899 at Baltimore. Executed for the murder of 24-year-old Sadie James (black), she having been slashed to death with a razor. Motive: lovers' quarrel. The killer was hanged at the Baltimore City Jail on August 3, 1900. Source: *Baltimore Sun*, 8/4/00 (7:4). See also 1880 U.S. Census (Kent Co., MD), which notes Sadie James as a minor.

William Black (black, age 24). *Rape.* The crime was committed on 2/21/1900 in Harford County. Indecent assault on the person of 15-year-old Jessie Bradford (white). The rapist was hanged at Bel Air on August 31, 1900. Source: *Baltimore Sun*, 2/22/00 (1:4), 3/1/00 (12:5) and 9/1/00 (8:3).

1901

Charles H. Overs (black, age 27). *Murder.* The crime was committed on 10/31/1900 in Frederick County. Executed for the handgun slaying of 19-year-old Charles Frank Donaldson (white). Motive: big attitude. The killer was hanged at Frederick on April 19, 1901. Source: *Frederick (MD) News*, 11/1/00 (3:3) and 11/2/00 (3:4); *Baltimore Sun*, 4/20/01 (8:1); *Washington Post*, 4/20/01 (3:4).

Wiley Kirk (black, age 18). *Rape.* The crime was committed on 3/7/1901 in Baltimore County. Indecent assault on the person of 44-year-old Barbara E. Green (white), she having been attacked on a public road. The rapist was hanged at Towson on May 31, 1901. Source: *Bal-*

timore News, 3/8/01 (12:1); *Baltimore Sun*, 6/1/01 (4:6); *Washington Post*, 6/1/01 (4:2). See also 1910 U.S. Census (Baltimore Co., MD), which notes the victim.

John F. Butler (black, age 41). *Murder.* The crime was committed on 10/27/1900 at Baltimore. Uxoricide. Executed for the murder of 34-year-old Lavinia Butler (black), she having been bludgeoned with a cobblestone. Motive: impending divorce. The killer was hanged at the Baltimore City Jail on August 23, 1901. Source: *Baltimore Sun*, 8/24/01 (7:3). See also 1900 U.S. Census (Baltimore, MD, Ward 22), which notes both parties.

1902

Henry Boyd (black, age 24). *Murder.* The crime was committed on 8/8/1901 in Prince George's County. Executed for the murder of 18-year-old Martha Oden (black), her throat having been cut. Motive: lovers' quarrel. The killer was hanged at Upper Marlboro on January 17, 1902. Source: *Baltimore News*, 1/17/02 (9:8); *Baltimore Sun*, 1/18/02 (9:2). See also 1900 U.S. Census (Prince George's Co., MD), which notes both parties.

John Johnson (black, age 52) and **Frank Jones** (black, age 22). *Murder.* Their crime was committed on 3/4/1902 in Howard County. Executed for the handgun slaying of 36-year-old Israel Radetsky (white), whose body was then dumped in a river. Motive: robbery. Johnson had previously served 18 years in the Kentucky State Penitentiary for the 1882 killing of a fellow inmate. He was then let loose, with the aforesaid result. He and his younger accomplice in the Radetsky homicide were hanged at Ellicott City on June 20, 1902. Source: *Daily News* (Frederick, MD), 5/12/02 (4:3); *Baltimore Morning Herald*, 6/21/02 (1:8); *Baltimore Sun*, 6/21/02 (1:5); *Ellicott City Times*, 6/21/02 (3:3).

Asbury Dixon (black, age 50). *Murder.* The crime was committed on 12/1/1901 in Worcester County. Executed for the shotgun slaying of 27-year-old Delia Dixon, alias "Lizzie Borden" (black), a woman of dubious reputation (as evidenced by her sobriquet). Motive: quarrel over missing money. The killer was hanged at Snow Hill on August 29, 1902. Source: *Baltimore Morning Herald*, 8/30/02 (3:1); *Baltimore Sun*, 8/30/02 (10:1). See also 1900 U.S. Census (Worcester Co., MD), which notes both parties.

John Wesley Devine, alias "Charles Wilson" (black, age 29). *Murder.* The crime was committed on 5/19/1902 at Baltimore. Cop killer. Executed for the handgun slaying of 27-year-old Charles J. Donohue (white). Motive: domestic disturbance turned deadly. The killer was hanged at the Baltimore City Jail on September 19, 1902. Source: *Baltimore Sun*, 5/20/02 (12:5) and 9/20/02 (7:7).

1904

Howard Matthews, alias "Howard Brown" (black, age 34). *Murder.* The crime was committed on 1/1/1904 in Howard County. Executed for the hatchet murder of 63-year-old Hugh McAvoy (white). Motive: robbery and personal animosity. This killer was hanged at Ellicott City on May 20, 1904. Source: *Washington Post*, 1/3/04 (11:6); *Baltimore News*, 5/20/04 (2:1); *Baltimore Morning Herald*, 5/21/04 (3:1). See also MD State Archives, death cert. index (1898–1910), which notes the miscreant.

James Cooper (black, age 29). *Murder.* The crime was committed on 3/8/1904 at Baltimore. Executed for the handgun slaying of 45-year-old Edward "Jesse" Powell (black). Motive: drunken row. The killer was hanged at the Baltimore City Jail on July 29, 1904. Source: *Baltimore Morning Herald*, 3/9/04 (12:1); *Baltimore Sun*, 7/30/04 (7:1).

Andrew Leonard, known to some as "Andrew Leonhardt" (white, age 34). *Murder.* The crime was committed on 6/27/1903 at Baltimore. Uxoricide. Executed for the handgun slaying of 39-year-old Ann Collins Leonard (white). Motive: marital discord. The killer was hanged at the Baltimore City Jail on October 14, 1904. Source: *Baltimore Sun*, 10/15/04 (7:6). See also 1900 U.S. Census (Baltimore, MD), which notes both parties as "Andrew Leonhardt" and "Ann Collins" (the latter being a widow at that time).

Edward Cassidy (black, age 36). *Rape.* The crime was committed on 9/17/1904 in Baltimore County. Executed for burglary, robbery and indecent assault on the person of 21-year-old Emma Florijnek (white). This multiple offender was hanged at Towson on December 23, 1904. Source: *Baltimore News*, 9/19/04 (14:3); *Baltimore Sun*, 12/24/04 (8:1). See also 1900 U.S. Census (Boone Co., MO), which notes the culprit and his origin.

1905

Julius Cooper (black, age 36). *Murder.* The crime was committed on 7/16/1904 in Anne Arundel County. Executed for the handgun slaying of 29-year-old George Harris (black). Motive: rivalry for a female. The killer was hanged at Annapolis on January 27, 1905. Source: *Evening Capitol* (Annapolis, MD), 7/18/04 (1:5) and 1/27/05 (1:4). See also MD State Archives, death cert. index (1898–1910), which notes both men.

William Henry Jones (black, age 30). *Murder.* The crime was committed on 1/7/1905 at Baltimore. Executed for the hammer slaying of 59-year-old James Emory Cunningham (white). Motive: burglary. The killer was hanged at the Baltimore City Jail on February 17, 1905. Source: *Baltimore Sun*, 1/9/05 (12:1) and 2/18/05 (8:2). See also Baltimore City death cert. no. 76639.

John Burch (black, age 24). *Murder.* The crime was committed on 12/31/1904 at Baltimore. Executed for the handgun slaying of 19-year-old Lulu Morsell (black). Motive: lovers' quarrel. The killer was hanged at the Baltimore City Jail on July 7, 1905. Source: *Baltimore Sun*, 1/9/05 (12:2) and 7/8/05 (6:3). See also 1900 U.S. Census (Baltimore, MD), which notes the female party.

Henry J. Handy (black, age 37). *Murder.* The crime was committed on 9/23/1904 in Wicomico County. Uxoricide. Executed for the shotgun slaying of 22-year-old Cecilia Handy (black). Motive: suspected infidelity. The killer was hanged at Salisbury on July 7, 1905. Source: *Wicomico News* (Salisbury, MD), 9/29/04 (1:3), 7/6/05 (1:3) and 7/13/05 (1:3). See also MD State Archives, death cert. index (1898–1910), which notes the homicide victim as "Sealey Handy."

William Leazer (black, age 35). *Murder.* The crime was committed on 3/21/1905 in Anne Arundel County. Cop killer. Executed for the handgun slaying of 45-year-old John George McNamara (white). Motive: resisting arrest. The killer was hanged at Annapolis on July 21, 1905. Source: *Evening Capitol* (Annapolis, MD), 3/22/05 (1:4), 3/23/05 (1:7) and 7/21/05 (1:4).

John M. Simpers (white, age 22). *Murder.* The crime was committed on 8/18/1904 in Cecil County. Executed for the handgun slaying of 64-year-old Albert Constable (white), a noted attorney. Motive: highway robbery. The killer was hanged at Elkton on October 20, 1905. Source: *Cecil (MD) Whig*, 8/20/04 (1:1), 8/27/04 (1:1) and 4/1/05 (1:1); *Baltimore Sun*, 10/21/05 (10:1). See also 1900 U.S. Census (Cecil Co., MD), which notes the murdered man.

1906

Isaac Winder (black, age 27). *Murder.* The crime was committed on 12/21/1905 in Baltimore County. Executed for the handgun slaying of 63-year-old Frederick Thomas Rinehart (white). Motive: robbery. The killer was hanged at Towson on March 30, 1906. Source: *Baltimore News*, 12/22/05 (18:1); *Washington Post*, 12/24/05 (7:1); *Baltimore Sun*, 3/31/06 (14:1). See also 1900 U.S. Census (Baltimore Co., MD), which notes Rinehart, plus 1880 U.S. Census (Baltimore City, MD), which notes the killer's antecedents.

Joseph Bradley (black, age 40). *Murder.* The crime was committed on 3/28/1906 in Howard County. Executed for the handgun slaying of 27-year-old John Redwine (black). Motive: rivalry for a female. The killer was hanged at Ellicott City on July 6, 1906. Source: *Baltimore News*, 7/6/06 (5:5); *Baltimore Sun*, 7/7/06 (10:1). See also MD State Archives, death cert. index (1898–1910), which notes both parties.

Harold Ernest Lyles (black, age 25). *Murder.* The crime was committed on 5/9/1906 in Baltimore County. Executed for the murder of Harriet Ardenia Derricks (black, age about 20), who was slashed to death with a razor. Motive: unreciprocated love. The killer was hanged at Towson on July 13, 1906. Source: *Baltimore News*, 7/13/06 (14:4); *Baltimore Sun*, 7/14/06 (7:5).

William Lee (black, age 17). *Rape.* The crime was committed on 6/10/1906 in Somerset County. Indecent assaults on the persons of 18-year-old Frances Powell and 33-year-old Lela "Ida" Barnes (both white), the latter of whom was holding a baby in her arms when attacked. The trial of the rapist was held at Baltimore, but he was hanged in Somerset County on July 26, 1906. Inordinate haste was applied in adjudicating this case because it had sparked civil unrest. Source: *Washington Post*, 6/12/06 (3:4) and 6/13/06 (5:1); *Salisbury (MD) Advertiser*, 6/16/06 (1:7) and 6/23/06 (1:4); *The News* (Frederick, MD, 7/6/06 (1:5); *Baltimore News*, 7/26/06 (1:5); *Baltimore Sun*, 7/27/06 (1:7). See also 1900 U.S. Census (Somerset Co., MD), which identifies the older victim as Lela Barnes, the wife of Gordon Barnes.

John Henry (black, age 27). *Rape.* The crime was committed on 11/22/1905 in Worcester County. Indecent assault on the person of a 43-year-old white woman identified only as "Mrs. Frederick J. Selby." The rapist was hanged at Snow Hill on July 27, 1906. Source: *Washington Post*, 11/23/05 (11:6); *Baltimore News*, 7/27/06 (11:8); *Baltimore Sun*, 7/28/06 (10:1); *Democratic Messenger* (Snow Hill, MD), 7/28/06 (5:5). See also 1910 U.S. Census (Worcester Co., MD), which notes the rape victim's age but not her actual name.

1907

Frisby Gibbs (black, age 34). *Murder.* The crime was committed on 10/9/1906 at Baltimore. Executed for the murder of 43-year-old Ida Cuff (black), she having been shot four times with a handgun and then very nearly decapitated with a razor. Motive: long-standing domestic violence. The killer was hanged at the Baltimore City Jail on May 10, 1907. Source: *Baltimore News*, 5/10/07 (9:1); *Baltimore Sun*, 5/11/07 (14:4). See also Baltimore City death cert. nos. 94313 and C-982.

1908

Edward A. Wilson (black, age 29). *Murder.* The crime was committed on 8/20/1907 at Baltimore. Uxoricide. Executed for the handgun slaying of 22-year-old Martha Hawkins Wilson (black). Motive: marital estrangement. The killer was hanged at the Baltimore City Jail on February 28, 1908. Source: *Baltimore News*, 2/28/08 (4:6); *Baltimore Sun*, 2/29/08 (8:6). See also Baltimore City death cert. no. C-4035.

1912

Andrew Taylor (black, age 27). *Murder.* The crime was committed on 4/27/1912 in Anne Arundel County. Executed for the shotgun slaying of 41-year-old Fanny May Clifton (black). Motive: lovers' quarrel. The killer was hanged at Annapolis on August 9, 1912. Source: *Evening Capitol* (Annapolis, MD), 4/29/12 (1:3) and 8/9/12 (1:3); *Baltimore Sun*, 8/10/12 (2:8). See also MD State Archives, death cert. index (1910–1951), which notes the female party.

Wesley Miles (black, age 42). *Rape.* The crime was committed on 5/28/1912 in Somerset County. Indecent assault on the person of 15-year-old Margaret E. Phillips (white). The trial of the rapist was held at Baltimore, but he was hanged at Princess Anne on December 6, 1912. Source: *Baltimore Sun*, 10/10/12 (24:3), 10/11/12 (26:2) and 12/7/12 (9:3); *Baltimore News*, 12/6/12 (2:1). See also 1910 U.S. Census (Somerset Co., MD), which notes the miscreant.

1913

Philip Gibson (black, age 31). *Murder.* The crime was committed on 8/26/1912 at Baltimore. Executed for the handgun slaying of 31-year-old John Johnson (black). Motive: rivalry for a female. The killer was hanged at the Baltimore City Jail on January 3, 1913. Source: *Baltimore Sun*, 8/27/12 (11:2) and 1/4/13 (5:3); *Baltimore News*, 1/3/13 (20:2). See also 1910 U.S. Census (Baltimore, MD), which notes Gibson, and Baltimore City death cert. C-56874, which notes Johnson.

James Jacobs (black, age 27). *Murder.* The crime was committed on 8/31/1912 in Anne Arundel County. Executed for the shotgun slaying of 28-year-old John Brooks (black). Motive: personal feud. The killer was hanged at Annapolis on January 10, 1913. Source: *Evening Capitol* (Annapolis, MD), 11/19/12 (1:1) and 1/10/13 (1:3); *Baltimore News*, 1/10/13 (1:5); *Baltimore Sun*, 1/11/13 (5:1). See also 1910 U.S. Census (Anne Arundel Co., MD), which notes Brooks.

1915

Aloysius Sheppard (black, age 19). *Rape.* The crime was committed on

7/15/1915 in Caroline County. Indecent assault on the person of 15-year-old Mildred Clark (white), she having been left completely naked in the woods. The rapist was hanged at Denton on August 27, 1915. Source: *Baltimore Sun*, 7/16/15 (9:8), 7/17/15 (12:1) and 8/28/15 (2:8); *Denton (MD) Journal*, 7/17/15 (5:8) and 8/28/15 (5:6); *Baltimore News*, 8/27/15 (2:1).

Benjamin E. Davis (white, age 37). *Murder.* The crime was committed on 1/28/1915 in Baltimore County. Uxoricide. Executed for the handgun slaying of 33-year-old Mary Ann Davis (white). Motive: marital estrangement. The killer was hanged at Towson on November 12, 1915. Source: *Baltimore News*, 1/28/15 (10:1); *Baltimore Sun*, 11/13/15 (3:4). See also 1910 U.S. Census (Baltimore, MD), which notes both parties.

Carmine Stumpo, known more familiarly as "Frank Grano" (white, age 53). *Murder.* The crime was committed on 9/6/1915 in Worcester County. Executed for the handgun slayings of 41-year-old Levin P. Robinson and 31-year-old Della S. Robinson (whites, a married couple), as well as 37-year-old Alonzo M. Redden (white), a third party. Motive: wishful lover gone berserk. Additionally, Stumpo (alias Grano) had a fourth murder to his discredit: that of his wife, Caroline Stumpo (white, age 51), whom he had slain with a handgun at Philadelphia, Pennsylvania, on 8/30/1913. Motive: jealousy. He was a fugitive when he came to Maryland. He was hanged at Snow Hill on November 26, 1915. Source: *Atlanta Constitution*, 8/31/13 (5:2); *Baltimore News*, 9/6/15 (1:4) and 9/7/15 (16:1); *Baltimore Sun*, 9/7/15 (1:6) and 11/27/15 (3:1); *Democratic Messenger* (Snow Hill, MD), 11/27/15 (1:6). See also 1910 U.S. Census (Worcester Co., MD), which notes the three Maryland victims, plus the census for Philadelphia, which notes "Carman" Stumpo and spouse.

1916

Arnold Martin (black, age 27). *Murder.* The crime was committed on 10/16/1915 in Anne Arundel County. Cop killer. Executed for the handgun slaying of 33-year-old John E. Miller (white). Motive: resisting arrest. The killer was hanged at Annapolis on January 7, 1916. Source: *Evening Capitol* (Annapolis, MD), 10/18/15 (1:4) and 1/7/16 (3:3); *Democratic Messenger* (Snow Hill, MD), 12/4/15 (1:5). See also MD State Archives, death cert. index (1910–1951), which notes Martin.

Solomon Sudler (black, age 17). *Murder.* The crime was committed on 1/1/1916 in Carroll County. Executed for the murder of 26-year-old William F. Brown (white), who was bludgeoned with a rock. Motive: runaway from a work-release program concomitant with robbery. News reports that a gun was used in this crime are erroneous. The killer was hanged at Westminster on April 14, 1916. Source: *New Oxford (PA) Item*, 1/6/16 (4:2); *The Carroll Record* (Taneytown, MD), 1/7/16 (1:3); *Gettysburg (PA) Times*, 4/14/16 (1:3). See also 1900 U.S. Census (Baltimore, MD), which notes Sudler.

Marion Deems (white, age 32). *Murder.* The crime was committed on 6/19/1915 in Baltimore County. Executed for the murder of 29-year-old Laura M. Schaefer (white, a deaf-mute), who had been pushed into a roadside ditch and there cruelly clubbed to death. Motive:

highway robbery. The killer was hanged at Towson on May 26, 1916. Source: *Baltimore Sun,* 6/20/15 (14:5), 6/21/15 (12:3) and 5/27/16 (5:4); *Baltimore News,* 5/26/16 (24:1).

John W. Brown (black, age 28). *Murder.* The crime was committed on 12/24/1915 in Washington County. Executed for the shotgun slaying of 74-year-old Susan A. Dixon (white). Motive: robbery on Christmas Eve. The killer was hanged at Hagerstown on June 30, 1916. Source: *Baltimore Sun,* 12/25/15 (1:3) and 7/1/16 (3:6); *Baltimore News,* 6/30/16 (12:7). See also 1910 U.S. Census (Washington Co., MD), which notes both parties.

George A. Myers (black, age 30). *Murder.* The crime was committed on 4/23/1916 in Howard County. Child killer and church defiler. Executed for the handgun slaying of 13-year-old Carrie Dorsey (black) when he shot up a church during Easter Sunday services. Motive: disgruntled parishioner. He was hanged at Ellicott City on August 4, 1916. Source: *Ellicott City Times,* 4/29/16 (8:5) and 8/5/16 (5:4). See also 1910 U.S. Census (Howard Co., MD), which notes both parties.

1918

Archie Isaacs (black, age 30). *Murder.* The crime was committed on 4/5/1918 in Anne Arundel County. Executed for the murder of 27-year-old Dora Ebert (white), she having been battered to death with a heavy railroad track repair wrench. Motive: robbery and sexual assault. The killer was hanged at Annapolis on July 12, 1918. Source: *Baltimore Sun,* 4/6/18 (16:8), 4/8/18 (5:5), 4/9/18 (16:2), 4/10/18 (16:5) and 7/13/18 (3:4); *Evening Capitol* (Annapolis, MD), 4/6/18 (1:7), 4/10/18 (1:7), 4/29/18 (1:4) and 7/12/18 (1:1). See also 1910 U.S. Census (Anne Arundel Co., MD), which notes the culprit.

John Henry Evans (black, age 28). *Rape.* The crime was committed on or around 4/15/1918 in Anne Arundel County. Indecent assault on the person of 13-year-old Mary Henson (black). The rapist was hanged at Annapolis on October 4, 1918. Source: *Evening Capitol* (Annapolis, MD), 5/9/18 (1:2) and 10/4/18 (1:7). See also MD State Archives, death cert. index (1910–1951), which notes the offender.

1919

John Snowden (black, age 25). *Murder.* The crime was committed on 8/8/1917 in Anne Arundel County. Executed for the strangulation of pregnant 23-year-old Lottie May Haislup Brandon (white) during the course of a home intrusion. The trial was held at Towson, but the condemned man was hanged at Annapolis on February 28, 1919. A gubernatorial pardon was posthumously issued in this case (in the year 2001) based on allegations of flimsy evidence and racial bias. Opponents denounced the move as part of a politically subversive campaign to discredit capital punishment in general. Further investigation may or may not lead to revocation of the pardon at some future date. Source: *Baltimore Sun,* 8/9/17 (1:4), 8/10/17 (1:2), 8/12/17 (1:8), 8/13/17 (1:8), 8/14/17 (1:8), 8/15/17 (14:3), 8/16/17 (12:3), 8/17/17 (12:8) and 3/1/19 (10:1); *Evening Capitol* (Annapolis, MD), 2/28/19 (1:1).

George Cummings (black, age 35). *Murder.* The crime was committed on 8/17/1919 in Prince George's County. Executed for the handgun slaying of 52-year-old George Peters (white). Motive: robbery and home invasion. The killer was hanged at Upper Marlboro on December 5, 1919. Source: *Washington Post,* 8/18/19 (1:8), 8/19/19 (1:7), 8/20/19 (2:1) and 12/6/19 (9:6).

1920

Isaiah Fountain (black, age 28). *Rape.* The crime was committed on 4/1/1919 in Talbot County. Indecent assault on the person of 14-year-old Bertha Simpson (white). The trial of the rapist was held at Towson, but he was hanged at Easton on July 22, 1920. Source: *Baltimore Sun,* 7/23/20 (1:4); *Wilmington (DE) Evening Journal,* 7/23/20 (1:1). See also 1920 U.S. Census (Baltimore, MD), which notes the condemned man as a prisoner.

1921

George Terry (black, age 29). *Rape.* The crime was committed on 9/24/1919 at Baltimore. Indecent assault on the person of 52-year-old Sadie Sibley (white) during the course of a residential burglary. Terry had previously served ten years in the Maryland State Penitentiary for murder. He was hanged at the Baltimore City Jail on January 28, 1921. Source: *Baltimore Evening Sun,* 1/28/21 (28:2); *Baltimore News,* 1/28/21 (34:3).

Felix Bell (black, age 28). *Murder.* The crime was committed on 11/8/1919 at Baltimore. Executed for the handgun slaying of 42-year-old Russell Lee (black), the victim having been deliberately lured to his doom. Motive: robbery. The killer was hanged at the Baltimore City Jail on February 25, 1921. Source: *Baltimore Afro-American,* 11/21/19 (2:1) and 2/25/21 (12:1); *Baltimore News,* 2/25/21 (9:1). See also Baltimore City death cert. nos. D-36827 and D-51238.

Charles Robertson, alias "Charles R. Robinson" (black, age 16). *Murder.* The crime was committed on 11/15/1920 in Frederick County. Executed for the murder of 27-year-old Mary Edith Hightman (white), she having been struck down with a hatchet, raped, doused with lamp oil and burned alive. Motive: sexual assault. This killer was hanged at Frederick on February 25, 1921. Source: *Frederick (MD) Post,* 11/18/20 (1:6) and 2/26/21 (1:3).

William Davis (black, age 34) and **Charles Lewis** (black, age 31). *Murder.* Their crime was committed on 9/4/1920 at Baltimore. Executed for the handgun slaying of 41-year-old Evert K. Gerritsen (white). Motive: mugging. The killers were hanged at the Baltimore City Jail on March 18, 1921. Source: *Baltimore Sun,* 9/5/20 (28:6) and 3/18/21 (36:3); *Baltimore News,* 3/18/21 (36:7). See also Baltimore City death cert. nos. D-46368, D-51989 and D-51990.

Robert Robinson (black, age 21). *Murder.* The crime was committed on 4/26/1919 in Anne Arundel County. Executed for the murder of 50-year-old James Elder Tydings (white), who was bludgeoned with a rock. Motive: mugging. The killer's trial was held at Baltimore, but he was hanged at Annapolis on April 1, 1921. Source: *Baltimore Sun,* 4/29/19 (20:3) and 4/1/21 (22:5); *Evening Capitol* (Annapolis, MD), 4/1/21 (1:7).

Guy Vernon Thompson (white, age 41). *Murder.* The crime was committed on 11/18/1920 in Montgomery County. Executed for the dynamite murders of 35-year-old James Bolton, 2-year-old Evelyn Shipley and 18-month-old Harold Shipley (whites), who were all blown up along with their home. Motive: personal feud. The culprit was hanged at Rockville on April 15, 1921. Source: *Washington Post*, 11/19/20 (1:8), 11/20/20 (1:6) and 4/16/21 (3:4). See also 1920 U.S. Census (Montgomery Co., MD), which notes all parties.

Henry A. Brown (black, age 19). *Murder.* The crime was committed on 1/14/1921 in Anne Arundel County. Executed under federal authority for the murder of 35-year-old Harriet M. Kavanaugh (white), she having been bludgeoned with a lead pipe on the grounds of the U.S. Naval Academy. Motive: mugging. The killer was hanged at the Baltimore City Jail on September 1, 1921. (Local officials at Annapolis would not allow their county jail to be used for such a purpose because they did not want to get stuck with the expense.) Source: *Baltimore Evening Sun*, 1/15/21 (1:8), 1/18/21 (1:6), 1/19/21 (1:7), 1/20/21 (1:5) and 9/1/21 (4:3).

1922

John Davis, alias "Elmer Hoffman" (black, age 22). *Murder.* The crime was committed on 8/30/1921 at Baltimore. Executed for the handgun slayings of 20-year-old Bessie Simms and 63-year-old Lottie Luckey (both black), the latter being the grandmother of the former. Motive: thwarted lover gone wild. The gunman was hanged at the Baltimore City Jail on February 17, 1922. Source: *Evening Sun* (Baltimore), 8/30/21 (18:1) and 2/17/22 (10:1).

Samuel Smith (black, age 26). *Attempted Rape.* The crime was committed on 10/13/1921 in Baltimore County. Felonious assault on the person of 21-year-old Marita Davis Lyons (white), she having been forcibly abducted and shot four times with a handgun. The attacker was hanged at Towson on February 24, 1922. Source: *Evening Sun* (Baltimore), 10/13/21 (34:1), 10/14/21 (38:1) and 2/24/22 (20:3). See also 1920 U.S. Census (Baltimore City, MD, 11th Ward, page 4, line 70), which notes the culprit.

William Stultz (white, age 45). *Murder.* The crime was committed on 8/9/1922 in Frederick County. Cop killer. Executed for the shotgun slaying of 47-year-old John H. Adams (white). Motive: resisting arrest. The killer was hanged at Frederick on November 10, 1922. Source: *The News* (Frederick, MD), 8/9/22 (1:6) and 11/10/22 (1:7); *Frederick (MD) Post*, 8/10/22 (1:7) and 11/11/22 (1:7).

1923

Bishop Hawkins (black, age 43). *Murder.* The crime was committed on 10/31/1922 at Baltimore. Executed for the murder of Ethel Starling (black, age not recorded), she having been slashed to death with a razor. Motive: lovers' quarrel. The killer was hanged at the Baltimore City Jail on April 6, 1923. Source: *The News* (Frederick, MD), 10/31/22 (1:6); *Baltimore News*, 4/6/23 (21:6); *Evening Sun* (Baltimore), 4/6/23 (28:3). See also Baltimore City death cert. no. D-74517.

John Butler (black, age 27). *Rape.* The crime was committed on 12/22/1922 in St. Mary's County. Indecent assault on the person of 60-year-old Madeline Kundahl (white). The rapist was hanged at Leonardtown on May 11, 1923. Source: *St. Mary's Enterprise* (Leonardtown, MD), 5/12/23 (3:2). See also 1920 U.S. Census (St. Mary's Co., MD), which notes the culprit.

George Chelton (black, age 19). *Rape.* The crime was committed on 1/13/1923 in Somerset County. Indecent assault on the person of 14-year-old Thelma Hughlett (white), she having been attacked on a public road. The rapist was hanged at the Maryland State Penitentiary on June 8, 1923. Source: *Democratic Messenger* (Snow Hill, MD), 1/20/23 (5:5) and 4/21/23 (1:4); *Baltimore Sun*, 6/8/23 (28:5). See also 1920 U.S. Census (Somerset Co., MD), which notes the culprit.

1925

Carroll Gibson (black, age 18). *Rape.* The crime was committed on 8/27/1924 in Talbot County. Indecent assault on the person of 41-year-old Clara E. Baker (white), she having been attacked in her own home. The rapist was hanged on February 13, 1925. Source: *Wilmington (DE) Evening Journal*, 8/28/24 (10:2), 8/29/24 (1:8) and 8/30/24 (1:1); *Evening Sun* (Baltimore), 8/29/24 (1:3) and 2/13/25 (22:1); *Baltimore Afro-American*, 2/14/25 (1:8). See also 1920 U.S. Census (Talbot Co., MD), which notes the victim.

1926

Isaac Benson (black, age 35). *Murder.* The crime was committed on 4/1/1926 at Baltimore. Executed for the handgun slayings of 37-year-old Carrie Braxton and 34-year-old Haywood Price (both black). Motive: love triangle. The killer was hanged on July 23, 1926. Source: *Baltimore Afro-American*, 4/17/26 (20:5) and 7/31/26 (10:1); *Evening Sun* (Baltimore), 7/23/26 (26:7). See also 1920 U.S. Census (Baltimore, MD), which notes the murdered pair.

Richard Reese Whittemore (white, age 23). *Murder.* The crime was committed on 2/20/1925 at Baltimore. Prison guard killer, etc. Executed for the murder of 61-year-old Robert H. Holtman (white), who was bludgeoned with an iron bar. Motive: jailbreak. Additionally confirmed to have murdered two bank couriers, Charles W. Clifford (white, age 41) and Louis M. Yarington (white, age 53), during a robbery at Buffalo, New York, on October 28, 1925. This killer was hanged on August 13, 1926. Source: *Evening Sun* (Baltimore), 2/20/25 (1:6) and 8/13/26 (32:1); *Republican Press* (Salamanca, NY), 10/28/25 (1:1); *Titusville (PA) Herald*, 10/30/25 (1:5); *New York Herald-Tribune*, 8/13/26 (1:5); *Master Detective*, 1/30, 2/30, 3/30 and 4/30; *Official Detective*, 7/15/37. See also 1920 U.S. Census (Baltimore, MD), which notes Holtman, and the census for Erie Co., NY, which notes Clifford and Yarington.

1927

William Henry Ross (black, age 23). *Murder.* The crime was committed on 6/13/1927 in Frederick County. Executed for the ax murder of 38-year-old Lottie L. McElfresh (white). Motive: attempted sexual assault. He was hanged on September 9, 1927. Source: *Baltimore Sun*, 6/14/27 (26:5) and 9/9/27 (26:8).

Odi Simmons (black, age 18) and **Arthur Swann** (black, age 19). *Murder.* Their crime was committed on 1/8/1927 in Charles County. Executed for the handgun slaying of 35-year-old Edward J. Carpenter (white). Motive: highway robbery. The killers were hanged on September 9, 1927. Source: *Baltimore News*, 1/8/27 (1:3) and 9/9/27 (10:3); *Baltimore Sun*, 1/9/27 (16:8) and 9/9/27 (26:8). See also 1920 U.S. Census (Charles Co., MD), which notes Mr. Carpenter.

Alfred Simms (black, age 19). *Attempted Rape.* The crime was committed on 7/20/1927 in Prince George's County. Ringleader of a five-man gang assault on the persons of 20-year-old Alberta Rice and 26-year-old John W. Buckler (both white—a courting couple), they having been beaten, pelted with stones and otherwise mistreated. The lead culprit (Simms) was hanged on November 11, 1927. The others either were not identified or escaped with lesser verdicts. Source: *Washington Post*, 7/21/27 (2:7) and 7/22/27 (20:2); *Baltimore Sun*, 11/11/27 (24:6); *Baltimore Afro-American*, 11/19/27 (10:2).

1928

Benjamin Spragins (white, age 27) and **Charles P. Carey** (white, age 28). *Murder.* Their crime was committed on 7/5/1927 at Baltimore. Executed for the handgun slaying of 66-year-old Alfred H. Walker (white), a Maryland State Penitentiary office worker. Motive: attempted jailbreak. Their trial was held at Towson. Carey was a repeat offender already serving a so-called life sentence for the 8/18/1922 handgun murder of 42-year-old William B. Norris (white) during a Baltimore payroll robbery. The gallows ended the earthly careers of these men on August 3, 1928. Source: *Gettysburg (PA) Times*, 8/19/22 (2:1); *Baltimore Sun*, 7/6/27 (28:1), 7/9/27 (20:1) and 8/3/28 (1:1); *Master Detective*, 4/30, 5/30 and 6/30.

Hopkins Watkins (black, age 27). *Murder.* The crime was committed on 10/2/1927 in Baltimore County. Executed for the hatchet killing and decapitation of John King (black, age not recorded). Motive: gambling dispute. This killer was hanged on November 16, 1928. Source: *The Jeffersonian* (Towson, MD), 10/8/27 (1:6), 5/26/28 (1:3) and 11/17/28 (1:2); *Baltimore Sun*, 11/16/28 (30:4). See also Baltimore City death cert. no. E-39272, which notes the culprit as "Hobson W. Watkins."

1929

John Orestes Marsh (white, age 51). *Murder.* The crime was committed on 4/10/1929 in Carroll County. Uxoricide. Executed for the shotgun slaying of 29-year-old Beulah L. Marsh (white). Motive: domestic turmoil. The killer was hanged on August 9, 1929. Source: *Baltimore Sun*, 4/11/29 (1:6), 4/12/29 (2:2) and 8/9/29 (40:6). See also 1920 U.S. Census (Carroll Co., MD), which notes both parties.

1930

John Jackson (black, age 56). *Murder.* The crime was committed on 11/12/1929 at Baltimore. Executed for the murders of 29-year-old Mattie Tarleton and 50-year-old Mary Wright (both black), they having both been slashed to death with a razor. Motive: jilted lover gone berserk.

Jackson was hanged on January 31, 1930. Source: *Baltimore Afro-American*, 11/23/29 (20:2) and 2/8/30 (20:3); *Baltimore News*, 1/31/30 (1:4); *Baltimore Sun*, 1/31/30 (24:4).

1931

Lorenzo Price (black, age 35). *Murder.* The crime was committed on 1/2/1930 at Baltimore. Executed for the handgun slaying of 24-year-old Reuben Heyman (white) together with an indecent assault on the person of 24-year-old Dorothy M. Burgess (white). Motive: carjacking and sexual assault. Price was a disabled World War I veteran with only one leg. The Maryland gallows gave him equal rights for the handicapped on June 12, 1931. Source: *Baltimore Sun*, 1/4/30 (1:7), 1/5/30 (20:1) and 6/12/31 (26:8).

1932

Thomas Blocksom, alias "Bloxom," alias "Blockston" (black, age 42). *Murder.* The crime was committed on 10/24/1931 in Worcester County. Executed for the handgun slaying of Randolph Taylor (black, age about 25). Motive: gambling dispute. Blocksom was another handicapped man with only one leg. He was also a repeat offender who had previously served 17 years in the Virginia State Penitentiary for a homicide committed at Norfolk. He was hanged on January 15, 1932. Source: *Democratic Messenger* (Snow Hill, MD), 10/31/31 (1:5) and 11/21/31 (1:3); *Baltimore Sun*, 1/15/32 (20:4).

Wilbur F. Wright, alias "Walter Wright" (black, age 29). *Murder.* The crime was committed on 1/2/1932 at Baltimore. Cop killer. Executed for the handgun slaying of 52-year-old William Alfred Bell (white). Motive: resisting arrest. He was hanged on April 8, 1932. Source: *Baltimore Sun*, 1/3/32 (20:1), 1/4/32 (28:1) and 4/8/32 (24:4); *Baltimore Afro-American*, 4/16/32 (5:6).

1933

Euel Lee, alias "Orphan Jones" (black, age 61). *Murder.* The crime was committed on 10/12/1931 in Worcester County. Executed for the shotgun slayings of 55-year-old William Green Davis and 38-year-old Eva Davis (both white—a married couple), as well as 15-year-old Elizabeth Davis and 13-year-old Mary Lee Davis, their daughters. Motive: vindictiveness for the sake of *one dollar*, which he felt that he was owed. Venue changed from Worcester County to Baltimore County. Lee was also the prime suspect in the 1/24/1918 ax murders of two bachelor brothers (whites) named Evan Davis (age 52) and Thomas Davis (age 56) during a residential burglary in Mercer County, Pennsylvania. Lee was tried and acquitted for those murders but convicted for stealing from the crime scene. He was locked up in Pennsylvania's Western Penitentiary on that count from November 5, 1925, to May 5, 1931. The Maryland gallows settled his score on October 27, 1933. Source: *Pittsburgh (PA) Press*, 1/27/18 (1:6); *Baltimore Sun*, 10/13/31 (1:1), 10/14/31 (40:1), 10/16/31 (50:7) and 10/27/33 (24:1); *Democratic Messenger* (Snow Hill, MD), 10/17/31 (1:5), 10/24/31 (1:6) and 11/7/31 (1:6). See also 1910 U.S. Census (Mercer Co., PA), which notes the Davis brothers.

1934

Page Jupiter (black, age 42). *Murder.* The crime was committed on 7/8/1933 in Charles County. Executed for the ax murder of 47-year-old Evelyn Reifschneider (white). Motive: sexual assault. The killer was hanged on February 2, 1934. Source: *Washington Post*, 7/9/33 (1:2) and 7/10/33 (1:3); *Washington Afro-American*, 7/15/33 (1:6) and 2/10/34 (9:6); *Baltimore Sun*, 2/2/34 (22:2).

1935

Gordon Dent (black, age 29) and **James A. Gross** (black, age 24). *Murder.* Their crime was committed on 5/30/1934 in Prince George's County. Executed for the handgun slaying of 43-year-old John T. Geary, Jr. (white). Motive: robbery. The killers were hanged on April 19, 1935. Source: *Washington Post*, 5/31/34 (17:4) and 6/5/34 (12:5); *Baltimore Sun*, 4/19/35 (26:2).

William Harold, alias "Alexander Jones" (black, age 35) and **James Poindexter** (black, age 27). *Rape.* Their crime was committed on 9/30/1934 in Montgomery County. Indecent assault on the person of a 16-year-old white female whose identity was never divulged because her father was a high-ranking federal bureaucrat. The rapists were hanged on June 28, 1935. Source: *Evening Star* (Washington, D.C.), 10/1/34 (2:3); *Montgomery Independent* (Rockville, MD), 10/19/34 (1:1), 12/14/34 (1:7) and 4/19/35 (1:5); *Baltimore Sun*, 6/28/35 (28:5).

1936

Augusto Perez (Latino, age 25). *Rape.* The crime was committed on 10/17/1935 at Baltimore. Indecent assault on the person of 10-year-old Constance Kosakowski (white), she having been grievously molested in a boxcar. This child rapist was hanged on June 12, 1936. Source: *Baltimore News & Post*, 11/22/35 (5:1); *Baltimore Sun*, 11/23/35 (20:5) and 6/12/36 (28:6). See also Criminal Court of Baltimore indictment docket (1935), pages 536 and 813; MD State Archives.

Willie Williams (black, age 35). *Murder.* The crime was committed on 2/25/1936 at Baltimore. Executed for the beatings and handgun slayings of 75-year-old Samuel Blacher and 64-year-old Bessie Blacher (both white—a married couple). Motive: shoplifting attempt turned violent. The killer was hanged on June 12, 1936. Source: *Baltimore Sun*, 2/26/36 (24:8), 2/27/36 (22:1) and 6/12/36 (28:6).

1937

James Irvin Howard (black, age 23). *Murder.* The crime was committed on 4/1/1937 in Anne Arundel County. Executed for the murder of 55-year-old Marie M. Gunther (white), she having been beaten and then finished off by having her throat cut. Motive: highway robbery. The killer was hanged on July 9, 1937. Source: *Baltimore Sun*, 4/2/37 (28:8) and 7/9/37 (26:2).

1938

Richard Hammond (black, age 31). *Murder.* The crime was committed on 8/12/1937 at Baltimore. Executed for the murder of 46-year-old Edith Milman (white), who was beaten on the head with a heavy candlestick. Motive: burglary. The killer was hanged on August 12, 1938. Source: *Baltimore Sun*, 8/14/37 (18:8), 8/21/37 (18:1), 8/23/37 (16:3) and 8/12/38 (8:6). See also 1930 U.S. Census (Baltimore, MD), which notes Mrs. Milman.

James Albert Turner (black, age 25). *Rape.* The crime was committed on 5/31/1938 in Montgomery County. Indecent assault on the person of 13-year-old Etta May Coleman (white), she having also been beaten to within an inch of her life. The rapist was hanged on August 26, 1938. Source: *Washington Post*, 6/1/38 (1:6) and 6/2/38 (1:5); *Baltimore Sun*, 8/26/38 (22:4).

1939

Frederick L. Brown (white, age 48). *Murder.* The crime was committed on 6/14/1938 in Dorchester County. Uxoricide. Executed for the strangulation of pregnant 17-year-old Elizabeth Arvey Brown (white—his child bride), whose body was dumped into a river at midstream. Motive: she had reported him for cruelty to animals. The killer was hanged on March 10, 1939. Source: *Daily Banner* (Cambridge, MD), 6/20/38 (1:7), 7/13/38 (1:7), 7/14/38 (1:7) and 3/10/39 (1:5); *Daring Detective*, 12/38; *Front Page Detective*, 3/39; *Crime Detective*, 12/40.

1940

Alvin Kenton (white, age 22) and **Thomas Sanchez** (Latino, age 39). *Rape.* Their crime was committed on 9/8/1939 in Talbot County. Indecent assault on the person of 82-year-old Alice Aikens (white), she having been attacked in her own home. Concomitant aggravated assault on the person of 84-year-old Peter Aikens (white—her husband), who was tortured in an attempt to make him reveal the hiding place of his money. Venue changed from Talbot County to Queen Anne's County. The miscreants were hanged on March 15, 1940. Source: *Queen Anne's Record-Observer*, 9/14/39 (1:1); *Baltimore Sun*, 3/15/40 (28:2); *Daily Banner* (Cambridge, MD), 3/15/40 (1:4).

Otis Harrell (black, age 23) and **William Sorrell** (black, age 28). *Murder.* Their crime was committed on 12/16/1939 at Baltimore. Executed for the handgun slaying of 74-year-old Wallace L. Smith (black). Motive: home invasion. The killers were hanged on May 10, 1940. Source: *Baltimore Sun*, 12/17/39 (26:8) and 5/10/40 (10:3); *Baltimore Afro-American*, 5/18/40 (1:7).

Alexander Williams (black, age 33). *Rape.* The crime was committed on 5/8/1940 in Anne Arundel County. Indecent assault on the person of 22-year-old Adele Stockett (white), she having been dragged from her home by Williams, an escaped convict, and outraged by him twice. He was hanged on June 28, 1940. Source: *Daily Mail* (Hagerstown, MD), 5/25/40 (2:7); *Baltimore Sun*, 6/28/40 (24:3).

Arthur Henry Collick (black, age 28). *Murder.* The crime was committed on 2/11/1940 in Worcester County. Executed for the shotgun slaying of 61-year-old Harvey Pilchard (white). Motive: home invasion. Venue changed from Worcester County to Baltimore County. The killer was hanged on September 13, 1940. Source: *Baltimore Sun*, 2/13/40 (5:1) and 2/17/40 (20:1); *Baltimore Afro-American*, 9/21/40 (24:6).

1941

Wilson Knott (white, age 33). *Rape.* The crime was committed on 8/24/1940 in Anne Arundel County. Indecent assault on the person of a 19-year-old white female (name withheld) and the unlawful restraint of her 24-year-old male companion, who was tied up and forced to watch. Knott was also the prime suspect in the 5/26/1940 handgun slaying of 25-year-old Frank A. Scheihing (white) at Baltimore, Maryland, and the attempted sexual assault of that young man's female companion (Anna Peterson, white, age 24) under circumstances nearly identical to those for which he was hanged. This rapist met justice at the end of a rope on January 10, 1941. Source: *Daily Mail* (Hagerstown, MD), 5/27/40 (14:6) and 12/14/40 (1:2); *Baltimore Sun*, 1/10/41 (14:7); *Crime Detective*, 7/41.

French Lee White (black, age 32). *Rape.* The crime was committed on 11/23/1940 in Montgomery County. Indecent assault on the person of a 26-year-old white female (name withheld) amid violent circumstances. The rapist was hanged on June 27, 1941. Source: *Montgomery County Sentinel*, 4/10/41 (1:6); *Bethesda (MD) Journal*, 4/11/41 (1:5); *Frederick (MD) Post*, 6/14/41 (1:6); *Baltimore Sun*, 6/27/41 (16:5).

Earl Loveless (white, age 22) and **James Lee Miller** (white, age 28). *Murder.* Their crime was committed on 10/11/1940 in Washington County. Both were executed for the murder of 76-year-old Raleigh Poffenberger (white), who was beaten to death with a heavy metal wrench. Motive: robbery and gross perfidy. Venue changed from Washington County to Allegany County. The killers were hanged on September 26, 1941. Source: *Morning Herald* (Hagerstown, MD), 10/12/40 (1:1), 10/14/40 (1:1) and 9/26/41 (1:7).

James Baker (black, age 38). *Murder.* The crime was committed on 9/26/1941 in Dorchester County. Executed for the shotgun slaying of 34-year-old Larry Donohue (black). Motive: spitefulness (Baker had been ejected from a house party and didn't like it). He was hanged on December 19, 1941. Source: *Daily Banner & Cambridge (MD) Record*, 11/8/41 (1:1); *Baltimore Afro-American*, 12/27/41 (11:2).

1942

Wilbur Pritchett (black, age 37). *Attempted Rape.* The crime was committed on 1/16/1942 in Dorchester County. Felonious assault on the person of 62-year-old Jessie R. Dail (white, a maiden woman), who was beaten, terrorized and driven from her home during a nocturnal burglary. The attacker was hanged on May 8, 1942. Source: *Daily Banner* (Cambridge, MD), 1/17/42 (1:1); *Democrat & News* (Cambridge, MD), 2/26/42 (1:2); *Baltimore Sun*, 5/8/42 (13:5). See also 1910 U.S. Census (Dorchester Co., MD), which notes the victim earlier in her lifetime.

Frank Haywood (black, age 32). *Rape.* The crime was committed on 12/24/1941 in Prince George's County. Indecent assault on the person of an 18-year-old white female (name withheld) who was forcibly abducted for that purpose on Christmas Eve. The rapist was hanged on June 5, 1942. Source: *Baltimore Sun*, 6/5/42 (6:6); *Baltimore Afro-American*, 6/13/42 (18:1).

Andrew Henry (black, age 53). *Murder.* The crime was committed on 4/18/1942 in Dorchester County. Executed for the shotgun slaying of 36-year-old Francis P. Ross (black). Motive: monetary dispute. The killer was hanged on July 10, 1942. Source: *Daily Banner* (Cambridge, MD), 4/20/42 (1:5) and 7/10/42 (1:3); *Democrat & News* (Cambridge, MD), 5/7/42 (1:7).

Edward Woffard (black, age 26) and **Charles Jackson Benjamin** (black, age 22). *Murder.* Their crime was committed on 12/28/1941 at Baltimore. Executed for the handgun slaying of 44-year-old Vincent di Pietro (white). Motive: robbery. The killers were hanged on July 24, 1942. Source: *Baltimore Sun,* 12/29/41 (18:1) and 7/24/42 (4:2); *Daily Mail* (Hagerstown, MD), 7/24/42 (1:4).

1943

James Gilliam (black, age 38). *Murder.* The crime was committed on 8/22/1942 in Worcester County. Executed for the shotgun slaying of 40-year-old David Lewis (black). Motive: gambling dispute. The killer was hanged on January 15, 1943. Source: *Democratic Messenger* (Snow Hill, MD), 8/27/42 (1:3); *Baltimore Afro-American,* 1/8/44 (10:1), in retro. (This wartime execution for black-on-black murder was almost entirely ignored by the press. An official list of executions obtained from the Maryland Department of Corrections included Gilliam as having been hanged on the aforesaid date, while a brief newspaper mention of the fact almost an entire year later confirms it in the upshot.)

James Ford (black, age 31). *Rape.* The crime was committed on 3/22/1942 at Baltimore. Indecent assault on the person of 42-year-old Mary Stewart (white), she having been bludgeoned with a stick in order to disable her. The rapist was hanged on March 12, 1943. Source: *Salisbury (MD) Times,* 3/12/43 (3:2). Appeal: 181 MD 303–314. See also Criminal Court of Baltimore indictment docket for the year 1942, pages 158 and 863; File No. 943 (MD State Archives).

Freeman Holton (black, age 20), **Wilbur Jackson** (black, age 20) and **Frank Williams** (black, age 23). *Murder.* Their crime was committed on 8/4/1941 at Baltimore. Executed for the handgun slaying of 37-year-old Louis Pertnoy (white), a theater manager. Motive: armed robbery. The guilty parties were hanged on June 4, 1943. Source: *Baltimore News-Post,* 8/5/41 (13:5); *Baltimore Sun,* 8/5/41 (24:1) and 6/4/43 (15:3); *Baltimore Afro-American,* 6/12/43 (20:7).

John Lampkin (black, age 19). *Rape.* The crime was committed on 3/17/1943 at Baltimore. Indecent assault on the person of "a young white woman" named "Miss Sanford Norris," who was forcibly abducted, severely beaten, held against her will and violated by more than one assailant. Lampkin was hanged on August 13, 1943. Source: *Baltimore News-Post,* 3/18/43 (22:1) and 8/13/43 (11:3).

1944

William Charles Holsey (black, age 32). *Murder.* The crime was committed on 8/30/1943 in Carroll County. Executed for the shotgun slaying of 55-year-old Charles L. Meister (white). Motive: robbery. The killer was hanged on February 25, 1944. Source: *The Times*

(Westminster, MD), 11/19/43 (1:5); *Baltimore News-Post*, 2/24/44 (3:1) and 2/25/44 (21:2); *Frederick (MD) Post*, 2/26/44 (10:1).

Martin Smith (black, age 19). *Rape.* The crimes were committed on 1/22/1944 and 1/23/1944 at Baltimore. Indecent assaults on the persons of two married white women (names withheld, ages not specified), who were attacked in their homes by an armed burglar (Smith) fourteen hours apart. This marauder was hanged on March 31, 1944. Source: *Baltimore Sun*, 1/23/44 (20:8), 1/24/44 (18:7), 1/25/44 (22:2), 1/26/44 (18:5) and 3/31/44 (22:2).

John Hinton (black, age 25). *Attempted Rape.* The crime was committed on 3/12/1944 in Somerset County. Felonious assault on the person of 15-year-old Geraldine Griffin (white), she having been attacked in her own home but saved from actual defilement by the timely arrival of a third party. Trial venue changed from Somerset County to Dorchester County. The attacker was hanged on June 16, 1944. Source: *Marylander & Herald* (Princess Anne, MD), 3/17/44 (1:7) and 3/24/44 (1:7); *Baltimore Afro-American*, 6/24/44 (16:8) and (17:4).

Calvin William Watkins (black, age 24). *Murder.* The crime was committed on 4/1/1944 at Baltimore. Executed for the killing of 57-year-old Joseph J. Stewart (white), who was beaten to death with a mallet. Motive: mugging. Watkins was hanged for this act of violence on November 17, 1944. Source: *Baltimore Evening Sun*, 4/3/44 (18:4) and (23:8); *Baltimore Morning Sun*, 4/3/44 (6:1); *Baltimore Afro-American*, 11/25/44 (12:3).

1945

Patrick J. Murphy (white, age 37). *Rape.* The crime was committed on 4/19/1942 in Prince George's County. Indecent assault on the person of 25-year-old Margaret Laignel (white). Murphy was additionally charged with capital felony for the 2/18/1945 rape of an 18-year-old Prince George's County female whose name was not made public. This suspected serial rapist was hanged on July 20, 1945. Source: *Baltimore News-Post*, 3/27/44 (3:5), 4/29/44 (3:4) and 7/20/45 (17:3); *Morning Herald* (Hagerstown, MD), 6/30/45 (1:6); *Baltimore Sun*, 7/20/45 (22:2).

Luther McClam (black, age 28). *Murder.* The crime was committed on 3/10/1944 at Baltimore. Executed for the murders of 22-year-old Ray Moore, 33-year-old Thomas Tate and 44-year-old Fred Moore (blacks), who were all battered to death with an iron pipe. Motive: gambling dispute. McClam was already a convicted murderer when he killed the three gamesters. Subsequent investigation found that he had escaped from a South Carolina penal farm where he was serving a so-called life sentence for killing his wife. He was hanged on August 17, 1945. Source: *Baltimore News-Post*, 3/11/44 (3:4); *Baltimore Afro-American*, 12/23/44 (6:3) and 8/25/45 (16:6).

Donald H. Brooks (white, age 31). *Murder.* The crime was committed on 7/1/1944 at Baltimore. Executed for the murder of 63-year-old Mary M. Finn (white), she having been battered to death with a hammer on the day that she was supposed to have been married. Motive: residential burglary. The killer was hanged on November 30, 1945. Source: *Baltimore News-Post*, 7/1/44

(1:7) and 11/30/45 (26:3); *Front Page Detective*, 1/45; *Official Detective*, 5/45 and 10/71; *Crime Detective*, 2/46 and 12/64; *Master Detective*, 2/53.

John Henry Fields (black, age 25). *Murder.* The crime was committed on 2/5/1945 in Worcester County. Executed for the shotgun slaying of 39-year-old Gordon G. Barnes (white), a deputy game warden with the Maryland Department of Natural Resources. Motive: hunting out of season. Fields was hanged on December 28, 1945. Source: *Democratic Messenger* (Snow Hill, MD), 2/8/45 (1:7); *The Capitol* (Annapolis, MD), 12/28/45 (1:5).

1946

William Tasker (black, age 21). *Murder.* The crime was committed on 9/5/1945 in Anne Arundel County. Executed for the ax murder of 29-year-old Richard Johnson (black). Motive: personal grudge. The killer was hanged on January 18, 1946. Source: *The Capitol* (Annapolis, MD), 11/9/45 (1:3) and 1/17/46 (1:6); *Baltimore Afro-American*, 1/26/46 (17:4).

Lloyd Walker (black, age 23). *Attempted Rape.* The crime was committed on 6/4/1945 at Baltimore. Felonious assault on the person of a 19-year-old white female (name withheld) with intent to commit rape. She and her 19-year-old male escort were accosted in a public park, terrorized at the point of a knife, robbed of their valuables and stripped nearly naked. The attacker was hanged on August 9, 1946. Source: *Baltimore Sun*, 10/17/45 (14:4); *Baltimore News-Post*, 8/9/46 (24:5). Appeal: 186 MD 440–445.

William Daniel Demby (black, age 23) and **Roy Nathan Peters** (black, age 23). *Rape.* Their crime was committed on 1/8/1946 in Harford County. Indecent assault on the person of 28-year-old Edna E. Strickland (white), she having been forcibly abducted by four miscreants in all. The trial venue was changed from Harford County to Baltimore City. The two principal offenders were hanged on October 4, 1946. Source: *Harford Gazette* (Bel Air, MD), 1/11/46 (1:7), 1/18/46 (1:7), 1/25/46 (1:3), 2/1/46 (1:5), 2/15/46 (1:7) and 2/22/46 (1:7); *Baltimore Afro-American*, 2/23/46 (20:6) and 10/12/46 (15:4).

John Lester Barnes (black, age 24). *Rape.* The crime was committed on 8/4/1945 in Prince George's County. Indecent assault on the person of a 53-year-old white female (name withheld), the further details of which are not in the public domain. The rapist in this case was hanged on December 13, 1946. Source: *Washington Post*, 8/7/45 (4:2); *Daily Mail* (Hagerstown, MD), 12/13/46 (18:5). Appeal: 186 MD 287–312.

1947

Charles Lee Carmen (black, age 23). *Rape.* The crime was committed on 6/23/1946 in Cecil County. Indecent assault on the person of 26-year-old Dottie Jean Streeter (white), she having been attacked in her home while recuperating from a hospital stay. Trial venue changed from Cecil County to Harford County. The rapist was hanged on January 17, 1947. Source: *Cecil Whig* (Elkton, MD), 6/27/46 (1:5) and 10/31/46 (1:8); *Philadelphia (PA) Evening Bulletin*, 1/17/47 (3:7).

William E. Copper (black, age 21). *Rape.* The crime was committed on 1/30/1947 in Talbot County. Indecent assault on the person of a 25-year-old white female (name withheld), she having been attacked by a stowaway in her automobile (Copper) who had hidden in the backseat for that purpose. Trial venue changed from Talbot County to Cecil County. The rapist was hanged on June 27, 1947. Source: *Baltimore Sun*, 6/27/47 (9:2); *Salisbury (MD) Times*, 6/27/47 (1:1).

Ross J. Abbott (white, age 24). *Murder.* The crime was committed on 7/19/1946 in Somerset County. Executed for the handgun slaying of 19-year-old Pansy Twigg (white). Motive: jilted lover. Abbott was hanged on August 1, 1947. Source: *Journal Every Evening* (Wilmington, DE), 7/20/46 (9:6); *Baltimore Sun*, 8/1/47 (10:2). Appeal: 188 MD 310–315.

Weldon Jones, Jr. (black, age 18). *Murder.* The crime was committed on 1/12/1945 in Somerset County. Executed for the rifle slaying of 38-year-old Raynor Graham (white) during the course of a crime spree. Motive: robbery. Jones went to the gallows on August 1, 1947. Source: *Journal Every Evening* (Wilmington, DE), 1/13/45 (1:4); *Baltimore Afro-American*, 1/20/45 (1:1), 1/27/45 (20:6), 2/3/45 (20:7) and 8/9/47 (10:3). Appeals: 185 MD 481–491 and 188 MD 263–273.

1948

Henry Tilghman Jackson (black, age 28). *Murder.* The crime was committed on 9/6/1944 in Worcester County. Executed for the shotgun slaying of 31-year-old Otha Mason (black male) and concomitant murder of Emma Jackson (black, age not recorded), the latter having been battered to death with the stock of the gun. Motive: personal feud. The killer was hanged on April 30, 1948. Source: *Democratic Messenger* (Snow Hill, MD), 9/7/44 (1:5); *Baltimore News-Post*, 4/30/48 (26:1).

Roy Lee Lathco (white, age 39). *Rape.* The crime was committed on 7/15/1947 in Baltimore County. Child rapist. Indecent assault on the person of an 11-year-old white female (name withheld), who was left severely injured and traumatized by what he did to her. Lathco paid for this at the end of a rope on April 30, 1948. Source: *County Record* (Towson, MD), 7/18/47 (1:2) and 9/19/47 (8:2); *Baltimore News-Post*, 4/30/48 (26:1).

Ollie Smith, Jr. (black, age 22). *Rape.* The crime was committed on 5/3/1947 in Dorchester County. Indecent assault on the person of 22-year-old Florence May Henry (white), who was beaten and dragged from her home. This rapist was hanged on April 30, 1948. Source: *Democrat & News* (Cambridge, MD), 5/8/47 (1:5); *Baltimore News-Post*, 4/30/48 (26:1). Appeal: 189 MD 596–609.

1949

Howard Andrew Frahm (white, age 31). *Murder.* The crime was committed on 12/17/1947 at Baltimore. Executed for the hatchet murder of 77-year-old George Lehr (white). Motive: robbery. The killer was hanged on July 8, 1949. Source: *Baltimore Sun*, 12/18/47 (36:4) and 12/26/47 (18:5); *Front Page Detective*, 7/48; *Real Detective*, 9/48; *Master Detective*, 1/49; *Baltimore News-Post*, 7/8/49 (1:7).

Eugene H. James (black, age 31). *Murder.* The crime was committed on 7/6/1948 at Baltimore. Child killer. Executed for the fatal stabbing of 11-year-old Marsha Brill (white), she having been attacked while riding her bicycle in a public park. Motive: attempted sexual assault. James was additionally confirmed to have murdered a second child at Washington, D.C., under almost identical circumstances on 6/27/1948. The victim in that case was 11-year-old Carol Bardwell, she having been slashed to death with a butcher knife. This killer was hanged on August 12, 1949. Source: *Baltimore News-Post*, 7/6/48 (1:7), 7/7/48 (1:7), 7/9/48 (1:7) and 8/12/49 (31:2); *Official Detective*, 11/48; *Baltimore Afro-American*, 8/20/49 (1:3). Appeal: 193 MD 31–46.

John Thomas Knowles (black, age 26). *Murder.* The crime was committed on 6/13/1948 at Baltimore. Executed for the mutilation murder of 21-year-old Ruby Davis (black), who was found to have been stabbed 23 times with a butcher knife, among other rending injuries. Motive: control freak gone berserk. Knowles was hanged on August 12, 1949. Source: *Baltimore Afro-American*, 6/26/48 (12:1) and 8/20/49 (1:3); *Baltimore Sun*, 8/12/49 (30:2). Appeal: 192 MD 664–671.

1953

Lot Glover, alias "Willie Green" (black, age 31). *Murder.* The crime was committed on 1/29/1952 in Prince George's County. Described as a "burly merchant seaman," this offender originally came from South Carolina. His last known address was a rooming house at no. 1507 Marion St. NW, Washington, D.C. He was out of work on the above date and eager to make a score. Even so, lack of funds did not stop Glover from partying the night away in a Baltimore dancehall. He was on his way home with two sleepy women (at about 5 o'clock in the morning) when an impulse to rob somebody overtook him. Glover pulled his jalopy into Arnold Baker's Service Station, a 24-hour business situated in Beltsville along the old Baltimore–Washington highway. He overpowered the lone attendant there, James Alfred Beacraft (white, age 49), and beat him on the head with heavy metal pliers. Glover then helped himself to $44 from the service station's cash register. He also took coins from Beacraft's pockets, plus the injured man's wristwatch, a car battery and two boxes of cheap cigars. Afterward, Glover drove onward with his female companions, who remained unaware of what he had done.

The station attendant staggered over to the nearby home of his employer, where he managed to gasp out the news of what had happened. Then he fell into a coma, succumbing to a skull fracture ten hours later. Prince George's County police were promptly alerted. They stopped Glover's car before it reached the DC line. In response, Glover fled into the woods. His passengers were taken into custody, where they presumably told the police what they wanted to know. Glover made it back to his rooming house by a roundabout route but soon found that place surrounded by lawmen. He reportedly "hoisted himself through a skylight and fled over rooftops as police searched the building." Thus did Glover escape a second time. Somebody told police that he would likely go to Baltimore; as a result, every Maryland-bound bus was searched. The killer was finally nabbed that way. He admitted to both the service station robbery and the assault on James Alfred Beacraft. He was hanged on August 28, 1953.

Maryland's governor—Theodore R. McKeldin—allowed this execution to go forward despite his personal opposition to capital punishment. He explained his reasons for doing so in the following statement: "A complete reading of Glover's rather extensive testimony at trial gives one the impression of a clever, rather intelligent person whom the trial court found able to express himself far better than many persons of his origin. I am in complete accord with the statement of the trial judge that there were no mitigating facts in the case and I could find no justification for altering the penalty imposed by the court." McKeldin had previously commuted seven other Maryland death sentences while allowing none to be carried out. His decision not to spare Glover caught his critics by surprise. Source: *Washington Post*, 1/30/52 (1:8), 1/31/52 (B:8:1) and 8/28/53 (1:3). Appeal: 202 MD 522–532.

1954

George Edward Grammer (white, age 35). *Murder.* The crime was committed on 8/20/1952 near Baltimore. Uxoricide. "A diabolically clever man did it," said Maryland governor Theodore R. McKeldin in reference to this case. Its details were indeed as sordid as they were shrewd. George Grammer—a Manhattan executive—had cheated on his wife during what was supposed to be a period of mourning. He had also pestered that woman for a quickie divorce (her unblemished character and devotion to their three small children notwithstanding) and cruelly bludgeoned her to death when she balked at his lack of decorum. A staged car wreck also figured in what newsmen dubbed "The Almost Perfect Murder."

George Edward and Dorothy Mae Grammer (née Schmidt) had grown up within the better part of Baltimore society. Their parents were conscientious homemakers. The future couple attended local schools before advancing to more specialized pursuits. George, or "G. Edward," as he styled himself, served with the U.S. Army Counter Intelligence Corps during World War II. His wife graduated from a prestigious nursing academy in 1939. The couple moved to New York City shortly after their marriage because young Mr. Grammer had accepted a job there. He subsequently attained the high point of his life as office manager for the Climax Molybdenum Corporation (a metals and minerals concern) at no. 500 Fifth Avenue.

Fast-forward to the spring of 1952. Grammer had been in New York for eleven years by then, discounting military service. A Bronx apartment building (1569 Metropolitan Avenue) served as his primary residence. Three daughters, ages eleven, seven and four, rounded out his household. A propitious future seemed assured; the upwardly mobile G. Edward Grammer found himself blessed with a good job, a good home, a loyal wife, fine kids, and so forth. Then came a telephone call from his in-laws in Maryland: Dorothy Mae's father was terminally ill, and her mother needed help in dealing with the situation. There being no estrangement between the Grammers and their Maryland kin, it was agreed that Dorothy Mae should stay with her parents for a while. She accordingly took up temporary quarters there while her husband remained in New York with their children. Weekly train trips to Baltimore ensured that all kept in close personal contact.

Spring became summer. Dorothy Mae's father passed away as expected. A dutiful daughter (as well as a faithful wife), the former then obtained her husband's consent to stay in Maryland for the rest of that season. Her request was an understandable one under the circumstances, Dorothy Mae's mother being sorely bereaved, and George Grammer was more than willing to agree to this. Ostensible compassion (as it was later shown) afforded him a perfect cover for something entirely different. He had in fact taken advantage of his wife's absence in order to cavort with another woman, a pretty office worker (employed at the United Nations) who naively believed Grammer when he misrepresented himself to her as a bachelor. Several weeks of dinner dates and romance followed. It was enough to make Grammer rue being a married father of three. He then cast about for a means of extricating himself from such a position, albeit in a way that would not tip off his mistress to the fact that he was also an adulterer and a liar. The simple thought of remaining true to his lawful spouse apparently didn't even occur to him.

Slowly, Dorothy Mae Grammer caught on to what her husband was doing. She maintained a stoic veneer but did let slip some hints of inner anguish. For instance, during the course of a long-distance telephone call between "Ed" Grammer and Dorothy Mae, the latter was heard to say, "Don't you love me anymore?" Later asked what she meant by that question, the woman sighed, "I'll never divorce him for another woman." A subsequent remark on the following day sounded equally ominous: "I'll never give him a divorce. We have to keep a home for the children."

This year Grammer had scheduled the second and third weeks in August as time off from work. He spent those days with his family, having gone to Baltimore as prearranged. Dorothy Mae was on hand to greet him at the Victory Avenue train station. The automobile she used on that occasion was a blue 1952 Chrysler sedan (brand new), an anniversary gift from her husband.

Grammer's widowed mother-in-law welcomed him into her home. No one suspected that he was set on a nefarious course of action. Grammer brought his wife's car to a repair shop that same week, claiming that it had a faulty accelerator. Mechanics checked for such a problem but found none. Only later was this explained as a tactic to create an alibi. Grammer's next move was to spend several days in feigned harmony with his wife and children. He was careful not to say or do anything that would excite apprehension in the minds of other family members. His return trip to New York was set for the pre-dawn hours of August 20, 1952. Grammer packed his bags accordingly and assisted Dorothy Mae in tucking their youngsters into bed. Then the couple set off for the Victory Avenue train station, seemingly the same as on previous occasions.

Two Baltimore police officers told of subsequent events in a written report: "At exactly 12:33 a.m. while on routine patrol we turned our squad car from Belair Road onto Taylor Avenue. No sooner had we done so however than we saw a late model sedan careening toward us apparently out of control. Its speed increased along a downhill course so that we had to swerve to avoid a collision. The sedan then veered off the road of its own accord, sideswiped a telephone pole and flipped over onto its side. A lone female occupant was dead at the scene."

Close examination of the wreck gave grounds for suspicion that all was not as it appeared. The sedan's engine kept up a steady racing momentum even after the crash. Its wheels likewise kept spinning at full speed. There was only slight body damage to the vehicle and no broken glass save for that caused by rescuers attempting to reach the driver. Even so, that person—later identified as Dorothy Mae Grammer—had head injuries to a traumatic extent. These included two skull fractures, plus seven distinct lacerations of the scalp and forehead. Moreover, blood found on the driver's seat was already partially dry despite officers having reached the crash scene within seconds of impact, and the dead woman's pocketbook was strangely missing. There was also a pebble wedged beneath the vehicle's accelerator in such a way as to jam it forward in the high-speed position. Had this somehow occurred by accident? It didn't seem likely. Still, such details being purely speculative at that point, they were withheld from the press. Local newspapers therefore reported (at least initially) that Mrs. Dorothy Mae Grammer (white, age 33) had died as the result of a tragic accident. Authorities found Mr. G. Edward Grammer at his Bronx apartment later that same day. He was officially notified of his wife's death according to standard police procedure.

No actor could have played a dramatic role more convincingly than did George Grammer during the next several days. He immediately returned to Baltimore, where his relatives received him amid displays of tender affection. A funeral for the late Mrs. Grammer was largely attended. Her apparently stunned widower received all kinds of condolences. Then he was carried to his mother-in-law's house in a prostrate condition. Grammer remained in bed for an entire week. No amount of effort could rouse him from what appeared to be a semi-catatonic state of shock. He neither washed, shaved nor ate solid food. His only nourishment during that time was spoon-fed sips of broth. Then, late one night, Grammer's brother-in-law caught him raiding the refrigerator. "To what may we attribute this sudden transformation?" asked the brother-in-law. Grammer replied that he was feeling better.

It was then decided that the brother-in-law should drive Grammer back to New York at the first opportunity so that extra clothing could be fetched back to Baltimore for his personal use. The two men reached their destination without incident. However, once inside Grammer's Bronx apartment, the brother-in-law glimpsed Dorothy Mae's pocketbook on the bedroom floor. It was the same pocketbook that the deceased woman had had with her when she drove her husband to the train station on the night that she had died. This seemed odd—to say the least—since Grammer had already suggested to Baltimore police interviewers that Dorothy Mae might have been carjacked by robbers after he had boarded the New York–bound train—hence the absence of her pocketbook from the wrecked automobile.

Grammer played off his brother-in-law with a hastily contrived explanation for the presence of the pocketbook in his apartment. The brother-in-law pretended to believe him but reported his suspicions when he returned to Baltimore. Their interest piqued, investigators decided to take a closer look at Mr. Grammer. They found that he had recently gone on a business trip to Chicago. A check of his hotel's guest register disclosed that Grammer had not taken a single room. A female guest had registered along with him under the pseudonym "Mrs. Edward Grammer." The true Mrs. Grammer having been in Baltimore at that time, it was thus established that G. Edward Grammer had brought another woman along with him on the sly. Detectives then carefully reexamined the accident scene. The wrecked sedan had been going downhill when it suddenly spun off the road. Had a straight course been kept for just a few seconds longer, the car would have smashed head on into a concrete retaining wall. And what about that pebble that had been jammed under the accelerator?

Had that been done deliberately with the concrete wall as an intended target? Such a crash would have indeed been serious enough to account for the injuries incurred by the dead woman; however, the vehicle had suddenly swerved off course just before impact so that only minor damage had resulted—damage not commensurate with the decedent's wounds. Something about this purported car accident didn't ring true.

Detectives next retraced the path of the wrecked automobile. They questioned everyone who lived along upper Taylor Avenue. Their route eventually took them over the crest of a hill to the then sprawling campus of the Maryland School for the Blind. One of the matrons there (who lived in a former gatekeeper's cottage) reported that a dark-colored sedan had driven onto the grounds shortly after midnight on August 20 and parked near Taylor Avenue. She had not considered this unusual in itself because that same area was popularly known as a lovers' lane. However, on this particular occasion the same matron had heard a frightful scream shortly after the sedan's arrival. A forensics team then scoured the site. A lead pipe with an elbow joint on the end of it was found in an ivy bed near where the sedan had parked. Laboratory analysis revealed latent blood stains on that object.

George Edward Grammer eventually cracked during interrogation. He admitted to having bludgeoned his wife with the lead pipe as charged. He had ordered her to pull their car off Taylor Avenue while en route to the Victory Avenue train station so that they could discuss personal differences. The campus of the Maryland School for the Blind had merely been a convenient spot for them to talk, or so he said. Then, according to Grammer's narrative, he had lost his temper during a heated exchange and struck Dorothy Mae with the pipe. Seeing that she was dead, he sought to make the whole thing look like an accident. He drove the car a short distance to the top of the Taylor Avenue hill and poised it there with his wife's body propped up in the driver's seat. Yes, he had jammed a pebble under the accelerator so that the car would hurtle down the hill, smash into the aforesaid retaining wall and thereby complete the deception. It was a disingenuous statement. Grammer was trying to weasel his way out of culpability for what was in fact a premeditated murder.

How was it, then—demanded the interrogators—that Grammer had so conveniently happened to have a lead pipe handy when he supposedly lost his temper? What about the phony repair shop story about a malfunctioning accelerator? Furthermore, how was it that the pebble that jammed the accelerator was of the exact same variety of crushed stone as found in the driveway of his mother-in-law's house? It seemed likely under the circumstances that Grammer had deliberately picked up that pebble there and brought it along with him for the express purpose of tampering with the accelerator later. His choice of the Maryland School for the Blind was also as cynical as it was cagey: none of the residents there could *see* anything.

The clincher came at the trial, when Grammer's illicit girlfriend testified as a surprise witness for the prosecution. She had played no direct part in the murder plot, but her very existence made Grammer look bad in the eyes of the jury. The verdict was guilty with no recommendation for mercy.

On June 11, 1954, this murderer was hanged at the Maryland State Penitentiary. "I cannot ignore the callous manner in which he cunningly contrived the cruel and vicious battering of his faithful wife, a devoted mother," declared Governor McKeldin earlier that day. "The application for clemency is denied."

Source: *The News* (Frederick, MD), 6/11/54 (7:5); *Front Page Detective*, 12/52 and 12/78; *True Detective*, 1/53; *Crime Detective*, 2/53 and 11/60; *Real Detective*, 12/58; *Official Detective*, 11/70; *Master Detective*, 9/73. Appeal: 203 MD 200–226.

1955

William C. Thomas (black, age 32). *Murder.* The crime was committed on 1/17/1954 at Baltimore. Beloved by all, 67-year-old Delia Honeyman (white, a maiden woman) made her home on North Gilmore Street, just west of Baltimore's downtown business district. She owned a little candy store. Two decades in the same location had established her as a neighborhood fixture. Then, on the above date, along came Willie Thomas, a roving thief and pervert about whom not even the city's foremost Negro newspaper (the *Baltimore Afro-American*) could find a single good thing to say. He forced his way into Miss Honeyman's unpretentious abode sometime during the pre-dawn hours. The details of what transpired next were substantiated by forensic evidence. Thomas beat the aging woman so severely that the phrase "covered with bruises" was used to put it tactfully. He also tore Miss Honeyman's clothes off (without even attempting to unbutton them first) and raped her in every conceivable way. That done, he choked her to death with his bare hands. Thomas also ransacked both store and living quarters in a frenzied search for valuables. He found a jar containing $4,700 in assorted monies (part of the woman's life savings) but reportedly missed much more in his haste. Even so, the sheer atrocity of this murder was enough to incite Baltimore citizenry, both black and white.

Police worked without clues for nearly a month. Then came an unexpected breakthrough. One of the killer's drinking buddies got arrested on a petty charge. That person offered inside information about the Delia Honeyman case in exchange for dismissal of the charge against him. As he told it, Willie Thomas had been seen at a Washington, D.C., afterhours club for several nights in a row. He was spending money beyond his means and in an unguarded moment (while under the influence of liquor) had let slip details about its source. Baltimore and DC police immediately staked out the speakeasy and nabbed Thomas.

Arraigned, the suspect acknowledged burglary, robbery and rape. He stood mute, however, when a plea to murder was demanded of him. A trial jury had no difficulty in sorting this out. The verdict was guilty and the sentence was death by hanging. "I can find no grounds to intervene," said the governor. "There are no mitigating circumstances." Thomas was executed on June 10, 1955. Source: *Frederick (MD) Post*, 1/19/54 (8:4), 2/10/54 (1:3) and 2/16/54 (1:3); *Frederick (MD) News*, 3/26/55 (11:3) and 6/10/55 (6:2); *Baltimore Afro-American*, 6/18/55 (17:3). Appeal: 206 MD 575–588.

1957

Eddie Lee Daniels (black, age 28). *Murder.* The crime was committed on 4/22/1956 at Silver Spring. "His guilt is not open to any reasonable doubt. No mitigating circumstances are presented by the actual facts." So spoke Maryland governor Theodore R. McKeldin in denying executive clemency to this killer. It was a pronouncement based on consternation more than anything else. McKeldin's personal opposition to capital punishment had moved him to commute the sentences of twelve other condemned criminals up until this time, but he could find no pretext whatsoever—not even a lame one—for intervention in this case.

Daniels was a man of no set occupation. His last known address was a seedy rooming house in the 1200 block of Constitution Avenue NE, Washington, D.C. Low on cash, he hatched a scheme to get some quickly. It entailed armed robbery. Daniels recalled a suburban car wash where he had obtained employment the previous year (address: 8808 Old Bladensburg Road). He had lasted there for only two days as a hired hand, but he had seen enough during that time to know where money was kept. His next move was to recruit an accomplice who owned an automobile. He wound up with two willing cronies: Richard Leroy Simmons (black, age 22), a so-called "art student," and James Arthur Sullivan (black, age 28), a "former bartender," as they were described. The three schemers agreed that Simmons would act as the getaway driver, while Sullivan would act as a lookout and Daniels as actual gunman during the heist.

Shrewdly, the conspirators waited until five minutes before the car wash closed for business on the above date. Then they put their plan in motion. Simmons drove the getaway vehicle to a parking lot directly behind but a short distance downhill from the target. Sullivan kept watch thereabout. Daniels traversed the remaining distance on foot, a loaded pistol in his waistband. He knew exactly where to go: a small office where the car wash owners were counting that day's receipts. Those persons consisted of two business partners named Arthur E. Chyatte (Jewish, age 61) and Meyer Klem (Jewish, age 58), as well as the former's wife, Mrs. Sophia Chyatte.

The intruder (Daniels) knocked on the office door. A voice from within asked what he wanted. Daniels replied that he needed change for a quarter. The people in the office mistook him for one of their scrub crew. So the door was opened to him. Daniels immediately barged into the room, weapon drawn. He had by then slipped a surgical mask over his face to keep from being recognized. Daniels flung a pillowcase (which he had purposely brought with him) at Meyer Klem and ordered that it be filled with money. Klem obeyed, but Arthur Chyatte said, "Wait a minute, you!" Daniels then shot Mr. Chyatte dead where he stood. The man's body fell atop his terrified business partner, who was retrieving cash from a floor safe at that moment. Sophia Chyatte saw her beloved husband slain before her eyes. She was traumatized by that experience. The robbery netted $407 at a far higher cost.

Daniels ran out of the car wash with his loot in one hand and gun in the other. Klem pursued him. Both men stumbled on the sloping terrain, but Daniels managed to reach his getaway car, which drove off at a high rate of speed, sideswiping another motorist while doing so. That person was quick thinking enough to note the license plate number. Police quickly ran this down. Simmons was dismayed at the revelation that a homicide had occurred, so he divulged the names of his accomplices. Sullivan also cooperated with authorities. Daniels, however, continued at large for several days. Police in the meantime learned the identity of a young woman of whom he was enamored. They went to her residence and questioned all persons there, including the young woman's mother. The latter despised Daniels for personal reasons and saw this as a chance to get rid of him. She immediately called the attention of her interviewers to a male pedestrian who was approaching her house at that very moment via a garden path. It was Eddie Lee Daniels. He took off running but was caught after a brief chase. He soon admitted every particular of his guilt. The State of Maryland having changed its method of execution from hanging to lethal gas that same year, Daniels found himself sentenced to the latter. He was executed on June 28, 1957. Source: *Washington Post*, 4/23/56 (1:8), 4/24/56 (1:6), 4/25/56 (1:3), 4/26/56 (1:1) and 6/29/57 (B:1:8). Appeal: 213 MD 90–109.

1959

Carl Daniel Kier (black, age 21). *Murder.* The crime was committed on 6/12/1956 at Towson. Albeit short, Kier's life story exemplified the evolution of a sociopath. He had been born out of wedlock (reportedly at Roanoke, Virginia), paternity unknown. His mother brought him to the slums of Baltimore when he was eight years old. Once there, a biological half-brother got imposed on him thanks (in part) to an anonymous male caller. Ensuing years brought no improvement to Kier's circumstances. The Kier boys grew up disadvantaged in every imaginable way. They were scrawny, fatherless, ill-fed creatures, ragged and unwashed like waifs from a nineteenth-century workhouse. Carl in particular faced insurmountable odds; he had a stunted intellect bordering on mental retardation. No efforts were made to bolster his formal education through remedial courses or any other means.

The lad dropped out of school before he had even become a teenager. Worse, truant officers did not consider Kier worth saving, allowing him to run wild instead. His mother was either unable or unwilling to rein in her son, especially since a dissipated lifestyle had reduced her to semi-invalidism. So, with neglected schooling, no known father and a mother in name only, it came as little surprise when young Kier wound up in jail. He had broken into at least two occupied houses. The penalty he faced was five years in juvenile detention. Kier began serving that sentence in the summer of 1954. He was paroled barely a year later (on August 7, 1955), having received "favorable reviews" from a so-called progressive-minded case worker. The real reason for the indulgence shown to him is somewhat vague, but it may have been at least partially based on Kier's physical inability to fend off attacks by other prisoners.

Free again, jobless, desperate and unreformed, Kier assumed sole financial support of his ailing mother. She had by then been abandoned by her most recent "male companion." Kier's half-brother was equally ineffective, having problems of his own. These factors, combined with a low IQ (it was officially set at 81, in the dull-normal range), caused Kier to slip into despondency. Then, when he emerged from that dark mood, an even darker one took hold of him—namely, attributing his failures to the success of others. It was an emotional crutch commonly overplayed by self-pitying types. He reasoned that white people—especially rich ones—were to blame for his wretched condition. It was the same worn-out refrain proclaimed by incendiary street preachers while Kier—being naturally gullible—ingested every word of their harangues. Then came disillusionment from a fruitless job search. Kier had gone to the suburbs north of Baltimore convinced that "one should follow the money," as the saying went. Such places being the environs of affluent people (nearly all of whom were white), Kier hoped to peddle his services there as a door-to-door handyman. He did not get far. Potential customers were repelled by his churlish appearance. In addition, his politeness seemed feigned and unconvincing. Matters worsened when Kier got caught peeping in windows. A spate of thefts from unguarded homes also boded ill, Kier being the prime suspect in all of them.

Kier went to Towson on the above date. His journey there began as another job search. He called at several addresses in the upscale Murray Hill district. Nobody would hire him, but Kier did leave his personal information (name, address and telephone number) with at least one homeowner. He was dressed noticeably better than on previous occasions, his raiment including blue trousers and a matching sports jacket. Mid-afternoon found Kier ambling his way along Bellona Avenue. He paused at the intersection with Charles Street. A spacious house was partially visible there behind some tall hedges. This was the residence of a wealthy businessman named John H. Bopst III and his socially prominent wife Myrtle Agnes Bopst, plus their four children. No one seemed to be at home, so Kier—lacking inhibitions in this regard—decided to snoop around. He found that a rear door was open save for a locked screen set in the same portal (this was not unusual, the weather being serene). Kier then surmised that someone was home after all. He looked inside and saw the lady of the house, Myrtle Bopst (white, age 47), relaxing in her parlor. There being no further sign of activity (the other family members were elsewhere at the time), Kier let his festering hatred erupt with maniacal fury.

He jimmied open the aforesaid screen door, thereby gaining access to the kitchen. The intruder then took a butcher knife from a cutlery rack. Armed therewith, he attacked the unsuspecting matron. She was unconcernedly eating ice cream as the knife was pressed to her throat from behind. An exact sequence of what happened next was never determined for sure, but forensic evidence substantiated all of the following: rape both before and after death, multiple stab wounds, broken bones, plus bludgeoning almost beyond recognition. Kier used the butcher knife on Mrs. Bopst with deadly effect. Then he carefully washed it clean of blood (in the kitchen sink) and put it back in the cutlery rack.

Next, he returned to where the victim lay and battered her face and head with a brass statuette of a man riding a horse. No attempt being made to cleanse that object, it was thrown into a corner caked with gore. The killer also took a samurai sword from among Mr. Bopst's collection of Oriental antiques. Kier deliberately and purposefully churned the blade of that weapon into every single one of the victim's wounds to make them doubly traumatic. Then he tore down a curtain and threw it over what was left of Mrs. Bopst. Myrtle Agnes Bopst had been a petite woman weighing scarcely 105 pounds—no match for even a physically runty assailant like Carl Daniel Kier.

The murderer cleaned himself up in the victim's bathroom. Then he filched two bottles of beer from her refrigerator and drank them at his leisure. Next, Kier located the dead woman's pocketbook, which he plundered of car keys and a small amount of money. He made his getaway in Mrs. Bopst's automobile, backing it out of an attached garage in order to do so. Kier threw his empty beer bottles out the door as he was leaving. They landed on the lawn and were later recovered intact. He also removed his blue sports jacket and threw that on the lawn as well. The door of the Bopst garage was carelessly left open.

Mr. Bopst came home from work later and found the carnage in his house. So vicious had the killer been that seasoned lawmen could recall nothing to equal the crime scene. They rated it as the work of either a madman, a werewolf or someone with a tremendous amount of pent-up hatred. Kier's rage might have really been actuated by perceived disparities between Mrs. Bopst and his own mother, with racism and its concomitant malice only playing ancillary roles. Both women were of opposite extremes in almost every way: rich vs. poor, white vs. black, a fine home vs. a roach-infested hovel and so on. Moreover, Mrs. Bopst had a reliable provider in the person of her husband, whereas Kier's mother had only a grueling struggle to survive while the men who had made it all so impossible for her were nowhere to be found. Psychological theorems aside, the sheer savagery of what Kier had done was such that two Maryland governors—namely, Theodore McKeldin and J. Millard Tawes—refused to spare his life despite their self-avowed opposition to capital punishment.

Kier was caught when police questioned neighbors of the murdered woman. In this way they came up with the name and address that Kier had left with a prospective landscaping customer, leading detectives to Baltimore and the 2900 block of Westwood Avenue. Kier was found at home, as were the blue pants that he had worn (matching the discarded sports jacket). Mrs. Bopst's car turned up abandoned at around the same time, with Kier's fingerprints all over it. Most damning of all were the car keys; lawmen found them in the gooseneck of Kier's toilet, he having attempted to flush them in a hurry. Kier subsequently admitted to having been in the Murray Hill area while looking for work. He denied everything else, however.

Two trials were held. Both resulted in capital convictions. The first of these (held in Baltimore County) was reversed on appeal. The second trial was taken to Frederick County on a change of venue; its verdict withstood appellate challenge. The penalty was death by cyanide gas. Carl Daniel Kier met that fate at the Maryland State Penitentiary on January 23, 1959. Source: *Salisbury (MD) Times*, 1/24/59 (5:6); *Inside Detective*, 9/56; *Official Detective*, 10/56; *Master Detective*,

10/56, 4/62 and 9/68. Appeals: 140 AR 896–900 and 216 MD 513–523.

Leonard Melvin Shockley (black, age 17). *Murder.* The crime was committed on 1/16/1958 at Boxiron, a small community in lower Worcester County. William Hearne and his wife Sarah (white, age 39) kept a country store adjacent to their house. It was a typical rural enterprise of that period, featuring assorted merchandise, a gasoline pump and a well-worn wooden floor. Vacationers provided the Hearnes with steady trade in the warm-weather months. During off seasons, however, Sarah Hearne would mind the store singlehandedly while her husband worked as a tinsmith and general repairman. The couple had three sons, ages nine, ten and nineteen, but none of them could readily assist their parents business-wise because one was in the military and the others were too young.

Harold Shockley (black, age 22) used to purchase small items from Mr. and Mrs. Hearne. He had lived at Snow Hill (a nearby town) for most of his life before moving to Delaware. Even so, Shockley and his kid brother Leonard remained in frequent contact with their former environs by working as timber haulers on both sides of the Delaware state line. The above date found them with empty wallets. What were they to do? Harold Shockley then remembered Sarah Hearne and the probability that she would be alone in her store. A decision was made to rob her. The two brothers arrived at the Hearnes' store at about 1:45 in the afternoon. Leonard Shockley was armed with a large hunting knife. Mrs. Hearne was hanging laundry at the time, though she put that chore aside in order to wait on the two supposed customers. Harold Shockley said nothing to the unsuspecting woman. He punched her in the face instead, shattering her eyeglasses and breaking her nose. Leonard then stabbed her in the left shoulder. Mrs. Hearne attempted to flee out a side door only to be overtaken once again by Leonard, who plunged the blade of that weapon all the way into the woman's back and also slashed her across the throat. Mortally wounded, Mrs. Hearne somehow managed to break free from the killer's grip. She ran next door to her home, burst into the kitchen and there fell dead in front of her 81-year-old stepfather. A trail of gore marked her path.

The Shockleys wasted no time, immediately jimmying open the store's cash register. A customer arrived just then and caught them in the act. This was a law-abiding black man of that locale named Clarence Bishop. Fortunately, he had presence of mind not to fight the killers hand-to-hand, choosing instead to dart in another direction. Seeing him, however, the Shockleys feared that Bishop meant to fetch a shotgun. So they jumped into their car and fled posthaste.

Bishop had made excellent mental notes despite the exigency of the moment. He was able to give lawmen good descriptions of both the killers themselves and the getaway car. Those same details also brought willing replies from other black residents of that vicinity when they were questioned by police. Those persons shared the popular resentment for the murder and were eager to help solve it. "Yes," they said, "we do know two people who match those descriptions. Their names are Harold and Leonard Shockley. And yes, Harold Shockley does own a car like the one that you describe." The suspects were quickly traced to their Delaware home. The murder weapon was also found to still be in Leonard Shockley's possession. He admitted his guilt a short time later. In addition, Clarence Bishop positively identified both of the Shockleys in a police line-up.

Efforts to impanel an unbiased jury in Worcester County proving futile, the case was sent to Dorchester County on a change of venue. The verdict was inevitable in the face of conclusive evidence. Leonard Shockley—his youth notwithstanding—heard himself sentenced to death. Harold Shockley— despite being equally guilty in the eyes of the law because he had made no effort to restrain his knife-wielding sibling—received a sentence of life imprisonment. The next stop for both defendants was the Maryland State Penitentiary.

On April 10, 1959, with his postconviction appeals having failed, Leonard Shockley was escorted to the gas chamber. "How long will it take?" were his last audible words. He was pronounced dead less than two minutes later. Source: *Salisbury (MD) Times*, 1/17/58 (1:7) and 1/20/59 (1:4); *Frederick (MD) Post*, 4/11/59 (1:5); *Baltimore Afro-American*, 4/25/59 (8:4). Appeal: 148 AR 371–377.

1961

Nathaniel Lipscomb (black, age 30). *Murder.* His crimes were committed over a four-month period in Baltimore. An incipient serial killer, this individual terrorized Maryland's largest city to a high degree. Newspapers called him "The Dawn Strangler" because he always struck at sunrise. His sexually motivated rampage left three women dead and at least three others grievously traumatized.

The horror began suddenly on December 9, 1958. A male resident of no. 1308 East Eager Street (by all accounts a respectable man) stepped into his small backyard at 8 o'clock in the morning to discard some household trash. He was shocked to find the ravished body of a Negro woman there. The decedent had undoubtedly met with foul play: she was naked from the waist up, her limbs were grotesquely contorted, and pantaloons hung loosely around one of her ankles. Physical evidence of rape was unmistakable. Bloody froth and neck bruises indicated manual strangulation. Oddly, the corpse was still warm despite chilly weather. Death had evidently occurred minutes before the discovery. Even so, no occupant or neighbor of the aforesaid address had seen anything unusual. The slain woman was later identified as 37-year-old Mae Hall, a hospital employee. Police theorized that she had been walking to her job at the nearby Johns Hopkins Medical Center when tragedy overtook her.

"WHO KILLED THE LADY FOUND IN YARD?" demanded the *Baltimore Afro-American* (a weekly newspaper) in its subsequent edition. People of all ethnicities wanted an answer, but none was immediately forthcoming.

Five days later the killer struck again. This time he chose a matronly white woman as the object of his malice. Her name was Lottie Kight. She was last seen sweeping the sidewalk in front of her home (in the 900 block of East Preston Street) at exactly 8 o'clock on the morning of December 14, 1958. Mrs. Kight (a 60-year-old practical nurse) liked to keep things tidy. She had long been a common sight in her neighborhood with a dustpan and broom in hand. This particular occasion, however, proved calamitous. Mrs. Kight's live-in daughter grew concerned when a full hour went by with no further sign of her mother. A look outside revealed a broom, a dustpan and a pair of bedroom slippers lying on the sidewalk. All belonged to Lottie Kight. Closer inspection revealed telltale droplets of blood on the same walkway. These led to an alley two doors away. Some helpful men followed this ominous trail, which ended in a small backyard. The dead body of Lottie Kight lay there—fully clothed—but badly beaten. Her lifeless fingers were clenched and smeared with gore, proof that she had fought with an attacker. It was later determined that manual strangulation caused her demise.

Daybreak on December 26, 1958, saw a municipal road crew mending pavement stones in the 1400 block of Ensor Street. Their attention was drawn to the sound of screams. The men dropped their tools and ran to the source. They saw a 30-year-old black woman struggling with a male assailant, the latter of identical age and ethnicity. He had seized the woman by the throat and thrown her to the ground. She was desperately resisting further efforts to drag her into an alley. The road crew (black men all) leaped to the woman's rescue. They chased her attacker but failed to catch him. They did, however, provide police with an excellent description.

Nine days later (on January 4, 1959) a 24-year-old nurse's aide was assaulted in exactly the same manner in the 1400 block of North Caroline Street. She was a black lady, the same race as her attacker. She had been walking to her job at about 8 o'clock in the morning when the incident took place. Fortunately, she managed to break free and outrun her assailant. The news spread quickly. Police and civilians realized that a maniac was loose in Baltimore and that he had no qualms about killing his victims. All of the attacks had similarities: The persons preyed upon had been exclusively female. All had been assaulted at or very close to the hour of 8 o'clock in the morning. All had been grabbed by the throat with deadly force, and then dragged into or toward alleyways. The alarm became so great that few women—black or white—dared to venture outdoors unescorted. A heavy police presence was imposed in neighborhoods where the crimes had occurred, particularly those near Greenmount Cemetery.

The killer now lay low for a while. Public tension waned with the passage of time. Eleven weeks went by with no further trouble. Then, on the first day of spring (March 21, 1959), a 15-year-old black girl was brutally outraged in the 1300 block of Ensor Street—just a few doors away from the scene of the December 26 crime. The victim in this case had been seized by her throat, dragged into a rear yard and raped right there on the frozen ground. She had been walking homeward from a bus stop shortly before 8 o'clock that morning. Incredibly, this victim survived to tell her story despite being manually throttled and left for dead. The culprit was a 30-year-old black man of medium build, said she.

"Here we go again!" sighed the harried residents of Baltimore's east side. The black community was especially galled by the knowledge that one of its own was to blame. Some had set their hearts on attributing the attacks to a racist conspiracy but found it impossible to do so.

Another murder came to light on April 9, 1959. This time a 39-year-old black woman named Pearl Wees was found strangled in an alley in the 1400 block of Harford Avenue. She had been dead for less than an hour before a sanitation crew discovered her body. The pattern was the same as in the previous cases.

"HANDS OF DEATH," wrote the *Baltimore Afro-American* beneath a woodcut rendition of the killer's gnarled fingers. "STRANGLER STRIKES IN AREA OF CEMETERY," and so forth. The entire district was near panic.

Eight days later a woman screamed in one of the more closely patrolled areas of the city. Jumpy policemen came running, arriving in time to see a suspicious-looking black man dart into an alley. Giving chase, they caught up with him and demanded that he account for himself. Four sets of women's panties were found in his pockets. Interrogated further at police headquarters, the suspect said that his name was Nathaniel Lipscomb. He originally came from Gaffney, South Carolina. He had been diagnosed as a mental defective after dropping out of grade school, and had come to Baltimore in 1954 following three years in a Goldsboro, North Carolina, sanitarium. He presently lived with relatives on Asquith Street. He earned money as a dishwasher and part-time construction laborer. All of Lipscomb's statements were later confirmed through additional investigation.

Asked about his sexual proclivities, Lipscomb started to cry. "Why did they have to die?" he sobbed. "I didn't mean to kill them." He then tearfully told lawmen that the only way he could "respond as a male" was by throttling his sex partners with his hands. Several psychiatrists examined Lipscomb at length. Their report said that he was "disturbed" but still able to comprehend the enormity of his acts and bear responsibility for them. His disorder is nowadays called *sexual sadism*, a psychiatric term that did not exist in 1959.

At trial Lipscomb made a bad impression by lying about certain details—possibly on the advice of his counsel. He claimed that the two black women killed by him had had consensual intercourse with him at the time of their deaths. He had met them in nightclubs (or so he claimed) and successfully propositioned them. This was too much for judge, jury and prosecutors alike. It seemed incredible that any female—no matter how depraved—would consent to do such things in trash-strewn alleys and freezing cold weather. The families of the victims likewise resented the aspersions cast upon their loved ones by this shabby defense tactic. Lipscomb could not explain, however, why he had tried to force other women into such situations, especially those who had survived his assaults. "Were these consensual also?" sneered the state's attorney. "How about the white lady, Lottie Kight? Did you pick her up in a honky tonk too?" Lipscomb admitted that he had accosted Mrs. Kight on the sidewalk in front of her home and asked her to have sex with him. Appalled by such impudence, she had smacked him upside his head with her broom. He then became angry, leading him to punch Mrs. Kight and drag her away, leaving broom, dustpan and slippers on the sidewalk behind him.

An insanity defense was unavailing. Verdict: guilty of capital murder with no recommendation for mercy. Sentence of the court: death by cyanide gas. Appeals kept Lipscomb alive until June 9, 1961, at which time he was executed in the manner prescribed by law. Source: *Salisbury (MD) Times*, 12/15/58 (5:1), 2/18/60 (39:2) and 11/18/60 (15:6); *Baltimore Afro-American*, 12/20/58 (8:3), 4/25/59 (8:1) and 5/9/59 (8:6); *Frederick (MD) Post*, 4/21/59 (1:8) and 6/12/61 (11:4). Appeal: 165 AR 918–922.

Virginia

(in chronological order)

1866

Thomas Shields (white, age 29). *Murder.* The crime was committed on 1/25/1866 in James City County. Executed for the ax murder of Andrew Taylor (white, age not recorded). Motive: robbery. Trial by military commission before reorganization of the postwar civilian courts. He was hanged at Libby Prison on April 20, 1866. Source: *The World* (New York), 4/23/66 (7:2); *Richmond Whig & Public Advertiser*, 4/24/66 (4:6).

Isaac Chaney (black, age 31). *Murder.* The crime was committed on 10/14/1865 in Rockbridge County. Executed for the sniper killings of 53-year-old Richard Gerald and 55-year-old Elizabeth A. Gerald (both white—a married couple) together with the burning of their house. Motive: robbery and revenge. Chaney had been freeborn in Ohio. He was captured by Confederates during the Civil War (1861–1865) while serving with Union forces in some unknown capacity. His captors sold him to Mr. Gerald as a slave and he presumably chafed under those circumstances. Trial by military commission before reorganization of the postwar civilian courts. He was hanged at Libby Prison on July 16, 1866. Source: *Louisville (KY) Daily Democrat*, 10/24/65 (1:5); *Staunton (VA) Spectator*, 10/24/65 (2:1) and 11/21/65 (3:1); *Daily Richmond Enquirer*, 7/17/66 (3:2). See also 1850 U.S. Census (Nelson Co., VA), which notes the Geralds.

Harrison Flood (black, age not recorded). *Murder.* The crime was committed in Buckingham County sometime in the year 1866 (exact date unknown). Executed for the gunshot slaying of 36-year-old James Sudsbury (white), who was reportedly "waylaid" for that purpose. Motive: murder-for-hire, or so the killer said. Date of execution tentatively assigned to October 26, 1866. This is an obscure case for which only a thin paper trail remains. The original trial papers were lost in a courthouse fire that wiped out nearly all of this county's recorded history prior to 1869. Enough has been found, however, to make it a certainty. Flood was apparently tried at the September 1866 term of Buckingham County Circuit Court, per a brief newspaper mention of him by the *Richmond (VA) Whig*, 10/9/66 (1:3), which in turn indicated that the murder of Mr. Sudsbury occurred earlier that year instead of in 1865, because military authorities would have otherwise handled the matter. Confirmation that Flood was indeed hanged turns up 26 years later in the form of a retrospective mention of the event in a local newspaper: *The Appomattox and Buckingham Times*, 2/3/93 (1:3). The Governor's Journal and correspondence files at the Virginia State Archives (also known as the Library of Virginia) contain nothing on this case—a sure indication that no post-conviction efforts were made on behalf of the condemned man. See also 1860 U.S. Census (Buckingham Co., VA), which notes "Jas. Sudsbury."

Glenroy Baker (black, age 19). *Murder.* The crime was committed on 8/15/1866 in Spotsylvania County. Executed for the rifle slaying of 23-year-old Judson A. Motley (white). Motive: highway robbery. Baker had scavenged the murder weapon (a carbine) from the Spotsylvania battlefield two years earlier. He had previously been a slave of Mr. William Richards of that county. He said that he had shot down young Mr. Motley for no other reason than because he wanted his clothes. Baker took the dead man's hat, gloves and handkerchief. Motley was a C.S.A. veteran, having served with the Bowling Green Guards, 30th Virginia Regiment. The killer was hanged at Spotsylvania Courthouse on November 16, 1866. Source: *Daily Richmond Whig*, 8/22/66 (2:3) and 11/22/66 (2:6); *Richmond Whig & Public Advertiser*, 11/23/66 (1:6). See also 1860 U.S. Census (Henrico Co., VA), which notes Motley.

Solomon Stamper (black, age 18). *Rape.* The crime was committed on 4/23/1866 in Grayson County. Indecent assault on the person of 9-year-old Emma Bland (white). A letter to the governor later charged that the victim was older than claimed and a precocious slut by nature. The same letter denounced her as a pathological liar who had consented to the sex act. The sheriff of Grayson County was also targeted by this poison pen. He was alleged to be a virulent racist who had supposedly said that "blacks should be extinguished as a race if they could no longer be owned as slaves." Stamper's execution was stayed for 90 days to investigate these claims, but they were found to be groundless. The rapist was hanged in Grayson County on November 24, 1866. It is not known if the letter writer was charged with obstruction of justice. Source: Executive Papers (Gov. Pierpont), Box 4, Folder 6. See also Secretary of the Commonwealth Executive Papers (8/10/66), plus Executive Journal of the Governor entries dated 8/10/66 and 9/15/66 (VA State Archives).

Caesar Wooldridge (black, age not recorded). *Rape.* The crime was committed on 8/14/1866 in Chesterfield County. Indecent assault on the person of 14-year-old Mary Cogbill (white), she having been accosted on a public road, menaced with a shotgun, knocked to the ground by the butt of that weapon, manually throttled, raped and then thrown into a swamp. The attacker was hanged at Chesterfield Courthouse on December 7, 1866. Source: *Daily Richmond Whig*, 8/21/66 (3:1) and 11/7/66 (2:3); *Norfolk Virginian*, 12/10/66 (1:7). See also Chesterfield County Circuit Court Files (Criminal Cases 1852–1873), Box 1 (VA State Archives).

John Robertson (white, age 24). *Murder.* The crime was committed on 8/25/1866 in Stafford County. Executed for the murders of 50+-year-old Gustavus Limerick and 50+-year-old Nancy Limerick (both white—a married couple), they having been clubbed to death and their cabin burned. Motive: plunder.

The killer's surname is alternately given as Robinson, Roberson, Robertson, Robeson and Robison. He had gotten married only a few days prior to the crime. He spent the ensuing time drinking, carousing and gambling in Fredericksburg. His money gone, he became so desperate for more that he even applied to work side-by-side with Negro gravediggers who were then excavating the Fredericksburg battlefield. His next thought was of a reclusive couple who lived in a cabin just over the Stafford County line. They were rumored to be misers with plenty of money hidden away.

Robertson cut an oaken club for what he had in mind. Then he went to the aforesaid cabin after nightfall and lured Mr. Limerick outdoors with a tale about horses being loose in his cornfield. He struck Limerick down from behind a short distance from the cabin. Then he went back to the cabin, where he found Mrs. Limerick seated before the fireplace. She, too, was bludgeoned from behind. That done, the killer ransacked the cabin and set it ablaze. Then he reappeared at his Fredericksburg haunts flush with silver. This was noteworthy because earlier that evening Robertson hadn't even had a penny to pay the ferryman who took him across the river to Stafford County. In fact, Robertson had told the ferryman that he would pay him on the return trip, which he indeed did. Robertson had traitorously served as a scout for Union forces during the lately concluded war. This last fact outraged many Virginians even more than the murders. A gallows ended Robertson's career at Stafford Courthouse on December 28, 1866. Source: *Richmond Daily Dispatch*, 8/28/66 (4:1); *Norfolk Virginian*, 1/4/67 (2:3). See also Executive Papers (Gov. Pierpont), Box 4, Folder 4 and Box 5, Folder 6 (VA State Archives), plus the 1860 U.S. Census (Stafford Co., VA), which notes the killer's surname as "Robinson."

1867

Benjamin F. Harden (white, age about 22). *Murder.* The crime was committed on 4/16/1867 in Tazewell County. Executed for the murder (by undisclosed means) of 55-year-old Dennis T. Burnes (white). Motive: highway robbery. The killer was hanged at Tazewell Courthouse on June 28, 1867. Source: *Richmond (VA) Whig*, 7/5/67 (4:2); *The World* (New York), 7/6/67 (8:4); *Louisville (KY) Daily Courier*, 7/8/67 (3:7). See also Tazewell County Circuit Court Order Book (1861–1871), page 821, plus the 1860 U.S. Census (Fleming Co., KY), which notes Mr. Burnes.

Isaac Yarborough (black, age 24). *Murder.* The crime was committed on 12/28/1866 in Lunenburg County. Executed for the ax murder of 20-year-old Samuel S. Rowlett (white). Motive: robbery. This killer was hanged at Lunenburg Courthouse on November 1, 1867. Source: *Daily Enquirer & Examiner* (Richmond, VA), 11/4/67 (1:2); *New York Herald*, 11/5/67 (4:1). See also 1860 U.S. Census (Prince Edward Co., VA), which notes Rowlett, and 1860 U.S. Census Slave Schedule (Lunenburg Co., VA), which notes "F. Yarbrough" as the owner of an 18-year-old male slave who was probably the killer in this case.

1868

Thomas H. Laurence (white, age not recorded). *Murder.* The crime was committed on 7/14/1867 in Pittsylvania

County. Executed for the handgun slaying of 42-year-old Lucy A. Prewitt (white). Motive: ruckus in a bagnio. The killer was hanged at Chatham on January 10, 1868. Source: Executive Papers of Gov. Francis H. Pierpont, Box 7, Folder 1 (VA State Archives). See also 1860 U.S. Census (Pittsylvania Co., VA), which notes the victim and lists her occupation as "whore."

Abel Anthony (black, age not recorded). *Rape.* The crime was committed in Northampton County in the spring of 1868, exact date unknown. Executed for an indecent assault on the person of an unidentified white female. The rapist was hanged at Eastville on July 24, 1868. Source: Northampton County Circuit Court Order Book, Vol. 46 (1868–1871), entries dated 6/8/68 and 6/9/68; *Petersburg (VA) Index,* 8/3/68 (1:4). The actual trial papers in this case are long lost.

Harrison Young (black, age about 33). *Murder.* The crime was committed on 11/2/1866 in Warwick County. Executed for the murder of 31-year-old John Wootten (white), the victim having been jumped by a 16-man gang and shot multiple times by guns of different makes and calibers. Motive: robbery. Harrison Young was singled out as the ringleader. He was hanged at Warwick Courthouse on August 25, 1868. Source: *Norfolk Virginian,* 8/27/68 (1:2); *New York Herald,* 8/29/68 (5:3); *Daily Press* (Newport News, VA), 7/13/1906 (5:2), in retro. See also *Grattan's Reports,* Vol. 18, pages 1033–1047, plus the 1860 U.S. Census (Warwick Co., VA), which notes Mr. Wootten.

John Perkins (white, age 36). *Rape.* The crime was committed on 6/8/1868 in Norfolk County. Indecent assault on the person of 27-year-old Sarah Elizabeth Ford (white) during the course of a home invasion. A black co-defendant named Benjamin Jefferson was reprieved. The white man (Perkins) was hanged at Portsmouth on October 9, 1868. Source: *New York Herald,* 10/10/68 (10:1); *Norfolk Journal,* 10/10/68 (1:5); *Norfolk Virginian,* 10/10/68 (1:4). See also 1860 U.S. Census (Norfolk Co., VA), which notes the female party.

1869

Adam Franklin (black, age 44). *Murder.* The crime was committed on 12/1/1868 in Appomattox County. Executed for the murder of 59-year-old Haxall Johnson (black), the victim having been beaten to death with a hickory stick (his body was found nine days later). Motive: the killer coveted the dead man's wife. Franklin was hanged at Appomattox Courthouse on May 28, 1869. Source: Secretary of the Commonwealth Executive Papers, Box 15, Folder 2 (VA State Archives). See also Appomattox County Death Register (1868 and 1869), which notes both parties.

Albert Tyler (black, age about 40). *Murder.* The crime was committed on 2/23/1869 in Henrico County. Executed for the fatal and deliberate poisoning of Paulina Hubbard (black, age not recorded). Motive: witness removal (the murder victim had caught Tyler in the act of molesting his 12-year-old stepdaughter). He was hanged at Richmond on May 29, 1869. Source: *New York Herald,* 5/30/69 (3:6); *Daily Dispatch* (Richmond, VA), 5/31/69 (1:4); *Richmond Whig & Advertiser,* 6/1/69 (1:4).

Peter Riddick (black, age 41). *Murder.* The crime was committed on 1/21/1869 in Norfolk County. Executed for the murder of 28-year-old Cornelius Hays (white), the victim having been clubbed to death. Motive: highway robbery. The killer was hanged at Portsmouth on July 23, 1869. Source: *Norfolk Journal*, 7/24/69 (1:4); *Norfolk Virginian*, 7/24/69 (1:4); *The World* (New York), 7/24/69 (3:1).

1870

Alexander Gardiner (black, age 35). *Murder.* The crime was committed on 9/26/1868 in New Kent County. Executed for the murders of 54-year-old John Baker (black) and 31-year-old Julia Hookady Stewart (white). The male victim was shot with a musket. The woman was raped and battered with heavy iron fireplace tongs, and her house was set ablaze. Motive: robbery and sexual assault. This killer was hanged at New Kent Courthouse on February 11, 1870. Source: *Daily Dispatch* (Richmond, VA), 2/12/70 (1:3); *New York Herald*, 2/13/70 (4:5). See also 1860 U.S. Census (New Kent Co., VA), which notes Baker and the murdered woman.

Spencer Wright (black, age not recorded). *Murder.* The crime was committed on 4/14/1869 in Northampton County. Executed for the murder of 52-year-old Joshua P. Wescoat (white, a store keeper), who was slashed to death with a barlow knife. Motive: robbery. Wright was hanged at Eastville on June 3, 1870. Source: Northampton County Common Law Order Book (1852–1874), pages 348 and 369–370; *Richmond (VA) Whig*, 4/23/69 (1:5); *New Orleans Times-Picayune*, 6/4/70 (2:1). Appeal: 60 VA 626–639. See also Northampton County Death Register (1869), plus the 1860 U.S. Census (Northampton Co., VA), which notes Mr. Wescoat.

William Taylor (black, age not recorded). *Murder.* The crime was committed on 3/25/1870 in King George County. Executed for the murder of 16-year-old Willie H. Jett (white), the victim having been chased down by bandits and battered to death with the butt of a shotgun; his body was then left in a burning barn. Motive: robbery. This killer was hanged at King George Courthouse on June 17, 1870. Source: *Virginia Herald* (Fredericksburg), 3/31/70 (3:2), 6/20/70 (3:2) and 8/15/70 (3:2); *New York Herald*, 6/18/70 (6:1). See also 1860 U.S. Census (Richmond, VA), which notes Jett as a stripling.

Lewis Kennedy (black, age 25). *Murder.* The crime was committed on 9/26/1868 in New Kent County. Accomplice in the murders of 54-year-old John Baker (black) and 31-year-old Julia Hookady Stewart (white). Motive: robbery and sexual assault. Kennedy was hanged at New Kent Courthouse on July 1, 1870. Source: *New York Herald*, 7/2/70 (7:6); *Richmond (VA) Whig*, 7/5/70 (4:1). See also 1870 U.S. Census (New Kent Co., VA), which notes Kennedy. See also **Alexander Gardiner** (executed 2/11/70).

James Jeter Phillips (white, age 24). *Murder.* The crime was committed on 2/17/1867 in Henrico County. Uxoricide. Executed for the handgun slaying of 30-year-old Mary Emily Pitts Phillips (white). Motive: a sordid tale of adultery. This killer was hanged at Richmond on July 22, 1870. Source: *Daily Dispatch* (Richmond, VA), 7/23/70 (1:1); *New York Herald*, 7/23/70 (5:1). *Master Detective*, 11/54. Appeal: 60 VA 485–542. See also 1850 U.S. Census (Henrico Co., VA), which notes the culprit, and 1860 U.S. Census (Essex Co., VA), which notes the victim as "M. E. Pitts."

York Campbell (black, age 25). *Murder.* The crime was committed on 12/29/1869 in Culpeper County. Executed for the murder of 60+-year-old Pollux Patrick (black), who was both bludgeoned and slashed to death. Motive: uncertain. The killer was hanged at Culpeper Courthouse on August 5, 1870. Source: *New York Herald*, 8/9/70 (5:6); *Richmond (VA) Whig*, 8/9/70 (4:4).

Hance Parramore, alias "John Walkabout" (black, age not recorded). *Murder.* The crime was committed on 10/22/1866 in Accomack County. Executed for the murder of 46-year-old Ayres Latham (white), a farmer who turned up with his throat cut. Motive: connivance with the victim's wife, or so the killer said. Mrs. Latham had been tried separately for this murder. She was convicted but somehow wrangled a pardon from "the then Military Governor of the State and soon after remarried." The assassin was hanged at Accomack Courthouse on August 5, 1870. Source: *Alexandria (VA) Gazette*, 8/12/69 (4:4); *Peninsula Enterprise* (Accomack, VA), 12/22/1900, in retro. See also Accomack County Common Law Order Book (1867–1880), pages 210–217, plus Accomack County Circuit Court Papers (November 1869), which contain the original indictment, and 1860 U.S. Census (Accomack Co., VA), which notes Mr. Latham.

Warner Taylor (black, age not recorded). *Murder.* The crime was committed on 3/25/1870 in King George County. Accomplice in the murder of 16-year-old Willie H. Jett (white). Motive: robbery. Warner Taylor was hanged for his part in the crime at King George Courthouse on August 12, 1870. Source: *New York Herald*, 8/13/70 (5:1). See **William Taylor** (executed 6/17/70).

Henry Costen, alias "Henry East" (black, age 18), **Peter Newby**, alias "Peter Lawrence" (black, age about 38), **Moses Newby** (black, age about 27) and **Jacob Wallace** (black, age 18). *Murder.* Their crime was committed on 12/11/1869 in Isle of Wight County. All four were executed for the gang assault and killing of 67-year-old Josiah P. Gray (white), who was beaten to death with clubs and his body left to be devoured by hogs. Motive: highway robbery. This killer quartet met death on a specially constructed gallows at Isle of Wight Courthouse on September 16, 1870. Source: *Norfolk Journal*, 12/15/69 (1:5) and 9/17/70 (1:6); *Richmond (VA) Whig*, 12/17/69 (1:4) and 9/20/70 (4:4); *New York Herald*, 9/17/70 (4:1). See also 1850 U.S. Census (Isle of Wight Co., VA), which notes Mr. Gray.

Archer Hines (black, age 34). *Murder.* The crime was committed on 12/20/1868 in Prince Edward County. Executed for the musket murder of Anderson Fowlkes (black, age not recorded). Motive: adultery. This black-on-black killer was hanged at Farmville on October 7, 1870. Source: *Louisville (KY) Courier Journal*, 12/28/68 (2:2); *New York Herald*, 10/8/70 (10:1). See also 1870 U.S. Census (Prince Edward Co., VA), which notes the culprit.

Kit Hubbard (back, age about 32). *Murder.* The crime was committed on 7/4/1870 in Pittsylvania County. Executed for the murder of 62-year-old Joseph E. Anderson (white), who was battered to death with a billet of wood and a rock. Motive: robbery. The killer was hanged at Chatham on November 26, 1870. Source: *New York Herald*, 11/30/70 (4:5). See also 1860 U.S. Census (Pittsylvania Co., VA), which notes Mr.

Anderson, and 1870 U.S. Census (Halifax Co., VA), which notes the killer.

1871

John Jackson (black, age 27). *Murder.* The crime was committed on 7/4/1870 in Pittsylvania County. Accomplice in the murder of 62-year-old Joseph E. Anderson (white). Motive: robbery. Jackson was hanged at Chatham on February 24, 1871. Source: *New York Herald*, 2/25/71 (6:1). See **Kit Hubbard** (executed 11/26/70).

Thomas McGiffin (white, age 22). *Murder.* The crime was committed on 12/24/1869 in Brunswick County. Accomplice in the rifle slaying of 70-year-old John B. Drummond (white), a sheriff's constable. The actual shooter was found to be *non compos mentis*. Venue changed from Brunswick County to Greensville County. McGiffin was hanged at Emporia on July 21, 1871. Source: *New York Herald*, 7/22/71 (7:1). See also the actual trial record (*Commonwealth vs. McGiffin*), April Term, 1871, Circuit Court Records Room, Greensville County Courthouse. See also 1860 U.S. Census (Brunswick Co., VA), which notes Drummond.

Richard Green (black, age 26) and **William Henry Johnson** (black, age 23). *Murder.* Their crime was committed on 3/24/1871 in Prince George County. Both executed for the murder of 53-year-old Charles Friend (white), the victim having been clubbed to death. Motive: mugging. The killers were hanged at Prince George Courthouse on July 28, 1871. Source: *Daily Index* (Petersburg, VA), 3/27/71 (3:1); *Richmond (VA) Whig*, 3/28/71 (2:5); *New York Herald*, 7/29/71 (6:5). See also 1870 U.S. Census (Prince George Co., VA), which notes Mr. Friend, plus the census for Petersburg, VA, which notes the culprits.

Jacob Brock (black, age 43). *Murder.* The crime was committed on 9/4/1871 in Louisa County. Uxoricide. Executed for the murder of 31-year-old Judy Brock (black), she having been literally flogged to death under circumstances of extreme atrocity. Motive: suspected infidelity. The killer was hanged at Louisa Courthouse on December 8, 1871. Source: *Richmond (VA) Whig*, 9/8/71 (2:3) and 12/12/71 (1:5); *New York Herald*, 12/9/71 (8:1). See also 1870 U.S. Census (Louisa Co., VA), which notes both parties but incorrectly classifies the victim as white, whereas the *Richmond Whig*'s eyewitness correspondent stated implicitly that she was black.

1873

Charles Manley (black, age not recorded). *Murder.* The crime was committed on 7/5/1872 at Alexandria. Executed for the murder of 60-year-old John Monroe, alias "Scottish John" (white, an itinerant clock repairman), who was bludgeoned with a rock; afterward, his body was stripped. Motive: mugging. The killer was hanged at Alexandria on March 28, 1873. Source: *Alexandria Gazette*, 7/6/72 (3:1), 7/8/72 (3:1) and 3/28/73 (3:1); *Evening Star* (Washington, D.C.), 3/28/73 (4:2); *New York Herald*, 3/29/73 (3:1).

Archie Johnson (black, age not recorded). *Murder.* The crime was committed on 4/17/1872 in Russell County. Executed for the rifle slaying of 33-year-old John Hurt (white), the victim's body having later been found hidden in a cave. Motive: undisclosed. The killer was hanged at Lebanon on June 13, 1873. Source: *Louisville (KY) Courier Journal*, 5/8/72 (2:1); *Daily Dispatch* (Richmond, VA), 6/16/73 (1:6); *New York Herald*, 6/17/73 (4:1). See also 1870 U.S. Census (Russell Co., VA), which notes Mr. Hurt.

James Brown (black, age 22). *Murder.* The crime was committed on 6/1/1873 in Nansemond County. Executed for the murders of 47-year-old Elizabeth Jones and 59-year-old Sarah N. Dozier (both white), they having been clubbed to death in the residence that they shared. Motive: home invasion. The killer was hanged at Suffolk on July 11, 1873. Source: *Norfolk Journal*, 7/11/73 (1:5) and 7/12/73 (1:1); *New York Herald*, 7/12/73 (9:6); *Norfolk Virginian*, 7/12/73 (1:4).

William Jackson (black, age about 40). *Murder.* The crime was committed on 2/15/1872 at Alexandria. Executed for the murder of 27-year-old Mary Fletcher (black, his common-law wife), whom he had bludgeoned with a billet of wood. Motive: temper tantrum. Jackson was hanged at Alexandria on August 15, 1873. Source: *Evening Star* (Washington, D.C.), 8/15/73 (1:6); *New York Herald*, 8/16/73 (8:1). Appeal: 64 VA 919–934. See also 1870 U.S. Census (Alexandria, VA), which notes the victim.

David Goggin (black, age 43). *Murder.* The crime was committed on 1/6/1873 in Franklin County. Executed for the ax murder of 53-year-old Thomas Starkey (black). Motive: heated argument. The killer was hanged at Rocky Mount on August 22, 1873. Source: *Louisville (KY) Courier Journal*, 9/3/73 (2:1). See also "Determined Papers 1873–1874," Franklin County Circuit Court records on microfilm (VA State Archives), plus the 1870 U.S. Census (Franklin Co., VA), which notes both parties.

1874

Edward Brown, alias "William Jones" (black, age about 35). *Murder.* The crime was committed on 12/26/1873 in Culpeper County. Executed for the murder of 23-year-old William C. Durkin (white), the victim having been beaten on the head with a railroad coupling pin. Motive: robbery. The killer was hanged at Culpeper Courthouse on June 12, 1874. Source: *New York Herald*, 6/13/74 (3:1); *Richmond Daily Dispatch*, 6/13/74 (3:1). See also 1870 U.S. Census (Petersburg, VA), which notes Mr. Durkin.

John Wesley Diggs (black, age 34). *Murder.* The crime was committed on 7/29/1874 in Nelson County. Uxoricide. Executed for the deliberate strangulation of Mariah Diggs (black, age not recorded). "He threw a piece of cloth over her face and around her neck, drawing her up against a tree where he held her until she fell, when planting his knee upon her breast, he finished the job with his hands." Motive: the killer wanted to be free to cavort with the dead woman's sister. He was hanged at Lovingston on November 13, 1874. Source: *Alexandria (VA) Gazette*, 8/3/74 (2:5); *Richmond Daily Dispatch*, 11/14/74 (1:5); *Lynchburg Daily Virginian*, 11/16/74 (3:2). Original case file (*Commonwealth vs. Diggs*), September Term 1874, provided courtesy of Lisa D. Bryant, deputy clerk of Nelson County Circuit Court. (Note: This killer was only 4'9' tall.)

1875

Lewis Adams (black, age 64). *Murder.* The crime was committed on 6/28/1874 in Pittsylvania County. Executed for the musket slaying of 31-year-old Rice Wilson (black). Motive: gambling dispute. This killer was hanged at Chatham on January 8, 1875. Source: *Richmond Daily Dispatch*, 1/9/75 (1:6). See also 1870 U.S. Census (Pittsylvania Co., VA), which notes both parties.

Jesse Fowlkes, known to some as "Jesse Foukes" (black, age 18). *Murder.* The crime was committed on 12/3/1874 in Prince William County. Executed for the ax murders of 70-year-old Jeremiah Herndon and 65-year-old Gina Herndon (both white—a married couple), as well as 18-year-old Addison Russell (black), their houseboy. Motive: robbery and vindictiveness. Fowlkes had been accused of stealing meat from a smokehouse belonging to the Herndons. He then went to their home with an ax, slaughtered his accusers and stole their money. He was hanged at Brentsville on March 19, 1875. Source: *Evening Star* (Washington, D.C.), 3/19/75 (1:6); *National Republican* (Washington, D.C.), 3/20/75 (1:5); *New York Herald*, 3/20/75 (3:3); *Richmond Daily Dispatch*, 3/20/75 (3:3). See also Prince William County Death Register (1874), which notes the murder victims, and 1870 U.S. Census (Prince William Co., VA), which notes the killer.

Joe Clarke (black, age 29). *Murder.* The crime was committed on 3/9/1874 in Pittsylvania County. Executed for the murder of 28-year-old Albert Barksdale (black), the victim having been bludgeoned with a rock and his body chopped into pieces by means of an ax. Motive: adultery. The killer was hanged at Chatham on April 30, 1875. Source: *Richmond (VA) Whig*, 3/31/74 (2:5); *Lynchburg Daily Virginian*, 2/22/75 (3:3) and 5/1/75 (3:4); *New York Herald*, 5/1/75 (5:6); *Petersburg (VA) Index-Appeal*, 5/5/75 (1:4). See also Pittsylvania County Death Register (1875), which notes the killer, and 1870 U.S. Census (Halifax Co., VA,) which notes the victim, as well as Secretary of the Commonwealth Executive Papers (1874), Box 41, Folder 2 (VA State Archives).

Thomas Withers (black, age 15). *Murder.* The crime was committed on or about 2/15/1875 in Campbell County. Executed for the ax murder of 60-year-old Agnes Thomas, known to all as "Aunty Thomas" (black). Motive: umbrage over an uncomplimentary rumor. This black-on-black killer was hanged at Rustburg on August 13, 1875. Source: *New York Herald*, 8/14/75 (6:3); *Richmond Daily Dispatch*, 8/14/75 (1:6); *Richmond Enquirer*, 8/14/75 (1:3). See also Secretary of the Commonwealth Executive Papers (1875), Box 44, Folder 8 (VA State Archives), which contains an affidavit from the killer's former owner (Col. Robert W. Withers) stating that "Tom" had been born in the year 1860.

1876

Isaac Griffin (black, age 31). *Rape.* The crime was committed on or about 9/15/1875 in Norfolk County. Serial rapist. Specifically executed for an indecent assault on the person of 25-year-old Idavilla Brown Griffin (black—his sister-in-law). He was also indicted for forcing himself on two other black females named Adeline Bell and Violet Stone, plus an attempted attack on a white woman identified only as "Mrs. Dr. West." A sentence of 12 years' imprisonment was meted out to him in the latter case. This sexual predator was hanged at Portsmouth on March 2, 1876. Source: *New York Herald*, 3/3/76 (8:4); *Norfolk Virginian*, 3/3/76 (4:1). See also 1870 U.S. Census (Norfolk

Co., VA), which notes Idavilla Griffin by her maiden name, and the census for Halifax Co., VA, which notes the miscreant.

Hillary Page (black male, age 17). *Arson.* His crimes were committed over a period of time from 3/13/1874 to 1/13/1875 in Chesterfield County. A serial incendiary who struck 16 times in a 10-month period, burning down barns, stores, stables, granaries and other buildings belonging to the same property owner: a white man named Frank G. Ruffin. Motive: none apparent; possible pyromaniac. He was hanged at Chesterfield Courthouse on September 1, 1876. Source: *Richmond Daily Dispatch*, 9/2/76 (10:1). Appeals: 67 VA 943–951 and 68 VA 954–981.

Cornelius Coggins (black, age 30). *Murder.* The crime was committed on 3/27/1876 in Campbell County. Uxoricide. Executed for the handgun slaying of 26-year-old Hattie Coggins (black). Motive: "without provocation." This killer was hanged at Rustburg on September 29, 1876. Source: *Lynchburg Daily Virginian*, 3/30/76 (3:2), 4/22/76 (3:1) and 10/2/76 (3:1). See also 1870 U.S. Census (Pittsylvania Co., VA), which notes both parties as "Coggans."

1877

Jack Pleasants (black, age 51). *Murder.* The crime was committed on 4/7/1876 in Dinwiddie County. Executed for the rifle slaying of Ann Lundy (black, age not recorded). Motive: she refused to marry him. The killer was hanged at Dinwiddie Courthouse on June 8, 1877. Source: *New York Herald*, 6/9/77 (3:3); *Richmond Daily Dispatch*, 6/9/77 (3:3). See also 1870 U.S. Census (Dinwiddie Co., VA), which notes the murderer.

Anderson Shifflett (white, age 29). *Murder.* The crime was committed on 3/15/1875 in Rockingham County. Executed for the rifle slaying of 37-year-old David G. Lawson (white). Motive: murder-for-hire. The assassin was hanged at Harrisonburg on September 25, 1877. Source: *New York Herald*, 9/26/77 (3:4); *Richmond Daily Dispatch*, 9/26/77 (3:4); *Richmond Enquirer*, 9/26/77 (1:5). See also 1870 U.S. Census (Rockingham Co., VA), which notes both parties.

James Edwards, alias "Frank Smith" (black, age not recorded). *Rape.* The crime was committed on 3/24/1877 in Princess Anne County. Incipient serial rapist. Executed for an indecent assault on the person of 14-year-old Agnes Ruffin (black). Also condemned for doing the same thing to another local girl named Martha J. Gentry (black, age 11) on 6/1/1876. This rapist was hanged at Princess Anne Courthouse on November 9, 1877. Source: *Richmond Daily Dispatch*, 11/10/77 (3:4); *Norfolk Virginian*, 11/11/77 (1:5). See also Princess Anne County Circuit Court Judgments (1877–1879), Box 8, Folder 3 (VA State Archives).

1878

Henry Williams, alias "Lewis Hill" (black, age not recorded). *Rape.* The crime was committed on 8/19/1877 in Isle of Wight County. Serial rapist. Executed for an indecent assault on the person of Margaret Ann Stephens (white), described as a "young girl." This sex offender was hanged at Isle of Wight Courthouse on February 22, 1878. Source: *New York Herald*, 2/23/78 (8:1).

John Henry Robinson (black, age 23). *Murder.* The crime was committed on 1/14/1875 in Caroline County. Executed for the shotgun slaying of 18-year-old Eliza Roy (black). Motive: unreciprocated love. This thwarted suitor was hanged at Bowling Green on May 31, 1878. Source: *New York Herald*, 6/1/78 (2:4); *Richmond Daily Dispatch*, 6/1/78 (3:5).

1879

Julius Christian (black, age 21) and **Patrick Smith** (black, age 22). *Murder.* Their crime was committed on 1/17/1879 in New Kent County. Executed for the hatchet killing of 43-year-old John Calvin Lacy (white). Motive: attempt to cover up a prior felony. These killers were hanged at New Kent Courthouse on March 25, 1879. Source: *New York Herald*, 3/26/79 (3:5); *Richmond Daily Dispatch*, 3/26/79 (1:1). See also 1870 U.S. Census (New Kent Co., VA), which notes Mr. Lacy.

Winter Payne (black, age 38). *Murder.* The crime was committed on 4/11/1879 in Fauquier County. Executed for the murder of 50-year-old James Adams (black), the victim having been clubbed to death. Motive: feud between neighbors. The killer was hanged at Warrenton on July 11, 1879. Source: *New York Herald*, 7/12/79 (4:1).

John Williams (black, age about 25). *Murder.* The crime was committed on 2/6/1879 in Fauquier County. Executed for the sniper slaying of 20-year-old Howard Holtzclaw (white). Motive: robbery. Williams was hanged at Warrenton on July 11, 1879. Source: *Richmond Daily Dispatch*, 2/8/79 (3:5) and 2/10/79 (3:4); *New York Herald*, 7/12/79 (4:1).

Frank Baker (black, age 22). *Murder.* The crime was committed on 8/1/1879 in Sussex County. Executed for the murders of 25-year-old Agnes Shands and 18-month-old Sarah Shands (both black—a mother and child). The woman was battered beyond recognition with a jagged piece of scrap iron. The baby was buried alive. The killer also dug up the baby postmortem and hacked its little body to pieces with the edge of a spade. Motive: jealous rage. He was hanged at Sussex Courthouse on December 19, 1879. Source: *Norfolk Virginian*, 8/5/79 (1:6); *New York Herald*, 12/20/79 (6:4); *Richmond Daily Dispatch*, 12/20/79 (3:3). See also Sussex County Death Register (1879), which notes the victims.

Daniel Dean (white, age 45). *Murder.* The crime was committed on 6/25/1877 in Scott County. Executed for the sniper slaying of 25-year-old Henry E. Fugate (white). Motive: to eliminate a witness in a pending court case. The killer was hanged at Gate City on December 19, 1879. Source: *New York Herald*, 12/20/79 (6:4). Appeal: 73 VA 912–928. See also 1870 U.S. Census (Scott Co., VA), which notes both parties.

1880

General H. Webb (white, age 44). *Murder.* The crime was committed on 6/20/1879 in Carroll County. Executed for the sniper slaying of 86-year-old Joshua Nester (white), his father-in-law. Motive: impatient heir. The killer was hanged at Hillsville on January 9, 1880. Source: *New York Herald*, 1/10/80 (5:2); *Richmond Daily Dispatch*, 1/10/80 (3:4). See also 1870 U.S. Census (Carroll Co., VA), which notes both parties.

Samuel Robinson (black, age 28). *Murder.* The crime was committed on 10/22/1879 in Loudoun County. Executed for the shotgun slaying of 56-year-old Edward Thomas (black), his uncle. Motive: a quarrel about some whiskey. The killer was hanged at Leesburg on April 9, 1880. Source: *New York Herald*, 4/10/80 (8:1); *Washington Post*, 4/10/80 (1:1); *The Mirror* (Leesburg, VA), 4/15/80 (1:4). See also 1870 U.S. Census (Loudoun Co., VA), which notes Edward Thomas.

Charles Bolling (black, age 17). *Rape.* The crime was committed on 4/1/1880 in Hanover County. Indecent assault on the person of 8-year-old Phelia Gathright (white) under circumstances that were deemed sufficient to warrant his execution at Hanover Courthouse on May 28, 1880. Source: *New York Herald*, 5/29/80 (5:3); *Richmond Daily Dispatch*, 5/29/80 (3:2). See also 1880 U.S. Census (Hanover Co., VA), which notes Miss Gathright.

Peter Wright (black, age 57). *Murder.* The crime was committed on 6/28/1879 in Bedford County. Child killer. Executed for the murder of 13-year-old Robert M. Maupin (white). Motive: landlord-tenant dispute. Wright was employed as a wood hauler by the victim's father. The elder Maupin suspected Wright of withholding some of the proceeds from the sale of a load of wood. Angered by this accusation, Wright assaulted Mr. Maupin with a dogwood stick. The boy ran to help his dad, only to get his head smashed in with the same dogwood stick. The killer was hanged at Bedford Courthouse on October 29, 1880. Source: *Lynchburg Virginian*, 10/29/80 (3:2) and 10/30/80 (3:2); *New York Herald*, 10/30/80 (8:4). Appeals: 73 VA 941–945 and 74 VA 880–897.

Albert Mitchell (black, age 22). *Murder.* The crime was committed on 3/9/1879 in Louisa County. Executed for the murder of 33-year-old Charles K. Walton (white), who was bludgeoned with a plow blade and had his house burned down around him. Motive: robbery. The killer was hanged at Louisa Courthouse on November 5, 1880. Source: *New York Herald*, 11/6/80 (6:6); *Richmond Daily Dispatch*, 11/6/80 (3:1) and 11/7/80 (3:2). Appeal: 74 VA 845–871. See also 1860 U.S. Census (Louisa Co., VA), which notes Walton as a minor.

Marcus Hawley (white, age 28). *Murder.* The crime was committed on 6/18/1879 in Roanoke County. Executed for the sniper slaying of 29-year-old Zachariah Hays (white). Motive: land dispute. The killer was hanged at Salem on November 26, 1880. Source: *New York Herald*, 11/27/80 (3:5); *Richmond Daily Dispatch*, 11/27/80 (3:3). Appeal: 75 VA 847–855. See also 1870 U.S. Census (Roanoke Co., VA), which notes the victim.

1881

Lucinda Fowlkes (black female, age 35). *Murder.* The crime was committed on 1/15/1881 in Lunenburg County. Executed for the ax murder of 50-year-old Wilson Fowlkes (black), her husband. Motive: marital discord. She was hanged at Lunenburg Courthouse on April 22, 1881. Source: *New York Herald*, 4/23/81 (8:1); *Richmond Daily Dispatch*, 4/23/81 (3:4). See also 1870 U.S. Census (Lunenburg Co., VA), which notes both parties.

1882

Dock Wright (black, age 18). *Murder.* The crime was committed on 2/5/1881 in Pittsylvania County. Executed for the murder of 32-year-old Coleman Arthur (white), who was bludgeoned with a billet of wood. Motive: brawling. The killer was hanged at Chatham on March 31, 1882. Source: *New York Herald*, 4/1/82 (4:6); *Richmond Daily Dispatch*, 4/1/82 (3:5). See also 1870 U.S. Census (Pittsylvania Co., VA), which notes Arthur.

Armistead Gray (black, age 40). *Murder.* The crime was committed on 1/12/1882 in Powhatan County. Filicide. Executed for the murder of 10-year-old Abraham Lincoln Gray (black), who was beaten to death with an ax handle. Motive: excessive discipline. The killer was hanged at Powhatan Courthouse on June 9, 1882. Source: *New York Herald*, 6/10/82 (3:3); *Richmond Daily Dispatch*, 6/10/82 (1:4). See also 1880 U.S. Census (Powhatan Co., VA), which notes both parties.

Walter Hamilton Yeatts (white, age 26). *Murder.* The crime was committed on 2/2/1882 in Pittsylvania County. Executed for the handgun slaying of roughly 24-year-old Presley Edward Atkinson (white). Motive: robbery. There were stories to the effect that Yeatts killed Atkinson because the latter planned to prosecute him for an act of forgery. It was also alleged that the killer acted out of anger because he had been duped into marrying a young woman who was pregnant with Atkinson's child. The robbery motive is the most plausible explanation because Yeatts was found with the victim's personal valuables in his pockets. Whatever the truth, Walter Yeatts was hanged at Chatham on August 4, 1882. Source: *Lynchburg Virginian*, 2/7/82 (3:2) and 8/5/82 (3:2); *Richmond Daily Dispatch*, 2/7/82 (2:5) and 8/5/82 (3:4); *New York Herald*, 8/5/82 (2:5).

1883

Charles William Beaner (black, age 16). *Rape.* The crime was committed on 9/5/1882 in Loudoun County. Indecent assault on the person of 10-year-old Annie Hunt (white) under circumstances deemed heinous enough to hang him pursuant to the law. He was executed at Leesburg on March 30, 1883. Source: *New York Herald*, 3/31/83 (3:4); *Richmond Daily Dispatch*, 3/31/83 (3:4); *Washington Post*, 3/31/83 (1:5). See also 1880 U.S. Census (Loudoun Co., VA), which notes both parties.

Lewis Carter (black, age not recorded). *Murder.* The crime was committed on 2/26/1883 in Southampton County. Uxoricide. Executed for the ax murder of Fannie Carter (black, age not recorded). Motive: suspicion of infidelity. This wrathful husband was hanged at Courtland on June 22, 1883. Source: *New York Herald*, 6/23/83 (3:3); *Norfolk Virginian*, 6/23/83 (1:8); *Richmond Daily Dispatch*, 6/23/83 (3:2).

Charles Henry Lee (black, age 20). *Murder.* The crime was committed on 2/14/1883 in Henrico County. Executed for the ax murder of 37-year-old Daniel Miller (black). Motive: adultery with the victim's wife. He was hanged at Richmond on August 3, 1883. Source: *New York Herald*, 8/4/83 (3:3); *Richmond Daily Dispatch*, 8/4/83 (1:2). See also 1880 U.S. Census (Henrico Co., VA), which notes Daniel Miller. See **Barbara Miller** (executed 9/14/83).

Barbara Miller (black, age 28). *Murder.* The crime was committed on 2/14/1883 in Henrico County. Mariticide. Executed for being the catalyst in the Valentine's Day murder of her husband, 37-year-old Daniel Miller (black), whose body was then mangled beneath the wheels of a passing locomotive in an attempt to conceal the crime. She was hanged at Richmond on September 14, 1883. Source: *New York Herald*, 9/15/83 (4:1); *Richmond Daily Dispatch*, 9/15/83 (1:2). See **Charles Henry Lee** (executed 8/3/83).

Isaac Evans (black, age 18), **Reuben King** (black, age 20) and **Sawney Younger** (black, age 20). *Murder.* Their crime was committed on 8/10/1883 in Pittsylvania County. Executed for the handgun slaying of 40-year-old William F. Shappard (white). Motive: highway robbery. They were all hanged at Chatham on September 28, 1883. Source: *New York Herald*, 9/29/83 (4:5); *Richmond Daily Dispatch*, 9/29/83 (3:1). See also 1850 U.S. Census (Halifax Co., VA), which notes the murdered man as "Sheppard," and 1860 and 1870 U.S. Census (Pittsylvania Co., VA), which note him as "Shepherd."

1884

John Jarvis (white, age 50). *Murder.* The crime was committed on 9/18/1883 in Princess Anne County. Executed for the shotgun slaying of 38-year-old Claudius W. Bonney (white). Motive: land dispute. The killer was hanged at Princess Anne Courthouse on January 11, 1884. Source: *New York Herald*, 1/12/84 (2:3); *Norfolk Virginian*, 1/12/84 (1:5); *Richmond Daily Dispatch*, 1/12/84 (3:3). See also 1880 U.S. Census (Princess Anne Co., VA), which notes both parties.

Absalom Russell (white, age about 30). *Murder.* The crime was committed on 7/19/1882 in Lee County. Executed for the ax murder of 59-year-old Ira Dean (white), his father-in-law. Motive: family tensions. The killer was hanged at Jonesville on May 9, 1884. Source: *New York Herald*, 5/10/84 (4:2). Appeal: 78 VA 400–405. See also 1880 U.S. Census (Lee Co., VA), which notes Mr. Dean.

1885

George Gibson (white, age 26) and **Wayne Powers** (white, age 24). *Murder.* Their crime was committed on 4/19/1884 in Scott County. Executed for the handgun slaying and cremation of 28-year-old William E. Gibson (white), the victim having also had his throat cut. Motive: robbery. The killers were hanged at Gate City on February 6, 1885. Source: *Richmond (VA) Dispatch*, 2/7/85 (3:6). See also *Historical Sketches of Southwest Virginia*, Vol. 11 (1977), for an excellent account of this case.

Joe Barbour (black, age 68). *Murder.* The crime was committed on 11/17/1883 in Albemarle County. Executed for the murder of 28-year-old Randolph Jackson (black), who was slashed to death in a drunken brawl. The killer was hanged at Charlottesville on June 18, 1885. Source: *Richmond Dispatch*, 11/20/83 (3:2) and 6/19/85 (4:1); *Galveston (TX) Daily News*, 6/19/85 (2:2); *New York Herald*, 6/19/85 (10:2). See also Albemarle County Death Register (1883), which notes Jackson.

Horace Terrell (black, age 27). *Murder.* The crime was committed on 10/4/1884 in Albemarle County. Child killer. Executed for the murder of 11-year-old Mary Foster (black), she having been battered to death with stones. Motive: sexual assault. The killer was hanged at Charlottesville on June 18, 1885. Source: *New York Herald*, 6/19/85 (10:2). See also

1880 U.S. Census (Madison Co., VA), which notes Terrell.

Jacob Butler (black, age 32). *Murder.* The crime was committed on 6/13/1885 in York County. Executed for the shotgun slaying of 45-year-old James Griffin (black). Motive: dispute over a loan. The killer was hanged at Yorktown on November 20, 1885. Source: *Richmond Dispatch*, 6/16/85 (3:5) and 11/21/85 (1:3). See also 1880 U.S. Census (York Co., VA), which notes both parties.

1886

Clinton Banks, alias "Tably Banks" (black, age 22) and **Wesley Honesty** (black, age 24). *Murder.* Their crime was committed on 11/14/1884 at Winchester. Both were executed for the murder of 19-year-old Joseph C. McFaul (white), who was beaten on the head with a rock. Motive: racial disharmony. The killers were hanged at Winchester on June 4, 1886. Source: *Winchester (VA) News*, 11/21/84 (3:2) and 6/11/86 (2:2). Appeal: 81 VA 283–304. See also 1880 U.S. Census (Shenandoah Co., VA), which notes Banks and McFaul, plus the City of Winchester Death Register (1886), which notes Honesty.

1887

Thomas Judson Cluverius (white, age 24). *Murder.* The crime was committed on 3/13/1885 in Henrico County. Executed for the beating and forcible drowning of 22-year-old Fannie Lillian Madison (white). Motive: personal betrayal. The killer was hanged at Richmond on January 14, 1887. This case received sensational press coverage at the time and has been frequently retold. Source: *Richmond Dispatch*, 1/14/87 (1:1) and 1/15/87 (1:1); *Daring Detective*, 12/36; *Real Detective*, 6/38; *Headline Detective*, 10/39; *Master Detective*, 1/41 and 12/55. Appeal: 81 VA 787–899.

Holmes Puryear (white, age 26). *Murder.* The crime was committed on 6/13/1885 in Dinwiddie County. Uxoricide. Executed for the deliberate poisoning of 27-year-old Emma Webb Puryear (white). Motive: she gave birth to a black baby. Venue changed from Dinwiddie County to Prince George County. The killer was hanged at Prince George Courthouse on August 12, 1887. Source: *Richmond Dispatch*, 6/16/85 (3:5) and 8/13/87 (1:2); *New York Herald*, 8/13/87 (10:2). See also 1870 U.S. Census (Dinwiddie Co., VA), which notes the victim, and 1880 U.S. Census (Dinwiddie Co., VA), which notes the culprit.

William Finchum (white, age 26). *Murder.* The crime was committed on or about 3/10/1886 in Rockingham County. Fratricide. Executed for the shotgun slaying of 32-year-old Presley Finchum (white). Motive: he coveted his brother's wife. The killer was hanged at Harrisonburg on December 30, 1887. Source: *Richmond Dispatch*, 12/31/87 (4:3). See also 1870 U.S. Census (Rappahannock Co., VA), which notes both parties.

1889

John Cephas Johnson (black, age 35). *Rape.* The crime was committed on 10/14/1888 in Richmond County. Indecent assault on the person of Alice Wilson (white, age not recorded), she having been attacked in her own home (her door being broken in). The rapist was hanged at Warsaw on January 9, 1889. Source: *Northern Neck News* (Warsaw, VA), 11/9/88 (3:3) and 1/11/89 (3:2). See also Richmond County Death Register (1889), which notes Johnson.

Jedediah Pritchett (black, age about 30). *Rape.* The crime was committed on 6/24/1888 in Pittsylvania County. Indecent assault on the person of 8-year-old Jennie R. Pollock (white). This child rapist was hanged at Chatham on March 29, 1889. Source: *Daily Times* (Richmond, VA), 3/30/89 (1:3); *Richmond Dispatch,* 3/30/89 (3:5). See also 1900 U.S. Census (Charlotte Co., VA), which notes the victim and her later whereabouts.

Walter Harris (black, age 18). *Murder.* The crime was committed on 11/13/1888 in Greensville County. Executed for the ax murder of 35-year-old Albert Parham (black). Motive: robbery. This black-on-black killer was hanged at Hicksford on May 3, 1889. Source: *Daily Times* (Richmond, VA), 5/4/89 (1:3); *Richmond Dispatch,* 5/4/89 (4:1). See also 1880 U.S. Census (Greensville Co., VA), which notes Parham.

Robert Williams (black, age 19). *Murder.* The crime was committed on 2/21/1889 in Greensville County. Executed for the ax murder of 37-year-old Emerson Mason (black), the victim having been slaughtered in his bed. Motive: disgruntled employee. This black-on-black killer was hanged at Hicksford on May 3, 1889. Source: *Daily Times* (Richmond, VA), 5/4/89 (1:3); *Richmond Dispatch,* 5/4/89 (4:1). See also 1880 U.S. Census (Greensville Co., VA), which notes Parham.

Henry Albert Coleman, alias "Matthew Barney," alias "Ford Knox" (black, age 31). *Murder.* The crime was committed on 9/6/1888 in Norfolk County. Executed for the ax murder of 60+-year-old James Grant (white) and grievous wounding of 36-year-old Louisa Spratt. Motive: robbery. This killer was hanged at Portsmouth on May 31, 1889. Source: *Norfolk Virginian,* 9/7/88 (1:3), 9/8/88 (1:3), 9/11/88 (1:2) and 6/1/89 (4:4); *Richmond Dispatch,* 6/1/89 (4:1).

Paul Keys (black, age 33). *Rape.* The crime was committed on 5/8/1889 at Fredericksburg. Indecent assault on the person of 5-year-old Alice Ballard (white). This child rapist was hanged at Fredericksburg on October 4, 1889. Source: *Richmond Dispatch,* 5/10/89 (2:5), 5/18/89 (1:5) and 10/5/89 (1:7). See also 1900 U.S. Census (Fredericksburg, VA), which notes Miss Ballard and the fact that she outlived her attacker.

1890

Thomas Wilson (black, age 20). *Murder.* The crime was committed on 10/15/1887 in Henry County. Executed for the handgun slaying of Jim Davis (black, age not recorded). Motive: rivalry for a female. This black-on-black killer was hanged at Martinsville on July 25, 1890. Source: *Richmond Dispatch,* 7/26/90 (4:1). Appeal: 86 VA 666–667.

John Phillips (black, age 35). *Murder.* The crime was committed on 4/14/1890 in Mecklenburg County. Executed for the murder of 52-year-old Robert Camillus Overby (white), the victim having been hit on the head with a wagon tongue. Motive: insolence. The killer was hanged at Boydton on August 15, 1890. Source: *The Times* (Richmond, VA), 8/16/90 (1:4); *Richmond (VA) Planet,*

8/23/90 (1:1). See also 1880 U.S. Census (Mecklenburg Co., VA), which notes Mr. Overby.

George Early (black, age 44) and **Bird Woods** (black, age 26). *Arson.* Their crime was committed on 10/8/1889 in Franklin County. Both were executed for setting a fire that destroyed the entire business district in the town of Rocky Mount, Virginia. Motive: they had been denied permission to hold a political meeting in the auditorium there. These arsonists were hanged at Rocky Mount on August 22, 1890. Source: *The Times* (Richmond, VA), 8/22/90 (1:2) and 8/23/90 (1:2); *Richmond (VA) Planet,* 8/30/90 (4:1). Appeal: 86 VA 921–937. See also Franklin County Death Register (1890), which notes the executed pair.

1891

William Muscoe, alias "William T. Jordan" (black, age 18). *Murder.* The crime was committed on 12/31/1888 at Charlottesville. Cop killer. Executed for the handgun slaying of 37-year-old George Thomas Seal (white). Motive: resisting arrest. This offender was hanged at Charlottesville on April 21, 1891. Source: *Richmond Dispatch*, 1/2/89 (1:3) and 4/22/91 (4:1). Appeals: 86 VA 443–451 and 87 VA 460–465. See also 1880 U.S. Census (Madison Co., VA), which notes the slain man as "G.T. Seal."

James Craney (black, age 24). *Murder.* The crime was committed on 9/28/1890 in Rockbridge County. Executed for the handgun slaying of 16-year-old Charles Oliver (black). Motive: fracas in a dance hall. The killer was hanged at Lexington on April 24, 1891. Source: *Rockbridge County News*, 10/2/90 (3:3) and 4/30/91 (3:2). See also 1880 U.S. Census (Rockbridge Co., VA), which notes Oliver.

Walter Johnson (black, age not recorded). *Rape.* The crime was committed on 9/19/1890 in Nottoway County. Indecent assault on the person of Elizabeth Majors (white, age not recorded), she having been left bound and gagged in a roadside ditch. Venue changed from Nottoway County to the City of Petersburg. The rapist was hanged at Petersburg on May 22, 1891. Source: *Daily Index-Appeal* (Petersburg), 9/24/90 (1:5); *Richmond Dispatch*, 5/23/91 (2:3); *The Times* (Richmond, VA), 5/23/91 (2:1).

Randall Watson (black, age 33). *Murder.* The crime was committed on 12/26/1886 in Greensville County. Executed for the handgun slaying of 27-year-old Joseph Robinson (black). Motive: anger stemming from gossip. The killer was hanged at Hicksford on July 10, 1891. Source: Original Case File (*Commonwealth vs. Watson*), October Term 1887, Greensville County Circuit Court Records Room, Emporia, VA. Appeal: 87 VA 608–620. See also 1880 U.S. Census (Greensville Co., VA), which notes both parties.

Henrietta Murrell (black, age 41). *Murder.* The crime was committed on 10/23/1890 in Charlotte County. Executed for the murders of two black children whose mother's name was Lucy Rice. Motive: vindictiveness. Lucy had turned Henrietta out of her house because she didn't like the way that she prepared the children's meals. Resenting this, Henrietta set fire to Lucy's house, killing the two unnamed children in the resulting inferno. She was hanged at Charlotte Courthouse on September 28, 1891. Source: *Richmond Dispatch*, 9/29/91 (2:6); *The Times* (Richmond, VA), 9/29/91

(1:1); *Daily Virginian* (Lynchburg), 9/30/91 (1:1). See also 1880 U.S. Census (Campbell Co., VA), which notes the miscreant. The original case file is missing (a search of the Circuit Court Records Room at Charlotte Courthouse failed to locate it despite the employees there being pleasant folks and willing to help). The murdered children were not otherwise identified by name or gender in any other surviving record, at least not so far as is known.

Robert Jordan (black, age 25). *Rape.* The crime was committed on 7/3/1891 in Elizabeth City County. Indecent assault on the person of 23-year-old Martha E. Moore (white), she having been rendered a lifetime invalid by what Jordan did to her. She died in the state insane asylum on April 26, 1894, of "acute phithisis," or general weakening, as it is nowadays called. Hence the charge against her attacker might just as well have been murder. He was hanged at Hampton on October 23, 1891. Source: *The Times* (Richmond, VA), 10/24/91 (2:3); *Norfolk Virginian*, 7/31/91 (6:3) and 10/24/91 (1:4). See also Secretary of the Commonwealth Executive Papers, Box 163, Folder 1 (VA State Archives), plus Western State Hospital Admissions Register (1889–1896), entry no. 4375, dated 10/30/91 (VA State Archives), and Elizabeth City County Death Register (1891), which notes Jordan.

William Henry Custis (black, age 30). *Murder.* The crime was committed on 9/8/1889 in Norfolk County. Executed for the murder of 64-year-old Tanus L. Waller (white), the victim having been slain with a hatchet (his house was also burned down). Motive: robbery. The killer was hanged at Portsmouth on November 10, 1891. Source: *Norfolk Virginian*, 9/10/89 (1:4), 9/27/91 (3:1) and 11/11/91 (3:1). See also 1880 U.S. Census (Norfolk Co., VA), which notes both parties.

Henry Nowlin, alias "Butting Henry" (black, age 19). *Murder.* The crime was committed on 8/2/1891 in Botetourt County. Executed for the handgun slaying of an Italian stonecutter known only as "Signore Mosca" (age not recorded). Motive: mugging. The killer was hanged at Fincastle on November 20, 1891. Source: *Richmond Dispatch*, 8/5/91 (4:1) and 11/21/91 (2:4); *Roanoke (VA) Times*, 11/21/91 (1:2).

1892

Charles Watkins (black, age 28). *Murder.* The crime was committed on 4/7/1890 in Roanoke County. Uxoricide. Executed for the murder of 37-year-old Susan Watkins (black), she having been shot with a handgun and beaten about the head, with her body later dumped in a creek. Motive: adultery on his part. This killer was hanged at Salem on January 8, 1892. Source: *Roanoke (VA) Times*, 1/8/92 (1:3).

Margaret Lashley (black, age 22) and **James Lyles** (black, age 24). *Murder.* Their crime was committed on 10/26/1890 at Danville. Mariticide. Both were executed for the handgun slaying of 40+-year-old George Lashley (black), his wife being the catalyst and her lover the triggerman. Motive: adultery. The guilty pair was hanged at Danville on January 22, 1892. Source: *Roanoke (VA) Times*, 1/23/92 (1:2); *The Times* (Richmond, VA), 1/23/92 (2:1); *Richmond Dispatch*, 12/22/01 (9:5), in retro. Appeal: 88 VA 396–401.

George Gaines (black, age 34). *Murder.* The crime was committed on 8/7/

1890 in Essex County. Executed for the handgun slaying of 20-year-old Percy Carlton (white). Motive: a misunderstanding. Gaines thought that Carlton had tried to entice his wife by sending her a note. The message had really been intended for someone else, but a grocery boy mistakenly gave it to the killer's spouse instead. Unfortunately, Gaines was a hothead who shot first and asked questions later. Carlton succumbed to his wound on September 21, 1890. Gaines was hanged at Tappahannock on May 27, 1892. Source: *Richmond Dispatch*, 8/10/90 (4:4); *Northern Neck News* (Warsaw, VA), 6/3/92 (2:4). Appeal: 88 VA 682–694. See also 1880 U.S. Census (Essex Co., VA), which notes Gaines.

Talton Hall (white, age 40). *Murder.* The crime was committed on 7/26/1891 in Wise County. Cop killer. Executed for the handgun slaying of 37-year-old Enos B. Hylton (white). Motive: obstruction of justice. Prime suspect in at least six other murders: Henry Maggard (white, age 23), in Letcher County, KY, in 1866; Daniel Pridemore (white, age 64), in Scott County, VA, in 1875; Nathaniel Baker (white, age 36), in Scott County, VA, in 1881; Henry Triplett (white, age 30), in Floyd County, KY, in 1882; Henry Houk (white, age uncertain), at an undetermined location in 1883; and Mack Hall (white, age 32), in Breathitt County, KY, in 1885. Talton Hall—mountaineer and murderer—was hanged at Wise Courthouse on September 2, 1892. Source: *Richmond Dispatch*, 9/3/92 (1:3). Appeal: 89 VA 171–181. See also 1880 U.S. Census (Wise Co., VA), which notes Hylton, plus 1880 U.S. Census (Letcher Co., KY), which notes Hall; 1870 U.S. Census (Scott Co., VA), which notes Pridemore; 1860 U.S. Census (Letcher Co., KY), which notes Maggard; 1880 U.S. Census (Scott Co., VA), which notes Baker; 1880 U.S. Census (Floyd Co., KY), which notes Triplett; and 1880 U.S. Census (Breathitt Co., KY), which notes Mack Hall.

William Davis, alias "Horse Head Bill" (black, age not recorded). *Murder.* The crime was committed on 6/16/1891 in Tazewell County. Cop killer. Executed for the handgun slaying of Charles Jones (black, age not recorded), a "negro policeman" in the town of Pocahontas. Motive: fracas in a so-called house of dubious reputation. The killer was hanged at Tazewell Courthouse on September 9, 1892. Source: *Richmond Dispatch*, 9/10/92 (2:3). Appeal: 89 VA 132–135.

1893

John Royster (black, age 50). *Murder.* The crime was committed on 7/29/1891 in Nansemond County. Executed for the shotgun slaying of 25-year-old John P. Eppes (white). Motive: mistaken identity. The killer was hanged at Suffolk on February 9, 1893. Source: *Norfolk Virginian*, 7/31/91 (1:1) and 2/10/93 (5:3); *The Times* (Richmond, VA), 2/9/93 (2:3) and 2/10/93 (2:2).

Silas Nash (black, age about 22). *Murder.* The crime was committed on 12/24/1892 in Buckingham County. Patricide. Executed for the ax murder of 57-year-old Charles Nash (black), the victim having been mangled in his bed. Motive: Papa Nash had refused to subdivide his land. His son was hanged at Buckingham Courthouse on February 24, 1893. Source: *Richmond News-Dispatch*, 12/27/92 (4:2); *The Times* (Richmond, VA), 1/10/93 (2:5); *Richmond Dispatch*, 2/28/93 (2:2). See also 1870 U.S. Census (Buckingham Co., VA), which notes the elder Nash.

George Drier (white, age 21). *Murder.* The crime was committed on 10/13/1891 in Northampton County. Executed for the murder of 70-year-old Fanny McFadden (white), she having been butchered in her bed with a barrow knife. Motive: robbery and ingratitude. Drier was said to be a Polish Jew; the old lady was a storekeeper who had hired him to be her salesclerk. Drier paid for his crime at the end of a rope at Eastville on June 16, 1893. Source: *The Times* (Richmond, VA), 10/15/91 (2:2), 10/16/91 (2:2) and 6/17/93 (2:5); *Norfolk Virginian*, 10/16/91 (1:1).

Marshall B. Taylor, alias "Doc Taylor" (white, age 56). *Murder.* The crime was committed on 5/14/1892 in Wise County. Mass killer. Executed for the rifle slayings of 35-year-old Ira Mullins and 31-year-old Louranza Estep Mullins (both white—a married couple), as well as 36-year-old John Wilson Mullins and two other white males named John Chappell and Greenbury Harris (ages not recorded), the latter described as a "silly boy" (i.e., a simple-minded lad). The victims were also sexually mutilated after they had been shot. Motive: highway robbery and overall depravity. Taylor was hanged at Wise Courthouse on October 27, 1893. Source: *Richmond Dispatch*, 10/28/93 (1:5); *Savannah (GA) Morning News*, 10/28/93 (1:3); *Big Stone Gap Post*, 11/2/93 (3:2). See also 1880 U.S. Census (Pike Co., KY), which notes the Mullins family, plus "The Hangings at Gladeville," by Luther F. Addington, published in *Historical Sketches of Southwest Virginia*, Vol. 9 (1975).

William Foreman (black, age 24). *Murder.* The crime was committed on 6/26/1893 at Portsmouth. Executed for the fatal stabbing of 22-year-old Carrie Carrington (black). Motive: heated argument. The killer was hanged at Portsmouth on November 24, 1893. Source: *Norfolk Landmark*, 6/27/93 (4:4) and 11/25/93 (4:4); *Norfolk Virginian*, 6/29/93 (7:5) and 11/25/93 (5:1). See also Portsmouth City Death Register (1893), which notes the female in this case.

1894

James B. Robinson (black, age about 20) and **Benjamin White** (black, age about 20). *Rape.* Their crime was committed on 1/13/1894 in Prince William County. Indecent assaults on the persons of 45-year-old Elizabeth Elliott Hefflin and her 20-year-old sister-in-law, identified only as "Mrs. Elliott." Both ladies were raped at gunpoint during a home invasion and in the presence of two small children. Their attackers were hanged at Manassas on April 27, 1894. Source: *Evening Star* (Washington, D.C.), 4/27/94 (1:1); *The Times* (Richmond, VA), 4/28/94 (2:1); *The Freelance* (Fredericksburg, VA), 5/1/94 (3:5).

Lawrence Spiller (black, age 46). *Murder.* The crime was committed on 4/28/1894 in Augusta County. Child killer. Executed for the murder of 14-year-old Lottie Rowe (white), she having been bludgeoned with a rock. Motive: sexual assault. This killer was hanged at Staunton on June 8, 1894. Source: *Richmond Dispatch*, 5/1/94 (1:1), 5/2/94 (1:1) and 6/9/94 (1:5); *The Times* (Richmond, VA), 6/9/94 (1:1). See also 1880 U.S. Census (Grant Co., WV), which notes the felon.

Madison Brown (black, age 16). *Murder.* The crime was committed on 4/7/1893 at Norfolk. Executed for the handgun slaying of 52-year-old John Dollard (white). Motive: burglary gone awry. The killer was hanged at Norfolk on July 31, 1894. Source: *Norfolk Virginian*, 4/7/93 (1:5), 4/8/93 (2:1), 4/18/93 (1:3), 7/31/94 (1:5) and 8/1/94 (1:1). See also 1880 U.S. Census (Norfolk Co., VA), which notes Brown as a small child, plus 1860 U.S. Census (Norfolk Co., VA), which notes Dollard as a young man.

William G. Taylor (white, age 49). *Murder.* The crime was committed on 7/18/1893 in Pulaski County. Uxoricide. Executed for the ax murder of 42-year-old Nancy Taylor (white). Motive: morbid jealousy. This killer was hanged at Pulaski Courthouse on August 17, 1894. Source: *Richmond Dispatch*, 8/18/94 (3:3); *The Times* (Richmond, VA), 8/18/94 (2:1). See also 1880 U.S. Census (Pulaski Co., VA), which notes both parties.

Moses Christopher (black, age 17). *Rape.* The crime was committed on 9/13/1894 in Caroline County. Indecent assault on the person of 7-year-old Moselle Carter (white). Her attacker was hanged at Bowling Green on November 14, 1894. Source: *Richmond Dispatch*, 11/15/94 (1:2); *The Times* (Richmond, VA), 11/15/94 (1:7).

1895

William Robertson (white, age 18). *Murder.* The crime was committed on 1/14/1892 in Franklin County. Executed for the handgun slaying of 68-year-old Jerry Barbour (white). Motive: highway robbery. This killer was hanged at Rocky Mount on January 25, 1895. Source: *Richmond Dispatch*, 1/16/92 (3:2), 12/11/92 (9:5) and 1/26/95 (4:3); *The Times* (Richmond, VA), 1/26/95 (2:1); *Washington Post*, 1/26/95 (1:6).

Sam Marshall (black, age not recorded). *Murder.* The crime was committed on 10/1/1894 in Lee County. Executed for the handgun slaying of 24-year-old Joshua Ingle (white). Motive: gambling dispute. The killer was hanged at Jonesville on March 1, 1895. Source: *Big Stone Gap Post*, 3/7/95 (3:3); *Richmond Dispatch*, 3/7/95 (1:6). See also Lee County Death Register (1894), plus 1880 U.S. Census (Lee Co., VA), which notes Ingle.

Thornton Parker (black, age 21). *Attempted Rape.* The crime was committed on 3/5/1895 in Frederick County. Felonious assault on the person of 19-year-old Mary V. Melton (white), she having been terrorized in her own home with intent to commit rape. This offender was hanged at Winchester on April 19, 1895. Source: *Richmond Dispatch*, 3/16/95 (1:3) and 4/20/95 (3:6); *Cumberland (MD) Evening Times*, 4/19/95 (4:7); *The Times* (Richmond, VA), 4/20/95 (1:1).

Morris Hopkins (black, age about 20). *Murder.* The crime was committed on 6/7/1893 in Henrico County. Executed for the murder of 48-year-old Henry S. Parsons (white), the victim having been beaten over the head with a hickory stick. He succumbed after three weeks in a coma. Motive: disgruntled employee. The killer was hanged at Richmond on April 24, 1895. Source: *Richmond Dispatch*, 6/9/93 (1:6), 6/28/93 (1:6) and 4/25/95 (3:1); *Richmond Planet*, 5/4/95 (1:1). See also 1880 U.S. Census (Henrico Co., VA), which notes Parsons.

Philip Norbourne Nicholas (white, age 48). *Murder.* The crime was committed on 12/8/1892 in Henrico County. Executed for the purposeful drowning deaths of 44-year-old James L. Mills and a second white man named William

Judson Wilkerson (age not recorded), they having been lured onto a boat that was booby-trapped to sink. Motive: a sordid plot to steal the wife of one of the murdered men. This killer was hanged at Richmond on July 25, 1895. Source: *Richmond Dispatch*, 12/11/92 (5:1), 12/13/92 (1:3), 12/15/92 (1:1) and 7/26/95 (1:1). See also 1870 U.S. Census (Goochland Co., VA), which notes Mr. Mills.

James Henry Harris (black, age 22). *Attempted Rape.* The crime was committed on 6/27/1895 in King & Queen County. Felonious assault on the person of 6-year-old Emma B. Fleet (white), she having been mistreated, with intent to commit rape. This child attacker was hanged at King & Queen Courthouse on August 23, 1895. Source: *Richmond Dispatch*, 7/6/95 (2:3) and 8/24/95 (6:2). See also Original Case File (*Commonwealth vs. Harris*), copy provided courtesy of Vanessa D. Porter, the deputy clerk of King & Queen County Circuit Court.

Kit Leftwich (black, age 25). *Rape.* The crime was committed on 9/7/1895 at Bristol. Indecent assault on the person of 13-year-old Annie Fogarty (white). This rapist was hanged at Bristol on October 11, 1895. Source: *Fort Wayne (IN) News*, 10/11/95 (1:3); *Richmond Dispatch*, 10/12/95 (6:3).

Robert Ridley (black, age 31). *Murder.* The crime was committed on 12/25/1894 in Sussex County. Executed for the musket-ball murder of 48-year-old William S. Williams (white). Motive: personal grudge. The killer was hanged at Sussex Courthouse on October 18, 1895. Source: *Norfolk Virginian*, 10/19/95 (1:5); *Richmond Dispatch*, 10/19/95 (5:2); *The Times* (Richmond, VA), 10/19/95 (1:7). See also 1870 U.S. Census (Brunswick Co., VA), which notes Ridley, and 1880 U.S. Census (Sussex Co., VA), which notes Williams.

Edward Hubbard (black, age 21). *Murder.* The crime was committed on 7/14/1895 in Halifax County. Executed for the handgun slaying of 21-year-old Isaac Calland (black). Motive: rivalry for a female. The killer was hanged at Halifax Courthouse on November 1, 1895. Source: *Richmond Dispatch*, 11/2/95 (2:1); *The Times* (Richmond, VA), 11/2/95 (2:5). See also 1880 U.S. Census (Pittsylvania Co., VA), which notes Calland as a minor.

1896

John S. Weatherman (white, age 41). *Murder.* The crime was committed on 11/19/1891 in Carroll County. Uxoricide. Executed for the ax murder of 40-year-old Rachel Malinda Rorer Weatherman (white). Motive: obnoxious drunk. The killer was hanged at Hillsville on February 14, 1896. Source: *The Times* (Richmond, VA), 2/15/96 (1:1); *Richmond Dispatch*, 2/16/96 (14:3). See also 1880 U.S. Census (Surry Co., NC), which notes both parties before they came to Virginia.

John Johnson (black, age 19). *Murder.* The crime was committed on 4/1/1896 in Lancaster County. Executed for the ax murder of 20-year-old Charles L. Carter (white). Motive: robbery. This killer was hanged at Lancaster Courthouse on June 12, 1896. Source: *Richmond Dispatch*, 4/2/96 (7:5), 4/7/96 (7:3) and 6/13/96 (1:6).

Henry Magruder (black, age 37). *Attempted Rape.* The crime was committed on 4/14/1896 in Alleghany County. Specifically executed for a felonious assault on the person of 22-year-old Nancy Putnam Ballinger (white) with intent to commit rape. Magruder was also a child killer. He had raped and murdered a 14-year-old black girl named Ellen Wallace on the same day that he attacked Mrs. Ballinger; the girl's head was smashed by a rock and her body thrown into a ravine. A murder trial was held in abeyance pending the outcome of prosecution on the assault charge, which was a capital felony in itself. This predator was hanged at Covington on June 19, 1896. Source: *Clifton Forge (VA) Review*, 4/17/96 (1:2) and 6/19/96 (1:1). See also 1880 U.S. Census (Fluvanna Co., VA), which notes Magruder, plus the census for Bath Co., VA, which notes Mrs. Ballinger by her maiden name.

Taylor Harmon (black, age 45). *Murder.* The crime was committed on 1/6/1896 in Albemarle County. Executed for the murder of 23-year-old Thomas W. Thompson (white), the victim having been bludgeoned with a heavy iron hook; afterward, his head was cut off and his body consumed in an arson fire. Motive: robbery. Harmon was hanged at Charlottesville on June 27, 1896. Source: *Richmond Dispatch*, 6/28/96 (12:2). See also 1880 U.S. Census (Albemarle Co., VA), which notes both parties.

Solomon Marable (black, age 25). *Murder.* The crime was committed on 6/14/1895 in Lunenburg County. Executed for the ax murder of 50-year-old Lucy Jane Fowlkes Pollard (white). Motive: robbery. Venue changed from Lunenburg County to Prince Edward County. The killer was hanged at Farmville on July 3, 1896. Source: *Richmond Dispatch*, 6/16/95 (7:1), 6/18/95 (2:5), 6/20/95 (4:1) and 7/4/96 (1:1).

Harry Chapman (black, age 21). *Murder.* The crime was committed on 9/14/1895 in Culpeper County. Executed for the musket slaying of 62-year-old Henry Pendleton (black). Motive: the killer didn't like the manner in which Pendleton had spoken to his mother. This black-on-black killer was hanged at Culpeper Courthouse on August 7, 1896. Source: *Richmond Dispatch*, 8/8/96 (3:3); *Richmond Planet*, 8/15/96 (1:3). See also 1895 and 1896 Culpeper County Death Registers (online version), compiled by Beth Fridley.

1897

William Downing (black, age 22). *Murder.* The crime was committed on 5/2/1896 at Norfolk. Executed for the handgun slaying of roughly 22-year-old Emma Lane (black). Motive: she had dared to chide him for ungentlemanly conduct. He was hanged at Norfolk on January 5, 1897. Source: *Norfolk Landmark*, 5/3/96 (1:6) and 1/6/97 (1:9); *Norfolk Virginian*, 5/3/96 (1:3) and 1/6/97 (6:1).

Charles Williams (black, age 21). *Murder.* The crime was committed on 4/18/1896 at Norfolk. Executed for the ax murder of about 25-year-old George Bess (black). Motive: gambling dispute. Williams was hanged at Norfolk on January 5, 1897. Source: *Norfolk Landmark*, 4/19/96 (1:5) and 1/6/97 (1:9); *Norfolk Virginian*, 4/19/96 (1:1) and 1/6/97 (6:1).

James Lewis (black, age 24). *Rape.* The crime was committed on 4/13/1897 in Fairfax County. Serial rapist. Specifically executed for an indecent assault on the person of 62-year-old Ida Reidel (white), she having been deliberately targeted in retaliation for the loss of his job. It was further determined that Lewis had raped at least three young women in Albemarle County as follows: Lucy Meade (black, age 17) in 1887; Edmonia Gardner (black, age 18) in 1888; and a 25-year-old white woman (in 1892) whose name was never made public. He was executed at Fairfax Courthouse on June 4, 1897. Source: *Alexandria Gazette*, 4/14/97 (3:2) and 6/4/97 (2:5); *Evening Star* (Washington, D.C.), 4/14/97 (11:4) and 6/4/97 (1:3).

Joseph Fife (black, age 19). *Attempted Rape.* His crimes were committed on 7/14/1897 in Henrico County. Felonious assaults on the persons of 16-year-old Nina Russell and 27-year-old Mary Griffith Marks (both white), each with intent to commit rape. This attacker was hanged at Richmond on August 26, 1897. Source: *Richmond Dispatch*, 7/15/97 (1:7), 7/16/97 (1:1) and 8/27/97 (1:7); *The Times* (Richmond, VA), 7/15/97 (1:3), 7/16/97 (1:1) and 8/27/97 (1:5).

Edward Hankins (white, age 51). *Murder.* The crime was committed on 8/26/1897 in Pittsylvania County. Executed for the ax murder of 74-year-old John Roy Cabell (white). Motive: landlord-tenant dispute. Hankins had previously served ten years in the Virginia State Penitentiary for the 1873 killing of another Pittsylvania County man named James A. Jackson. He was hanged at Chatham on November 11, 1897. Source: *Richmond Dispatch*, 8/28/97 (1:7) and 11/12/97 (6:5). See also 1880 U.S. Census (Henrico Co., VA), which notes Hankins as a prison inmate.

John Hardin (white, age 21). *Murder.* The crime was committed on 9/24/1897 in Buchanan County. Executed for the rifle slaying of 35-year-old George Mounts (white), the victim having been shot from ambush. Motive: suspicion of adultery. The killer was hanged at Grundy on December 17, 1897. Source: *The Times* (Washington, D.C.), 9/26/97 (1:4); *Richmond Dispatch*, 12/18/97 (6:5). See also 1880 U.S. Census (Logan Co., WV), which notes George Mounts.

Peter Coleman (black, age not recorded). *Murder.* The crime was committed on 5/27/1897 in Hanover County. Executed for the shotgun slaying of 29-year-old Louvisa White (black), she having also been beaten with a chain and a shovel. Motive: he didn't like her cooking. Coleman was hanged at Hanover Courthouse on December 24, 1897. Source: *Richmond Dispatch*, 12/25/97 (7:1). See also 1880 U.S. Census (Hanover Co., VA), which notes Louvisa as a minor, plus Original Case File (*Commonwealth vs. Coleman*), copy provided courtesy of Frank D. Hargrove, Jr., the clerk of Hanover County Circuit Court.

1898

Archie Lockley (black, age 31). *Murder.* The crime was committed on 10/12/1897 in King & Queen County. Child killer, etc. Executed for the rifle slayings of 67-year-old Ellen Banks Chapman, 12-year-old Eddie Chapman and 8-year-old George Lee (blacks). Motive: temper tantrum. This killer was hanged at King & Queen Courthouse on January 14, 1898. Source: *Richmond Dispatch*, 10/14/97 (6:3) and 1/15/98 (2:3). See also 1880 U.S. Census (King & Queen Co., VA), which notes Lockley and the former Ellen Banks.

James Easkins (black, age not recorded). *Attempted Rape.* The crime was committed on 3/28/1898 in Fauquier County. Felonious assault on the person of 10-year-old Barbara S. Waggler (white) with intent to commit rape. He was executed at Warrenton on May 18, 1898. Source: *The Times* (Washington, D.C.), 3/31/98 (1:6); *Richmond Dispatch*, 5/19/98 (4:5); *The Times* (Richmond, VA), 5/19/98 (2:3).

Isaac Paylor (black, age 23). *Murder.* The crime was committed on 1/21/1898 in Mecklenburg County. Uxoricide. Executed for the murder of Della Paylor (black, age not recorded), she having been felled with a club and her body hidden in a leaf pile, where it was found two weeks later mutilated by carrion birds. Motive: temper tantrum. The killer was executed at Boydton on May 20, 1898. Source: *Richmond Dispatch*, 3/24/98 (6:1); *Daily Press* (Newport News, VA), 5/21/98 (1:5).

Anthony Mayfield (black, age 58). *Murder.* The crime was committed on 6/29/1898 in Sussex County. Executed for the murders of 48-year-old Robert Harris and 43-year-old Etta Wells (both black), the man having been wounded by a shotgun blast and the woman hacked with an ax before both were burned alive in the cabin that they shared. Motive: moral outrage (the killer thought that Harris had forced himself on his wife). Mayfield was hanged at Sussex Courthouse on September 16, 1898. Source: *Richmond Dispatch*, 9/17/98 (3:4); *The Times* (Richmond, VA), 9/17/98 (7:1). See also 1880 U.S. Census (Sussex Co., VA), which notes all parties, plus Original Case File (*Commonwealth vs. Mayfield*), copy provided courtesy of Gary M. Williams, the clerk of Sussex County Circuit Court (and a very astute historian in his own right).

James H. Terrell, alias "James Douglass" (black, age 19). *Murder.* The crime was committed on 5/23/1898 in Albemarle County. Executed for the handgun slaying of 41-year-old Malinda Brown (black), his mother-in-law. Motive: family problems. This shooter was hanged at Charlottesville on September 23, 1898. Source: *Richmond Dispatch*, 9/24/98 (8:4). See also 1880 U.S. Census (Albemarle Co., VA), which notes both parties.

Robert Morton (black, age 24). *Murder.* The crime was committed on 6/25/1898 at Petersburg. Executed for the handgun slaying of 24-year-old George H. Westmoreland (white). Motive: pugnacity. This killer was hanged at Petersburg on November 4, 1898. Source: *Richmond Dispatch*, 6/26/98 (11:5) and 11/5/98 (5:2).

John Andersen (white, age 43). *Murder.* The crime was committed on 8/6/1897 aboard a ship at sea. Executed under federal authority for the handgun slayings of 44-year-old John W. Whitman and 39-year-old William Wallace Saunders (both white) while on an American vessel in the Atlantic Ocean. The murdered men were, respectively, its skipper and first mate. The ship itself was illegally scuttled. Motive: barratry. The killer was hanged at Norfolk on December 9, 1898. Source: *Fitchburg (MA) Daily Sentinel*, 8/19/97 (7:3) and 8/20/97 (8:4); *Middletown (NY) Daily Argus*, 12/21/97 (1:4) and 12/10/98 (1:6); *Washington Post*, 12/10/98 (1:7).

Jordan Webb (black, age 25). *Rape.* The crime was committed on 9/28/1898 in Southampton County. Indecent assault on the person of 65-year-old Lucy Bowden (white), she having been severely beaten in the process; her invalid (physically infirm) husband (Billie Bowden, white, age 70) died as a direct result of mental trauma incurred thereby. The rapist was hanged at Courtland on December 9, 1898. Source: *Richmond Dispatch*, 12/10/98 (6:3); *Washington Post*, 12/10/98 (9:4). See also 1880 U.S. Census (Brunswick Co., VA), which notes the culprit as a minor.

Arthur Lovitt (black, age 19). *Murder.* The crime was committed on 9/24/1898 in Princess Anne County. Cop killer. Executed for the handgun slaying of 40-year-old Malachi J. Beasley (white). Motive: resisting arrest. Lovitt was hanged at Princess Anne Courthouse on December 16, 1898. Source: *Richmond Dispatch*, 12/17/98 (4:5); *The Times* (Richmond, VA), 12/17/98 (6:2).

John Hancock (black, age 18). *Rape.* The crime was committed on 7/15/1898 at Lynchburg. Incipient serial rapist. Specifically executed for an indecent assault on the person of 11-year-old Rosa Cohn (white), she having been forced at knifepoint. Two other indictments for similar crimes against young girls were held in abeyance. This attacker was hanged at Lynchburg on December 30, 1898. Source: *Richmond Dispatch*, 12/31/98 (4:6); *The Times* (Richmond, VA), 12/31/98 (2:1); *Washington Post*, 12/31/98 (9:1).

1899

James Webster (black, age 18). *Rape.* The crime was committed on 11/19/1898 in Bedford County. Indecent assault on the person of 71-year-old Mary Aunspaugh (white), a maiden woman. This rapist was hanged at Bedford Courthouse on January 6, 1899. Source: *New York Times*, 11/30/98 (5:4); *Richmond Dispatch*, 1/7/99 (4:6). See also 1870 U.S. Census (Bedford Co., VA), which notes Miss Aunspaugh.

George Hite (white, age 60+). *Murder.* The crime was committed on 4/26/1898 in Mecklenburg County. Executed for the handgun slaying of 66-year-old William Bowers (black), a so-called inoffensive man. Motive: temper tantrum. The killer was hanged at Boydton on January 23, 1899. This case appears to have been the only legal execution of a white person for the killing of a black person in Virginia during the century after the Civil War. But it was *not* unique in Virginia history; several other such cases have been found in both the Colonial and the Federalist eras. Source: *Richmond Dispatch*, 5/10/98 (5:2), 7/22/98 (6:2) and 1/24/99 (2:6); *The Times* (Richmond, VA), 12/7/98 (5:6). See also 1880 U.S. Census (Mecklenburg Co., VA), which notes Bowers.

Noah Finley (black, age 25). *Highway Robbery.* The crime was committed on 8/2/1899 in Pulaski County. Executed for robbing and feloniously assaulting 61-year-old James H. Darst (white), a former army major and member of the Virginia state legislature. Darst had his watch and money stolen, plus three shots fired at him as he fled from the scene of the crime. The bandit was hanged at Pulaski Courthouse on September 15, 1899. Source: *Richmond Dispatch*, 8/3/99 (6:6), 8/4/99 (2:3) and 9/16/99 (1:1). See also 1880 U.S. Census (Montgomery Co., VA), which notes Finley, plus the census for Pulaski Co., VA, which notes Mr. Darst.

1900

Junius Robinson (black, age 21). *Murder.* The crime was committed on 10/31/1899 in Dinwiddie County. Executed for the handgun slaying of 27-year-old William M. Jolly (white). Motive: an argument about trespassing on private property. The killer was hanged at Dinwiddie Courthouse on January 2, 1900. Source: *Richmond Dispatch*, 11/2/99 (6:1) and 1/3/00 (3:3); *The Times* (Richmond, VA), 11/2/99 (5:1). See also 1880 U.S. Census (Dinwiddie Co., VA), which notes Mr. Jolly as a minor.

Reuben Griggs (black, age 17). *Rape.* The crime was committed on 11/20/1899 in Cumberland County. Indecent assault on the person of 6-year-old Martha Hatcher (black), she having been ravished at knifepoint. This predator was hanged at Cumberland Courthouse on March 23, 1900. Source: *The Times* (Richmond, VA), 3/24/00 (1:2). See also 1900 U.S. Census (Cumberland Co., VA), which notes the little girl, plus Original Case File (*Commonwealth vs. Griggs*), in Cumberland County Circuit Court Judgments (1899–1901, Box 5), State Records Center, Richmond, VA.

Charles Hairston (black, age 20). *Attempted Rape.* The crime was committed on 5/9/1900 in Henry County. Felonious assault on the person of 18-year-old Susan Jane Gauldin (white) with intent to commit rape. This attacker was hanged at Martinsville on June 20, 1900. Source: *Richmond Dispatch*, 5/13/00 (23:4), 5/16/00 (7:3) and 6/21/00 (4:3). See also 1900 U.S. Census (Henry Co., VA), which notes both parties.

Stephen Baptist (black, age 18). *Murder.* The crime was committed on 4/22/1900 in Mecklenburg County. Executed for the murder of 79-year-old Peter Jones (white), who was bludgeoned with an iron bar. Motive: a three-dollar mugging. The culprit was hanged at Boydton on July 10, 1900. Source: *The Times* (Richmond, VA), 4/25/00 (1:7) and 7/11/00 (3:6). See also 1900 U.S. Census (Mecklenburg Co., VA), which notes both parties.

Grant Reed (black, age 35). *Murder.* The crime was committed on 4/2/1899 in Madison County. Executed for the rifle slayings of 26-year-old Minnie Jackson Reed and 54-year-old Peter Jackson (both black), his wife and father-in-law, respectively. Motive: family problems. The killer was hanged at Madison Courthouse on August 3, 1900. Source: *Richmond Dispatch*, 8/4/00 (3:1). See also 1880 U.S. Census (Madison Co., VA), which notes the murdered pair.

William Woodson (black, age 38). *Murder.* The crime was committed on 5/19/1900 at Richmond. Executed for the murder of 23-year-old Ambrose Ferrebee (black), a fellow prisoner at the Virginia State Penitentiary. Motive: prison violence. Ferrebee had broken up a fight between Woodson and another convict. Resenting this, Woodson turned his anger against Ferrebee and slashed his throat with a contraband knife, very nearly decapitating him. The killer was hanged at Richmond on December 13, 1900. Source: *Richmond Dispatch*, 5/20/00 (1:5) and 12/14/00 (2:4).

John Holden (black, age 20). *Attempted Rape.* The crime was committed on 10/18/1900 in Accomack County. Felonious assault on the person of 10-year-old Virginia Clayton (white), she having been attacked on a public road with intent to commit rape. The attacker was hanged at Accomack Courthouse on December 21, 1900. Source: *Peninsula Enterprise* (Accomack, VA), 10/27/00 (3:4) and 12/22/00 (3:6). See also 1900 U.S. Census (Accomack Co., VA), which notes both parties.

Sylvester Griffin (black, age 22). *Murder.* The crime was committed on 7/30/1900 at Danville. Executed for the handgun slaying of 22-year-old Georgia King (black). Motive: suspicion of lesbianism (he had caught her dancing with another female and he didn't approve). Griffin was hanged at Danville on December 28, 1900. Source: *Richmond Dispatch*, 7/31/00 (3:2) and 12/29/00 (6:1); *The Times* (Richmond, VA), 8/18/00 (2:1) and 12/29/00 (4:4). See also 1900 U.S. Census (Pittsylvania Co., VA), which notes the victim, and 1880 U.S. Census (Pittsylvania Co., VA), which notes Griffin as a minor.

1901

Archer Hunt (black, age 23). *Murder.* The crime was committed on 8/24/1900 at Lynchburg. Executed for the handgun slaying of 38-year-old Thomas Gills (black), who was shot four times. Motive: a dispute about a lock. The killer was hanged at Lynchburg on January 25, 1901. Source: *The Times* (Richmond, VA), 9/22/00 (6:2) and 1/26/01 (2:1). See also 1900 U.S. Census (Lynchburg, VA), which notes Gills, plus the census for Campbell Co., VA, which notes Hunt.

Edward Payne (black, age 20). *Attempted Rape.* The crime was committed on 6/1/1901 in Pulaski County. Felonious assault on the person of 18-year-old Cynthia Duncan (white) with intent to commit rape. The attacker was hanged at Pulaski Courthouse on July 12, 1901. Source: *Richmond Dispatch*, 7/13/01 (1:3). See also 1900 U.S. Census (Pulaski Co., VA), which notes Miss Duncan.

John Fugate, alias "John Herbert Fuqua" (black, age 21). *Murder.* The crime was committed on 6/6/1901 in Wise County. Executed for the handgun slaying of 26-year-old Martha Wells (black). Motive: jilted lover. Fugate was hanged at Wise Courthouse on August 23, 1901. Source: *Big Stone Gap (VA) Post,* 6/13/01 (2:5) and 8/29/01 (3:5).

Cicero Harris (black, age 46). *Murder.* The crime was committed on 9/27/1901 at Bristol. Executed for the handgun slaying of 33-year-old Samuel Ware (black). Motive: adultery. Harris was hanged at Bristol on December 20, 1901. Source: *Richmond Dispatch*, 12/21/01 (9:7). See also 1900 U.S. Census (Bristol, VA), which notes Samuel Ware.

1902

Joseph Higginbotham (black, age 28). *Rape.* The crime was committed on 1/11/1902 at Lynchburg. Indecent assault and attempted murder of 21-year-old Bertha Webber (white), her throat having been slashed with homicidal intent. The attacker was hanged at Lynchburg on February 24, 1902. Source: *Richmond Dispatch*, 2/25/02 (9:3). See also 1910 U.S. Census (Atlanta, GA), which notes the victim and her later whereabouts, and 1880 U.S. Census (Campbell Co., VA), which notes Higginbotham as a minor.

Neal Stanback (black, age 18). *Attempted Rape.* The crime was committed on 1/18/1902 at Portsmouth. Felonious assault on the person of 60-year-old Elizabeth H. Preufer (white) with intent to commit rape. This attacker was hanged at Portsmouth on March 12, 1902. Source: *Richmond Times-Dispatch*, 1/21/02 (3:3) and 3/13/02 (4:5).

Mark Banks (black, age about 23). *Rape.* The crime was committed on 4/16/

1902 at Portsmouth. Indecent assault on the person of a 60+-year-old white female, whom surviving accounts identify only as "Mrs. B. J. Canady" (a mother of 13 children), she having also been robbed of her money and held in the woods for several hours against her will. The rapist was hanged at Portsmouth on May 30, 1902. Source: *Portsmouth (VA) Star*, 4/17/02 (1:6) and 5/30/02 (1:6).

George Robertson (black, age 35). *Murder.* The crime was committed on 6/28/1902 in Wise County. Executed for the fatal beating of 24-year-old Thomas Bates (black—his brother-in-law), a man with only one arm and one eye. Motive: Bates had allegedly spoken ill of Robertson's mother. Robertson was hanged at Wise Courthouse on August 1, 1902. Source: *Richmond Dispatch*, 7/12/02 (5:3), 8/1/02 (5:3) and 8/2/02 (1:3). See also 1900 U.S. Census (Wise Co., VA), which notes Bates.

George Easter (black, age 49). *Murder.* The crime was committed on 12/25/1901 in Greensville County. Executed for the handgun slaying of roughly 67-year-old Thomas Woodruff (white). Motive: hooliganism on Christmas Day. The killer was hanged at Emporia on August 22, 1902. Source: *Evening News-Leader* (Richmond, VA), 8/22/02 (7:5); *The Times* (Richmond, VA), 8/23/02 (1:5). See also 1900 U.S. Census (Greensville Co., VA), which notes George Easter.

Robert Foy (black, age 24). *Murder.* The crime was committed on 12/20/1901 in Wise County. Executed for the handgun slaying of 28-year-old Dayton H. Miller (white). Motive: dispute over wages. The killer was hanged at Wise Courthouse on August 29, 1902. Source: *Bluefield (WV) Daily Telegraph*, 12/21/01 (1:4) and 12/22/01 (1:3); *Big Stone Gap (VA) Post*, 12/26/01 (3:4) and 9/4/02 (2:3).

John Lomax (black, age 18). *Attempted Rape.* The crime was committed on 6/28/1902 in Westmoreland County. Felonious assault on the person of 15-year-old Susie Costenbader (white) with intent to commit rape. She died before the case came to trial, having been fatally burned when an oil lamp exploded. Her untimely demise did not help Lomax. He was hanged at Montross on September 9, 1902. Source: *The Times* (Richmond, VA), 7/1/02 (1:5) and 9/10/02 (3:6); *Richmond Dispatch*, 8/6/02 (5:5) and 9/10/02 (6:1).

Burrell Johnson (black, age 17). *Attempted Rape.* The crime was committed on 8/17/1902 in New Kent County. Felonious assault on the person of 25-year-old Addie Clow (white), she having been beaten to within an inch of her life with intent to commit rape. The attacker was hanged at New Kent Courthouse on September 23, 1902. Source: *Richmond Dispatch*, 8/19/02 (1:1) and 9/24/02 (2:3).

John Wesley Hicks (white, age 47). *Murder.* The crime was committed on 6/23/1902 in Louisa County. Executed for the shotgun slaying of roughly 25-year-old Melton Bourne (white—his son-in-law), who was taken down by three separate blasts, the first one in the back. Motive: personal animosity. Hicks was hanged at Louisa Courthouse on October 3, 1902. Source: *Richmond Dispatch*, 6/24/02 (7:6) and 10/4/02 (3:4). See also 1880 U.S. Census (Louisa Co., VA), which notes the killer.

John Avent (black, age 32). *Murder.* The crime was committed on 6/30/1902 in Brunswick County. Uxoricide. Executed for the ax murder of 27-year-old

Harriet Avent (black). Motive: suspicion of infidelity. This killer was hanged at Lawrenceville on October 24, 1902. Source: *Richmond Dispatch*, 7/3/02 (5:5) and 10/25/02 (3:5). See also 1900 U.S. Census (Brunswick Co., VA), which notes both as "Arent."

Jeremiah Kimbrough (black, age 23). *Attempted Rape*. The crime was committed on 11/10/1902 in Hanover County. Felonious assault on the person of pregnant 22-year-old Muriel Taylor (white—the wife of Butler Julian Taylor) with intent to commit rape. The attacker was hanged at Hanover Courthouse on December 22, 1902. Source: *Richmond Dispatch*, 11/11/02 (1:7) and 12/23/02 (5:1). See also 1900 U.S. Census (Hanover Co., VA), which notes Mrs. Taylor.

1903

Jack Brown (black, age 26). *Murder*. The crime was committed on 11/4/1902 in Goochland County. Executed for the murder of 30-year-old James H. Parker (black), the victim having been slashed with a contraband knife. Motive: prison violence. The killer was hanged at Goochland Courthouse on January 2, 1903. Source: *Richmond Dispatch*, 1/3/03 (2:2); *The Times* (Richmond, VA), 1/3/03 (10:6). See also 1900 U.S. Census (Isle of Wight Co., VA), which notes Parker, plus the census for Richmond, VA, which notes Brown.

Ernest Davis (black, age 29). *Murder*. The crime was committed on 8/8/1902 at Manchester, just below Richmond. Executed for the fatal stabbing of 53-year-old John Henry Stokes (black). Motive: street brawl. The killer was hanged at the Manchester municipal jail on January 9, 1903. Source: *The Times* (Richmond, VA), 8/9/02 (1:7), 8/10/02 (21:4) and 1/10/03 (2:5). See also 1900 U.S. Census (Rocky Mount, NC), which notes Stokes, and 1880 U.S. Census (Chesterfield Co., VA), which notes Davis as a minor.

William Treadwell (black, age 27). *Murder*. The crime was committed on 7/1/1902 at Portsmouth. Uxoricide. Executed for the handgun slaying of 25-year-old Sarah Treadwell (black), she having been shot in the back. Motive: marital estrangement. Her husband was hanged at the Portsmouth city jail on January 16, 1903. Source: *Virginian-Pilot* (Norfolk), 7/2/02 (8:3) and 1/17/03 (8:3); *Portsmouth Star*, 1/16/03 (1:6). See also 1900 U.S. Census (Norfolk, VA), which notes them as "Tredwell."

Arthur Wilton (black, age about 20). *Murder*. The crime was committed on 11/13/1902 at Danville. Executed for the murder of 50+-year-old Jake Lee (black), who was beaten on the head with a billiard cue. Motive: robbery. Wilton was hanged at Danville on February 6, 1903. Source: *Richmond Dispatch*, 12/11/02 (8:5); *Atlanta Constitution*, 2/7/03 (5:4); *Richmond Times-Dispatch*, 2/7/03 (6:3).

Alexander Spencer (black, age 18). *Murder*. The crime was committed on 2/2/1903 in Halifax County. Executed for the murder of 47-year-old Sallie A. Wilborn (white), she having been beaten to death with an unknown blunt instrument. Motive: sexual assault. The killer was hanged at Halifax Courthouse on April 10, 1903. Source: *Richmond Times-Dispatch*, 2/5/03 (6:2) and 4/11/03 (6:2). See also 1900 U.S. (Halifax Co., VA), which notes the victim.

Samuel Waters (black, age not recorded). *Murder.* The crime was committed on 1/10/1903 at Norfolk. Executed for the murder of a white man whose name was tentatively given as "Charles R. Hunter" and/or "T. H. Allen" (age not recorded), the victim having been struck on the head with a gas pipe and his body thrown onto the street. Motive: robbery in a whorehouse. The killer was hanged at Norfolk on April 24, 1903. Source: *Virginian Pilot* (Norfolk), 1/14/03 (1:6), 1/15/03 (2:3) and 4/25/03 (3:4).

Evans Hopson (white, age 34). *Murder.* The crime was committed on 11/5/1902 in Wise County. Executed for the handgun slaying of 46-year-old John Salyer (white). Motive: burglary gone awry. Hopson was hanged at Wise Courthouse on June 12, 1903. Source: *Richmond Dispatch*, 11/7/02 (7:6); *Washington Post*, 6/13/03 (5:3); *Middleboro (KY) Daily News*, 8/26/50 (1:1), feature article. See also 1900 U.S. Census (Wise Co., VA), which notes Mr. Salyer.

Anderson Finch (black, age 18). *Attempted Rape.* The crime was committed on 7/23/1903 in Mecklenburg County. Felonious assault on the person of 29-year-old Fannie W. Geohegan (white), she having had cornmeal thrown in her eyes, after which Finch wrestled her to the ground with intent to commit rape. The attacker was hanged at Boydton on September 2, 1903. Source: *Richmond Times Dispatch*, 7/25/03 (1:3), 7/30/03 (6:5) and 9/3/03 (6:1).

Julian Warren (black, age 35). *Murder.* The crime was committed on 5/28/1903 in Southampton County. Executed for the shotgun slaying of 31-year-old Allen Wilson (black), the victim having been ambushed. Motive: adultery turned deadly. The killer was hanged at Courtland on September 4, 1903. Source: *Richmond Times-Dispatch*, 5/30/03 (1:6); *Alexandria (VA) Gazette*, 9/5/03 (2:4). See also 1900 U.S. Census (Southampton Co., VA), which notes both parties.

Clifton Branham (white, age 41). *Murder.* The crime was committed on 12/24/1902 in Wise County. Uxoricide. Executed for the gunshot slaying of blind 40-year-old Nancy J. Branham (white). Motive: temper tantrum on Christmas Eve. Clifton Branham had previously served 15 years in the Kentucky State Penitentiary for the 1885 sniper killing of a Letcher County man named Henry Vanover. He further confessed to the sniper killing of another man named Anderson Moore (white, age 51) in Floyd County, Kentucky, on or about 4/1/1903. Branham was hanged at Wise Courthouse on September 25, 1903. Source: *Naugatuck (CT) Daily News*, 4/20/03 (3:5); *Richmond Times-Dispatch*, 8/7/03 (3:3) and 9/26/03 (2:5); *Alexandria (VA) Gazette*, 8/12/03 (2:3), 9/25/03 (2:4) and 9/26/03 (2:2). See also 1880 U.S. Census (Wise Co., VA), which notes the Branhams, and 1900 U.S. Census (Floyd Co., KY), which notes Anderson Moore.

Doc Bacon (black, age not recorded). *Attempted Rape.* The crime was committed on 7/23/1903 in Mecklenburg County. Accomplice in a felonious assault on the person of 29-year-old Fannie W. Geohegan (white) with intent to commit rape. He was hanged at Boydton on October 3, 1903. Source: *Richmond Times-Dispatch*, 10/4/03 (11:3). See **Anderson Finch** (executed 9/2/03). See also 1900 and 1910 U.S. Census (Mecklenburg Co., VA), which notes the victim.

Will Jones (black, age not recorded). *Murder.* The crime was committed on 11/13/1902 at Danville. Accomplice in the murder of 50+-year-old Jake Lee (black). Motive: robbery. He was hanged at Danville on October 9, 1903. Source: *The Times* (Richmond, VA), 1/14/03 (6:4); *Richmond Times-Dispatch*, 10/10/03 (1:4). See **Arthur Wilton** (executed 2/6/03).

Robert Gleeson (black, age 55). *Murder.* The crime was committed on 10/6/1903 in Amherst County. Executed for the handgun slaying of 33-year-old James C. Reed (white), the victim having been shot four times. Motive: argument over a fishing spot. The killer was hanged at Amherst Courthouse on December 30, 1903. Source: *Richmond Times-Dispatch*, 10/7/03 (5:6) and 12/31/03 (5:2); *Washington Post*, 10/7/03 (4:2); *Richmond (VA) News Leader*, 12/30/03 (4:7).

1904

Frank Bradley (black, age about 22). *Murder.* The crime was committed on 9/11/1903 in Nelson County. Executed for the handgun slaying of 44-year-old William P. Harris (white). Motive: robbery. The killer was hanged at Lovingston on January 30, 1904. Source: *Richmond Times-Dispatch*, 9/12/03 (7:3) and 1/31/04 (14:7); *Washington Post*, 9/12/03 (1:6), 1/1/04 (5:2) and 1/31/04 (11:2). See also 1900 U.S. Census (Bath Co., VA), which notes Mr. Harris.

Parker Robinson (black, age 27). *Murder.* The crime was committed on 11/9/1903 in Brunswick County. Matricide. Executed for the rifle slaying of 58-year-old Sarah Robinson (black), his own mother. Motive: temper tantrum. This killer was hanged at Lawrenceville on March 4, 1904. Source: *Daily Index-Appeal* (Petersburg, VA), 3/5/04 (1:2); *Washington Post*, 3/5/04 (9:2). See also 1880 U.S. Census (Brunswick Co., VA), which notes both parties.

John Clements (black, age not recorded). *Murder.* The crime was committed on 12/12/1903 in King William County. Executed for the handgun slaying of 42-year-old George W. Hobaugh (white), the victim having been initially shot in the back and then finished off with a second shot. Motive: obnoxious drunk. Clements was hanged at King William Courthouse on March 11, 1904. Source: *Richmond Times-Dispatch*, 12/15/03 (3:2) and 3/12/04 (5:1). See also 1900 U.S. Census (King William Co., VA), which notes Mr. Hobaugh.

Henry Williams (black, age 29). *Rape.* The crime was committed on 1/30/1904 at Roanoke. Indecent assault and near murder of 21-year-old Alice Shields (white), together with the grievous wounding of 2-year-old Mildred Shields (her daughter) by means of a hatchet and a razor, the victims having been attacked in their home. Williams was hanged at Roanoke on March 18, 1904. Source: *Roanoke (VA) Times*, 1/31/04 (1:3) and 3/19/04 (1:1). See also 1910 U.S. Census (Roanoke, VA), which notes the adult victim and the absence of the injured child, who had apparently died by then.

Chesley Peoples (white, age 47). *Murder.* The crime was committed on 12/3/1903 in Wythe County. Executed for the shotgun slaying of 29-year-old John Seagle (white). Motive: gambling dispute. Peoples was reportedly the prime suspect in three other murders. He was hanged at Wytheville on March 25, 1904. Source: *Atlanta Constitution*, 3/26/04

(5:2); *Richmond Times-Dispatch*, 3/26/04 (7:4). See also 1880 U.S. Census (Wythe Co., VA), which notes Peoples, and 1900 U.S. Census (Wythe Co., VA), which notes Seagle.

Henry Woodward (black, age not recorded). *Murder.* The crime was committed on 12/26/1903 in Tazewell County. Executed for the handgun slaying of 28-year-old Frank Tabor (white). Motive: vindictiveness (the murdered man was a mine boss who had fired Woodward from his job). The killer was hanged at Tazewell Courthouse on May 6, 1904. Source: *Washington Post*, 12/27/03 (6:1) and 5/7/04 (4:1); *Clinch Valley News* (Tazewell, VA), 1/8/04 (2:2) and 5/6/04 (1:4). See also 1900 U.S. Census (Bland Co., VA), which notes Mr. Tabor.

Leonard Clark (black, age about 20). *Murder.* The crime was committed on 12/24/1903 in Amherst County. Executed for the ax murder of roughly 20-year-old Lloyd Morris (black). Motive: robbery. The victim of this homicide had come home for Christmas with some money and a new set of clothes. Clark feigned camaraderie with him as they walked along a rural lane. Then he struck down the unsuspecting Morris from behind with an ax that he was carrying, inflicting four head wounds. Clark then stripped the decedent of clothes and money. He discarded his own clothes right there on the spot and put on those of the murdered man, including the victim's hat, which clearly bore marks of where the ax had struck. Whether blood got on any of the other items of apparel is uncertain. The unperturbed killer then went to a Christmas Eve dance dressed in the victim's clothes. He played a banjo for the revelers throughout the remainder of that night. He wore the same ill-gotten garments at his trial, as well as on the gallows itself. Clark was executed at Amherst Courthouse on May 27, 1904. Source: *Richmond Times-Dispatch*, 12/27/03 (6:3), 12/29/03 (5:1) and 5/28/04 (5:3); *Daily Index-Appeal* (Petersburg, VA), 5/28/04 (3:2); *Washington Post*, 5/28/04 (5:5).

James Caul (black, age 21). *Murder.* The crime was committed on 5/14/1904 in Nelson County. Handgun slaying of 20-year-old Sallie Thompson (black). Motive: she had refused to marry him. This frustrated suitor was hanged at Lovingston on September 17, 1904. Source: *Richmond Times-Dispatch*, 7/27/04 (5:1); *Daily Index-Appeal* (Petersburg), 9/18/04 (3:3). See also 1900 U.S. Census (Nelson Co., VA), which notes both parties.

James Bailey (black, age 18). *Murder.* The crime was committed on 6/23/1904 in Southampton County. Executed for the handgun slaying of 19-year-old Cadmus Williams (black). Motive: a dispute over a nickel. This killer was hanged at Courtland on September 26, 1904. Source: *Richmond News Leader*, 9/26/04 (1:6); *Daily Index-Appeal* (Petersburg), 9/27/04 (1:5). See also 1900 U.S. Census (Southampton Co., VA), which notes the victim as "Cad" Williams.

John Henry Banks (black, age 22). *Murder.* The crime was committed on 6/24/1904 in Buckingham County. Executed for the shotgun slaying of 74-year-old John J. Brown (black), known to all as "Old Uncle John Brown." Motive: vindictiveness (the victim had previously had the killer arrested for disrupting a church service). Banks was hanged at Buckingham Courthouse on September 30, 1904. Source: *Richmond Times-Dispatch*, 6/26/04 (7:1) and 10/1/04 (5:6). See also 1900 U.S. Census (Buckingham Co., VA), which notes both parties.

1905

James Goode (black, age 28). *Murder.* The crime was committed on 7/1/1904 at Richmond. Cop killer. Executed for the handgun slaying of 63-year-old John F. Shinberger (white). Motive: resisting arrest. Goode had fatally shot another black man named Richard Fox in a saloon brawl five days earlier. He was being sought for that homicide when he gunned down Officer Shinberger. He was hanged at Richmond on January 6, 1905. Source: *Richmond Times-Dispatch,* 6/26/04 (13:4), 7/2/04 (1:4) and 1/7/05 (8:1).

Benjamin Lipkins (black, age 57). *Murder.* The crime was committed on 7/9/1904 in Clarke County. Executed for the handgun slaying of 33-year-old Richard Ellerson (black), the victim having been shot four times, including twice in the back. Motive: personal animosity. Lipkins was hanged at Berryville on January 27, 1905. Source: *Clarke Courier* (Berryville, VA), 7/13/04 (1:7) and 2/1/05 (1:3). See also 1900 U.S. Census (Clarke Co., VA), which notes both parties.

James Samuel McCue (white, age 43). *Murder.* The crime was committed on 9/4/1904 at Charlottesville. Uxoricide. Executed for the handgun slaying of 33-year-old Frances Crawford McCue (white). Motive: she had reproached him for being a philanderer. McCue was the three-term mayor of Charlottesville and a member of the Charlottesville Bar Association and the Virginia State Bar Association. He also held memberships in the ultra-exclusive Meadow Creek Country Club and Elks Lodge No. 389, both of Charlottesville. This is the same hometown of Thomas Jefferson, the University of Virginia and the University of Virginia Law School. McCue was allowed to take a last walk around the campuses of those institutions before being led to the gallows. He met a felon's end at the end of a rope at the Charlottesville city jail on February 10, 1905. "One searches our chronicles in vain for the execution of any member of the affluent strata of our society," said the late William O. Douglas, much-quoted associate justice of the U.S. Supreme Court. The McCue case indicates that Justice Douglas did not "search" very hard. Source: *Charlottesville Daily Progress*, extra edition, 2/10/05; *Washington Post*, 2/11/05 (1:1); *Front Page Detective*, 10/36; *Real Detective*, 7/38 and 5/52; *Master Detective*, 1/40. See also 1900 U.S. Census (Charlottesville, VA), which notes both parties, plus *University of Virginia: Its History, Influence, Equipment and Characteristics with Biographical Sketches and Portraits of Founders, Benefactors, Officers and Alumni* (Lewis Publishing Co., NY, 1904), Vol. 2, page 192, for a sterling write-up of this killer and his place in society.

Edward Austin (black, age 20). *Rape.* The crime was committed on 10/29/1904 at Richmond. Indecent assault on the person of 8-year-old Lillie Ross (black). This rapist was hanged at Richmond on March 16, 1905. Source: *Richmond Times-Dispatch*, 1/11/05 (8:1) and 3/17/05 (10:5). See also 1900 U.S. Census (Raleigh, NC), which notes the culprit, plus the census for Henrico Co., VA, which notes the victim.

Peter Dancey (black, age 35). *Murder.* The crime was committed on 11/16/1904 at Richmond. Executed for the handgun slaying of Inez Ledbetter (black, age not recorded). Motive: she had declined his advances. The killer was hanged at Richmond on March 16, 1905. Source: *Richmond Times-Dispatch*, 11/17/04 (9:3), 1/13/05 (10:3) and 3/17/05 (10:5).

Robert Bowles (black, age not recorded). *Murder.* The crime was committed on 3/21/1904 in Alleghany County. Executed for the handgun slaying of 25-year-old John A. Ruff (white), a railroad brakeman. Motive: Ruff had attempted to stop him from illegally boarding a train. Furthermore, the victim's father (Samuel Ruff) later died of grief over the tragic loss of his beloved son. The killer was hanged at Covington on March 17, 1905. Source: *Richmond Times-Dispatch*, 10/1/04 (5:3) and 3/18/05 (5:3); *Staunton (VA) Daily Leader*, 3/17/05 (1:5). Appeal: 103 VA 816–837.

James E. Linkous (white, age 46). *Murder.* The crime was committed on 12/25/1904 at Radford. Executed for the beating deaths and cremations of 48-year-old Virginia Cundiff Linkous and 7-year-old Willie Vaughn Linkous (whites), his wife and adopted son. Their heads had been smashed in and their house set ablaze with them in it. Motive: the killer had a roving eye and wanted to be free to pursue another woman. His surname was really "Luckadoo," according to some reports. He was hanged at Radford on March 17, 1905. Source: *Richmond Times-Dispatch*, 12/27/04 (1:7) and 3/18/05 (5:3); *Washington Post*, 12/27/04 (1:8) and 12/28/04 (5:2). See also 1880 U.S. Census (Montgomery Co., VA), which notes this ill-fated couple.

Robert Turner (black, age 35). *Murder.* The crime was committed on 7/4/1904 in Washington County. Executed for the handgun slaying of 29-year-old Lou Jefferson (black female). Motive: he thought that she was cheating on him with other men. His actions brought him to the gallows at Abingdon on March 24, 1905. Source: *Washington Post*, 1/28/05 (9:2) and 3/25/05 (5:6). See also 1900 U.S. Census (Washington Co., VA), which notes the victim.

Cloyd Hale (black, age 51). *Murder.* The crime was committed on 4/1/1905 in Pulaski County. Executed for the shotgun slaying of John Hart (white, age not recorded), an itinerant umbrella mender. Motive: Hart had demanded that Hale return a coat that he had stolen. The killer was hanged at Pulaski Courthouse on May 12, 1905. Source: *Richmond Times-Dispatch*, 4/4/05 (5:2) and 5/13/05 (5:2). See also 1900 U.S. Census (Wythe Co., VA), which notes Hale.

William Hansboro (black, age 32). *Murder.* The crime was committed on 3/17/1905 in Bath County. Executed for the murder of James R. McKeen (white, age not recorded), the victim having been bludgeoned with a heavy wine bottle. Motive: disgruntled employee. The killer was hanged at Warm Springs on June 15, 1905. Source: *Highland Recorder* (Monterey, VA), 3/24/05 (3:2); *The Old Dominion* (Staunton, VA), 3/24/05 (3:3) and 3/31/05 (1:4); *Washington Post*, 6/16/05 (5:3).

Charles Dean (black, age not recorded). *Murder.* The crime was committed on 4/20/1905 in Craig County. Executed for the handgun slaying of Fletcher Hawkins (black, age not recorded), the victim having been shot in the back. Motive: rivalry for a female. The killer was hanged at New Castle on September 13, 1905. Source: *Washington Post*, 6/30/05 (4:3) and 9/14/05 (5:1). See also Original Case File (*Commonwealth vs. Dean*), copy provided courtesy of Sharon Kaye Braden, the clerk of Craig County Circuit Court.

Edward Winston Gaines (black, age 33). *Murder.* The crime was committed on 5/13/1905 in Charles City County. Executed for the murder of 80-year-old Laura Ennis (black), known to all as "Old Aunt Ennis," who was brutally clubbed to death. Motive: the killer blamed her for the refusal of her granddaughter to marry him. Gaines was hanged at Charles City Courthouse on November 23, 1905. Source: *Richmond Times-Dispatch*, 5/16/05 (1:2), 6/6/05 (1:7) and 11/24/05 (2:4). See also 1900 U.S. Census (Charles City Co., VA), which notes Ennis, and 1880 U.S. Census (Charles City Co., VA), which notes Gaines as a minor.

Cephas Poindexter (black, age not recorded). *Murder.* The crime was committed on 7/25/1905 in Franklin County. Cop killer. Executed for the shotgun slaying of 56-year-old Zachary Taylor Wade (white). Motive: resisting arrest. Poindexter was hanged at Rocky Mount on November 24, 1905. Source: *Roanoke (VA) Times*, 7/27/05 (1:1), 7/30/05 (1:5) and 11/25/05 (1:6). See also 1900 U.S. Census (Franklin Co., VA), which notes Wade.

1906

Morris Cremeans (white, age 41). *Murder.* The crime was committed on 4/24/1905 in Giles County. Executed for the shotgun slaying of 60+-year-old George A. Kidd (white). Motive: temper tantrum. Cremeans confessed to four other murders as well, but their details are too vague to be accredited. He was hanged at Pearisburg on April 6, 1906. Source: *Richmond Times-Dispatch*, 4/7/06 (1:5); *Washington Post*, 4/7/06 (11:3).

Robert Booker (black, age 32). *Murder.* The crime was committed on 1/20/1906 in Prince Edward County. Executed for the handgun slaying of 27-year-old Charles Brown (black), the victim having been shot in his own doorway. Motive: personal animosity. The killer was hanged at Farmville on May 18, 1906. Source: *Farmville (VA) Herald*, 1/26/06 (3:3) and 5/25/06 (3:2). See also 1900 U.S. Census (Prince Edward Co., VA), which notes Brown.

Gabriel Battaile (black, age 16). *Rape.* The crime was committed on 4/30/1906 in King George County. Indecent assault on the person of 16-year-old Lena Rogers (white), a retarded girl. This sex offender was hanged at King George Courthouse on June 8, 1906. Source: *Alexandria (VA) Gazette*, 5/5/06 (1:2) and 6/9/06 (2:3). See also 1900 U.S. Census (King George Co., VA), which notes both parties, although the culprit is listed as Gabriel "Battle."

Ben Hubbard, alias "Bennie Hubert" (black, age not recorded). *Murder.* The crime was committed on 2/17/1906 in Alleghany County. Executed for the murder of another black man named Robert Brown (age not recorded) by undisclosed means for an undisclosed reason. Neither the court file nor local newspaper accounts of this case have survived. It is, however, historically certain that Hubbard was hanged at Covington on June 28, 1906. Source: *Rockbridge County News*, 4/26/06 (1:7); *Richmond Times-Dispatch*, 6/29/06 (10:6).

Andrew Davenport (black, age 31). *Murder.* The crime was committed on 1/29/1906 at Newport News. Executed for the handgun slaying of William Thomas (black, age not recorded), the victim having been first shot in the back and then finished off by another bullet fired into his head. Motive: insurance fraud. The killer was hanged at Newport News on July 13, 1906. Source: *Daily Press* (Newport News, VA), 1/30/06 (2:1), 1/31/06 (2:1), 2/1/06 (2:1) and 7/13/06 (1:1).

Thomas Jones (black, age 24) and **Charles Woodruff** (black, age 29). *Murder*. Their crime was committed on 12/27/1905 in Grayson County. Patricide. They were, respectively, the principal and accomplice in the handgun slaying of 45-year-old Wiley Jones (black), who was shot dead in his own doorway. Motive: the elder Jones had found fault with his son (Thomas) for partying when one of his children lay gravely ill. These killers were hanged at Independence on July 13, 1906. Source: *Richmond Times-Dispatch*, 3/30/06 (5:2) and 7/14/06 (5:2). See also 1900 U.S. Census (Grayson Co., VA), which notes the culprits, and 1880 U.S. Census (Grayson Co., VA), which notes Papa Jones.

William Wilcher (white, age 23). *Murder*. The crime was committed on 2/24/1906 in Rockbridge County. Executed for the shotgun slaying of Henry J. Smith (white, age not recorded). Motive: heated argument. The killer was hanged at Lexington on August 3, 1906. Source: *Lexington (VA) Gazette*, 2/28/06 (3:5), 6/20/06 (2:2) and 8/8/06 (3:3).

Sinnel Bagby (black, age 16). *Attempted Rape*. The crime was committed on 8/22/1906 in Middlesex County. Felonious assault on the person of 22-year-old Cora Stanley (white—a deaf-mute) with intent to commit rape. The attacker willfully took advantage of Stanley's handicap, knowing that she could not cry out. He was hanged at Saluda on September 28, 1906. Source: *Virginia Citizen* (Irvington, VA), 8/31/06 (2:2) and 10/5/06 (3:3). See also 1900 U.S. Census (Middlesex Co., VA), which notes Bagby.

1907

James Ward (black, age 30). *Murder*. The crime was committed on 5/24/1906 at Richmond. Executed for the handgun slaying of 19-year-old Carrie Meekins (black), she having been shot in the back. Motive: lovers' quarrel. The killer was hanged at Richmond on January 18, 1907. Source: *Mathews (VA) Journal*, 10/25/06 (3:3); *Richmond Evening Journal*, 1/18/07 (1:7). See also 1900 U.S. Census (New Kent Co., VA), which notes the victim.

William Ruffin, alias "Jesse Ruffin" (black, age 38) and **Massie Hill**, alias "Massie Jackson" (black, age 22). *Murder*. Their crime was committed on 6/5/1906 in Prince Edward County. Executed for the handgun slaying and incineration of 78-year-old John E. Grubb (white), the victim's house having been burned down around him. Motive: burglary. The killers were hanged at Farmville on February 15, 1907. Source: *Farmville (VA) Herald*, 6/8/06 (3:2) and 2/15/07 (3:2). See also 1900 U.S. Census (Prince Edward Co., VA), which notes Mr. Grubb.

Arthur Davis (black, age 20). *Murder*. The crime was committed on 12/26/1906 in Surry County. Executed for the fatal beating of Joseph F. Saleeby (white, age not recorded), a Syrian peddler. Motive: robbery. This killer was hanged at Surry Courthouse on March 8, 1907. Source: *Daily Index-Appeal* (Petersburg), 3/9/07 (8:6); *Richmond Times-Dispatch*, 3/9/07 (5:6).

Peter Good, alias "Charles Shaffer" (white, age 23). *Murder.* The crime was committed on 11/30/1906 in Page County. Executed for the shotgun slaying of 22-year-old Fannie Stroop (white), she having been shot in the back. Motive: unreciprocated love. This killer was hanged at Luray on March 22, 1907. Source: *The Page Courier* (Luray, VA), 12/6/06 (3:1), 3/21/07 (3:2) and 3/28/07 (4:1).

James King (black, age 18). *Murder.* The crime was committed on 9/12/1906 in Giles County. Executed for the handgun slaying of 43-year-old Charles B. Early (white). Motive: disgruntled employee. The teenage killer was hanged at Pearisburg on June 7, 1907. Source: *Atlanta Constitution*, 6/8/07 (16:5); *Richmond Times-Dispatch*, 6/8/07 (4:7); *Washington Post*, 6/8/07 (5:5). See also 1900 U.S. Census (Stark Co., OH), which notes Mr. Early.

John Hardy (black, age 34). *Murder.* The crime was committed on 10/12/1906 at Roanoke. Cop killer. Executed for the handgun slaying of 52-year-old Robert M. Beard (white). Motive: resisting arrest. Hardy was hanged at Roanoke on June 14, 1907. Source: *Richmond Times-Dispatch*, 10/13/06 (5:3) and 6/15/07 (5:3). See also 1900 U.S. Census (Roanoke, VA), which notes both parties.

Frank Allen (black, age not recorded). *Attempted Rape.* The crime was committed on 7/1/1907 in Mecklenburg County. Felonious assault on the person of 21-year-old Ella Ellis Callis (white), she having been attacked at gunpoint with intent to commit rape. Her would-be rapist was hanged at Boydton on August 22, 1907. Source: *Richmond Evening Journal*, 7/3/07 (1:7); *Richmond Times-Dispatch*, 8/23/07 (4:3). See also 1910 U.S. Census (Mecklenburg Co., VA), which notes Miss Callis.

William McIntosh (black, age not recorded). *Murder.* The crime was committed on 4/28/1907 at Norfolk. Executed for the murder of 48-year-old Charles W. Parks (white), who was bludgeoned with an iron pipe. A black man named Miles Newby (age 40) was also slain in the same incident. A separate indictment in Newby's case was held in abeyance. Motive: mugging. The killer was hanged at Norfolk on September 5, 1907. Source: *Virginian Pilot* (Norfolk), 4/30/07 (1:1) and 9/6/07 (3:2); *Portsmouth (VA) Star*, 9/5/07 (1:2). See also 1900 U.S. Census (Norfolk Co., VA), which notes both of the murdered men.

William Harris (black, age 22). *Attempted Rape.* The crime was committed on 8/22/1907 in Chesterfield County. Felonious assault on the person of 18-year-old Lena Rowland (white) with intent to commit rape. Her attacker was hanged at Chesterfield Courthouse on October 18, 1907. Source: *Richmond Times-Dispatch*, 8/23/07 (1:2) and 10/19/07 (4:3). See also 1900 U.S. Census (Chesterfield Co., VA), which notes Miss Rowland as a minor.

George Peters (white, age 33). *Murder.* The crime was committed on 5/23/1907 in Carroll County. Executed for the shotgun slaying of 49-year-old Joseph Easter (white). Motive: moonshiners' feud. Peters was hanged at Hillsville on October 18, 1907. Source: *The Landmark* (Statesville, NC), 5/28/07 (2:2); *Richmond Times-Dispatch*, 10/19/07 (4:3). See also 1900 U.S. Census (Carroll Co., VA), which notes both parties.

John Taylor (black, age 17). *Murder.* The crime was committed on 2/2/1907 in Caroline County. Executed for the fatal stabbing of roughly 20-year-old Jenifer Coleman (black male—his cousin) while at a young persons' dance. Motive: stupid male hubris in the presence of females. This black-on-black killer was hanged at Bowling Green on November 22, 1907. Source: *Richmond Times-Dispatch*, 2/6/07 (5:4) and 11/23/07 (4:7); *Richmond Evening Journal*, 11/22/07 (1:1).

John Gillison (black, age 32). *Murder.* The crime was committed on 8/17/1907 in Madison County. Uxoricide. Executed for the murder of Pearl Thomas Gillison (black, age not recorded), she having been battered to death with the butt of a shotgun. Motive: marital discord. The killer was hanged at Madison Courthouse on November 29, 1907. Source: *Richmond Times-Dispatch*, 10/2/07 (5:3) and 11/30/07 (3:2). See also 1880 U.S. Census (Loudoun Co., VA), which notes "Gilleson" as a minor, plus Original Case File (*Commonwealth vs. Gillison*), copy provided courtesy of Linda M. Parrish, the clerk of Madison County Circuit Court.

Noah Fulton (white, age 19). *Murder.* The crime was committed on 4/27/1907 in Washington County. Executed for the shotgun slaying of 16-year-old John Johnson (white). Motive: rivalry for a female. The killer was hanged at Abingdon on December 13, 1907. Source: *Richmond Evening Journal*, 12/13/07 (1:1); *Richmond Times-Dispatch*, 12/14/07 (3:3). See also 1900 U.S. Census (Washington Co., VA), which notes both parties.

Thomas Johnson (black, age not recorded). *Murder.* The crime was committed on 10/5/1907 in King William County. Executed for the murder of 57-year-old Chapman P. Snead (white), who was beaten on the head with an unknown object and left sprawled in the middle of the road. Motive: highway robbery. The killer was hanged at King William Courthouse on December 13, 1907. Source: *Richmond Times-Dispatch*, 10/7/07 (1:4) and 12/14/07 (3:3). See also 1900 U.S. Census (King William Co., VA), which notes the murdered man.

1908

George Midgets (black, age not recorded). *Murder.* The crime was committed on 10/20/1906 at Alexandria. Executed for the handgun slaying of 36-year-old Charles T. Smith (white). Motive: interfering with a police officer. Four days earlier, Midgets had used the same weapon to murder a 38-year-old Romany man named Frank Smith at Merion Township, Pennsylvania. He was hanged at Alexandria on February 14, 1908. Source: *Alexandria Gazette*, 10/22/06 (2:6) and 2/14/08 (2:6); *Washington Post*, 10/22/06 (11:5), 3/9/07 (9:2) and 2/15/08 (9:3); *Philadelphia Inquirer*, 2/20/08 (3:1).

Walter Rippey (black, age 18). *Rape.* The crime was committed on 2/13/1908 in Tazewell County. Serial rapist. Executed for an indecent assault on the person of 26-year-old Mary Dancey (white), she having been attacked in the presence of another woman and a 2-year-old child. On 8/22/1907 he had attacked a 14-year-old white girl and her younger sister as they were picking berries, also shooting at them when they broke free and ran away. Rippey was acquitted at trial on that count because the evidence was deemed inconclusive. He had three other rape charges pending against him involving girls of his own ethnicity. His usual *modus operandi* was to stuff mud into the mouths of his victims so that they could not scream. He was hanged at Tazewell Courthouse on March 27,

1908. Source: *Richmond Times-Dispatch*, 8/23/07 (4:3); *Roanoke (VA) Times*, 2/15/08 (1:5) and 2/19/08 (1:7); *Tazewell (VA) Republican*, 2/20/08 (1:5); *Washington Post*, 3/28/08 (11:2). See also 1900 U.S. Census (Tazewell Co., VA), which notes "Ripey" as a minor.

Grant Goode (black, age 16). *Murder.* The crime was committed on or about 2/20/1908 in Brunswick County. Executed for the murder of 24-year-old Samuel Rivers (black—his neighbor) by unknown means for an unknown reason. Newspaper accounts of this case are skimpy and its circuit court case file has since been "purged," as the clerk of that court informed me. Grant Goode was hanged at Lawrenceville on April 3, 1908. Source: *Richmond Times-Dispatch*, 2/25/08 (1:3) and 2/27/08 (1:3); *Richmond (VA) News Leader*, 3/27/08 (4:7) and 4/24/08 (1:1), in passing. See also 1900 U.S. Census (Brunswick Co., VA), which notes both parties.

Leo Thurman, alias "Charles F. Taylor" (white, age 23). *Murder.* The crime was committed on 2/1/1906 at Norfolk. Executed for the ax murder of roughly 21-year-old Walter P. Dolsen (white—his roommate), the victim having been hacked up in his bed, with his mangled body later stuffed into a storage trunk. Motive: robbery and mendacity. The killer was hanged at Norfolk on April 10, 1908. Source: *Richmond Times-Dispatch*, 2/2/06 (5:1); *Washington Post*, 4/11/08 (11:1); *Daring Detective*, 2/36; *Dynamic Detective*, 9/38. Appeal: 107 VA 912–918. See also "Leo C. Thurman: A Thrilling Story of His Checkered Career," a 68-page booklet published while he was awaiting execution (VA State Library).

Daniel Jackson (black, age 37). *Murder.* The crime was committed on 10/12/1907 in Greensville County. Uxoricide. Executed for the handgun slaying of 30-year-old Lizzie Jackson (black). Motive: marital breakdown. The killer was hanged at Emporia on April 24, 1908. Source: *Richmond Times-Dispatch*, 10/13/07 (5:5) and 4/25/08 (3:1). See also 1900 U.S. Census (Southampton Co., VA), which notes both parties, plus Original Case File (*Commonwealth vs. Jackson*), Greensville County Circuit Court Records Room, Emporia, VA.

Lee Strother (black, age 22). *Attempted Rape.* The crime was committed on 5/2/1908 in Madison County. Felonious assault on the person of 26-year-old Leola Frye (white), she having been forcibly pulled off a horse with intent to commit rape. Her attacker was hanged at Madison Courthouse on September 11, 1908. Source: *Alexandria (VA) Gazette*, 6/17/08 (2:4); *Richmond Times-Dispatch*, 9/12/08 (3:1). See also 1900 and 1930 U.S. Census (Madison Co., VA), which note the victim.

Henry Smith (black, age 22). *Rape.* The crime was committed on 8/11/1908 at Norfolk. Indecent assault on the person of 78-year-old Catherine Powell (white), she having been attacked and severely beaten in her own home twice during the same week. Her attacker paid for his crimes in the newly installed Virginia electric chair on October 13, 1908. Source: *Alexandria (VA) Gazette*, 8/12/08 (2:4) and 9/3/08 (2:4); *Richmond Times-Dispatch*, 10/14/08 (12:4).

Winston Green (black, age 17). *Attempted Rape.* The crime was committed on 9/10/1908 in Chesterfield County. Felonious assault on the person of 13-year-old Alice Larsen (white), she having been accosted on a public road with intent to commit rape. This attacker was electrocuted pursuant to the law on October 30, 1908. Source: *Alexandria Gazette*, 9/11/08 (2:2) and 10/30/08 (2:5); *Richmond Times-Dispatch*, 9/27/08 (1:2).

1909

Frank Davenport (black, age 22). *Murder.* The crime was committed on 7/30/1908 at Norfolk. Executed for the fatal stabbing of 25-year-old John Taylor (black). Motive: workplace dispute. The killer was put to death by high voltage on January 4, 1909. Source: *Virginia Citizen* (Irvington, VA), 8/7/08 (3:5), 12/11/08 (3:5) and 1/8/09 (2:4). See also 1900 U.S. Census (Northumberland Co., VA), which notes the victim.

Charles Gillespie (black, age 24). *Attempted Rape.* The crime was committed on 1/10/1909 in Henrico County. Felonious assault on the person of 19-year-old Marie Stumpf (white), she having been attacked while on her way to church, severely beaten, stripped of her valuables and her face horribly lacerated by the assailant's teeth with intent to commit rape. The miscreant was electrocuted on February 18, 1909. Source: *Daily Progress* (Petersburg), 1/11/09 (1:6); *Washington Post*, 2/19/09 (9:5).

Benjamin Gilbert (white, age 18). *Murder.* The crime was committed on 7/23/1908 at Norfolk. Executed for the handgun slaying of 21-year-old Amanda B. Morse (white), she having been shot twice in the back. Motive: jealous lover. Gilbert atoned for what he did in the electric chair on March 19, 1909. Source: *Richmond Evening Journal*, 3/19/09 (1:3); *Richmond Times-Dispatch*, 3/20/09 (8:5).

Aurelius Christian (black, age 19). *Murder.* The crime was committed on 2/18/1909 in Botetourt County. Executed for the fatal stabbing of 14-year-old Mary Dobbs (white), she having been knifed multiple times and her throat cut. Motive: sexual assault. This predator was electrocuted on March 22, 1909. Source: *Richmond Times-Dispatch,* 2/19/09 (1:4); *Alexandria (VA) Gazette*, 2/20/09 (2:4) and 3/23/09 (2:4); *Van Wert (OH) Daily Bulletin*, 2/20/09 (1:4).

James Smith (black, age 21). *Murder.* The crime was committed on 1/25/1909 in Henrico County. Executed for the murder of roughly 65-year-old James Flynn (white), who was battered to death with a brick. Motive: mugging. The killer died in the electric chair on April 8, 1909. Source: *Richmond Times-Dispatch*, 1/26/09 (10:7), 1/27/09 (10:1), 1/28/09 (4:2), 1/29/09 (10:5) and 4/9/09 (4:6).

Joel Payne (black, age 31). *Murder.* The crime was committed on or about 2/15/1908 in Bedford County. Executed for the handgun slaying of 54-year-old Reed Swain (black), his father-in-law. Motive: the older man had given refuge to the killer's estranged wife and child. Payne was executed by hanging at Bedford Courthouse on April 9, 1909. Source: *Richmond Times-Dispatch*, 7/26/08 (12:3) and 4/10/09 (3:7). See also 1900 U.S. Census (Bedford Co., VA), which notes both parties.

Berry Seaborne (black, age 21). *Rape.* The crime was committed on 1/21/1909 in Greensville County. Indecent assault on the person of 33-year-old Rebecca Turner (black), she having also been robbed of her intrinsic valuables at gunpoint, with her house vandalized. The culprit met his end in the Virginia electric chair on April 16, 1909. Source: *Richmond Times-Dispatch*, 1/29/09 (3:5), 2/3/09 (4:3), 2/5/09 (2:6) and 4/17/09

(2:5). See also Original Case File (*Commonwealth vs. Seaborne*), copy provided courtesy of Mr. Robert C. Wrenn, the clerk of Greensville County Circuit Court.

John Brown (black, age 57), **William Brown** (black, age 33), **Isham Taylor** (black, age 32), **Joe Taylor** (black, age 34) and **Lewis Jenkins** (black, age 40). *Murder.* Their crimes were committed on 2/12/1909 in Powhatan County. Executed for the ax murders of 72-year-old Mary Bolling Skipwith and 38-year-old Walter G. Johnson (both white), a bedridden widow and her caretaker, respectively. Their butchered bodies were left to be incinerated in their burning house. Motive: plunder. All five of these killers/home invaders were rounded up, convicted at trial and put to death by electrocution. The Browns died on April 30, 1909. The Taylors died on May 5, 1909, and Jenkins followed them two days later on May 7, 1909. No form of vituperation was spared in the denunciation of these men. Source: *Harrisonburg (VA) Daily News*, 2/19/09 (4:5); *Richmond Times-Dispatch*, 2/14/09 (12:1), 2/15/09 (8:1), 2/21/09 (11:3), 2/25/09 (10:7) and 5/1/09 (8:5). See also 1880 U.S. Census (Goochland Co., VA), which notes the male homicide victim as a minor; also the gravestone of Mary Elizabeth Skipwith (née Bolling) in Grace Church Cemetery (Rocky Ford Road), Powhatan Co., VA.

John Fleming (black, age 25). *Murder.* The crime was committed on 3/7/1909 in Lunenburg County. Uxoricide. Executed for the handgun slaying of Rosa Fleming (black, age not recorded), known to some as "Kasiah Fleming." Motive: not specified in surviving accounts. The killer was electrocuted pursuant to the law on July 30, 1909. Source: Lunenburg County Commonwealth Causes (1902–1917), Box 26 (VA State Archives). See also "Executed Offenders," Box 372, File 12 (VA State Archives).

William Wise (black, age 29). *Murder.* The crime was committed on 3/16/1909 at Petersburg. Executed for the murder of Thomas Walker (black, age not recorded), the victim having been knocked on the head and his throat cut from ear to ear. Motive: robbery. The Virginia electric chair settled accounts with Wise on August 27, 1909. Source: *Daily Progress* (Petersburg), 3/16/09 (1:3) and 3/17/09 (1:5); *Richmond Evening Journal*, 8/27/09 (8:2).

Howard H. Bragg (white, age 23). *Murder.* The crime was committed on 3/19/1909 in Rockbridge County. Executed for the murder of 50-year-old Thomas E. Drawbond (white), who was shot four times with a handgun; his body was later put onto railroad tracks, where it was mangled by passing trains. Motive: robbery. The killer was electrocuted on September 24, 1909. Source: *Lexington (VA) Gazette*, 3/24/09 (3:2) and 9/29/09 (3:6). See also 1900 U.S. Census (Rockbridge Co., VA), which notes Drawbond.

Jack Traynham (black, age 24). *Murder.* The crime was committed on 8/24/1909 at Lynchburg. Executed for the fatal stabbing of 30-year-old Edgar Turner (black). Motive: workplace dispute. The killer was put to death by electrocution on November 12, 1909. Source: *Washington Post*, 8/25/09 (3:2); *Mathews (VA) Journal*, 11/18/09 (1:4). See also 1900 U.S. Census (Rustburg, VA), which notes Turner.

Harry Robinson, alias "Harry Baltimore" (black, age 23). *Murder.* The crime was committed on 8/8/1909 in Warren County. Executed for the handgun slaying of 46-year-old William Larkin Sealock (white), the victim having been shot five times. Motive: obnoxious drunk. The killer died in the electric chair on December 9, 1909. Source: *Alexandria Gazette*, 8/10/09 (2:3); *Richmond Evening Journal*, 12/9/09 (7:2). See also 1900 U.S. Census (Fauquier Co., VA), which notes Sealock.

Clifton Breckinridge (black, age 20). *Attempted Rape.* The crime was committed on 11/11/1909 at Staunton. Felonious assault on the person of 6-year-old Dorothy Powell (white) with intent to commit rape. Further details were withheld from the public. The attacker was put to death by electrocution on December 17, 1909. Source: *Richmond Times-Dispatch*, 11/14/09 (4:3) and 12/18/09 (2:5).

1910

Thurman Spinner (black, age 18). *Murder.* The crime was committed on 10/30/1909 in Bedford County. Executed for the ax murder of 19-year-old Charles W. Noell (white). Motive: the murdered youth had torn the killer's shirt in a wrestling match. Spinner's reaction to getting his shirt torn cost him his life. He was executed on January 14, 1910. Source: *Richmond Times-Dispatch*, 11/5/09 (3:1); *Lexington (VA) Gazette*, 11/10/09 (2:5); *Mathews (VA) Journal*, 11/11/09 (1:4); *Richmond Evening Journal*, 1/14/10 (1:6). See also 1900 U.S. Census (Bedford Co., VA), which notes Noell.

Walter P. Parker (black, age 25). *Murder.* The crime was committed on 11/9/1909 at Norfolk. Executed for the murder of Samuel Fisher (black, age not recorded), the victim having been bludgeoned with "a wooden side post from a railway flatcar." Motive: gambling dispute for the sake of 20 cents. This killer was put to death on January 25, 1910. Source: *Virginian Pilot* (Norfolk), 12/15/09 (2:1), 12/24/09 (3:4) and 1/26/10 (7:4).

William Goins (black, age not recorded). *Murder.* The crime was committed on 6/24/1909 at Roanoke. Executed for the handgun slaying of Thomas Walker (black, age not recorded). Motive: rivalry for a female. The killer was executed on January 28, 1910. Source: *Roanoke (VA) Times*, 6/25/09 (1:3) and 1/29/10 (4:4); *Richmond Evening Journal*, 1/28/10 (12:7).

Willie Blake (black, age 23). *Rape.* The crime was committed on 7/31/1909 at Norfolk. Indecent assault on the person of 60-year-old Alice Jernigan (white), the record containing no further details. This rapist was executed on February 11, 1910. Source: *Richmond Times-Dispatch*, 8/2/09 (5:3); *Washington Post*, 2/12/10 (3:4).

Howard Little (white, age 37). *Murder.* The crime was committed on 9/21/1909 in Buchanan County. Mass slayer. Executed for the ax murders of 66-year-old Elizabeth Baker Justus, also known as "Aunt Betty Justus" (white), plus 24-year-old George Meadows, 21-year-old Lydia Justus Meadows (both white—a married couple) and their three children—Will Meadows (age 8), Noah Meadows (age 5) and Lafayette Meadows (age 2)—all of whom were left dead in their burning home. The young husband had also been shot twice in the back with a handgun. All were found with their heads chopped off and their bodies partially cremated. Motive: robbery. It was also determined that the killer had previously murdered a man in Pike County, Kentucky. This was in June 1892, the victim being one Jacob Kinney (white, age 20) by name. Further details of that homicide are lacking, but it was described as "brutal" and sufficiently aggravated to earn Little a sentence of so-called life imprisonment in the Kentucky State Penitentiary. Little managed to wrangle a pardon sometime in the early 1900s and was turned loose, to the detriment of his future victims. He was finally executed on February 11, 1910. Source: *Tazewell (VA) Republican*, 9/23/09 (1:5), 9/30/09 (1:4), 10/7/09 (1:3) and 2/17/10 (1:6); *Master Detective*, 7/35. See also 1880 U.S. Census (Pike Co., KY), which notes Kinney, and 1900 U.S. Census (Buchanan Co., VA), which notes three of the victims.

Elijah Rouse (black, age 28). *Murder.* The crime was committed on 7/10/1909 at Norfolk. Executed for the handgun slaying of Benjamin Taylor (black, age not recorded). Motive: gambling dispute. The killer was executed on April 25, 1910. Source: *Virginian Pilot* (Norfolk), 7/11/09 (14:1); *Richmond Times-Dispatch*, 1/23/10 (22:7); *Richmond Evening Journal*, 4/25/10 (2:6). See also 1910 U.S. Census (Richmond, VA), which notes Rouse as a prisoner.

Henry Smith (black, age 44). *Murder.* The crime was committed on 3/6/1909 at Alexandria. Executed for the fatal stabbing of roughly 35-year-old Walter F. Schultz (white), the victim having also had his throat cut. Motive: mugging. The killer was executed on June 3, 1910. Source: *Alexandria Gazette*, 3/8/09 (2:6), 3/9/09 (2:7) and 6/3/10 (3:2); *Washington Post*, 6/4/10 (3:5).

Thomas Noel (black, age 25). Murder. The crime was committed on 8/28/1909 at Norfolk. Cop killer. Executed for the handgun slaying of 41-year-old Joseph W. Sykes (white). Motive: resisting arrest. Noel paid for what he did in the electric chair on June 10, 1910. Source: *Virginian Pilot* (Norfolk) 8/29/09 (1:7) and 8/31/09 (4:3); *Portsmouth (VA) Star*, 8/30/09 (1:1); *Richmond Evening Journal*, 6/10/10 (7:6). See also 1910 U.S. Census (Portsmouth, VA), which notes Noel as a prisoner.

Angelo Hamilton (white, age 26). *Murder.* The crime was committed on 6/11/1909 at Lynchburg. Executed for the handgun slaying of 23-year-old Sallie Hicks (white), she having been shot twice in the back. Motive: thwarted lover. The Virginia electric chair put an end to Hamilton's worldly torment on July 1, 1910. Source: *Richmond Evening Journal*, 7/1/10 (1:2); *Richmond Times-Dispatch*, 7/2/10 (10:1). See also 1900 U.S. Census (Franklin Co., VA), which notes Miss Hicks.

Arch Brown (white, age 30). *Murder.* The crime was committed on 5/8/1910 in Augusta County. Executed for the shotgun slayings of 23-year-old William Peter Hoy and 8-year-old Cletus Higgs (both white). Motive: obnoxious drunk. This murderer met his fate in the electric chair on September 22, 1910. Source: *Shenandoah Herald* (Woodstock, VA), 5/13/10 (2:1); *Richmond Times-Dispatch*, 9/23/10 (10:1). See also 1900 U.S. Census (Augusta Co., VA), which notes Brown, and 1910 U.S. Census (Augusta Co., VA), which notes the victims.

Pink Barbour (black, age 22). *Murder.* The crime was committed on 7/4/1910 in Rockingham County. Executed for the handgun slaying of 59-year-old James

M. Lee (white). Motive: Mr. Lee had caught him in the act of stealing his buggy whips. This killer was executed on September 23, 1910. Source: *Washington Post*, 7/6/10 (4:7); *Richmond Evening Journal*, 9/23/10 (12:5). See also 1910 U.S. Census (Rockingham Co., VA), which notes Mr. Lee.

John H. Eccles (black, age 17). *Murder.* The crime was committed on 3/28/1910 in Henry County. Electrocuted for the murder of Sidney Woods (black, age not recorded), who was slashed to death with a razor. Motive: rowdy behavior on a train. This black-on-black killer was executed on November 11, 1910. Source: *Alexandria (VA) Gazette*, 3/30/10 (2:5); *Richmond Evening Journal*, 11/11/10 (2:1). See also 1900 U.S. Census (Forsyth Co., NC), which notes Eccles.

Waverly Coles (black, age 20). *Murder.* The crime was committed on 8/13/1910 in Henrico County. Electrocuted for the murder of Edward Fuller (black, age not recorded), who was slashed across the forehead with a knife and then finished off with a shot from a handgun. Motive: argument over a dollar. The killer was put to death on November 25, 1910. Source: *News Leader* (Richmond, VA), 8/15/10 (1:7); *Richmond Planet*, 8/20/10 (1:5); *Richmond Evening Journal*, 11/25/10 (1:3).

John Joseph Smyth (white, age 33). *Murder.* The crime was committed on 9/1/1910 in Norfolk County. Executed for the handgun slayings of 29-year-old Beatrice Smyth and 12-year-old Rita A. Smyth (both white), his wife and daughter. Motive: obsessive male jealousy. The killer was executed on December 16, 1910. Source: *Richmond Times-Dispatch*, 9/2/10 (3:1) and 12/17/10 (7:7). See also 1910 U.S. Census (Norfolk, VA), which notes all parties as "Smith."

Harry Sitlington (black, age 16). *Murder.* The crime was committed on 10/22/1910 in Rockbridge County. Executed for the murder of 62-year-old Fannie Brown (white), she having been beaten to death with a club. Motive: the lady had scolded him for neglecting his chores. This killer was put to death on December 16, 1910. Source: *Lexington (VA) Gazette*, 10/26/10 (5:3); *Washington Post*, 12/17/10 (13:1).

1911

Richard H. Biggs (black, age 27). *Murder.* The crime was committed on 6/11/1910 at Newport News. Executed for the handgun slaying of roughly 25-year-old Annie Davis (black), she having been shot three times. Motive: she had refused to be lured away from her husband. This killer was electrocuted on January 7, 1911. Source: *Daily Press* (Newport News, VA), 6/12/10 (2:3) and 6/14/10 (1:4); *Richmond Evening Journal*, 1/7/11 (1:7).

Alexander Holloman (black, age 24). *Murder.* The crime was committed on 2/23/1911 in Princess Anne County. Uxoricide and filicide. Executed for the handgun slayings of 20-year-old Martha Holloman and their unnamed infant child, who was less than a year old (both black—gender of the latter not specified by surviving accounts), they having been shot five and three times, respectively. Motive: marital estrangement. Holloman was put to death on June 2, 1911. Source: *Virginian Pilot* (Norfolk), 2/25/11 (2:3); *Richmond Evening Journal*, 6/2/11 (10:5). See also 1910 U.S. Census (Princess Anne Co., VA), which notes the Hollomans.

Henry Clay Beattie, Jr. (white, age 26). *Murder.* The crime was committed on 7/18/1911 in Chesterfield County. Uxoricide. Executed for the shotgun slaying of 21-year-old Louise Owen Beattie (white) during the course of an open-air automobile jaunt along Midlothian Turnpike. Motive: fickle husband. This is another case involving murder among the well-to-do. Beattie's family had substantial holdings (and pedigree), which qualified them for acceptance in high society. Every detail of the tragedy received sensational press coverage. The circumstances in and of themselves were common enough: The younger Beattie was a well-funded playboy with a paramour and an illegitimate child. It is not known for certain if his actual wife had become aware of this, but what transpired does suggest that at least one of these females had pressured him into making a definitive choice between them. Beattie died a liar, claiming that a highway robber had shot his wife. He could not, however, satisfactorily explain how it had been he himself who had arranged the prior purchase of the murder weapon. The Virginia electric chair ended his life of privilege on November 24, 1911. Neither money nor social status saved him. A double tombstone in Maury Cemetery shows where he found his last repose next to the wife whom he had so basely betrayed. Source: *A Full and Complete History of the Great Beattie Case* (Phoenix Publishing Co., Baltimore, 1911), Collection of Daniel Allen Hearn. See also feature articles about this case that were published in the following true crime magazines: *Master Detective*, 6/32; *Daring Detective*, 9/35; *Real Detective*, 12/36; *Actual Detective*, 2/38; *Intimate Detective*, 4/41 and 5/41; *Headline Detective*, 8/44; *Crime Detective*, 8/52.

1912

John Williamson (black, age not recorded). *Murder.* The crime was committed on 11/30/1911 in Halifax County. Executed for the handgun slaying of 28-year-old Ellis Watkins (black). Motive: he thought that Watkins had insulted his woman. Williamson was executed on March 15, 1912. Source: Original Case File (*Commonwealth vs. Williamson*), December Term 1911, Halifax County Circuit Court Records Room. See also 1900 and 1910 U.S. Census (Halifax Co., VA), which note Watkins, plus "Executed Offenders," Box 372, File 36 (VA State Archives).

John Ferby (black, age 19) and **William Price** (black, age 19). *Murder.* Their crime was committed on 1/22/1912 in Chesterfield County. Doomed for the ax murder of 47-year-old General Thomas Belcher (white), a convict guard. Motive: escape from the Chesterfield County chain gang. Both of these young killers were executed on June 14, 1912. Source: *Daily Index Appeal* (Petersburg), 2/18/12 (1:2); *Washington Post*, 2/18/12 (8:6) and 4/7/12 (11:7); *Richmond Evening Journal*, 6/14/12 (1:2).

Byrd Jackson (black, age 18). *Robbery with Violence.* The crime was committed on 3/31/1912 in Caroline County. Felonious assault and robbery of 42-year-old Jacob L. Farmer (white—a storekeeper), who was struck on the head with an iron bar in his place of business and then dragged outdoors and left unconscious in the rain, his person and his store both being picked clean of valuables. This attacker was executed on June 21, 1912. Source: *Richmond Evening Journal*, 6/21/12 (5:1); *Mathews (VA) Journal*, 6/27/12 (8:3). See also 1910 U.S. Census

(Caroline Co., VA), which notes Mr. Farmer.

Clarence Nixon (black, age about 25). *Attempted Rape.* The crime was committed on 7/30/1911 at Norfolk. Felonious assault on the person of 36-year-old Lizzie Skiles (white), she having been attacked in her own home with intent to commit rape. The attacker was executed on June 21, 1912. Source: *Portsmouth (VA) Star*, 7/31/11 (1:3); *Virginian Pilot* (Norfolk), 2/11/12 (16:2); *Richmond Evening Journal*, 6/21/12 (1:5). See also 1920 U.S. Census (Portsmouth, VA), which notes the victim.

Virginia Christian (black, age 17). *Murder.* The crime was committed on 3/20/1912 in Elizabeth City County. Executed for the mutilation murder of 51-year-old Ida E. Belote (white), who was beaten almost beyond recognition with an iron poker. Her hair was also torn out and stuffed down her throat together with a dishrag. Motive: ungovernable temper. The murdered lady (who was also Christian's employer) had remonstrated with her for poor work habits. The Virginia electric chair very effectively cured Virginia Christian of her temper control problem on August 16, 1912. Source: *Lima (OH) Daily News*, 3/21/12 (8:2) and 8/16/12 (1:1). See also 1910 U.S. Census (Hampton, VA), which notes Ida Belote.

Herbert Peyton (black, age 26). *Murder.* The crime was committed on 7/4/1912 in King George County. Executed for the handgun slaying of 23-year-old Caroline Jackson (black), she having been shot in the back. Motive: dance hall spat. The killer was executed on November 8, 1912. Source: *The Free Lance* (Fredericksburg, VA), 7/9/12 (1:4), 9/5/12 (3:3) and 9/7/12 (3:3); *Richmond Evening Journal*, 11/8/12 (1:1).

1913

Richard Quarles (black, age 26). *Rape.* The crime was committed on or about 3/25/1912 in Hanover County. Indecent assault on the person of 16-year-old Myrtle Rouse (white), she having also been severely beaten and robbed. The attacker was executed on January 3, 1913. Source: *Richmond Times-Dispatch*, 9/22/12 (11:3). See also "Executed Offenders," Box 373, File 5 (VA State Archives), plus 1910 U.S. Census (Hanover Co., VA), which notes the culprit, and 1920 U.S. Census (Richmond, VA), which notes Miss Rouse.

Roy Maxwell Sullivan (white, age 21). *Murder.* The crime was committed on 7/29/1912 in Pittsylvania County. Executed for the shotgun slaying of 24-year-old John C. Howard (white), an officer on the Pittsylvania County chain gang. Motive: resentment for alleged ill treatment, or so he said. Sullivan went to the electric chair on February 28, 1913. Source: *Lexington (VA) Gazette*, 8/7/12 (5:4); *Richmond Evening Journal*, 2/28/13 (1:5); *Washington Post*, 3/1/13 (11:6). See also 1910 U.S. Census (Pittsylvania Co., VA), which notes "J.C. Howard."

Floyd Allen (white, age 53) and **Claude Allen** (white, age 22). *Murder.* Their crime was committed on 3/14/1912 in Carroll County. Both were executed for the handgun slaying of 57-year-old William McDonald Foster (white), the state's attorney at Hillsville. Motive: shootout in a courthouse. Venue changed from Carroll County to Wythe County. Four other persons were slain in the same gun battle: Thornton Lemmon Massie (white, age 45), who was the judge of the circuit court then in session; Lewis Franklin Webb (white, age 64), the sheriff of Carroll County; and Augustus Cezar Fowler (white, age 55) and Nancy Elizabeth Ayers (white, age 18), a juror and a trial witness, respectively. It was never determined exactly who shot the four secondary casualties, although the Allens were the prime suspects. They were put to death on March 28, 1913. Source: *The Allen Outlaws and Their Career of Crime in the Mountains of Virginia* (Phoenix Publishing Co., Baltimore, 1912), Collection of Daniel Allen Hearn; *Richmond Evening Journal*, 3/28/13 (1:1); *Rockingham Daily Record* (Harrisonburg, VA), 3/29/13 (1:1); *Master Detective*, 1/32; *Official Detective*, 4/36; *Front Page Detective*, 11/44. See also 1910 U.S. Census (Pulaski Co., VA), which notes Massie, plus the census for Carroll Co., VA, which notes the other parties.

James Goode (black, age about 25). *Murder*. The crime was committed on 1/20/1913 at Newport News. Executed for the murder of 24-year-old Julius Smith (white), whose skull was broken in five places by means of an iron bar. Motive: robbery. The killer was put to death on May 2, 1913. Source: *Daily Press* (Newport News), 1/21/13 (1:7). See also 1910 U.S. Census (Newport News, VA), which notes Smith, plus death cert. no. 57–11330 (VA State Archives) and *Richmond Evening Journal*, 5/2/13 (1:2), which incorrectly said that Smith was a black man.

Alfred Wright (black, age 20). *Rape*. The crime was committed on 6/27/1912 in Appomattox County. Indecent assault on the person of 31-year-old Bertha Ferguson (white), she having been attacked on a public street. The rapist was executed on May 16, 1913. Source: *Bluefield (WV) Daily Telegraph*, 6/30/12 (1:6); *Washington Post*, 7/1/12 (9:4). See also 1910 U.S. Census (Appomattox Co., VA), which notes Ferguson, plus "Executed Offenders," Box 373 File 10 (VA State Archives).

Frank L. Hargrove (black, age 37). *Murder*. The crime was committed on 12/13/1912 in Spotsylvania County. Executed for the murders of 40-year-old Mansfield Thornton and 41-year-old Melvina Thornton (both black—a married couple), they having been battered to death with a dogwood stick, with their house burned down around them. Motive: possibly deranged. The killer was electrocuted pursuant to the law on June 20, 1913. Source: *The Free Lance* (Fredericksburg, VA), 12/17/12 (3:2) and 12/24/12 (3:2). See also 1910 U.S. Census (Spotsylvania Co., VA), which notes the Thorntons, plus the census for Fredericksburg, VA, which notes Hargrove. See also "Executed Offenders," Box 373, File 11 (VA State Archives).

Nelson Vernon Carter (white, age 46). *Murder*. The crime was committed on 2/6/1913 in Spotsylvania County. Uxoricide. Executed for the handgun slaying of 33-year-old Hattie B. Carter (white), she having been shot five times. Motive: domestic quarrel. The killer was executed on June 27, 1913. Source: *The Free Lance* (Fredericksburg, VA), 2/8/13 (3:2); *Washington Post*, 6/28/13 (3:6). See also 1910 U.S. Census (Spotsylvania Co., VA), which notes both parties.

Owen Goggin (black, age 36). *Attempted Rape*. The crime was committed on 3/31/1913 in Bedford County. Felonious assault on the person of 32-year-old Elizabeth M. Nance (white), she having been attacked with intent to commit rape. The attacker died in the electric chair on June 27, 1913. Source: Original Case File (*Commonwealth vs. Goggin*), copy provided courtesy of Karen O. Glover, the assistant clerk of Bedford County Circuit Court. See also death cert. no. 63–14436 (VA State Archives).

Benjamin Bailey (black, age 24). *Rape.* The crime was committed on 5/22/1913 in Fairfax County. Indecent assault on the person of 6-year-old Helen Mary Follin (white). This rapist was put to death on August 8, 1913. Source: *Washington Post*, 5/29/13 (4:6) and 5/31/13 (5:2). See also 1910 U.S. Census (Fairfax Co., VA), which notes the victim, plus "Executed Offenders," Box 373, File 14 (VA State Archives).

William Glinn (black, age 26). *Murder.* The crime was committed on 5/17/1913 at Norfolk. Executed for the fatal stabbing of 20-year-old Rosa Pitts (black). Motive: wrathful lover. He was executed on August 16, 1913. Source: *Portsmouth (VA) Star*, 7/3/13 (8:1); *Virginian Pilot* (Norfolk), 7/4/13 (4:2). See also death cert. nos. 59–12055 and 73–19677 (VA State Archives).

Minnie Collins (black male, age 18). *Attempted Rape.* The crime was committed on or about 9/1/1913 in Northampton County. Felonious assault on the person of 15-year-old Sarah B. Gayle (white), she having been attacked with intent to commit rape in an incident that was described as "one of the most revolting on record." Collins was put to death on October 31, 1913. Source: *Virginian Pilot* (Norfolk), 9/18/13 (3:1); *News Leader* (Richmond, VA), 10/31/13. See also 1910 U.S. Census (Northampton Co., VA), which notes Miss Gayle, plus 1913 death cert. no. 14–24227 (VA State Archives).

Lee Archer (black, age 22). *Rape.* The crime was committed on 9/2/1913 in Princess Anne County. Indecent assault on the person of 15-year-old Cora Whitehurst (white), the full details having apparently been censored from the start. The rapist was put to death on December 5, 1913. Source: *Semi Weekly Robesonian* (Lumberton, NC), 9/18/13 (4:3). See also 1910 U.S. Census (Princess Anne Co., VA), which notes Miss Whitehurst, plus 1913 death cert. no. 92–28905 and "Executed Offenders," Box 373, File 18 (VA State Archives).

Newell Walker (white, age 30). *Murder.* The crime was committed on 5/18/1913 in Charles City County. Uxoricide. Executed for the murder of 25-year-old Mary L. Walker (white), she having been slashed to death with a razor. Motive: estrangement and irrational jealousy. The killer went to the electric chair on December 5, 1913. Source: *Bluefield (WV) Daily Telegraph*, 5/20/13 (6:5); *The News* (Frederick, MD), 12/6/13 (1:5). See also 1910 U.S. Census (Charles City Co., VA), which notes both parties.

1914

Charlton Moore (black, age 49). *Murder.* The crime was committed on 10/8/1913 in King William County. Uxoricide. Executed for the murder of 45-year-old Hannah Hill Moore (black), who was struck on the head with an unknown blunt object. Motive: wrathful conduct. Moore paid with his life for this in the Virginia electric chair on January 16, 1914. Source: "Executed Offenders," Box 373, File 19, and death cert. no. 14–24332 (VA State Archives). See also 1910 U.S. Census (King William Co., VA), which notes both parties.

Willie Rhodes (black, age 26). *Murder.* The crime was committed on or about 11/11/1913 in Charlotte County. Executed for the ax murder of 79-year-old Sam Morton (black), the victim having also been severely battered with a hammer. Motive: home invasion. Rhodes was put to death on January 30, 1914. Source: Original Case File (*Commonwealth vs. Rhodes*), Charlotte County Circuit Court Records Room. See also death cert. no. 102–1127 (VA State Archives) and 1910 U.S. Census (Charlotte Co., VA), which notes Morton.

Marion Lee (black male, age 29). *Murder.* The crime was committed on 7/23/1913 at Williamsburg. Executed for the handgun slaying of 38-year-old Delaware Brown (black male). Motive: gambling dispute. Lee was executed on March 19, 1914. Source: *Virginia Gazette* (Williamsburg), 7/24/13 (4:2). See also death cert. nos. 74–19924 and 112–6106 (VA State Archives).

Walter Boyd (black, age 24). *Murder.* The crime was committed on 12/13/1913 in Henrico County. Executed for the handgun slaying of roughly 30-year-old Benjamin Franklin (black), the victim having been shot in the back. Motive: rivalry for a female. The Virginia electric chair ended the life of this killer on March 27, 1914. Source: *Richmond Times-Dispatch*, 1/27/14 (12:1). See also death cert. nos. 92–28959 and 112–6174 (VA State Archives).

George Woods (black, age 32). *Murder.* The crime was committed on 1/9/1914 at Danville. Uxoricide. Executed for the fatal beating and strangulation of 32-year-old Mariah Woods (black) and illegal disposal of her body in a river. Motive: suspicion of infidelity. This killer was put to death on May 22, 1914. Source: *Danville (VA) Register*, 1/13/14 (2:3). See also "Executed Offenders," Box 373, File 23, and death cert. no. 103–1842 (VA State Archives).

Will Calloway (black, age 47). *Murder.* The crime was committed on 2/1/1914 in Lee County. Executed for the murder of 5-year-old "Little Boy" Mason (black, full name not recorded), who was bound ankles and wrists with his own stockings before being pitched alive into an icy creek. His small body was then fished out of the water, dried by a campfire and afterward cremated therein, so that only charred bones remained. Motive: unwanted mouth to feed. The story had it that Calloway and a female companion were on a pedestrian journey through the mountains accompanied by her 5-year-old nephew. The child was taken lame along the way, and Calloway came to regard him as an unnecessary liability. He paid for his brutality with his own life in the Virginia electric chair on July 10, 1914. Source: *Washington Post*, 5/24/14 (3:4); *News Leader* (Richmond, VA), 7/10/14 (1:2).

Willie Puryear (black, age 19). *Attempted Rape.* The crime was committed on 6/20/1914 in Mecklenburg County. Felonious assault on the person of 32-year-old Cora Z. Hite (white), she having been attacked in her own bedroom with intent to commit rape. Puryear died in the Virginia electric chair on August 7, 1914. Source: Mecklenburg County Circuit Court Miscellaneous Records (1912–1915); State Records Center (1998 Charles City Road), Richmond, VA. See also death cert. no. 137–18826 (VA State Archives).

Henry Coach (black, age 32). *Robbery with Violence.* The crime was committed on 5/6/1911 in Nottoway County. Executed for battery on the person of 62-year-old Alexander Murdock (white—a storekeeper), who was attacked in his place of business, beaten with a wooden plow beam and robbed of about $60 in silver. Murdock died the following year, a fact that almost certainly figured in the severity of the sentence imposed on Henry Coach. It is uncertain whether the injuries Murdock sustained contributed to his death, but that also seems likely. The attacker was executed on August 21, 1914. Source: *Blackstone (VA) Courier*, 5/12/11 (1:3), 5/15/14 (2:3) and 6/19/14 (1:1). See also 1910 U.S. Census (Nottoway Co., VA), which notes Murdock, plus the census for Lunenburg Co., VA, which notes Coach, as well as 1914 death cert. no. 18907 (VA State Archives).

John Edmunds (black, age 30). *Murder.* The crime was committed on 10/9/1914 in Prince Edward County. Executed for the handgun slaying of 49-year-old Henry Morton (black). Motive: rivalry for a female. The killer was executed on December 18, 1914. Source: Original Case File (*Commonwealth vs. Edmunds*), copy provided courtesy of Machelle Eppes, the clerk of Prince Edward County Circuit Court. See also 1910 U.S. Census (Prince Edward Co., VA), which notes Morton, and 1914 death cert. no. 27974 (VA State Archives).

1915

Arthur Neale (black, age 19). *Attempted Rape.* The crime was committed on or about 10/1/1914 in King William County. Felonious assault on the person of Annie Vitalish (white, age not recorded), she having been attacked on a public road with intent to commit rape and robbed of her intrinsic valuables. The culprit was executed on January 8, 1915. Source: "Executed Offenders," Box 373, File 28 (VA State Archives). See also 1915 Henrico County death cert. no. 925.

Charles Miller (black, age 28). *Murder.* The crime was committed on 1/26/1915 in Halifax County. Executed for the fatal stabbing of John Fountain (black, age not recorded). Motive: gambling dispute. The killer was executed on March 26, 1915. Source: *News Leader* (Richmond, VA), 3/26/15 (15:1). See also Original Case File (*Commonwealth vs. Miller*), Halifax County Circuit Court Records Room, and 1915 Henrico County death cert. no. 6179.

Herbert Caple (black, age 22). *Highway Robbery.* The crime was committed on 1/6/1915 in Sussex County. Executed for battery on the person of 54-year-old Joseph M. Fuller (white), who was "knocked senseless" with a rock and robbed of his money after giving Caple a ride on his horse-drawn wagon. The miscreant was executed on April 30, 1915. Source: *Waverly (VA) Dispatch*, 3/26/15 (1:1). See also 1910 U.S. Census (Sussex Co., VA), which notes Mr. Fuller, and 1915 Henrico County death cert. no. 9104.

Skipwith Sydnor (black, age 24). *Murder.* The crime was committed on 4/19/1914 in Halifax County. Executed for the murder of 80-year-old Charlie H. Saddle (black), the victim having been slashed to death with a razor. Motive: household flare-up. The killer went to his death in the Virginia electric chair on May 21, 1915. Source: Original Case File (*Commonwealth vs. Sydnor*), Halifax County Circuit Court Records Room. See also death cert. no. 117-8692 (VA

State Archives) and 1915 Henrico County death cert. no. 11683.

Thomas Cole (black, age 21). *Rape.* The crime was committed on 3/22/1915 in Mecklenburg County. Specifically executed for an indecent assault on the person of 15-year-old Georgia Royster (white). Also indicted for the 1/31/1915 handgun slaying of a Mecklenburg County woman named Babe Chandler (black) during a lovers' quarrel. This criminal was executed on June 4, 1915. Source: *Daily News Record* (Harrisonburg, VA), 5/3/15 (4:4). See also 1915 Henrico County death cert. no. 13842.

Lemuel Jones (black, age 23). *Murder.* The crime was committed on 9/6/1914 at Norfolk. Executed for the handgun slaying of 22-year-old Isaac Aleck (white). Motive: armed robbery. This killer was put to death on June 10, 1915. Source: *Virginian Pilot* (Norfolk), 9/7/14 (2:4) and 4/29/15 (4:2). See also 1915 Henrico County death cert. no. 13887.

Luther Canter (white, age 24). *Murder.* The crime was committed on 4/24/1915 in Washington County. Executed for the shotgun slaying of 27-year-old Maude C. Wilson (white). Motive: sexual assault. Canter died in the electric chair on June 11, 1915. Source: *Bluefield (WV) Daily Telegraph*, 5/7/15 (1:4) and 6/12/15 (1:4); *Daily News Record* (Harrisonburg, VA), 5/19/15 (6:2) and 6/12/15 (1:6). See also 1910 U.S. Census (Bristol, VA), which notes Maude Wilson.

George Matthews (black, age 32) and **John Lewis Rollins** (black, age 31). *Rape.* Their crime was committed on 7/12/1915 in Caroline County. Indecent assaults on the persons of 49-year-old Burnley V. Coleman and 28-year-old Eulalia Coleman (both white—a mother and daughter), who were attacked in their residence at Rappahannock Academy. The culprits paid with their lives for this outrage in the Virginia electric chair on August 20, 1915. Source: *Daily News Record* (Harrisonburg, VA), 7/14/15 (1:5), 7/15/15 (1:1), 7/17/15 (1:1) and 8/21/15 (1:2). See also 1900 U.S. Census (Norfolk, VA), which notes the victimized women.

Edward Pryor (black, age 31). *Robbery with Violence.* The crime was committed on 9/29/1914 in Surry County. Executed for battery on the person of 16-year-old Cecil Clyde Pitman (white), who was severely beaten and robbed of eleven dollars in silver. Pryor was put to death at the Virginia State Penitentiary on September 10, 1915. Source: Original Case File (*Commonwealth vs. Pryor*), copy provided courtesy of Gail P. Clayton, the clerk of Surry County Circuit Court. See also 1900 U.S. Census (Surry Co., VA), which notes young Pitman, and 1915 Henrico County death cert. no. 21112.

Sherman Stanfield (black, age 19). *Attempted Rape.* The crime was committed on 6/3/1915 in Pittsylvania County. Felonious assault on the person of 6-year-old Elizabeth Collie (white) with intent to commit rape. This attacker was put to death on September 17, 1915. Source: *Danville (VA) Register*, 6/4/15 (1:2), 6/5/15 (1:4) and 7/25/15 (12:3); *Bluefield (WV) Daily Telegraph*, 9/18/15 (1:2).

1916

Percy Ellis (black, age 16). *Murder.* The crime was committed on 9/23/1915 at Norfolk. Executed for the handgun slaying of 37-year-old Nathan Cohen (white), a storekeeper. Motive: big attitude. The merchant had remonstrated with young Ellis for creating a disturbance in front of his place of business. Ellis then pulled out a pistol and shot the man dead. He was electrocuted on March 15, 1916. Source: *Ledger-Dispatch* (Norfolk), 9/24/15 (20:5) and 2/5/16 (1:4). See also 1915 Norfolk City death cert. no. 21652 and 1916 Henrico County death cert. no. 6719.

Joseph Lee (black, age 82). *Murder.* The crime was committed on 11/5/1915 in Caroline County. Executed for the murder and illegal cremation of 41-year-old Jack Grymes (black), the victim having been bludgeoned with the blade of a hoe and his body consumed in a bonfire. Motive: conspiracy with the decedent's wife, or so it was said. This octogenarian killer went to the electric chair on April 26, 1916. Source: *Daily News Record* (Harrisonburg, VA), 11/12/15 (2:5) and 4/27/16 (1:4). See also 1910 U.S. Census (Caroline Co., VA), which notes Grymes.

John Henry Williams (black, age 23). *Rape.* The crime was committed on 3/29/1916 in Nottoway County. Indecent assault on the person of 15-year-old Mamie Mason (white), no further details having been publicly disclosed. The rapist was executed on May 26, 1916. Source: *Daily News Record* (Harrisonburg, VA), 4/5/16 (4:3). See also "Executed Offenders," Box 374, File 1 (VA State Archives).

Milton Mallory (black, age 25). *Rape.* The crime was committed on or about 5/1/1916 in Wise County. Serial child rapist. Convicted of sexually assaulting six young girls aged 5–11 during a period of several weeks ending on 5/13/1916 by means of giving them drugged candy to better accomplish his purpose. Specifically condemned for assaulting 9-year-old Myra Jenkins, a white girl. Mallory was executed on July 7, 1916. Source: *Daily News Record* (Harrisonburg, VA), 5/18/16 (1:2). See also "Executed Offenders," Box 374, File 2 (VA State Archives), and 1920 U.S. Census (Wise Co., VA), which notes Miss Jenkins.

Richard Green (black, age 19). *Murder.* The crime was committed on 6/24/1916 in Charlotte County. Child killer. Executed for the handgun slaying of 11-year-old Gabriel Jones (black). Motive: obnoxious behavior. Green had been ejected from a Jim Crow soda fountain for being drunk and disorderly. He went stomping back there a short time later armed with a pistol and shot up the place, killing Jones and wounding several others. This killer was put to death in the Virginia electric chair on August 25, 1916. Source: Original Case File (*Commonwealth vs. Green*), Charlotte County Circuit Court Records Room. See also 1916 Charlotte County death cert. no. 14072 and "Executed Offenders," Box 374, File 3 (VA State Archives).

Clifford Mickens (black, age 19). *Murder.* The crime was committed on 6/21/1916 at Roanoke. Cop killer. Executed for the handgun slaying of 22-year-old J. Harvey Leverett (white). Motive: resisting arrest. Mickens was executed on August 25, 1916. Source: *World News* (Roanoke, VA), 6/21/16 (1:1), 6/28/16 (2:6) and 8/25/16 (1:5).

Henry Lewis (black, age 21). *Murder.* The crime was committed on 5/15/1916 at Lynchburg. Executed for the fatal stabbing of 22-year-old Mary Willie Crawford (black). Motive: dope addict gone berserk. The Virginia electric chair cured his addiction on September 8, 1916. Source: *The News* (Lynchburg, VA),

5/16/16 (5:5), 5/17/16 (6:5) and 7/4/16 (3:5). See also 1916 Campbell County death cert. no. 11504 and 1916 Henrico County death cert. no. 22529.

James Corbett (black, age 21). *Murder.* The crime was committed on 7/23/1915 at Norfolk. Executed for the handgun slaying of 33-year-old Ernest C. Manning (white), who was shot twice in the back. Motive: the slain man had garnished the killer's wages. Corbett paid with his life for what he did in the Virginia electric chair on October 2, 1916. Source: *Virginian Pilot* (Norfolk), 7/24/15 (3:1) and 8/18/15 (13:6). See also 1915 Norfolk City death cert. no. 16962 and 1916 Henrico County death cert. no. 24778.

Minzer Harris (black, age 19). *Rape.* The crime was committed on 4/7/1916 in Buckingham County. Indecent assault on the person of 60+-year-old Lucretia Branch (white), she having also been robbed and "badly wounded" with a knife. This rapist was executed on October 2, 1916. Source: *Daily News Record* (Harrisonburg, VA), 5/12/16 (6:6); *News Leader* (Richmond, VA), 10/2/16 (1:5). See also 1916 Henrico County death cert. no. 24779.

1917

Hansom Warren (black, age 22). *Murder.* The crime was committed on 1/30/1917 in Isle of Wight County. Executed for the ax murder of 35-year-old Thomas Jefferson Seward (white). Motive: surly attitude. Warren was a tenant farmer on Seward's land. The latter went to Warren's cabin to inquire as to why he had not come to work that day. Warren resented this and attacked Seward with an ax, killing him. Warren was put to death on June 15, 1917. Source: *Richmond Times-Dispatch*, 1/31/17 (2:7). See also 1917 Isle of Wight County death cert. no. 3986 and Henrico County death cert. no. 14442.

Hamilton Cosby (black, age 25) and **Robert Jones** (black, age 32). *Murder.* Their crime was committed on 4/12/1917 at Charlottesville. Cop killers. Executed for the murder of 41-year-old Meredith A. Thomas (white), the officer having been bludgeoned with rocks. Motive: resisting arrest. The killers were executed on June 20, 1917. Source: *Daily Progress* (Charlottesville, VA), 4/13/17 (1:1); *Daily News Record* (Harrisonburg, VA), 6/22/17 (1:2).

Albert Barrett (black, age 35). *Murder.* The crime was committed on 7/16/1917 in Charlotte County. Executed for the murder of 34-year-old William Thomas Roach (white), who was beaten on the head with a rock. Motive: heated argument (the slain man had accused the killer of stealing wheat). Barrett was put to death at the Virginia State Penitentiary on August 31, 1917. Source: *The News* (Roanoke, VA), 7/18/17 (2:4). See also 1917 Charlotte County death cert. no. 16632 and "Executed Offenders," Box 374, File 11 (VA State Archives).

William H. Burgess (black, age 32). *Attempted Rape.* The crime was committed on 8/24/1917 in Fairfax County. Felonious assault on the person of 23-year-old Mildred Miller (white), she having been attacked while walking along a public road and severely beaten (including several teeth knocked out) with intent to commit rape. Burgess had also attacked a second white female (age 17) that same day in a separate incident. He was put to death on October 26, 1917. Source: *Alexandria (VA) Gazette*, 8/25/17

(1:3), 8/27/17 (1:2) and 9/20/17 (1:6). See also 1910 U.S. Census (Washington, D.C.), which notes Miller, and "Executed Offenders," Box 374, File 12 (VA State Archives).

1918

Paul Langhorne (black, age 49). *Murder*. The crime was committed on 3/9/1918 at Newport News. Child killer. Executed for the murder of 14-year-old Dorothy Jones (black, his stepdaughter), she having been slashed to death with a razor. Motive: sexual jealousy (the girl had eloped with a soldier when Langhorne had decided that she should be his own concubine). He was put to death on June 7, 1918. Source: *Daily Press* (Newport News), 3/10/18 (2:1) and 3/30/18 (1:4). See also 1918 Warwick County death cert. no. 8352 and Henrico County death cert. no. 14746.

Bailey Tolson (black, age 17) and **Guy Nixon** (black, age 19). *Murder.* Their crime was committed on 12/19/1917 at Norfolk. Executed for the handgun slaying of 37-year-old George Frederick Dashiell (white), a gunsmith. Motive: shoplifting. Tolson and his accomplice had selected pistols from Dashiell's inventory and loaded them with bullets for the ostensible purpose of test firing them. However, they had no intention of paying for these weapons; instead, they used them to murder the seller rather than tendering money for their purchase. They wound up paying with their lives instead. Both died in the Virginia electric chair on July 2, 1918. (This case also provides a glimpse of the utter ease with which even teenagers were able to legally obtain firearms in those days.) Source: *Virginian Pilot* (Norfolk), 7/3/18 (10:5). See also 1917 Norfolk City death cert. no. 30003, plus 1918 Henrico County death cert. nos. 17190 and 17191.

1919

Harvey Stuart (black, age 34). *Murder*. The crime was committed on 4/5/1918 at Buena Vista. Executed for the handgun slayings of 22-year-old Matt Ross and 21-year-old Monica Evelyn Le Flett (both black). Motive: fracas in a dancehall. The killer was executed on March 26, 1919. Source: *Rockbridge County News*, 12/5/18 (2:3). See also 1918 Rockbridge County death cert. nos. 10911 and 10912, plus 1919 Henrico County death cert. no. 8879.

Horace Williams (black, age about 21). *Murder*. The crime was committed on 2/15/1918 in Culpeper County. Executed for the handgun slaying of 50-year-old Orlando T. Clark (white). Motive: armed robbery. The killer was executed on March 26, 1919. Source: *Washington Times*, 2/18/18 (1:7) and 2/19/18 (3:3). See also 1910 U.S. Census (Culpeper Co., VA), which notes Clark, and 1919 Henrico County death cert. no. 8880, which notes Williams.

Jerry Warren (black, age 27). *Murder.* The crime was committed on 11/28/1918 in Northampton County. Cop killer. Executed for the handgun slaying of 62-year-old James A. Taylor (white). Motive: resisting arrest. Warren had also used the same weapon to emasculate a fellow black man named James Nottingham during a dancehall brawl earlier that day. He went to the electric chair on June 27, 1919. Source: *Washington Post*, 11/30/18 (3:5). See also 1910 U.S. Census (Cape Charles, VA), which notes

Taylor, and "Executed Offenders," Box 374, File 18 (VA State Archives).

Emper Jacobs (black, age 27). *Murder.* The crime was committed on 9/15/1919 at Portsmouth. Executed for the handgun slaying of 21-year-old John Turk (white), who was shot four times. Motive: Turk had dunned him for an overdue grocery bill. Jacobs was executed on October 30, 1919. Source: *Portsmouth (VA) Star*, 9/15/19 (1:1), 9/16/19 (1:5) and 10/30/19 (1:5). See also 1919 Norfolk County death cert. no. 23780 and Henrico County death cert. no. 25379.

1920

Robert Williams, alias "Alabama Red" (black, age 23). *Rape.* The crime was committed on 8/6/1920 at Lynchburg. Indecent assault on the person of roughly 20-year-old Annie Ross (white), she having been attacked as she walked home from the movies. The rapist was put to death on November 13, 1920. Source: *The News* (Lynchburg, VA), 8/7/20 (1:4), 8/8/20 (6:1) and 9/14/20 (7:1). See also 1920 Henrico County death cert. no. 26382.

1921

John H. Williams, alias "Carolina Slim" (black, age 26). *Murder.* The crime was committed on 3/25/1920 at Lynchburg. Cop killer. Executed for the handgun slaying of 38-year-old Leslie Arthur Mann (white). Motive: resisting arrest. Williams was a fugitive at that time, having already murdered two other law enforcement officers at Greenville, South Carolina, on 10/5/1919. The casualties in that case were Detectives Alfred M. Blair (white, age 42) and Joseph L. Kitchen (white, age 44), they having been gunned down during a raid on an illicit gaming den. The killer died in the Virginia electric chair on March 5, 1921. Source: *The News* (Lynchburg, VA), 3/26/20 (1:1) and 3/27/20 (1:4) and (6:3). See also "Executed Offenders," Box 374, File 21 (VA State Archives), plus 1900 U.S. Census (Charlotte Co., VA), which notes Mann as a teenager, and 1919 Greenville (SC) County death cert. nos. 18235 (Blair) and 18236 (Kitchen).

Giles Sydnor (black, age 23). *Rape.* The crime was committed on 2/21/1921 in Halifax County. Indecent assault on the person of 24-year-old Lottie V. Cunningham (black) under circumstances that were deemed heinous enough to warrant his execution at the Virginia State Penitentiary on April 8, 1921. Source: "Executed Offenders," Box 374, File 22 (VA State Archives). See also 1920 U.S. Census (Halifax Co., VA), which notes both parties.

William Turner (black, age 49). *Murder.* The crime was committed on 5/21/1920 at Arlington. Executed under federal authority for the handgun slaying of 35-year-old Thomas Morgan Moore (white) and also capitally convicted at the state level for a concomitant felonious assault on the person of 25-year-old Pearl Clark (white), Morgan's fiancée. Motive: highway robbery and attempted sexual assault. The crime scene was on federal land near the entrance to Arlington National Cemetery. The killer was therefore tried in U.S. District Court at Richmond, Virginia. On June 24, 1921, he was executed by hanging on the grounds of the Henrico County Jail, a gallows having been specially constructed for that purpose. Source: *Washington Post*, 5/23/20 (1:8), 5/24/20 (1:1) and

6/25/21 (3:2). See also 1921 Henrico County death cert. no. 12900.

Judge Griffith (black, age 22) and **Raleigh Haskins** (black, age 18). *Murder.* Their crime was committed on 7/14/1921 in Dinwiddie County. Both were executed for the murder of 58-year-old Stephen G. White (a local postmaster), who was battered to death with rocks, a door bar and a ladder in addition to being stabbed. Motive: robbery. The miscreants went to the electric chair on September 30, 1921. Source: *Washington Post*, 10/1/21 (17:7). See also "Executed Offenders," Box 374, File 23 (VA State Archives), and 1920 U.S. Census (Dinwiddie Co., VA), which notes Mr. White.

Wilmer Amos Hadley (white, age 36). *Murder.* The crime was committed on 11/23/1918 in Henrico County. Uxoricide. Executed for the murder of 28-year-old Sue Kathleen Tinsley Hadley (white), she having been drugged and her body dumped in the James River. Motive: philandering on his part. Hadley was a U.S. Army surgeon; the 1911 *Texas State Journal of Medicine* (page 100) lists him among that year's graduates from the University of Texas Medical School. He was executed on December 9, 1921. Source: *Daily News Record* (Harrisonburg, VA), 1/29/19 (1:7) and 12/10/21 (1:4); *Official Detective*, 3/16/38; *Headline Detective*, 1/40 and 1/44; *Crime Detective*, 8/46; *Master Detective*, 10/46.

1922

Harry Hart (black, age 21). *Attempted Rape.* The crime was committed on 12/8/1920 in Augusta County. Felonious assault on the person of 17-year-old Virginia Garber (white), she having been manhandled on a public road with intent to commit rape. The attacker was executed on January 23, 1922. Source: *Daily News Record* (Harrisonburg, VA), 12/13/20 (1:5). See also *Virginia Appeals*, Vol. 24, pages 514–536, plus "Executed Offenders," Box 374, File 25 (VA State Archives).

Edmund Thompson (black, age 28). *Murder.* The crime was committed on 12/18/1920 in Botetourt County. Executed for the handgun slaying of 18-year-old William Peck Austin (white). Motive: disorderly conduct. Thompson had indiscriminately fired into a crowd of young people, thinking that they had thrown firecrackers at him. He paid with his life for this in the Virginia electric chair on February 7, 1922. Source: *Washington Post*, 3/3/21 (6:2) and 5/6/21 (4:5); *Virginia Appeals*, Vol. 24, pages 642–661. See also "Executed Offenders," Box 374, File 26 (VA State Archives).

Henry Lockett (black, age 34) and **Thomas Sparks** (black, age 26). *Murder.* Their crime was committed on 12/10/1921 in Albemarle County. Executed for the handgun slaying of 37-year-old Cornelius V. Ward (white), the victim having also been struck on the head with a hatchet. Motive: highway robbery. The killers were respectively executed a day apart on February 23 and 24, 1922. Source: *Daily Progress* (Charlottesville, VA), 12/12/21 (1:1), 12/16/21 (1:1), 1/18/22 (1:1) and 1/19/22 (1:1). See also "Executed Offenders," Box 374, Files 27 and 28 (VA State Archives).

Will Elmoe (black, age 28). *Murder.* The crime was committed on 8/1/1921 in Brunswick County. Executed for the murder of 41-year-old Wilbur Tingley Elmore (white), whose head was knocked in. Motive: robbery. An accomplice had been lynched on 8/2/1921. Venue changed from Brunswick County to Henrico County. Elmoe was executed on March 31, 1922. Source: *Virginia Appeals*, Vol. 25, pages 48–59. See also 1920 U.S. Census (Brunswick Co., VA), which notes the murdered man as "W. T. Elmore," plus "Executed Offenders," Box 374, File 29 (VA State Archives).

Henry Barnes (black, age 39) and **Ernest Brown** (black, age 19). *Murder.* Their crime was committed on 3/1/1921 in Orange County. Prison guard killers. Both were executed for the murder of 35-year-old Walter E. Snow (white), who was hit on the head with a stone and then finished off with his own service pistol. Motive: jailbreak. The culprits respectively died in the electric chair on April 4, 1922, and May 26, 1922. Source: *Daily Progress* (Charlottesville, VA), 3/2/21 (1:3) and 3/3/21 (1:4). See also 1922 Henrico County death cert. no. 8548 and "Executed Offenders," Box 374, File 31 (VA State Archives).

1923

Willie Edward Clayton (black, age 22). *Murder.* The crime was committed on 9/13/1922 in Henrico County. Uxoricide, etc. Executed for the shotgun slayings of 21-year-old Gertrude Brown Clayton, 44-year-old Albert Brown and 37-year-old Melinda Carter (blacks), his wife, father-in-law and aunt, respectively. Motive: family squabble turned deadly. Clayton was put to death on January 5, 1923. Source: *News Leader* (Richmond, VA), 9/13/22 (1:5) and 1/5/23 (11:5). See also 1922 Henrico County death cert. nos. 20089, 20090 and 20091, plus 1923 Henrico County death cert. no. 1251.

Alvin Harris (black, age 22). *Murder.* The crime was committed on 7/19/1922 in Prince William County. Executed for the handgun slaying of 64-year-old Thomas S. Meredith (white), who was shot four times, initially in the back. Motive: temper tantrum. The killer died in the Virginia electric chair on February 6, 1923. Source: *Daily News Record* (Harrisonburg, VA), 7/21/22 (6:2) and 7/22/22 (2:5). See also 1920 U.S. Census (Prince William Co., VA), which notes Mr. Meredith, plus "Executed Offenders," Box 374, File 33 (VA State Archives).

George Wiggins (black, age 31). *Murder.* The crime was committed on 11/5/1922 at Petersburg. Uxoricide. Executed for the strangulation of 30-year-old Alice Wiggins (black) by means of a "charmed" rope. Motive: voodoo. This killer was executed on March 2, 1923. Source: *Progress & Index-Appeal* (Petersburg), 11/6/22 (1:3), 12/7/22 (1:6), 1/25/23 (1:4) and 3/2/23 (1:5).

Sam Riddick (black, age 29). *Murder.* The crime was committed on 10/9/1921 in Warwick County. Executed for the handgun slaying of 47-year-old Mary Ralls Simmons (black), the wife of Alto Simmons. Motive: the killer thought that the victim's husband had finked on him for operating an illegal still. Riddick went to Alto's home to confront him, but Mary got in the way. The killer was executed on June 25, 1923. Source: *Daily Press* (Newport News), 10/11/21 (11:4). See also 1921 Warwick County death cert. no. 23286, plus "Executed Offenders," Box 374, File 35 (VA State Archives).

Robert Corbett (black, age 34). *Murder.* The crime was committed on 9/21/1922 at Roanoke. Executed for the handgun slaying of 25-year-old Virgie Martin Griggs (black), she having been shot in the back. Motive: wrathful lover. Corbett died in the electric chair on September 28, 1923. Source: *Roanoke World News*, 7/30/23 (3:3); *Roanoke Times*, 7/31/23 (8:1). See also 1922 Roanoke City death cert. no. 20824, plus "Executed Offenders," Box 374, File 36 (VA State Archives).

1924

Otto Clear (black, age 18) and **Fritz Lewis** (black, age 17). *Murder.* Their crime was committed on 7/30/1924 in Caroline County. Both were executed for the torture murder of 68-year-old Thomas R. Campbell (white), who was beaten, shot in the legs with both a rifle and a pistol (in an effort to make him reveal the hiding place of his money), and then purposely left tied up in his burning house. Motive: home invasion. The killers were put to death on September 12, 1924. Source: *The Bee* (Danville, VA), 7/31/24 (1:7) and 8/1/24 (1:4). See also "Executed Offenders," Box 374, File 37 (VA State Archives).

1925

Isaac Cooper (black, age 38). *Murder.* The crime was committed on 9/3/1924 in Roanoke County. Executed for the strangulation of 17-year-old Australia Wiley (black—his stepdaughter) and illegal dumping of her body. Motive: she had resisted his sexual advances. Cooper died in the electric chair on March 6, 1925. Source: *Roanoke World News*, 9/5/24 (19:7) and 9/6/24 (2:8). See also 1924 Roanoke County death cert. no. 21611 and 1925 Henrico County death cert. no. 6130.

Prince Dandridge (black, age 31). *Murder.* The crime was committed on 8/23/1923 in Henrico County. Uxoricide. Executed for the murder of 44-year-old Mary Ross Dandridge (black), she having been beaten and choked to death. Motive: not specified. The killer went to the electric chair on March 12, 1925. Source: *Richmond Times-Dispatch*, 1/27/25 (11:3); *The Bee* (Danville, VA), 3/12/25 (3:3). See also 1923 Henrico County death cert. no. 20394.

Jesse Carter (black, age 20). *Rape.* The crime was committed on 2/23/1925 in Prince Edward County. Indecent assault on the person of 16-year-old Ethel Thornton (white). The rapist was put to death on April 17, 1925. Source: Original Case File (*Commonwealth vs. Carter*), copy provided courtesy of Machelle J. Eppes, the clerk of Prince Edward County Circuit Court; *Daily Mail* (Hagerstown, MD), 3/10/25 (1:4). See also "Executed Offenders," Box 375, File 2 (VA State Archives).

Percy Lee (black, age 34). *Attempted Rape.* The crime was committed on 10/10/1924 in Henrico County. Serial rapist. Executed for a felonious assault on the person of 20-year-old Elizabeth Hudson (white—a Westhampton College student) with intent to commit rape. A second indictment for attacking another white female at the same time was held in abeyance. Lee had also criminally assaulted three women of his own ethnicity during a series of attacks that ended on 12/6/1924. All of the victims were beaten and menaced with knives. The last attack occurred 200 yards from the scene of the first one. The perpetrator was put to death on May 1, 1925. Source: *Richmond Times-Dispatch*, 10/11/24 (1:1), 10/12/24 (1:3), 12/14/24

(1:4) and 1/20/25 (1:4). See also "Executed Offenders," Box 375, File 3 (VA State Archives).

Rodney Hoke (white, age 19). *Murder.* The crime was committed on or about 4/20/1925 in Alleghany County. Executed for the murder of "Old Man Brown," a 60+-year-old white male whose full name was never positively ascertained, but who was thought to be the father of one Robert A. Brown, a peddler who had vanished some days earlier (and who was thought to be a victim of foul play), and for whom the older man was searching at the time of his death. Hoke was the prime suspect in the peddler's disappearance as well. He shot the other man with a handgun, severely pistol-whipped him after he had fallen, and then dragged him by his ankles to a stream, where he forcibly held his head underwater until he drowned. Hoke met his own end in the Virginia electric chair on July 10, 1925. Source: *The Bee* (Danville, VA), 7/10/25 (16:3); *News Leader* (Richmond, VA), 7/10/25 (1:6). See also "Executed Offenders," Box 375, File 4 (VA State Archives).

Horace Allen (black, age 34). *Murder.* The crime was committed on 1/17/1925 in Isle of Wight County. Executed for the handgun slaying of 49-year-old Sam T. Saunders (white). Motive: attempted robbery. The killer was executed on July 17, 1925. Source: *The Bee* (Danville, VA), 4/24/25 (3:3) and 7/17/25 (1:2). See also 1920 U.S. Census (Isle of Wight Co., VA), which notes Mr. Saunders, and 1925 Henrico County death cert. no. 16054.

Henry Perman (black, age 29). *Attempted Rape.* The crime was committed on 3/10/1925 at Norfolk. Felonious assault on the person of a 19-year-old white female newlywed (whose name was never made public) with intent to commit rape. She had been chased from her home wearing nothing but her slip. The culprit had recently been released from prison after serving eight years for a similar offense. He was executed on September 29, 1925. Source: *Virginian Pilot* (Norfolk), 3/11/25 (1:6) and 3/17/25 (18:1); *Portsmouth (VA) Star*, 9/30/25 (9:3).

Doc Earl McMillan (black, age 28). *Murder.* The crime was committed on 7/18/1925 at Norfolk. Executed for the handgun slaying of 21-year-old Harold W. Gregory (white). Motive: attempted robbery. The killer was executed on October 9, 1925. Source: *Virginian Pilot* (Norfolk), 7/19/25 (1:8), 7/20/25 (1:8) and 9/3/25 (12:3). See also "Executed Offenders," Box 375, File 7 (VA State Archives).

1926

William Spencer (black, age 27). *Murder.* The crime was committed on 10/31/1924 in Lee County. Child killer. Executed for the murder of 13-year-old Maxine Kinser (white), she having been stripped naked and beaten to death with a stick. Motive: sexual assault. The killer was put to death on January 22, 1926. Source: *Middleboro (KY) Daily News*, 11/1/24 (1:2); *Roanoke (VA) World News*, 11/22/24 (2:4); *Virginia Appeals*, Vol. 34, pages 286–290. See also "Executed Offenders," Box 375, File 8 (VA State Archives).

Rudolph Disse (white, age 20). *Murder.* The crime was committed on 7/28/1925 in Henrico County. Cop killer, etc. Executed for the handgun slayings of 39-year-old Harvey J. Burke, 19-year-old Vivian Tomlin Peers and 18-year-old

Henry Grady Carter (whites). Motive: jilted lover gone berserk. Disse was executed on February 19, 1926. Source: *The Bee* (Danville, VA), 7/29/25 (1:1); *Cumberland (MD) Evening Times*, 2/19/26 (5:5). See also 1920 U.S. Census (Richmond, VA), which notes Disse, Burke and Tomlin, plus the census for Norfolk, VA, which notes Carter.

Louis Watkins (black, age 27). *Murder.* The crime was committed on 8/9/1925 in Henrico County. Cop killer. Executed for the handgun slaying of 38-year-old Louis Bertucci (white), who was shot in the face at point-blank range. Motive: resisting arrest. Watkins was executed on March 19, 1926. Source: *The Bee* (Danville, VA), 8/10/25 (1:1) and 3/19/26 (1:6).

James Patterson (black, age 33). *Murder.* The crime was committed on 1/29/1922 at Petersburg. Executed for the shotgun slaying of 33-year-old Irving Seid (white). Motive: mugging. Patterson was electrocuted pursuant to the law on August 27, 1926. Source: *Evening Progress* (Petersburg), 1/30/22 (1:2); *Progress and Index-Appeal* (Petersburg), 6/3/23 (1:7). See also "Executed Offenders," Box 375, File 11 (VA State Archives).

James Satchell (black, age 25). *Murder.* The crime was committed on 4/30/1926 in Northampton County. Executed for the handgun slaying of 24-year-old Arletta Belote (black). Motive: she could not be lured away from her husband. The killer was executed on September 24, 1926. Source: *News Leader* (Richmond, VA), 9/25/26 (21:3). See also 1926 Northampton County death cert. no. 10349 and "Executed Offenders," Box 375, File 12 (VA State Archives).

1927

William Gee (black, age 21). *Attempted Rape.* The crime was committed on 11/1/1926 in Warwick County. Felonious assault on the person of a 67-year-old white female (whose name was never made public) with intent to commit rape. This attacker was executed on January 14, 1927. Source: *Daily Press* (Newport News), 11/2/26 (2:8); *Kingsport (TN) Times*, 11/2/26 (5:4). See also "Executed Offenders," Box 375, File 13 (VA State Archives).

Henry Perfey (black, age 20). *Murder.* The crime was committed on 9/14/1926 at Norfolk. Executed for the handgun slaying of 47-year-old Goldie L. Curling (white male), who was shot multiple times. Motive: carjacking. The killer was executed on April 15, 1927. Source: *Virginian Pilot* (Norfolk), 3/6/27 (5:1:3). See also 1920 U.S. Census (Norfolk, VA), which notes Curling, and 1927 Henrico County death cert. no. 8524, which notes Perfey.

William Thomas (black, age 26). *Attempted Rape.* The crime was committed on 1/24/1927 in Madison County. Felonious assault on the person of 22-year-old Dora Hudson Clore (white) with intent to commit rape. This attacker died in the electric chair on April 15, 1927. Source: "Executed Offenders," Box 375, File 15 (VA State Archives). See also 1930 U.S. Census (Madison Co., VA), which notes the victim, and 1927 Henrico County death cert. no. 8523, which notes Thomas.

Louis Boersig (white, age 44). *Murder.* The crime was committed on 3/4/1927 in Fairfax County. Child killer. Executed for the murders of 9-year-old Loretta Ridgeway and 6-year-old Kathleen Ridgeway (both white—sisters), they having been beaten and clubbed to death. Motive: home invasion. The killer was put to death on July 7, 1927. Source: *The Bee* (Danville, VA), 4/7/27 (3:3) and 7/7/27 (1:3).

William Nelson (black, age 25). *Attempted Rape.* The crime was committed on 8/31/1927 at Hopewell. Felonious assault on the person of a "young married" white female whose name was never made public. She was choked into unconsciousness and otherwise mistreated with intent to commit rape. The attacker was executed on November 15, 1927. Source: *City and Tri-County News* (Hopewell, VA), 9/2/27 (1:7) and 9/9/27 (1:1). See also "Executed Offenders," Box 375, File 17 (VA State Archives).

1928

Shirley Winningham (black male, age 24). *Murder.* The crime was committed on 10/14/1927 in Isle of Wight County. Child killer. Executed for the murder of 13-year-old Hilda Barlow (white), she having been savagely beaten and her face smashed with a rock. Motive: sexual assault. Venue changed from Isle of Wight County to Henrico County. The killer paid with his life for this capital offense on January 25, 1928. Source: *The Bee* (Danville, VA), 10/17/27 (1:4), 11/29/27 (3:6) and 1/25/28 (1:5). See also 1920 U.S. Census (Isle of Wight Co., VA), which notes both parties.

Burn V. Gray (black, age 35). *Murder.* The crime was committed on 5/24/1927 at Petersburg. Cop killer. Executed for the handgun slaying of 57-year-old J. Peyton Stewart (white). Motive: resisting arrest. The miscreant was executed on May 18, 1928. Source: *Progress-Index* (Petersburg), 5/26/27 (1:8). See also "Executed Offenders," Box 375, File 19 (VA State Archives).

James Washington (black, age 23). *Rape.* The crime was committed on 5/31/1928 in Loudoun County. Indecent assault on the person of 14-year-old Gladys Boyd (white), she having been accosted at knifepoint. The rapist was put to death on July 27, 1928. Source: *Loudoun Times-Mirror*, 6/7/28 (1:1) and 6/21/28 (1:3). See also "Executed Offenders," Box 375, File 20 (VA State Archives). See also Original Case File (*Commonwealth vs. Washington*), copy provided courtesy of Mr. John Fishback, the Loudoun County Circuit Court Historical Records Manager.

1929

Henry Jones (black, age 20). *Murder.* The crime was committed on 9/20/1928 in Mecklenburg County. Executed for the handgun slaying of 19-year-old Robert Hurick, alias "Henrick" (black). Motive: gambling dispute. The killer was executed on March 29, 1929. Source: "Executed Offenders," Box 375, File 21 (VA State Archives). See also 1928 Mecklenburg County death cert. no. 21090 and 1929 Henrico County death cert. no. 8400.

Henry Palmer, alias "Henry Moten" (black, age 27). *Murder.* The crime was committed on 4/4/1929 at Norfolk. Executed for the mutilation murder of 38-year-old Bertha Cox (white), she having been struck down with an ax and battered about the head with a flatiron, with her throat cut by means of a razor. Motive: sexual assault. The killer died pursuant to the law on May 17, 1929. Source: *The Bee* (Danville, VA), 4/5/29 (1:2); *Official Detective*, 6/36. See also "Executed

Offenders," Box 375, File 22 (VA State Archives).

Sam Haskins (black, age 31). *Murder.* The crime was committed on 3/23/1929 in Powhatan County. Executed for the murder of 55-year-old B. M. "Jake" Gordon (white—a junk dealer), who was battered to death with stones. Motive: robbery and treachery. Haskins was the victim's hired helper on his junk collection route. His objective was $200 in small bills and silver that Mr. Gordon used to conduct business. Haskins was also the prime suspect in the unrelated murder of 60-year-old Arthur Edgar Trainer (white—a storekeeper), who was found beaten to death in his shop at Richmond, Virginia, on 11/24/1928. Sam Haskins met his end in the electric chair on September 6, 1929. Source: *Richmond (VA) News Leader*, 3/25/29 (2:1) and 9/6/29 (2:5). See also 1929 Henrico County death cert. no. 25422.

Luther Clayborn (black, age 27). *Murder.* The crime was committed on 9/5/1929 at Roanoke. Executed for the murder of 28-year-old Frances White (black), her brains having been dashed out by the butt of a shotgun after the killer had fired at her with the same weapon and missed. Motive: scorned lover. Clayborn went to the electric chair on November 29, 1929. Source: *Roanoke World News*, 9/5/29 (1:3) and 9/20/29 (2:8). See also "Executed Offenders," Box 375, File 24 (VA State Archives).

1930

John Fields (black, age 21). *Murder.* The crime was committed on 12/20/1929 in Gloucester County. Executed for the handgun slaying of 32-year-old Christian Hogge (white). Motive: armed robbery. The killer was executed on February 20, 1930. Source: *The Bee* (Danville, VA), 12/23/29 (1:5) and 1/10/30 (10:5). See also 1930 Henrico County death cert. no. 3696.

Elwood Payne (black, age 33). *Murder.* The crime was committed on 6/30/1930 in Fauquier County. Executed for the murder of 56-year-old Alfin C. Corbin (white), who was shot with a handgun while seated in his automobile and horribly burned when said vehicle was deliberately torched. Two daughters of the victim (Estelle, age 26, and Isabelle, age 33) were also decoyed from their home with a story that their father had been hurt and nearly murdered in the same manner; fortunately, they survived. Motive: barnyard vendetta. The killer was executed on September 19, 1930. Source: *Denton (TX) Record-Chronicle*, 7/1/30 (1:6). See also 1920 U.S. Census (Fauquier Co., VA), which notes the Corbins, and 1930 Henrico County death cert. no. 21330.

Alphonso Bellamy (black, age 19). *Murder.* The crime was committed on 8/21/1930 at Newport News. Executed for the handgun slaying of 71-year-old Richard P. Richards (white). Motive: armed robbery. The killer was executed on October 31, 1930. Source: *Daily Press* (Newport News), 8/22/30 (1:1) and 8/23/30 (1:6); *The Bee* (Danville, VA), 11/13/30 (1:6). See also 1920 U.S. Census (Newport News, VA), which notes Mr. Richards.

1931

Ollie Dorson (black, age 40). *Murder.* The crime was committed on 12/18/1930 in Princess Anne County. Executed for the shotgun slaying of 58-year-old James

T. Howe (white). Motive: home invasion. Dorson had also murdered a night watchman named John W. Brickhouse (white, age 62) near Norfolk twelve days earlier, the victim having been shot by a prowler. Dorson met his own fate in the Virginia electric chair on February 3, 1931. Source: *Virginian Pilot* (Norfolk), 12/20/30 (1:8); *The Bee* (Danville, VA), 2/3/31 (8:8). See also 1930 U.S. Census (Norfolk, VA), which notes Mr. Brickhouse.

Calvin Grooms (black, age 19). *Rape.* The crime was committed on 3/21/1931 in Amherst County. Indecent assault on the person of 36-year-old Mary E. Vail (white), she having also been battered with a rock (three of her fingers were broken). The rapist was put to death on June 26, 1931. Source: *The Bee* (Danville, VA), 3/23/31 (3:6). See also 1920 U.S. Census (Amherst Co., VA), which notes Ms. Vail, and 1931 Henrico County death cert. no. 14686, as well as "Executed Offenders," Box 375, File 29 (VA State Archives).

1932

Sam Pannell (black, age 17). *Rape.* The crime was committed on 1/28/1932 in Halifax County. Indecent assault on the person of 38-year-old Lena Crews (white), she having been attacked in her own home by a burglar. This offender was executed on May 20, 1932. Source: Original Case File (*Commonwealth vs. Pannell*), Halifax County Circuit Court Records Room; *News Leader* (Richmond, VA), 5/20/32 (9:2). See also 1920 U.S. Census (Halifax Co., VA), which notes Ms. Crews, and 1930 U.S. Census (Halifax Co., VA), which notes Pannell.

Randolph Cox (black, age 39). *Murder.* The crime was committed on 12/19/1930 in Richmond County. Cop killer. Executed for the shotgun slaying of 38-year-old James Newton Wood (white). Motive: resisting arrest. The killer was executed on June 3, 1932. Source: *Times-Dispatch* (Richmond, VA), 12/20/30 (1:8). See also "Executed Offenders," Box 375, File 31 (VA State Archives).

1933

Frank Mann (black, age 37). *Murder.* The crime was committed on 11/4/1932 in Nansemond County. Executed for the handgun slayings of 17-year-old Dorothy Floyd Mann and 56-year-old David Floyd (both black), his wife and father-in-law, respectively. Motive: family rift. The killer was executed on October 6, 1933. Source: *Suffolk (VA) News-Herald*, 11/7/32 (1:7). See also 1930 U.S. Census (Nansemond Co., VA), which notes the victims, plus "Executed Offenders," Box 375, File 32 (VA State Archives).

1935

Robert Mais (white, age 28) and **Walter Legenza** (white, age 41). *Murder.* Their crime was committed on 3/8/1934 in Henrico County. Cop killers, etc. These men were members of the infamous *Tri-State Gang*, one of the most ferocious outlaw bands of that era. They were specifically executed for the handgun slaying of 44-year-old Euell M. Huband (white). Motive: armored car heist. Mais and his accomplice are also confirmed to have murdered Richmond police officer William A. Toot (white, age 58) on 9/29/1934 (by means of smuggled handguns) during a jailbreak in that city. They are additionally confirmed to have murdered a Philadelphia racketeer named

William "Big Nose" Weiss (white, age 44) during a subsequent kidnapping for ransom. Weiss was forcibly abducted from the driveway of his home on October 26, 1934, while Mais and Legenza were fugitives from Virginia. He was held captive until November 6, 1934, at which time they tortured him and shot him to death (with handguns) because his ransom had been only partially paid. Weiss's body was found on January 22, 1935, in a tributary of the Delaware River wrapped in a bundle and weighted with irons. Mais and Legenza were also reported to have assassinated several other underworld characters during the Prohibition era, but further details are lacking. They were executed in the Virginia electric chair on February 2, 1935. Source: *The Bee* (Danville, VA), 3/9/34 (1:4), 10/1/34 (1:8) and 2/2/35 (1:1); *Chester (PA) Times*, 12/17/34 (1:6); *Gettysburg (PA) Times*, 2/28/35 (10:1); *Official Detective*, 5/35; *Real Detective*, 5/35; *Master Detective*, 5/47; *Crime Detective*, 9/50. See also Daniel Allen Hearn, *Legal Executions in New Jersey: A Comprehensive Registry, 1691–1963* (McFarland, 2005), 362–366.

Philip Jones (black, age 25). *Murder.* The crime was committed on 11/18/1934 in Alleghany County. Child killer. Executed for the murders of 13-year-old Alice Hill and 9-year-old Ellen Hill (both black—sisters), who were both battered to death with the butt of a shotgun. Motive: sexual assault. Venue changed from Alleghany County to Botetourt County. Jones was executed on March 11, 1935. Source: *The Bee* (Danville, VA), 11/21/34 (2:6) and 3/11/35 (1:8).

1936

John Daugherty (white, age 27). *Murder.* The crime was committed on 9/23/1935 in Fluvanna County. Cop killer. Executed for the handgun slaying of 33-year-old William Raymond Thompson (white). Motive: bank robbery gone awry. Daugherty paid the price for what he did on February 7, 1936. Source: *The Bee* (Danville, VA), 9/24/35 (1:1), 9/25/35 (1:3) and 2/7/36 (1:2).

Joe Jackson (black, age 22) and **John Shell** (black, age 29). *Murder.* Their crime was committed on 4/2/1935 in Spotsylvania County. Both were executed for the shotgun slayings of 77-year-old John Thomas Coleman and 65-year-old Jennie C. Coleman (both white—a married couple), they having also been tortured in an unspeakable manner, with their bodies ultimately dumped down a well. Motive: home invasion. The miscreants were put to death on February 21, 1936. Source: *The Bee* (Danville, VA), 4/15/35 (1:5) and 4/27/35 (10:7); *Kingsport (TN) Times*, 2/21/36 (1:6); *Official Detective*, 4/36. See also 1930 U.S. Census (Spotsylvania Co., VA), which notes the Colemans.

Isaac Frank Watson (black, age 54). *Murder.* The crime was committed on 4/30/1936 in Halifax County. Executed for the shotgun slaying of 73-year-old William Thomas Powell (white). Motive: residential prowling. Watson was executed on July 3, 1936. Source: *The Bee* (Danville, VA), 5/7/36 (2:4) and 7/3/36 (1:8).

Thomas Cole Hart (white, age 32). *Murder.* The crime was committed on 9/15/1932 in Scott County. Prison guard killer. Executed for the murder of 23-year-old Alton Leonard (white), who was hit on the head with an iron bar. Motive: jailbreak. Hart paid with his life for this in the Virginia electric chair on July 24, 1936. Source: *Kingsport (TN)*

Times, 9/20/32 (3:1) and 9/23/32 (3:3); *The Bee* (Danville, VA), 7/24/36 (4:1).

1937

Willie Leake (black, age 28) and **Lawrence Benjamin Wyche** (black, age 29). *Murder.* Their crime was committed on 9/30/1936 in Greensville County. Both were executed for the handgun slaying of 30-year-old Billie Wright Smith (black male), a storekeeper. Motive: armed robbery. The killers were executed on August 20, 1937. Source: *The Bee* (Danville, VA), 10/1/36 (9:2) and 8/20/37 (4:3). See also 1936 Greensville County death cert. no. 25299 and 1937 Emporia City death cert. nos. 19463 and 19464.

John Winzor (black, age 22). *Murder.* The crime was committed on 8/31/1937 in Loudoun County. Executed for the handgun slaying of 83-year-old Henry Saffel (white). Motive: armed robbery. The killer was executed on December 31, 1937. Source: *Loudoun Times-Mirror*, 9/2/37 (1:8) and 1/6/38 (1:8).

1938

James Jackson (black, age 27). *Murder.* The crime was committed on 1/20/1937 in Elizabeth City County. Executed for the handgun slaying of 66-year-old Willie M. Kemp (white). Motive: armed robbery. This killer was executed on March 25, 1938. Source: *Daily Press* (Newport News), 1/21/37 (1:1) and 2/27/37 (7:3); *The Bee* (Danville, VA), 3/25/38 (7:2).

Jasper T. McNeil (black, age 23). *Murder.* The crime was committed on 9/5/1937 in Amherst County. Executed for the handgun slaying of 47-year-old Clyde Poindexter Styers (white). Motive: desperate fugitive. McNeil was also the prime suspect in the 9/4/1937 handgun slaying of 65-year-old Henry A. Gurley (white) at Charlotte, North Carolina. Motive: armed robbery. McNeil reportedly gunned down Gurley (a grocer) during a holdup. He then hopped a freight train to Monroe, Virginia, where Styers (a railroad flagman) became suspicious of him and was fatally shot as well. McNeil was executed at the Virginia State Penitentiary on March 25, 1938. Source: *The Bee* (Danville, VA), 9/6/37 (4:1), 10/22/37 (3:7) and 3/25/38 (7:2); *The Robesonian* (Lumberton, NC), 9/6/37 (8:4); *Statesville (NC) Landmark*, 9/9/37 (4:6).

Joe Martin (black, age 31). *Murder.* The crime was committed on 2/19/1938 at Lynchburg. Executed for the handgun slaying of 44-year-old Grover C. Clement (white). Motive: armed robbery. There was no appeal. The killer was executed on April 8, 1938. Source: *The Bee* (Danville, VA), 2/21/38 (5:2), 3/4/38 (8:6) and 4/8/38 (1:1).

Otis Cypress (black, age 28). *Murder.* The crime was committed on 6/13/1938 in Surry County. Executed for the murder of 61-year-old Frank Spratley (black), the victim having been shot with a handgun and his head cracked open. Motive: armed robbery. This black-on-black killer was put to death on November 25, 1938. Source: *The Bee* (Danville, VA), 11/25/38 (1:2). See also 1938 Warwick County death cert. no. 13042 and 1938 Richmond City death cert. no. 24892.

George Pingley (white, age 43). *Murder.* The crime was committed on 2/13/1938 in Frederick County. Cop killer.

Executed for the shotgun slaying of 46-year-old James William Newcome (white), the victim having been blasted in the back. Motive: resisting arrest. Pingley was put to death on November 25, 1938. Source: *The Bee* (Danville, VA), 2/14/38 (1:2) and 11/25/38 (1:2); *Crime Detective*, 12/38.

1939

Irving Brooks (black, age 31). *Robbery with Violence.* The crime was committed on 2/7/1938 in King William County. Executed for the beating and mugging of 66-year-old Eula P. Hand (white), she having been grossly manhandled as well as robbed. Her attacker was executed on January 20, 1939. Source: *The Bee* (Danville, VA), 2/12/38 (10:6). See also 1920 U.S. Census (King William Co., VA), which notes Ms. Hand, plus "Executed Offenders," Box 376, File 9 (VA State Archives).

John Anderson (black, age 28). *Rape.* The crime was committed on 11/15/1938 in Loudoun County. Indecent assault on the person of 25-year-old Lula V. Sisk (white), she having been attacked in her own home while tending her 4-month-old baby. The miscreant was executed on February 10, 1939. Source: Original Case File (*Commonwealth vs. Anderson*), copy provided courtesy of Mr. John Fishback, the Loudoun County Circuit Court Historical Records Manager. See also "Executed Offenders," Box 376, File 10 (VA State Archives).

Harry Williams (black, age 20). *Murder.* The crime was committed on 11/20/1938 in Greene County. Executed for the handgun slaying of 30-year-old Clarence Mills (black), who was shot four times. Motive: gambling dispute. The killer was executed on April 7, 1939. Source: *Greene County Record* (Stanardsville, VA), 11/24/38 (1:1), 12/8/38 (1:1) and 4/13/39 (1:6). See also 1938 Charlottesville City death cert. no. 25105.

Samuel Swanson (black, age 27). *Murder.* The crime was committed on 5/28/1939 in Pittsylvania County. Cop killer. Executed for the handgun slaying of 44-year-old William N. Coward (white), who was shot five times in the back. Motive: interfering with a police officer. Swanson was executed at the Virginia State Penitentiary on December 15, 1939. Source: *The Bee* (Danville, VA), 5/29/39 (1:2) and 12/15/39 (1:5).

1940

James Clifton Abdell (white, age 41). *Murder.* The crime was committed on 5/11/1938 at Norfolk. Uxoricide. Executed for the murder of 38-year-old Audrey Sharpe Abdell (white), she having been beaten and deliberately left unconscious in a gas-filled apartment so that she died amid the fumes. Motive: adultery on his part. This killer was executed on January 5, 1940. Source: *The Bee* (Danville, VA), 6/30/38 (9:3) and 1/5/40 (1:4); *Daring Detective*, 11/38; *Front Page Detective*, 6/39; *Master Detective*, 4/39 and 4/58.

John Henry McCann (black, age 62). *Attempted Rape.* The crime was committed on 2/13/1939 at Norfolk. Serial child molester. Executed for a felonious assault on the person of a 7-year-old white female with intent to commit rape. The victim and her 5-year-old playmate had been lured into a vacant house. McCann had previously been released from the Massachusetts State Prison on 12/7/1938 after completing a 7-year sentence there for statutory rape. He came to Norfolk a week later and began attacking little girls, including a 7-year-old, a 3-year-old and a 10-year-old, in addition to the attack for which he was specifically convicted. The Virginia electric chair permanently cured this pedophile on January 26, 1940. (The names of his victims are withheld by this chronicler because some of them might still be alive.) Source: *Ledger-Dispatch* (Norfolk, VA), 2/14/39 (3:6) and 2/15/39 (2:1); *The Bee* (Danville, VA), 1/26/40 (2:5). See also "Executed Offenders," Box 376, File 14 (VA State Archives).

Willie Bradshaw (black, age 55). *Murder.* The crime was committed on 12/18/1938 in Halifax County. Cop killer. Executed for the shotgun slaying of 36-year-old Herbert Boelte (white). Motive: resisting arrest. Bradshaw died in the electric chair on April 12, 1940. Source: *The Bee* (Danville, VA), 12/19/38 (1:2) and 4/12/40 (4:4).

Wilmer Davis (black, age 25). *Murder.* The crime was committed on 11/13/1939 in Southampton County. Uxoricide. Executed for the sniper slaying of roughly 25-year-old Bessie Davis (black), a shot having been fired through the window of her cabin. Motive: marital breakdown. The killer was executed on April 26, 1940. Source: Original Case File (*Commonwealth vs. Davis*), copy provided courtesy of Mr. Richard L. Francis, the clerk of Southampton County Circuit Court. See also "Executed Offenders," Box 376, File 16 (VA State Archives).

1941

Charles Brown (black, age 26). *Rape.* The crime was committed on 2/15/1941 in Isle of Wight County. Indecent assault on the person of a 23-year-old white female (name withheld), the mother of five small children. The rapist was executed on September 26, 1941. Source: *The Bee* (Danville, VA), 3/19/41 (9:5). See also "Executed Offenders," Box 376, File 17 (VA State Archives).

1942

William Henry Diggs (black, age 19) and **Charles Johnson, Jr.** (black, age 24). *Murder.* Their crime was committed on 10/18/1941 in Nelson County. Both were executed for the strangulation of 18-year-old Gladys Mae Tyree (white), she having also been forcibly abducted, raped and robbed. Motive: sexual assault. The killers were executed on January 16, 1942. Source: *The Bee* (Danville, VA), 11/8/41 (1:4) and 1/16/42 (1:2).

Odell Waller (black, age 23). *Murder.* The crime was committed on 7/15/1940 in Pittsylvania County. Executed for the handgun slaying of 46-year-old Oscar Davis (white), who was shot four times, including twice in the back. Motive: landlord-tenant dispute. The killer was executed on July 2, 1942. Source: *The Bee* (Danville, VA), 7/16/40 (2:6), 7/18/40 (5:7) and 7/2/42 (1:5). See also 1930 U.S. Census (Pittsylvania Co., VA), which notes Mr. Davis.

1943

James Branch Mooring, Jr. (black, age 22). *Murder.* The crime was committed on 12/22/1942 at Norfolk. Executed for the handgun slaying of 68-year-old Cornelius Grant Goodson (white). Motive: armed robbery. This killer was executed on March 19, 1943. Source: *The Bee* (Danville, VA), 12/23/42 (1:6) and 3/19/43 (6:6).

Harry Edward Farris (white, age 26). *Murder.* The crime was committed on 7/19/1942 in Henrico County. Executed for the murder of 36-year-old Vinichio Bichi (white), who was slashed to death with a butcher knife (his body was later left on a public road). Motive: robbery. Farris is confirmed to have murdered another man under identical circumstances the previous day. The victim in that case was identified as Frank E. Hargrove (white, age 41) of Henrico County. This killer was put to death on October 15, 1943. Source: *The Bee* (Danville, VA), 7/27/42 (5:4) and 10/15/43 (1:6); *Crime Detective*, 1/43 and 3/59; *Daring Detective*, 1/43; *True* (magazine), 1/43.

1944

Raymond Woodall (white, age 35). *Murder.* The crime was committed on 9/1/1943 in Pittsylvania County. Executed for the rifle slayings of 36-year-old Ruth Terry Woodall and 34-year-old Julia Terry Giles (both white), his wife and sister-in-law, respectively. Motive: drunken tantrum. Woodall died in the electric chair on March 3, 1944. Source: *The Bee* (Danville, VA), 9/2/43 (1:4) and 3/3/44 (1:7). See also 1920 U.S. Census (Danville, VA), which notes both women by their maiden names.

Howard Ross Walker (black, age 27). *Rape.* The crime was committed on 3/7/1944 at Winchester. Indecent assault on the person of 26-year-old Jessie H. Glaize (white), she having been attacked in her own home by a knife-wielding intruder. The rapist was executed on May 26, 1944. Source: *Winchester (VA) Evening Star*, 3/8/44 (1:3) and 3/9/44 (1:2); *The Bee* (Danville, VA), 5/26/44 (1:4).

Thomas William Clatterbuck (white, age 33). *Murder.* The crime was committed on 6/1/1943 in Loudoun County. Mass killer. Executed for the rifle slayings of 59-year-old Andrus Morris Love, 58-year-old Ruth G. Love, and 22-year-old James W. Love (whites—a married couple and their son), plus 27-year-old Walter Russell and 25-year-old Katherine Russell (both white—another married couple), they having also (with the exception of Mr. Russell) had their heads smashed in by means of a wooden mallet. Motive: felonious revelation (the killer had been exposed as a forger and he dreaded prosecution by Mr. Love for that offense). The Virginia electric chair ended his life on June 16, 1944. Source: *The Bee* (Danville, VA), 6/4/43 (3:7) and 6/16/44 (5:5); *True* (magazine), 9/43; *Official Detective*, 10/43 and 6/83; *Headline Detective*, 10/43; *Master Detective*, 7/54 and 11/59. See also 1930 U.S. Census (Loudoun Co., VA), which notes the Loves.

1945

Willie Rodgers Jones (black, age 29). *Rape.* The crime was committed on 10/2/1944 at Norfolk. Indecent assault on the person of a white female cab driver (whose name and age were never made public), she having been deliberately carjacked for that purpose. The rapist was executed on February 2, 1945. Source: *Norfolk Ledger-Dispatch*, 10/3/44 (2:4); *Norfolk Virginian Pilot*, 2/3/45 (2:1).

Holman B. Thomas (black, age 40). *Murder.* The crime was committed on 12/13/1943 in Lunenburg County. Cop killer. Executed for the handgun slaying of 43-year-old Abb Kimball Fleming (white). Motive: resisting arrest. This killer was electrocuted pursuant to the law on March 1, 1945. Source: *Times-Dispatch* (Richmond, VA), 12/15/43 (12:1). See also "Executed Offenders," Box 377, File 7 (VA State Archives).

Raymond McDaniel (white, age 29). *Murder.* The crime was committed on 2/6/1944 in Campbell County. Executed for the handgun slaying of 45-year-old Roy A. Alfred (white), the victim's body having been concealed in a well with the alleged connivance of his wife. Motive: adultery. McDaniel died in the Virginia electric chair on March 2, 1945. Source: *The Bee* (Danville, VA), 3/25/44 (7:6) and 3/2/45 (3:1); *Crime Detective*, 6/57.

Mancy Christian (black male, age 27). *Rape.* The crime was committed on 2/2/1945 in Nansemond County. Indecent assault on the person of a 15-year-old white female (name withheld), she having been forcibly abducted while walking home, choked into submission and raped twice over the course of several hours. The culprit was a chain-gang escapee at the time, having already been sentenced to 20 years at hard labor for highway robbery. He was executed on May 1, 1945. Source: *Suffolk (VA) News-Herald*, 2/5/45 (8:1); *The Bee* (Danville, VA), 5/1/45 (8:4).

Lonnie Pearson (black, age 30). *Rape.* The crime was committed on 2/5/1945 at Norfolk. Indecent assault on the person of 29-year-old Elizabeth Hardison (white), she having been attacked in her own home by a knife-wielding intruder, and her 3-year-old child threatened with death unless she yielded. Pearson was executed on August 3, 1945. Source: *Norfolk Virginian Pilot*, 2/25/45 (1:7) and 8/4/45 (3:4); *Portsmouth (VA) Star*, 2/25/45 (1:2). See also "Executed Offenders," Box 377, File 10 (VA State Archives).

1946

Andrew Jackson Holloman (black, age 31). *Rape.* The crime was committed on 8/24/1945 at Norfolk. Indecent assault on the person of 19-year-old Lussie Lenora White (white), she having been forcibly abducted and raped three times throughout the course of that day. This sex offender was put to death on January 11, 1946. Source: *The Bee* (Danville, VA), 1/11/46 (5:4). See also "Executed Offenders," Box 377, File 11 (VA State Archives).

Ernest Edward Fagan (black, age 30). *Murder.* The crime was committed on 9/4/1945 at Norfolk. Doomed for the handgun slaying of 42-year-old Horace H. Cox (white). Motive: robbery and carjacking. This transgressor was executed on February 15, 1946. Source: *The Bee* (Danville, VA), 2/15/46 (7:4).

Nelson Cross (black, age 33). *Murder.* The crime was committed on 12/1/1945 at Danville. Executed for the ax murder of 32-year-old Edward Johnson (black), whose butchered remains were found more than a month later stuffed into a jakes. Motive: uncontrollable anger (Cross had suspected Johnson of stealing some of his whiskey). He died in the electric chair on April 15, 1946. Source: *The Bee* (Danville, VA), 1/7/46 (1:7), 1/23/46 (1:7), 3/19/46 (1:7) and 4/15/46 (1:5).

Thomas Edward Harrison (white, age 19). *Murder.* The crime was committed on 1/19/1946 at Roanoke. Spree killer. Executed for the handgun slaying of 56-year-old Roby Monroe Daugherty (white), who was shot in the back. Motive: armed robbery. Harrison was also the prime suspect in two other Roanoke-area murders: those of William Ralph Chattin (white, age 30), who was abducted from his place of employment on 1/7/1946, and Roy R. Rice (white, age 50), who was abducted while en route to make a bank deposit on 1/9/1946. Both men were robbed and taken to remote fields, where they were shot in the back in the same manner as Mr. Daugherty. The gunman who is believed to have killed them, and who did indeed kill Mr. Daugherty, was put to death on May 20, 1946. Source: *Roanoke World News*, 1/9/46 (1:7), 1/10/46 (1:4), 1/11/46 (1:2) and 1/19/46 (1:2) and (1:8); *The Bee* (Danville, VA), 1/21/46 (4:7) and 5/20/46 (4:3); *Real Detective*, 8/46; *Official Detective*, 9/46.

George Grissett (black, age 32), **James Hough** (black, age 28) and **Arthur Johnson** (black, age 22). *Murder.* Their crime was committed on 9/21/1945 in Princess Anne County. Executed for the handgun slaying of 58-year-old Winston Mason (black—a cabbie), who was shot twice in the back of the head. Motive: robbery. The killers were executed on June 21, 1946. Source: *The Bee* (Danville, VA), 6/21/46 (1:4); *News Leader* (Richmond, VA), 6/21/46 (3:5). See also 1930 U.S. Census (Norfolk, VA), which notes Mason.

James Lee Fletcher (black, age 24) and **Robert Holland** (black, age 22). *Murder.* Their crime was committed on 7/22/1946 in Accomack County. Both were executed for the murder of 46-year-old George Broughton (white), who was bludgeoned with a bottle, his throat cut and his body dumped along a rural road. Motive: robbery and carjacking. The killers died in the electric chair on September 13, 1946. Source: *Baltimore Sun*, 8/9/46 (9:1); *Morning Herald* (Hagerstown, MD), 9/14/46 (1:8).

1947

Amon J. Gusler (white, age 52). *Murder.* The crime was committed on 6/13/1946 in Henry County. Executed for the booby-trap bomb killing of 38-year-old J. Russell Smith (white). Motive: he coveted the murdered man's wife. Gusler paid the death penalty pursuant to the law on January 3, 1947. Source: *The Bee* (Danville, VA), 6/14/46 (8:7); *Bluefield (WV) Daily Telegraph*, 1/4/47 (2:4); *Front Page Detective*, 10/46; *Official Detective*, 11/46; *Real Detective*, 1/47; *Crime Detective*, 2/62.

Ephraim N. Thomas (black, age 25). *Murder.* The crime was committed on 2/2/1946 in Nansemond County. Executed for the handgun slaying of roughly 25-year-old Lenora Hamlin (black). Motive: argument in a taxicab. Thomas started blasting away with a .45 automatic when a dispute arose over where the taxi should take them. He was executed on May 23, 1947. Source: *Suffolk (VA) News-Herald*, 2/4/46 (3:4), 2/5/46 (3:5) and 4/18/46 (3:5). See also "Executed Offenders," Box 378, File 8 (VA State Archives).

William Davis (black, age 43). *Murder.* The crime was committed on 8/5/1946 in Fauquier County. Cop killer. Executed for the handgun slaying of 62-year-old John Holcombe Woodson (white), a railroad detective. Motive: resisting interrogation. Davis was executed on July 18, 1947. Source: *The Bee* (Danville, VA), 8/8/46 (11:6). See also "Executed Offenders," Box 378, File 9 (VA State Archives).

Buford Russell Morton (black, age 29). *Rape.* The crime was committed on 5/9/1947 at Danville. Indecent assault on the person of 27-year-old Ruby Andrews (white), she having been stalked, beaten up, forcibly abducted and throttled into submission. The rapist was put to death on October 17, 1947. Source: *The Bee* (Danville, VA), 5/10/47 (1:5), 7/25/47 (2:6) and 10/17/47 (1:6).

Raymond Laurence (black, age 28). *Murder.* The crime was committed on 8/11/1946 at Newport News. Cop killer. Executed for the handgun slaying of 31-year-old Charles Nelson Doughty (white). Motive: resisting arrest. Laurence paid with his life for this on October 24, 1947. Source: *Virginian Pilot* (Norfolk), 8/12/46 (2:5). See also "Executed Offenders," Box 378, File 11 (VA State Archives).

1948

Sammie Lee Baldwin (black, age 35). *Murder.* The crime was committed on 10/4/1947 in Accomack County. Executed for the fatal stabbings of 36-year-old John McCabe and 23-year-old Bertha Wright (both black). Motive: male jealousy. This killer was executed on January 23, 1948. Source: *Eastern Shore News* (Onancock, VA), 10/10/47 (1:1). See also "Executed Offenders," Box 378, File 12 (VA State Archives).

John Major Brooks (black, age 20). *Rape.* The crime was committed on 11/22/1947 in Halifax County. Executed for an indecent assault on the person of 16-year-old Inez Yates (white), she and an 18-year-old female companion having been forcibly abducted at gunpoint and knifepoint by three black males. The one who got caught—Brooks—was put to death on April 23, 1948. Source: *The Bee* (Danville, VA), 11/24/47 (1:3) and 11/25/47 (1:4). See also "Executed Offenders," Box 379, File 1 (VA State Archives).

Johnnie Edward James (black, age 30). *Murder.* The crime was committed on 6/9/1948 at Norfolk. Executed for the deliberate killing of 23-year-old Lonnie Jordan (black), she having been found in a field naked, strangled and violated with a 10" piece of wood. Motive: sexual assault. The predator was electrocuted by court order on October 29, 1948. Source: *Virginian Pilot* (Norfolk), 6/11/48 (9:3) and 10/30/48 (20:3). See also "Executed Offenders," Box 379, File 2 (VA State Archives).

1950

Alfred Rayfield (black, age 37). *Murder.* The crime was committed on 8/16/1950 in Accomack County. Executed for the fatal stabbing of 59-year-old William West (black) during the course of a forced entry. Motive: personal animosity. This black-on-black killer was put to death on November 17, 1950. Source: *Eastern Shore News* (Onancock, VA), 8/18/50 (1:1) and 10/13/50 (1:8). See also "Executed Offenders," Box 379, File 3 (VA State Archives).

Ben Franklin Fuller (black, age 42). *Murder.* The crime was committed on 12/19/1949 in Mecklenburg County. Executed for the shotgun slaying of Joseph Robert Thompson (black, age not recorded). Motive: ramifications of gossip. Fuller was executed on December 8, 1950. Source: *Richmond (VA) News Leader*, 12/8/50 (31:7). See also "Executed Offenders," Box 379, File 4 (VA State Archives).

1951

George Thomas Hailey (white, age 23). *Murder.* The crime was committed on 2/3/1950 in Halifax County. Child killer. Executed for the rifle slaying of 12-year-old Marion Lloyd (white), she having also been battered with the stock of that weapon. Motive: sexual assault. This murderer was executed on February 2, 1951. Source: *The Bee* (Danville, VA), 7/29/50 (1:6); *High Point (NC) Enterprise*, 2/2/51 (1:7); *Front Page Detective*, 6/50; *Master Detective*, 9/57 and 2/77.

Joe Henry Hampton (black, age 20), **Howard Lee Hairston** (black, age 19), **Booker T. Millner** (black, age 20), **Frank Hairston** (black, age 19), **Francis Desales Grayson** (black, age 38), **James Luther Hairston** (black, age 21) and **John Clabon Taylor** (black, age 22). *Rape.* Their crime was committed on 1/8/1949 at Martinsville. Indecent assault on the person of 32-year-old Ruby Stroud Floyd (white), she having been gang raped as she attempted to walk through a disreputable neighborhood at night. Special interest groups tried to exploit this case for its propaganda value, but their efforts fizzled when it became clear that there was no doubt whatsoever about the guilt of the condemned and that all of them were fully aware of the penalty they risked by their actions. The first four named above went to the electric chair on February 2, 1951; the other three followed them on February 5, 1951. Source: *High Point (NC) Enterprise*, 2/2/51 (1:7); *The Bee* (Danville, VA), 2/5/51 (1:5). See also *The Martinsville Seven*, by Eric W. Rise (University of Virginia Press, 1995), for a book-length rehash of this matter.

Ulysses Jones (black, age 31). *Murder.* The crime was committed on 3/6/1951 in Nansemond County. Child killer. Executed for the murder of 10-year-old Doris Chapman (black), she having been forcibly smothered and left face-down in a brook. Motive: sexual assault. This miscreant was executed on July 13, 1951. Source: *Suffolk (VA) News Herald*, 3/15/51 (1:8) and 3/16/51 (3:5). See also "Executed Offenders," Box 380, File 1 (VA State Archives).

Floyd Joyner, Jr. (black, age 36). *Murder.* The crime was committed on 6/26/1950 at Roanoke. Executed for the hammer slaying of 48-year-old Addie G. McCormack (white), a housewife. Motive: home invasion. The culprit was a prison camp "trusty" at the time. He died in the Virginia electric chair on December 12, 1951. Source: *The Bee* (Danville, VA), 6/29/50 (14:8) and 12/12/51 (2:5).

1952

Albert Jackson, Jr. (black, age 23). *Rape.* The crime was committed on 5/6/1951 at Charlottesville. Indecent assault on the person of a 45-year-old white female (name withheld), she having been dragged into a maze of alleys and raped three times betwixt and between. This offender had had a prior rape conviction in 1948; he was paroled on August 28, 1950, after serving barely two years of a 10-year sentence. On August 25, 1952, the electric chair ensured that Jackson would have no further lapses of this kind. Source: *Daily Progress* (Charlottesville, VA), 5/8/51 (1:7), 7/6/51 (1:2) and 8/25/52 (1:2).

1954

John Clay Kensinger (white, age 28). *Murder.* The crime was committed on

6/24/1953 at Arlington. Executed for the handgun slaying of 46-year-old Leroy E. Applegate (white). Motive: carjacking. The killer was executed on May 26, 1954. Source: *Chronicle-Telegram* (Elyria, OH), 9/16/53 (8:4); *Progress-Index* (Petersburg, VA), 5/26/54 (1:1).

John Sterling Groom, alias "King Kong Groom" (black, age 45). *Murder.* The crime was committed on 12/17/1951 in Culpeper County. Executed for the fatal stomping and strangulation of 70-year-old Jeremiah Jasper Barthelow (white). Motive: robbery. On 4/5/1934 this same offender had been sentenced in Culpeper Circuit Court to a term of so-called life imprisonment for the fatal beating of a black woman. He was granted a conditional pardon on 7/23/1951, only to wind up on the FBI's "Ten Most Wanted List" for another brutal homicide. The electric chair precluded the possibility of any further problems with Groom when it ended his life on October 14, 1954. Source: *Kingsport (TN) News*, 4/8/54 (17:1); *Daily News Record* (Harrisonburg, VA), 10/15/54 (3:1). See also "Executed Offenders," Box 380, File 5 (VA State Archives).

1955

Alonzo Russell (black, age 42). *Murder.* The crime was committed on 1/9/1955 in Rockbridge County. Executed for the strangulation of 56-year-old Emma Moore Duncan (white). Motive: sexual assault. This felon had a record of sex offenses dating back to 1936. He was executed on July 14, 1955. Source: *Daily News Record* (Harrisonburg, VA), 1/12/55 (3:5) and 7/15/55 (10:6).

1957

John Lewis Gregory (black, age 23). *Murder.* The crime was committed on 1/25/1957 at Norfolk. Executed for the fatal stabbing of 72-year-old David Weinstein (white). Motive: armed robbery. This killer was put to death on June 4, 1957. Source: *Virginian Pilot* (Norfolk), 1/26/57 (26:4); *Progress-Index* (Petersburg, VA), 4/4/57 (1:2) and 6/4/57 (3:3).

Lloyd Junius Dobie (black, age 24). *Rape.* The crime was committed on 8/15/1955 in Southampton County. Indecent assault on the person of 48-year-old Lillian Vann Scott (white), she having also been beaten and robbed. The attacker was put to death on July 12, 1957. Source: *The Bee* (Danville, VA), 7/13/57 (11:2). See also "Executed Offenders," Box 381, File 3 (VA State Archives).

1958

Jeremiah McCray (black, age 23). *Murder.* The crime was committed on 2/2/1958 in Caroline County. Serial killer. Executed for the murder of 49-year-old Jeanette M. Griffin (white), she having been battered to death with sticks of firewood in the kitchen of her own home. Motive: sexual assault. McCray is confirmed to have also murdered four other persons in separate incidents: Daisy F. Gilbert (white, age 73) near Anniston, Alabama, on 2/27/1956, she having been clubbed to death during a home invasion; Sarah DeWitt (white, age 86) at Washington Courthouse, Ohio, on 7/2/1957, she having been hacked to death with a hatchet (although McCray claimed that he had used a hammer) during another home invasion; Robert

Hanbury (white, age 53) at Atlanta, Georgia, on 7/7/1957, he having been battered to death with a shovel (and his 79-year-old mother grievously injured) for the same motive; and Virginia Macklin Stevens (white, age 74) at Colonial Heights, Virginia, on 1/9/1958, she having been stabbed multiple times and kicked in the head by an intruder in her home. In addition to being brutally murdered, all of the victims' residences were plundered. The Virginia electric chair ended the homicidal career of Jeremiah McCray on April 18, 1958. Source: *Progress-Index* (Petersburg, VA), 2/4/58 (9:7), 2/7/58 (1:9) and 4/18/58 (1:3); *The Bee* (Danville, VA), 2/8/58 (1:2); *Official Detective*, 6/58.

E. J. Sherod, alias "Pete Sherod" (black, age 23). *Murder.* The crime was committed on 6/14/1957 in Henrico County. Executed for the handgun slaying of 31-year-old Clara Wingfield (black). Motive: racial incident. Sherod was driving around in a stolen car when he spotted Wingfield necking in a parked auto with a white soldier. Enraged, Sherod pulled her out of the car and shot her dead. Then he robbed the white man at gunpoint but left him otherwise unharmed. Sherod died in the Virginia electric chair on June 6, 1958. Source: *The Progress-Index* (Petersburg, VA), 6/6/58 (7:2). See also "Executed Offenders," Box 381, File 5 (VA State Archives).

Clarence Sparrow Dabney (black, age 24). *Murder.* The crime was committed on 7/29/1958 at Lynchburg. Executed for the ax murder of 27-year-old William Owen Grubbs (white). Motive: burglary. This killer was put to death on November 21, 1958. Source: *The Progress-Index* (Petersburg, VA), 7/30/58 (1:1) and 11/21/58 (1:8).

1959

William Brown (black, age 56). *Murder.* The crime was committed on 11/13/1958 in Caroline County. Executed for the handgun slayings of 74-year-old Katherine Lewis Brooks and 33-year-old Jean M. Brooks (both white), a mother-in-law and daughter-in-law. Motive: home invasion. This killer was electrocuted at the Virginia State Penitentiary on March 27, 1959. Source: *Times-Dispatch* (Richmond, VA), 11/14/58 (1:7) and 3/28/59 (3:6).

Willis Dameron Boyd (white, age 23). *Murder.* The crime was committed on 6/19/1958 in Goochland County. Executed for the handgun slaying of 51-year-old Radford Bennett Ranson, Jr. (white), who was also bound with cords, bludgeoned and slashed about the upper torso. Motive: jealousy. The killer hated Ranson because he (Ranson) had been given a job from which he (Boyd) had been fired. Boyd's ethnicity may have been mixed; photos of him look Caucasian, but he was said to be the bastard son of a Mexican flamenco dancer. He also faced capital charges for repeatedly raping a retarded girl. He was executed on April 24, 1959. Source: *The Progress-Index* (Petersburg, VA), 4/24/59 (1:5); *Master Detective*, 10/58; *Official Detective*, 10/58. See also "Executed Offenders," Box 381, File 8 (VA State Archives).

1960

Harry Eugene Fuller (black, age 29). *Murder.* The crime was committed on 2/4/1959 at Alexandria. Cop killer. Executed for the handgun slaying of 27-year-old Bobbie Jean Padgett. Motive: resisting arrest. Fuller went to his death in the electric chair on June 30, 1960. Source: *Salisbury (MD) Times*, 2/5/59 (29:1); *Progress-Index* (Petersburg, VA), 6/30/60 (20:4).

1961

Linwood Burch (black, age 20). *Rape.* The crime was committed on 9/20/1958 at Newport News. Serial burglar and serial rapist. Executed for an indecent assault on the person of a 49-year-old white female (name withheld) who was attacked in her home at six o'clock in the morning, just after her husband had left to go to work. Burch is also confirmed to have raped a 51-year-old white female at Williamsburg in June 1958 and a pregnant 17-year-old white female at Newport News the following month. He had also been thrown out of the army. He was executed at the Virginia State Penitentiary on February 17, 1961. Source: *Daily Press* (Newport News), 10/8/58 (3:9), 10/9/58 (14:3), 10/18/58 (10:3), 10/21/58 (3:7) and 1/6/59 (1:4); *Times-Herald* (Newport News), 10/8/58 (17:8) and 10/17/58 (17:7); *Virginian Pilot* (Norfolk), 2/18/61 (2:3).

Grover Earl Lucas (white, age 49). *Murder.* The crime was committed on 4/28/1958 at Roanoke. Uxoricide and filicide. Executed for the pickax killings of 48-year-old Connie Lucas, 9-year-old Dennis Lucas and 11-year-old Mildred Lucas (whites). Motive: disillusionment caused by unemployment. This killer was executed on March 10, 1961. Source: *The Progress-Index* (Petersburg, VA), 4/29/58 (1:1) and 3/10/61 (11:2); *Master Detective*, 9/58 and 10/74.

Claude Leon Hart, Jr. (white, age 31). *Murder.* The crime was committed on 5/17/1961 at Norfolk. Cop killer. Executed for the handgun slaying of 48-year-old Robert Courtland Wash (white). Motive: resisting arrest. Hart died in the electric chair on November 17, 1961. Source: *Daily News Record* (Harrisonburg, VA), 5/18/61 (1:1) and 11/18/61 (7:3).

Jim Cobbs (black, age 45). *Murder.* The crime was committed on 3/28/1961 in Halifax County. Executed for the shotgun slaying of 60-year-old James Algie Buckner (white) and forcible rape of that man's wife. Motive: burglary and sexual assault. Cobbs paid for his crimes in the electric chair on December 8, 1961. Source: *The Bee* (Danville, VA), 8/30/61 (1:8); *Daily News Record* (Harrisonburg, VA), 12/9/61 (16:1).

1962

Carroll Garland (black, age 26). *Murder.* The crime was committed on 5/28/1961 at Lynchburg. Executed for the murder of 27-year-old Jimmy N. Nuckles (white), the victim having been hit on the head with a thick glass bottle and his body dumped in the James River. Motive: robbery. The killer paid the death penalty in accordance with Virginia law on March 2, 1962. Source: *The Progress-Index* (Petersburg, VA), 5/29/61 (2:2); *Daily News Record* (Harrisonburg, VA), 3/3/62 (5:8).

West Virginia

(in chronological order)

1866

Thomas Boice (white, age not recorded) and **Daniel Grogan** (white, age not recorded). *Murder.* Their crime was committed on 9/16/1864 in Wood County. Executed for the gunshot slaying of 45-year-old William Abraham Deem (white). Motive: highway robbery. They were hanged at Parkersburg on February 9, 1866. Source: *New York Herald*, 2/10/66 (8:4). Appeal: 1 WV 329–335.

Mortimer Gibboney (white, age not recorded). *Murder.* The crime was committed on 9/16/1864 in Wood County. Accomplice in the gunshot slaying of 45-year-old William Abraham Deem (white). Motive: highway robbery. This offender was hanged at Parkersburg on June 15, 1866. Source: *Baltimore Sun*, 6/16/66 (1:5). See **Thomas Boice** (executed 2/9/66).

1868

Joseph Eisele, alias "John Schaefer" (white, age 34). *Murder.* His crimes were committed on 6/5/1867, 6/29/1867 and 12/6/1867 in Wood County. Executed for the hatchet killings of three white males named Joseph Lillienthal, Alois Ulrich and Rudolph Tsutor (ages not recorded), in corresponding chronological order. Motive in each case: robbery. This killer was hanged at Parkersburg on March 6, 1868. Source: *Baltimore Sun*, 3/9/68 (4:3). See also *The Life and Crimes of Joseph Eisele, alias John Schaefer, the Parkersburg Murderer* (Parkersburg, WV: Inland River Books, 1978; reprint of an original 1868 edition).

1871

William Johnson (black, age 22). *Murder.* The crime was committed on 10/24/1870 in Monroe County. Executed for the murder of 28-year-old George H. Hunter (white), who was struck down from behind with a billet of wood and then hammered to death with the blunt end of a hatchet. Motive: robbery. The killer was hanged at Union Courthouse on May 19, 1871. Source: *New York Herald*, 5/20/71 (5:1).

1879

Laban Walker (white, age 17). *Murder.* The crime was committed on 8/18/1878 in Wayne County. Executed for the gunshot slaying of Patrick Nolan (white, age not recorded). Motive: personal animosity (Walker suspected that the murdered man had fingered him in an arson investigation). He was hanged at Wayne Courthouse on November 28, 1879. Source: *New York Herald*, 11/29/79 (6:1).

1881

Henry Jenkins (black, age 22). *Murder.* The crime was committed on 5/16/1881 in Fayette County. Executed for the murder of Winfield Saunders (black, age not recorded), who was hit on the head with a rock and then heaved into a river, where he drowned. Motive: mugging. The killer was hanged at Fayetteville on November 11, 1881. Source: *New York Herald*, 11/12/81 (4:1).

1890

Felix Kampf (white, age 64). *Murder.* The crime was committed on 10/4/1889 in Kanawha County. Filicide. Executed for the murders of 20-year-old Mary Kampf and 19-year-old William Kampf (both white), who were fatally slashed with a dirk. Motive: household flare-up. This killer was hanged at Charleston on March 7, 1890. Source: *Wheeling Intelligencer*, 3/8/90 (1:3).

William Martin (white, age 29). *Murder.* The crime was committed on 10/18/1887 in Raleigh County. Uxoricide. Executed for the handgun slaying of Ann Martin (white, age not recorded). Motive: suspicion of infidelity. This killer was hanged at Beckley on October 3, 1890. Source: *Raleigh County Index*, 10/3/90 (special edition); *Wheeling Intelligencer*, 10/4/90 (1:3).

1891

Sim Johnson (black, age 18). *Rape.* The crime was committed on 4/7/1891 in Kanawha County. Indecent assault on the person of 16-year-old Alice Bailey (white). The rapist was hanged at Charleston on June 19, 1891. Source: *Newark (OH) Daily Advocate*, 4/9/91 (1:2), 4/13/91 (3:3) and 6/20/91 (1:2); *Wheeling Intelligencer*, 6/20/91 (1:1).

Henry Christian (black, age not recorded). *Murder.* The crime was committed on or about 1/20/1891 in McDowell County. Cop killer. Executed for the handgun slaying of William Crowe (white, age not recorded). Motive: resisting arrest. The killer was hanged at Susanna on July 17, 1891. Source: *Wheeling Intelligencer*, 7/18/91 (1:6). (The original court papers for this case have not survived.)

1892

William Maier (white, age 24). *Murder.* The crime was committed on 4/5/1892 in Ohio County. Uxoricide. Executed for the handgun slaying of 20-year-old Marie Yoho Maier (white). Motive: marital strife. The killer was hanged at Wheeling on November 18, 1892. Source: *Wheeling Daily Intelligencer*, 4/5/92 (1:1), 4/6/92 (5:1) and 11/19/92 (5:1).

Allen Harrison (white, age 26). *Murder.* The crime was committed on 4/2/-1892 in Cabell County. Executed for the handgun slaying of 15-year-old Bettie Adams (white). Motive: unreciprocated love. This killer was hanged at Huntington on November 22, 1892. Source: *Wheeling Daily Intelligencer*, 4/4/92 (1:3) and 11/23/92 (1:1); *Wheeling Register,* 11/23/92 (1:1).

1894

John Hardy (black, age not recorded). *Murder*. The crime was committed on or about 1/15/1893 in McDowell County. Executed for the handgun slaying of Thomas Drews (black, age not recorded). Motive: gambling dispute. This black-on-black killer was hanged at Welch on January 19, 1894. Source: *Wheeling Intelligencer*, 10/13/93 (2:1) and 1/20/94 (1:4); *Wheeling Register*, 10/13/93 (2:1) and 1/20/94 (1:4). (The original court papers for this case have not survived.)

Washington Adkins (white, age 50). *Murder.* The crime was committed on 11/11/1893 in Fayette County. Executed for the handgun slaying of 42-year-old Isaac Radford (white). Motive: robbery and home invasion. Adkins was hanged at Fayetteville on July 20, 1894. Source: *Charleston (WV) Evening Mail,* 7/20/94 (1:1). See also 1880 U.S. Census (Fayette Co., WV), which notes Radford, and the census for Wayne Co., WV, which notes Adkins.

John W. McFarland (black, age 19). *Murder.* The crime was committed on or about 8/15/1893 in McDowell County. Executed for the handgun slaying of George Andrews (black, age not recorded). Motive: umbrage over a petty debt. This black-on-black killer was hanged at Welch on July 20, 1894. Source: *Wheeling Daily Register*, 7/21/94 (4:4). (The original court papers for this case have not survived.)

1895

Andrew J. Scott (black, age 27). *Murder.* The crime was committed on 5/3/1895 in Jefferson County. Uxoricide. Executed for the poisoning of 20-year-old Elizabeth M. Scott (black) by putting arsenic in her tea. Motive: marital breakdown. Andrew Scott was a bantam of a man, 5'3' tall and weighing just 120 pounds. His wife was described as a neighborhood "easy girl" who flaunted her infidelity to such an extent that she would watch her lovers beat up her husband. The truth of this is impossible to determine so many years later, but it did nothing to mitigate the degree of Scott's guilt—at least not in the eyes of the law. He was hanged at Charles Town on October 4, 1895. Source: *Virginia Free Press* (Charles Town, WV), 5/8/95 (3:2) and 10/9/95 (3:2); *Wheeling Register*, 10/5/95 (3:2).

James Nichols (black, age 28). *Murder.* The crime was committed on 8/31/1895 in Fayette County. Executed for the handgun slaying of Henry Carr (black, age not recorded). Motive: rivalry for a white prostitute. The killer was hanged at Fayetteville on December 13, 1895. Source: *Wheeling Intelligencer*, 12/14/95 (1:6); *Wheeling Register,* 12/14/95 (1:2).

1897

Clark Lewis (black, age about 21). *Murder.* The crime was committed on 4/22/1896 in Fayette County. Executed for the strangulation of Charles Gibson (white, age not recorded), whose head was also smashed with a rock to make sure that he could not be revived. Motive: adultery and financial reward. The victim's wife was a bawdy type who ran a "disorderly house" (to use the polite vernacular of that era). Her husband had made the mistake of trying to clean up the place. Clark Lewis was hanged for the part he played in this crime at Fayetteville on June 25, 1897. Source: *Wheeling Register*, 3/29/97 (1:4), 4/2/97 (3:2) and 6/26/97 (1:1); *Charleston (WV) Daily Gazette*, 6/26/97 (1:1) and 11/13/97 (1:1); *Wheeling Intelligencer*, 6/26/97 (1:3) and 11/13/97 (1:2).

Jerry Brown (black, age not recorded). *Rape*. The crime was committed on 2/15/1897 in Fayette County. Indecent assault on the person of 42-year-old Araminta Bays Radford (white). She was the widow of Isaac Radford, for whose murder another man was executed in 1894. The rapist in this present case was hanged at Fayetteville on August 24, 1897. Source: *Charleston (WV) Daily Gazette*, 2/16/97 (1:1) and 8/25/97 (1:1).

Albert Voiers (white, age 21). *Murder.* The crime was committed on 4/22/1896 in Fayette County. Accomplice in the murder of Charles Gibson (white, age not recorded), who had made what turned out to be the fatal mistake of trying to clean up a whorehouse. Voiers connived with the victim's wife (who was the proprietress of said bagnio) and another of her cronies (Clark Lewis) to do away with the reformist. Voiers was hanged at Fayetteville on November 12, 1897. See **Clark Lewis** (executed 6/25/97).

John Morgan, alias "John T. Raines" (white, age 24). *Murder.* The crime was committed on 11/5/1897 in Jackson County. Executed for the hatchet killings of 59-year-old Clora Green, 26-year-old Matilda Pfost and 18-year-old James Green (whites). Motive: none apparent. This killer was hanged at Ripley on December 16, 1897. Source: *Fort Wayne (IN) Gazette*, 12/17/97 (2:1). See also 1880 U.S. Census (Jackson Co., WV), which notes all parties at earlier stages in their lives.

1899

Shep Caldwell (black, age 25). *Murder.* The crime was committed on or about 6/15/1899 in McDowell County. Executed for the shotgun slaying of Rose Crenshaw (black, age not recorded). Motive: lovers' quarrel. This killer was hanged at the State Penitentiary in Moundsville on October 10, 1899. Source: Circuit Court Files (Drawer 134, Case No. 133), McDowell County Courthouse. See also *Wheeling Daily Intelligencer*, 10/10/99 (2:1); *Wheeling Register*, 10/10/99 (5:3).

Thomas Broadenax (black, age 29). *Murder.* The crime was committed on 6/21/1899 in McDowell County. Executed for the handgun slaying of 16-year-old Sherman McFadden (black). Motive: abuse of authority. This miscreant was hanged at the West Virginia State Penitentiary on November 9, 1899. Source: McDowell County Death Register, Vol. 1A, page 23. (Courthouse Records Vault), Welch, WV. See also Circuit Court Files (Drawer 133, Case No. 109), McDowell County Courthouse; *Wheeling Daily Intelligencer*, 11/9/99 (2:4); *Wheeling Register*, 11/9/99 (1:7).

Frank Walker (black, age 24). *Murder.* The crime was committed on 3/19/1899 in Fayette County. Executed for the handgun slaying of 23-year-old Thomas Sanders (black). Motive: obnoxious drunk. Walker died on the state prison gallows on December 15, 1899. Source: *Fayette County (WV) Death Records,*

1866–1899, compiled by Larry G. Shuck (Athens, GA: Iberian Publishing Co., 1994), 128; *Wheeling Daily Intelligencer*, 12/15/99 (5:3) and 12/16/99 (3:1); *Wheeling Register*, 12/16/99 (5:1).

1902

George Carter (black, age not recorded). *Murder.* The crime was committed on 12/12/1900 in Kanawha County. Executed for the handgun slaying of Virgil Whistler (black, age not recorded). Motive: gambling dispute. Carter was hanged on March 21, 1902. Source: *Charleston (WV) Daily Gazette*, 1/18/01 (1:5); *Wheeling Daily Intelligencer*, 3/22/02 (5:5). Appeal: 49 WV 709.

Louis Young (black, age about 22). *Murder.* The crime was committed sometime prior to April 1900 (exact date uncertain) in McDowell County. Executed for the rifle slaying of Anthony Kell (black, age not recorded). Motive: umbrage at having been worsted in a fistfight. Young was hanged on May 1, 1902. Source: *Wheeling Daily Intelligencer*, 5/2/02 (8:6); *Wheeling Register*, 5/2/02 (10:5). (The original court papers for this case have been either lost or destroyed.)

Frank Friday (white, age about 39). *Murder.* The crime was committed on 3/1/1900 in Ohio County. Executed for the handgun slaying of 70-year-old James Hervey (white). Motive: home invasion. This killer was hanged on May 9, 1902. Source: *Wheeling Daily Intelligencer*, 3/2/00 (2:1); *Charleston (WV) Daily Gazette*, 5/10/02 (1:2). See also 1880 U.S. Census (Ohio Co., WV), which notes Mr. Hervey.

John Mooney (white, age about 39). *Murder.* The crime was committed on 3/1/1900 in Ohio County. Accomplice in the handgun slaying of 70-year-old James Hervey (white). Motive: home invasion. Mooney had previously done time in the Ohio State Penitentiary for the 10/21/1890 killing of an Ashtabula police officer named John E. Doran. He was executed by West Virginia authority on May 9, 1902. Source: *Charleston (WV) Daily Gazette*, 5/10/02 (1:2).

Perry Christian (white, age 26). *Murder.* The crime was committed on 3/25/1901 in Fayette County. Executed for the handgun slaying of 46-year-old George W. Dent (white). Motive: brawling. The West Virginia hangman made short work of this killer on June 13, 1902. Source: *Fayette (WV) Journal*, 3/28/01 (1:3) and 6/19/02 (1:5). See also 1900 U.S. Census (Kanawha Co., WV), which notes Mr. Dent.

State Henry (black, age 21). *Murder.* The crime was committed on 10/20/1900 in Wetzel County. Executed for the hammer killing of John Richardson (black, age not recorded). Motive: robbery. The killer was hanged on October 24, 1902. Source: *Moundsville (WV) Echo*, 10/31/02 (2:1). Appeal: 51 WV 283–304. See also 1900 U.S. Census (Wetzel Co., WV), which notes the miscreant.

1903

Wilfred Davis (white, age 20). *Murder.* The crime was committed on 4/11/1902 in Randolph County. Cop killer. Executed for the handgun slaying of 47-year-old Page Campbell Marstiller (white), the police chief at Elkins, West Virginia. Motive: resisting arrest. This murderer was hanged on June 5, 1903. Source: *Sandusky (OH) Evening Star*, 6/6/03 (1:2); *Moundsville (WV) Echo*, 6/12/03 (3:1).

1904

George Williams (black, age 24). *Rape.* The crime was committed on 6/27/1904 in Jefferson County. Indecent assault on the person of 20-year-old Laura Kanode (white), a rookie schoolmarm. The rapist was hanged on September 9, 1904. Source: *Farmer's Advocate* (Charles Town, WV), 7/2/04 (2:2) and 8/6/04 (2:2); *Moundsville (WV) Echo*, 9/16/04 (2:4). See also 1900 U.S. Census (Bedford Co., PA), which notes Miss Kanode.

1908

Frank Johnson, alias "Edward Walton" (black, age 35). *Murder.* The crime was committed on 3/3/1908 in Harrison County. Executed for the handgun slaying of 34-year-old Beulah Martin (black) during the course of a lovers' quarrel. This killer also confessed to four other murders: an unnamed black man at Blossburg, Alabama, in 1896; Edith Hannon (black) at Chicago in August 1904; an unidentified black man in July 1906; and a black lady named Mamie Gill near Wellsburg, West Virginia, in 1907. It is worth noting that if Johnson was indeed a serial killer who preyed exclusively on his fellow blacks (as his record indicates), he was far from being the only one. Numerous other examples have been found, but none received the degree of scrutiny accorded their Caucasian counterparts. As for Frank Johnson himself, he was hanged on July 17, 1908. Source: *Clarksburg (WV) News*, 3/4/08 (1:1); *Moundsville Weekly Echo*, 7/24/08 (3:1).

1909

Arthur Brown (black, age 22). *Murder.* The crime was committed on 4/20/1909 in McDowell County. Executed for the handgun slaying of 18-year-old Robert Shannon (white). Motive: robbery. The killer was hanged on August 27, 1909. A rough-and-tumble coal-mining county, McDowell had a homicide rate that was possibly one of the worst in the nation per capita. On-site research with original archival materials there made this fact plainly evident. Arthur Brown was one of many drawn from that localized pool. He was also one of the few who actually went to his death on the gallows. Source: Circuit Court Case Files (Drawer 147, Case No. 1731), McDowell County Courthouse Records Room; *Wheeling Intelligencer*, 8/28/09 (1:3); *Wheeling Register*, 8/28/09 (4:4).

1910

Thomas Wayne (black, age 30). *Murder.* The crime was committed on 8/17/1910 in Fayette County. Executed for the fatal strangulation of 17-year-old Lottie Ailiff (white). Motive: robbery and sexual assault. The killer was hanged on December 23, 1910. Source: *Fayette (WV) Journal*, 8/18/10 (1:1), 8/25/10 (1:1) and 12/29/10 (1:6); *Charleston (WV) Gazette*, 12/24/10 (1:1).

1911

Frank Stevenson (black, age 26). *Murder.* The crime was committed on 9/21/

1906 in Mercer County. Executed for the handgun slaying of roughly 22-year-old Boles Blagman (white). Motive: adultery and miscegenation. The killer was hanged on February 17, 1911. Source: *Wheeling Intelligencer*, 2/18/11 (1:1); *Wheeling Register*, 2/18/11 (1:6). Appeal: 64 WV 392–400. A search of the Mercer County Circuit Court Records Room for the original file for this case was futile.

Jesse Cook (white, age 22). *Murder.* The crime was committed on 12/24/1910 in McDowell County. Executed for the knife fight killing of Frank Bennett (white, age not recorded). Motive: uncertain. The killer never wavered in a claim of self-defense and there were no actual witnesses. One report said that Bennett had accused Cook of improper conduct toward his wife. Whatever the truth, Jesse Cook was hanged at the West Virginia State Penitentiary on March 10, 1911. Source: *Wheeling Intelligencer*, 3/11/11 (1:7); *Moundsville (WV) Journal*, 3/16/11 (2:4:1).

William Furbish (black, age 28). *Rape.* The crime was committed on 12/24/1910 in Lewis County. Indecent assault on the person of 42-year-old Flora Anglin (white). Venue changed from Lewis County to Harrison County. The rapist was hanged on March 17, 1911. Source: *Charleston (WV) Gazette*, 12/27/10 (1:2); *Wheeling Intelligencer*, 3/18/11 (1:1); *Moundsville (WV) Journal*, 3/23/11 (2:5:6). See also 1910 U.S. Census (Lewis Co., WV), which notes Flora Anglin.

1913

John Marshall (black, age 19). *Murder.* The crime was committed on or about 10/20/1911 in McDowell County. Uxoricide. Executed for the shotgun slaying of Minnie Marshall (black, age not recorded). Motive: marital discord. This maladjusted young husband was hanged at the West Virginia State Penitentiary on April 4, 1913. Source: Circuit Court Files (Drawer 231, Case No. 2628), McDowell County Courthouse Records Room. See also *Wheeling Intelligencer*, 4/5/13 (1:1); *Wheeling Register*, 4/5/13 (2:4).

James Williams (black, age 22). *Murder.* The crime was committed on 11/30/1912 in McDowell County. Uxoricide, etc. Executed for the handgun slayings of 19-year-old Rose Williams (black) and a black male named Luther Scott (age not recorded). Motive: a love triangle (or so the killer thought). Williams was hanged on April 4, 1913. Source: McDowell County Death Register, Vol. 1, page 218 (McDowell County Courthouse Records Vault). See also *Wheeling Intelligencer*, 4/5/13 (1:1); *Wheeling Register*, 4/5/13 (2:4).

Henry Sterling (black, age 22). *Murder.* The crime was committed on or about 10/15/1912 in McDowell County. Executed for the murder of William Patterson (black, age not recorded), who was shot with a handgun and then had his head chopped off by an ax. Motive: landlord-tenant dispute. This killer was hanged on April 11, 1913. Source: Circuit Court Files (Drawer 231, Case No. 2646), McDowell County Courthouse Records Room. See also *Wheeling Intelligencer*, 4/12/13 (10:5); *Wheeling Register*, 4/12/13 (2:4).

John Hicks (white, age 26). *Murder.* The crime was committed on 11/30/1912 in McDowell County. Executed for the handgun slaying of Mary Thompson (white, age not recorded). Motive: unreciprocated love. This killer was hanged on June 6, 1913. Source: *McDowell (WV) Recorder*, 12/6/12 (1:6) and 3/21/13 (1:2); *Wheeling Intelligencer*, 6/7/13 (1:7); *Wheeling Register*, 6/7/13 (2:4).

1914

Henry Green (black, age 23). *Murder.* The crime was committed on 10/20/1913 in Mingo County. Executed for the handgun slaying of Mary Belle Justice (black, age not recorded). Motive: lovers' quarrel. This black-on-black killer was hanged on March 6, 1914. Source: *Wheeling Intelligencer*, 3/7/14 (13:1). See also 1910 U.S. Census (McDowell Co., WV), which notes Green, he having spent most of his life there.

Silas Jones (black, age 27). *Murder.* The crime was committed on 12/10/1913 in Cabell County. Uxoricide. Executed for the shotgun slaying of Prudential Jones (black, age not recorded)). Motive: suspicion of infidelity. This killer was hanged on July 10, 1914. Source: *Huntington (WV) Herald-Dispatch*, 12/11/13 (12:3), 12/23/13 (3:4), 2/15/14 (1:7), 5/9/14 (12:3); *Wheeling Register*, 6/13/14 (5:5) and 7/11/14 (8:1).

1915

William John Stewart (black, age about 27). *Murder.* The crime was committed on 4/3/1915 in Greenbrier County. Cop killer. Executed for the handgun slaying of 58-year-old George T. Shires (white). Motive: resisting arrest. Stewart atoned for this at the end of a rope on July 2, 1915. Source: *Charleston (WV) Gazette*, 4/5/15 (1:1); *Charleston (WV) Mail*, 4/6/15 (1:5) and 4/7/15 (8:2); *Wheeling Intelligencer*, 7/3/15 (1:4); *Wheeling Register*, 7/3/15 (2:2).

William Thomas (black, age about 30). *Murder.* The crime was committed on 6/19/1914 in Ohio County. Uxoricide. Executed for the handgun slaying of roughly 22-year-old Frieda Thomas (black). Motive: marital discord. This killer was hanged on July 2, 1915. Source: *Wheeling Intelligencer*, 7/3/15 (1:4); *Wheeling Register*, 7/3/15 (2:2).

Matt Jarrell (white, age 28). *Murder.* The crime was committed on 12/21/1914 in Kanawha County. Cop killer, etc. Executed for the handgun slayings of 30-year-old Edward Ratcliff and 46-year-old Silas Frank Nantz (white). Motive: rivalry for a female and resisting arrest, respectively. This miscreant was hanged on July 9, 1915. Source: *Charleston (WV) Gazette*, 12/22/14 (1:1) and 12/24/14 (1:5); *Charleston (WV) Mail*, 12/22/14 (1:4) and 12/23/14 (1:5); *Wheeling Intelligencer*, 7/10/15 (8:1). Appeal: 76 WV 263–267. See also 1910 U.S. Census (Kanawha Co., WV), which notes the victims.

Charles Forrest (black, age not recorded). *Murder.* The crime was committed on 4/29/1915 in McDowell County. Executed for the fatal stabbing of Will Haden (black, age not recorded). Motive: moonshiners' feud. This purveyor of mountain liquor who resorted to homicide to protect his trade was hanged at the West Virginia State Penitentiary on September 10, 1915. Source: Circuit Court Case Files (Drawer 291, Case No. 3407), McDowell County Courthouse Records Room. See also *McDowell Times*, 5/7/15 (1:7); *Wheeling Register*, 9/11/15 (2:4).

1916

Claude Sutton (white, age 24). *Murder.* The crime was committed on 10/30/1915 in Randolph County. Executed for the shotgun slaying of 59-year-old John J. Kennedy (white). Motive: highway robbery. The killer was hanged on August 4, 1916. Source: *Randolph (WV) Enterprise*, 11/4/15 (1:1) and 8/10/16 (1:5); *Wheeling Register*, 8/5/16 (1:5); *Randolph Review*, 8/10/16 (1:1).

James Lay (black, age 25). *Murder.* The crime was committed on 5/8/1916 in McDowell County. Executed for the handgun slaying of 42-year-old William Bowman (white). Motive: robbery. The gallows settled accounts with this killer on September 1, 1916. Source: *McDowell Recorder* (Welch, WV), 5/12/16 (8:3) and 5/19/16 (1:5); *Wheeling Intelligencer*, 9/2/16 (11:1). See also 1910 U.S. Census (Mercer Co., WV), which notes Mr. Bowman.

1919

Hugh Ferguson (black, age 23). *Rape.* The crime was committed on 4/7/1919 in Morgan County. Indecent assault on the person of 26-year-old Lola Zimmerman (white), the details of which have been lost, along with most of this county's court records. Ferguson was hanged on August 6, 1919. Source: *Mansfield (OH) News*, 4/9/19 (1:2); *Morgan Messenger* (Berkeley Springs, WV), 4/10/19 (2:2); *Washington Post*, 8/7/19 (3:6). See also 1930 U.S. Census (Orange Co., CA), which notes Mrs. Zimmerman and her subsequent whereabouts.

1920

Huling Bragg (white, age 25). *Murder.* The crime was committed on 1/12/1920 in Webster County. Cop killer. Executed for the handgun slaying of 33-year-old John Dennis Morton (white). Motive: resisting arrest. Bragg was a double amputee who had lost both of his legs in a railroad mishap several years earlier. This did not prevent him from gunning down a law enforcement officer or from paying the full penalty for doing so. He was hanged on April 30, 1920. Source: *Webster (WV) Echo*, 1/15/20 (1:7); *Wheeling Intelligencer*, 5/1/20 (10:1). See also 1920 U.S. Census (Webster Co., WV), which notes Bragg.

1921

Jacob Lutz (white, age 46). *Murder.* The crime was committed on 2/9/1919 in Taylor County. Cop killer. Executed for the handgun slaying of 64-year-old James Phillips (white), the police chief at Grafton, West Virginia. Motive: resisting arrest. Lutz paid with his life for this on July 22, 1921. Source: *Grafton (WV) Sentinel*, 2/10/19 (1:3) and 2/12/19 (1:7); *Wheeling Intelligencer*, 7/23/21 (12:1). Appeal: 85 WV 330–346. See also 1910 U.S. Census (Taylor Co., WV), which notes Phillips.

Hobart Grimm (white, age 20). *Murder.* The crime was committed on 1/22/1920 in Brooke County. Executed for the murder of Stephen W. Gelchek (white, age not recorded), who was beaten, handcuffed and thrown alive into a freezing river. Motive: bunco. The *corpus delicti* was found on May 27, 1920, and identified on June 13, 1920. The killer was hanged on August 5, 1921. Source: *San-*

dusky (OH) Star Journal, 10/28/20 (5:1) and 2/10/21 (8:2); *Connellsville (PA) Weekly Courier*, 6/17/20 (5:5); *Martinsburg (WV) Journal*, 7/7/21 (1:5); *Wheeling Register*, 8/6/21 (1:5).

Henry Harbor (black, age 31). *Murder.* The crime was committed on 4/11/1921 in McDowell County. Executed for the murder of 30-year-old Mildred Robinson (black), whom he had slashed to death with a butcher knife. Motive: lovers' quarrel. Harbor was hanged at the state prison in Moundsville on October 7, 1921. Source: *Charleston (WV) Daily Mail*, 10/8/21 (2:2). See also 1921 McDowell County death cert. no. 6073.

1922

Leroy Williams (black, age 25). *Rape.* The crime was committed on 12/12/1921 in Kanawha County. Indecent assault on the person of 42-year-old Maud R. Stephens (white), she having been physically maimed in the process. A remorseless sex maniac, Williams was hanged on March 3, 1922. Source: *Charleston (WV) Daily Mail*, 12/12/21 (1:6) and 3/4/22 (1:2). See also 1920 U.S. Census (Kanawha Co., WV), which notes Mrs. Stephens.

Monroe Payton (black, age 49). *Rape.* The crime was committed on 7/3/1921 in Berkeley County. Indecent assault on the person of 10-year-old Hazel Johnson (white). This rapist was hanged on May 4, 1922. Source: *Martinsburg (WV) Journal*, 7/5/21 (1:2); *Gettysburg (PA) Times*, 5/6/22 (4:7).

1923

George Barrage, alias "Mike Visnic" (white, age 39). *Murder.* The crime was committed on 3/11/1923 in Brooke County. Executed for the murder of 35-year-old Katherine Visnic (white), his common-law wife. Motive: he feared that she might inform on him for another homicide. The gallows ensured that he atoned for both crimes on November 2, 1923. Source: *Mansfield (OH) News*, 11/2/23 (1:6); *Charleston (WV) Daily Mail*, 11/3/23 (9:8). See also 1923 Brooke County death cert. no. 3585 and Marshall County death cert. no. 13732.

1924

Philip Connizzaro (white, age 26), **Richard Ferri** (white, age 26) and **Nicola Salamante** (white, age 33). *Murder.* Their crime was committed on 2/16/1922 in Harrison County. All three were hanged for the gunshot slaying of 29-year-old Frank Napolitano (white), a fellow Italian. Motive: failed extortion. They paid the death penalty for their crime on January 4, 1924. Source: *Charleston (WV) Daily Mail*, 4/17/23 (16:3); *Charleston (WV) Gazette*, 1/5/24 (1:8). See also 1922 Harrison County death cert. no. 1740.

Sam Muratore (white, age 41). *Murder.* The crime was committed on 1/20/1923 in Harrison County. Executed for the gunshot slaying of 34-year-old James Papara (white). Motive: failed extortion. This offender was hanged at the West Virginia State Penitentiary on February 15, 1924. Source: *Charleston (WV) Daily Mail*, 4/26/23 (13:2); *Charleston (WV) Gazette*, 2/16/24 (1:7). See also January 1923 Harrison County Death Register.

Tiny McCoy (white, age 23). *Murder.* The crime was committed on 4/6/1924 in Pocahontas County. Executed for the gunshot killings of 22-year-old Hallie

Lee McCoy, 42-year-old Mary Burdette Totten and 19-year-old William Hobart Totten (whites), his wife, mother-in-law and brother-in-law, respectively. Motive: discordant family matters. This killer was hanged on September 12, 1924. Source: *Charleston (WV) Gazette*, 4/8/24 (1:8); *Charleston (WV) Daily Mail*, 9/13/24 (9:8). See also 1924 Pocahontas County death cert. nos. 5281, 5282 and 5283.

1926

Robert Ford (black, age 34). *Murder.* The crime was committed on 5/16/1925 in Harrison County. Executed for the gunshot killing of 52-year-old Edd Woody (black). Motive: rivalry for a female. This killer was hanged on January 29, 1926. Source: *Charleston (WV) Daily Mail*, 1/30/26 (10:2). See also 1925 Harrison County death cert. no. 5985.

Harry Sawyer (black, age 24). *Rape.* The crime was committed on 3/11/1926 in Mingo County. Indecent assault on the person of 25-year-old Olive McCoy Amburgy (white). The rapist was hanged on April 19, 1926. Source: *Charleston (WV) Gazette*, 4/20/26 (1:2). See also 1932 Mingo County death cert. no. 5453, which notes Mrs. Amburgy and her husband.

Philip Euman (black, age 18). *Murder.* The crime was committed on 4/10/1926 in Harrison County. Executed for the gunshot slaying of 19-year-old Charles Shaw (white), a grocer's assistant. Motive: armed robbery. This killer was hanged on August 20, 1926. Source: *Charleston (WV) Gazette*, 4/14/26 (8:8) and 8/21/26 (1:2). See also 1926 Harrison County death cert. no. 5102.

Henry Jackson (black, age 44). *Murder.* The crime was committed on 3/11/1926 in Marshall County. Prison guard killer. Executed for the murder of 25-year-old Earl Langfitt (white—a guard at the West Virginia State Penitentiary), who was stabbed with a contraband shank. This offender was already serving a sentence of life imprisonment for a prior homicide in McDowell County. The gallows ensured that there would be no further problems with him on September 10, 1926. Source: *Charleston (WV) Daily Mail*, 3/12/26 (8:4) and 9/11/26 (10:4); *Charleston (WV) Gazette*, 3/12/26 (1:4) and 9/11/26 (2:8).

1927

Pierce Jefferies (black, age 21). *Rape.* The crime was committed on 11/6/1926 in Greenbrier County. Indecent assault on the person of an adult white female known only as "Mrs. William Vance." Jeffries was hanged at the West Virginia State Penitentiary on February 18, 1927. Original court records of this case disappeared long ago. Source: *Greenbrier Independent* (Lewisburg, WV), 11/12/26 (1:3) and 2/25/27 (1:5); *Wheeling Intelligencer*, 2/19/27 (3:6).

1928

Wesley Homer Swain (white, age 42). *Rape.* The crime was committed on 10/7/1927 in Wood County. Indecent assault on the person of 5-year-old Aurelia Thornton (white). This rapist was hanged on February 3, 1928. Source: *Parkersburg (WV) Sentinel*, 10/8/27 (12:5), 10/10/27 (8:3) and 2/4/28 (1:3).

Andrew Brady (black, age 27). *Rape.* The crime was committed on 8/17/1926 in Hardy County. Indecent assault on the person of 17-year-old Odessa Oates (white). The rapist was hanged on March 30, 1928. Source: *Charleston (WV) Gazette*, 11/13/26 (8:6) and 3/31/28 (1:5).

Lawrence Fike (white, age 31). *Murder.* The crime was committed on 5/11/1928 in Preston County. Executed for the murder of 50-year-old Elroy Leonard (white), a storekeeper who was found on the floor of his establishment with his head cracked open. Motive: robbery. The killer was hanged on August 10, 1928. Source: *Charleston (WV) Daily Mail*, 5/15/28 (3:1), 5/25/28 (1:5) and 8/11/28 (3:8); *Charleston (WV) Gazette*, 8/11/28 (1:6).

1929

Henry Grogan (black, age 19). *Rape.* The crime was committed on 4/17/1928 in Raleigh County. Indecent assault on the person of 27-year-old Mary Delle Akers (white) under circumstances so foul that the victim took her own life. She died of a self-inflicted gunshot wound on June 25, 1928. Her attacker was hanged on February 8, 1929. Source: *Charleston (WV) Daily Mail*, 4/19/28 (2:1), 6/1/28 (8:2), 6/28/28 (2:3); *Charleston (WV) Gazette*, 2/9/29 (1:8). See also 1928 Raleigh County death cert. no. 8181.

Theodore Carr (white, age 50). *Murder.* The crime was committed on 10/30/1928 in Pocahontas County. Executed for the shotgun slayings of 46-year-old Maggie Carr and 27-year-old Lock Cunningham Sharp (both white), his wife and a neighbor, respectively. Motive: land dispute. This killer was hanged on June 14, 1929. Source: *Charleston (WV) Daily Mail*, 6/15/29 (1:5); *Charleston (WV) Gazette*, 6/15/29 (1:5). See also Marlinton (WV) Burial Records (Sharp Cemetery and Clawson Cemetery), which note all parties.

Millard F. Morrison (white, age 24) and **Walter Willmot** (white, age 21). *Murder.* Their crime was committed on 5/8/1929 in Kanawha County. Both were executed for the handgun slaying of 38-year-old Frank E. Bowen (white). Motive: carjacking. These culprits were hanged on September 13, 1929. Source: *Charleston (WV) Daily Mail*, 5/9/29 (1:8); *Trenton (NJ) Evening Times*, 6/4/29 (3:4); *Charleston (WV) Gazette*, 9/14/29 (1:8).

1930

Walter Crabtree (white, age 35). *Murder.* The crime was committed on 12/18/1929 in Hampshire County. Executed for the shotgun slayings of three white males: 59-year-old Henry Carter Inskeep (a justice of the peace), 60-year-old Benjamin E. Miller (the town jailer at Romney, West Virginia) and 20-year-old Edward Malcolm Wolford, a bystander. Motive: revenge for a perceived injustice. This killer was hanged on May 9, 1930. Source: *Charleston (WV) Gazette*, 1/10/30 (8:1) and 5/10/30 (1:8). See also 1929 Hampshire County death cert. nos. 16712, 16713 and 16714.

Roosevelt Darnell (white, age 25). *Murder.* The crime was committed on 6/8/1930 in Greenbrier County. Executed for the sniper killing of 23-year-old William Clarence Holbrooke (white). Motive: personal animosity. This self-defeating marksman was hanged on November 14, 1930. Source: *Charleston (WV) Gazette*, 11/15/30 (1:8). See also 1930 Greenbrier County death cert. no. 7615.

1931

William Claude Adams (white, age 40). *Murder.* The crime was committed on 10/1/1930 in Mingo County. Executed for the handgun slayings of 28-year-old Flossie Cobern Adams, 45-year-old Cynthia Maguire and 55-year-old Mallie Campbell (whites), his wife and two female relatives. Motive: family problems. Adams was hanged on February 20, 1931. Source: *Charleston (WV) Gazette*, 10/2/30 (1:1) and 10/3/30 (1:3); *Wheeling Register*, 2/21/31 (1:7). See also 1930 U.S. Census (Mingo Co., WV), for additional victim information.

Emory Stephens (white, age 24). *Murder.* The crime was committed on 10/4/1930 in Mingo County. Executed for the murder of 24-year-old Leonard Ooten (white), whose skull was fractured by a blow from an unknown blunt instrument. Motive: robbery. The killer was hanged on February 20, 1931. Source: *Charleston (WV) Gazette*, 10/6/30 (3:1) and 2/21/31 (1:6).

Frank Hyer (white, age 53). *Murder.* The crime was committed on 12/19/1930 in Pocahontas County. Uxoricide. Executed for the beating and stomping death of 52-year-old Eva McGann Hyer (white). Motive: alcoholism and a drunkard's penchant for blaming his problems on everyone except himself. The noose literally tore his head off when he plunged through the gallows trap on June 19, 1931. Source: *Charleston (WV) Daily Mail*, 12/21/30 (13:7) and 6/20/31 (1:5); *Charleston (WV) Gazette*, 6/20/31 (1:6). See also 1930 U.S. Census (Pocahontas Co., WV), which notes this ill-fated couple.

1932

Harry Powers (white, age 45). *Murder.* The crimes for which he paid with his life were committed on or about 8/1/1931 in Harrison County. Multiple killer and child killer. Executed for the murders of 50-year-old Dorothy Pressler Lemke, 47-year-old Asta Buick Eicher, 14-year-old Greta Eicher, 12-year-old Harry Eicher and 9-year-old Annabel Eicher (whites), the latter four being a mother and her three children. All of the victims were strangled, and they also had their skulls bored through by the business end of a ball-peen hammer. Motive: bunco and financial gain. A pudgy misfit of a man, Powers came to be almost unanimously regarded as the nastiest criminal that West Virginia ever produced. He used to troll for lovelorn women through letter-writing clubs and lure them to their doom with honeyed words—the same technique employed by predators who nowadays misuse the Internet for such purposes. Harry Powers was hanged by the neck until dead on March 18, 1932. Source: *Charleston (WV) Gazette*, 8/29/31 (1:8), 8/30/31 (1:5), 8/31/31 (1:8) and 3/19/32 (1:1); *Real Detective*, 12/31 and 12/51; *Daring Detective*, 12/35; *Official Detective*, 10/15/36; *Front Page Detective*, 12/36 and 10/61; *Crime Detective*, 10/46; *Master Detective*, 12/47 and 11/53.

James Blount (black, age 32). *Murder.* The crime was committed on 12/10/1931 in Greenbrier County. Executed for the shotgun slaying of 27-year-old Jesse Mupps (black). Motive: simmering dispute. Blount was hanged on May 13, 1932. Source: *Charleston (WV) Gazette*, 2/3/32 (10:7) and 5/14/32 (1:5). See also 1931 Greenbrier County death cert. no. 14799 and 1932 Marshall County death cert. no. 6694.

1933

Omer Brill (white, age 21). *Murder.* The crime was committed on 5/16/1933 in Hardy County. Executed for the handgun slayings of 53-year-old Lydia M. Burch and 17-year-old Esther Beatrice Burch (both white), a mother and daughter. Motive: robbery. This killer was hanged on August 10, 1933. Source: *Charleston (WV) Gazette*, 5/18/33 (1:2) and 8/11/33 (1:4); *Charleston (WV) Daily Mail*, 8/11/33 (1:4). See also 1933 Hardy County death cert. nos. 7073 and 7074.

Leo Fraser (white, age 30). *Murder.* The crime was committed on 7/25/1933 in Jackson County. Cop killer, etc. Executed for the handgun slaying of 49-year-old Roy L. Shamblin (white), a Kanawha County deputy sheriff. Motive: attempted rescue of another man from police custody—19-year-old Ralph Harper (white), who was also shot dead (albeit unintentionally). The gunman was hanged on November 24, 1933. Source: *Charleston (WV) Gazette*, 7/26/33 (1:7) and 11/25/33 (1:8); *Master Detective*, 4/34; *Intimate Detective*, 2/42.

Joe Corey (white, age 38). *Murder.* The crime was committed on 7/11/1932 in Kanawha County. Executed for the handgun slayings of 44-year-old Ada Ghiz Corey (his wife) and 37-year-old Katherine Ghiz (white), that woman's cousin by marriage. Motive: family squabble. All parties were of Syrian origin. The killer was hanged on December 8, 1933. Source: *Charleston (WV) Daily Mail*, 7/12/32 (1:2); *Charleston (WV) Gazette*, 7/12/32 (1:4), 7/14/32 (1:4) and 12/9/33 (1:2).

1935

Greeley Blankenship (white, age 30). *Murder.* The crime was committed on 9/5/1934 in Mingo County. Executed for the handgun slaying of 48-year-old John Christofane (white). Motive: love triangle. This killer was hanged on January 7, 1935. Source: *Charleston (WV) Gazette*, 9/6/34 (7:3) and 1/8/35 (1:6).

Robert Branch (black, age 42). *Murder.* The crime was committed on 2/18/1935 in Ohio County. Executed for the killing of 28-year-old Brady Hill (white), who was slashed to death with the jagged stump of a broken bottle. Motive: drunken brawl. The killer was stone sober when he plunged through the gallows trap on July 19, 1935. Source: *Charleston (WV) Gazette*, 6/28/35 (12:4), 7/7/35 (11:8) and 7/20/35 (1:6). See also 1935 Ohio County death cert. no. 2667.

1937

Frank Pramesa, alias "Frank Pratz" (white, age 26). *Murder.* The crime was committed on 7/15/1936 in Brooke County. Executed for the shotgun slaying of 45-year-old Louis Thames (white). Motive: love triangle. Frank Pramesa went to the gallows on April 14, 1937. Source: *Charleston (WV) Gazette*, 7/17/36 (16:1), 7/19/36 (1:8), 4/14/37 (1:6) and 4/15/37 (1:6); *Crime Detective*, 2/50.

William Beckner (white, age 23). *Murder.* The crime was committed on 5/6/1936 in Kanawha County. Executed for the shotgun slaying of 64-year-old Joseph S. Page (white). Motive: robbery. Beckner was hanged on June 25, 1937. Source: *Charleston (WV) Gazette*, 6/24/36 (1:7) and 6/26/37 (1:6); *Charleston (WV) Daily Mail*, 6/26/37 (1:7). See also 1936 Kanawha County death cert. no. 7363.

Mervin Brown (black, age 23). *Murder.* The crime was committed on 6/26/1937 in Mercer County. Executed for the killing of 85-year-old James Garland (black), who was found with his head caved in. Motive: financial gain. This murderer was hanged on September 10, 1937. Source: *Charleston (WV) Gazette,* 6/29/37 (3:1); *Charleston (WV) Daily Mail,* 7/29/37 (16:3) and 9/11/37 (1:7).

William Read (white, age 25). *Murder.* The crime was committed on 11/25/1936 in Braxton County. Executed for the murder of 34-year-old William Earle Dollman (white), who was knocked unconscious and then burned alive when the killer torched his automobile. Motive: robbery and carjacking. Read is confirmed to have also murdered a Maryland man four days before Dollman was killed. The victim in that case was an aging farmer named Ellwood Matthews (white, age 68). Read and two confederates followed Matthews after he had withdrawn some money from a Silver Springs bank. They beat him up and stole his cash. Read then shot Matthews in the back and made extra sure that he was dead by firing three more bullets into his head. Read's accomplices had not expected this, thinking that they were only going to jump Matthews and grab his money. Read terrified them into helping throw the body of the murdered farmer into Burnt Mills Creek, where it was found on December 13. This murderer was hanged at the West Virginia State Penitentiary on November 5, 1937. Source: *Daily Mail* (Hagerstown, MD), 12/14/36 (7:1); *Charleston (WV) Daily Mail,* 11/6/37 (1:6); *Charleston (WV) Gazette,* 11/6/37 (1:5); *Greensboro (NC) Record,* 12/25/36 (1:1); *Daring Detective,* 8/37; *Master Detective,* 11/37.

1938

Orville Adkins (white, age 25), **Arnett Booth** (white, age 46) and **John Travis** (white, age 25). *Murder.* Their crime was committed on 11/1/1937 in Cabell County. All three were executed for the forcible abduction of 79-year-old James I. Seder (white), who died of exposure after having been left tied up in an abandoned mineshaft. Motive: ransom. These kidnappers were hanged by their necks until dead on March 21, 1938. Source: *Charleston (WV) Daily Mail,* 3/22/38 (1:2); *Charleston (WV) Gazette,* 3/22/38 (1:5); *Official Detective,* 3/16/38; *Real Detective,* 4/38; *Daring Detective,* 6/38; *Actual Detective,* 6/1/38; *Headline Detective,* 5/43; *Master Detective,* 6/62.

Raymond Styers (white, age 29). *Murder.* The crime was committed on 12/23/1936 in Ohio County. Executed for the handgun slaying of 40-year-old Anna Bris (white). Motive: burglary gone awry. This killer was hanged on May 13, 1938. Source: *Charleston (WV) Daily Mail,* 12/28/36 (1:4) and 5/14/38 (1:7); *Front Page Detective,* 10/41.

1940

Byzantine Hartman (white, age 28). *Murder.* The crime was committed on 4/21/1940 in Upshur County. Cop killer. Executed for the shotgun slaying of 46-year-old Wilbur Hoy Grubb (white), lawfully empowered constable for the town of Buckhannon. Motive: resisting arrest. The murderer was hanged on June 28, 1940. Source: *Charleston (WV) Gazette,* 4/24/40 (3:1) and 6/29/40 (1:8).

Paul Tross (black, age 41). *Rape.* The crime was committed on 6/2/1940 in Mineral County. Indecent assault on the person of a 23-year-old white female whose name is withheld. The rapist was hanged on December 6, 1940. Source: *Charleston (WV) Daily Mail*, 6/4/40 (5:2) and 12/7/40 (3:6).

1945

James Chambers (black, age 33). *Murder.* The crime was committed on 1/20/1945 in Randolph County. Executed for the murder of 73-year-old Lucy Ward (white), who was slashed to death in the immediate aftermath of a sexual assault. Chambers was already serving a sentence of life imprisonment in the Huttonsville Correctional Facility for another murder when he escaped to commit a second one. This previous crime had been perpetrated in Wyoming County on 4/1/1935 when he deliberately slashed the throat of a 38-year-old black woman named Mabel McIntyre, who had objected to his "improper relations" with her 13-year-old daughter. Chambers was hanged on March 30, 1945. He is another example of how "life imprisonment" gives the public a false sense of security. Source: *Charleston (WV) Gazette*, 1/22/45 (1:2) and 3/31/45 (6:1); *Beckley (WV) Post-Herald*, 7/19/35 (9:1). See also 1930 U.S. Census (Raleigh Co., WV), which notes Mabel McIntyre, and *West Virginia Deaths Index* (1935), which notes her demise.

William Turner (white, age 29). *Murder.* The crime was committed on 7/31/1945 in Preston County. Executed for the rifle slaying of 15-year-old Darla Dean Pratt (white). Motive: personal grudge. This killer was hanged on December 28, 1945. Source: *Charleston (WV) Daily Mail*, 12/29/45 (1:6); *Charleston (WV) Gazette*, 12/29/45 (1:6); *Real Detective*, 6/46; *Master Detective*, 8/46 and 10/57.

1946

Richard Lee Collins (white, age 22). *Murder.* The crime was committed on 4/18/1946 in Kanawha County. Executed for the handgun slaying of 39-year-old Denver Delmas Hill (white male). Motive: carjacking. Collins was hanged on October 11, 1946. Source: *Charleston (WV) Daily Mail*, 4/19/46 (1:7) and 10/12/46 (1:8); *Charleston (WV) Gazette*, 4/19/46 (1:2) and 10/12/46 (1:6); *Real Detective*, 11/46. See also 1946 Kanawha County death cert. no. 4208.

1947

William Gordon (white, age 21). *Murder.* The crime was committed on 4/1/1946 in Mercer County. Executed for the shotgun slaying of 38-year-old Josephine Carr (white). Motive: robbery. This killer went to the gallows on January 3, 1947. Source: *Charleston (WV) Daily Mail*, 4/2/46 (1:3); *Charleston (WV) Gazette*, 1/4/47 (1:1); *Official Detective*, 11/46; *Front Page Detective*, 12/46; *Crime Detective*, 8/47; *Master Detective*, 11/54.

1948

Paul Burton (white, age 33). *Murder.* The crime was committed on 7/29/1947 in Logan County. Executed for the gunshot killing of 23-year-old Willard Simpson (white). Motive: labor feud. Burton died at the end of a rope on January 2, 1948. Source: *Charleston (WV) Daily Mail*, 1/3/48 (1:8); *Charleston (WV) Gazette*, 1/3/48 (1:5).

Mark McCauley (white, age 36). *Murder.* The crime was committed on 9/9/1946 in Mineral County. Cop killer. Executed for the handgun slaying of 51-year-old Orpha Gay Hovatter (the sheriff of Tucker County) and shotgun slaying of 44-year-old WVSP Sgt. Joseph Pierce Horne (both white). Motive: resisting arrest. McCauley was hanged on January 30, 1948. Source: *Charleston (WV) Daily Mail*, 9/10/46 (1:1) and 1/31/48 (1:2); *Real Detective*, 1/49; *Master Detective*, 7/49. See also Mineral County Register of Deaths (1946), entries at date.

Matthew Perison (black, age 33). *Murder.* The crime was committed on 4/20/1948 in Logan County. Uxoricide, etc. Hanged for the ax murders of 28-year-old Clancy Martin Perison, 70-year-old Jack Martin and 54-year-old Pearl Martin (blacks), his wife and in-laws. Motive: family flare-up. This killer was hanged on September 23, 1948. Source: *Charleston (WV) Gazette*, 4/21/48 (5:3), 7/10/48 (2:5) and 9/24/48 (1:4).

Lemuel Thomas Steed (black, age 28). *Murder.* The crime was committed on 7/1/1948 in Fayette County. Executed for the handgun slaying of 50-year-old Loren Robert McClurg (white). Motive: robbery. This killer was sent to the gallows on October 15, 1948. Source: *Charleston (WV) Daily Mail*, 7/2/48 (1:1) and 10/16/48 (1:7); *Charleston (WV) Gazette*, 7/2/48 (1:2) and 10/16/48 (1:2); *Front Page Detective*, 1/49; *Crime Detective*, 4/49.

1949

Bud Peterson (black, age 53). *Murder.* The crime was committed on 6/29/1947 in Logan County. Executed for the gunshot killing of 40-year-old Bessie Wright (black). Motive: home invasion. This black-on-black marauder was hanged on February 25, 1949. Source: *Charleston (WV) Daily Mail*, 6/30/47 (2:4) and 2/26/49 (1:6).

1951

Harry Burdette (white, age 25) and **Fred Painter** (white, age 31). *Murder.* Their crime was committed on 7/31/1949 in Kanawha County. Both were executed for the killing of 31-year-old Edward Conrad O'Brien (white), whom they beat and kicked to death during a street brawl. Motive: general rowdiness. These killers went to the electric chair on March 26, 1951. Source: *Charleston (WV) Daily Mail*, 8/1/49 (1:7) and 3/27/51 (1:2); *Charleston (WV) Gazette*, 8/1/49 (1:3).

James William Hewlett (white, age 22). *Murder.* The crime was committed on 10/24/1950 in Cabell County. Executed for the handgun slaying of 40-year-old Julian Edward Buie (white). Motive: robbery. The killer was executed by high voltage on April 10, 1951. Source: *Charleston (WV) Daily Mail*, 10/25/50 (1:4) and 4/11/51 (1:1); *Charleston (WV) Gazette*, 10/25/50 (1:5); *Real Detective*, 2/51. See also 1950 Cabell County death cert. no. 12702.

1953

Oschel Gardner (white, age 23). *Murder.* The crime was committed on 10/14/1952 in Mason County. Executed for the shotgun slaying of 54-year-old Roy Jackson (white). Motive: robbery. The electric chair provided Gardner with his final seat on April 17, 1953. Source: *Charleston (WV) Daily Mail*, 10/16/52 (1:8) and 4/18/53 (1:8).

1954

Thomas Lee Ingram (black, age 31). *Murder.* The crime was committed on 9/12/1953 in McDowell County. Child killer, etc. Electrocuted for the butcher knife slayings of 30-year-old Zenobia Irene Bigelow and 7-year-old Melba Lois Bigelow (both black), a mother and her daughter. Motive: uncertain. The killer was executed on March 27, 1954. Source: *Charleston (WV) Daily Mail*, 9/13/53 (1:4) and 3/28/54 (1:2); *Charleston (WV) Gazette*, 3/28/54 (1:2).

1956

Robert Lee Hopkins (white, age 27). *Murder.* The crime was committed on 2/28/1956 in Kanawha County. Electrocuted for the killing of 30-year-old Thomas Lantz Ervine (white), who was bludgeoned with a lug wrench, stripped of his clothes and thrown out into a wintry night, where he perished from exposure. Motive: robbery. The killer was executed on September 7, 1956. Source: *Charleston (WV) Gazette*, 3/1/56 (1:1) and 9/8/56 (1:1).

1958

Eugene Henry Linger (white, age 29). *Murder.* The crime was committed on 12/8/1956 in Upshur County. Executed for the shotgun slaying of 40-year-old William H. White (white). Motive: robbery. The electric chair evened the score with Linger on June 5, 1958. Source: *Charleston (WV) Gazette*, 12/10/56 (12:2) and 6/6/58 (1:4); *Charleston (WV) Daily Mail*, 6/6/58 (17:3).

Larry Paul Fudge (white, age 26). *Murder.* The crime was committed on 1/4/1958 in Cabell County. Executed for the knifepoint killing of 51-year-old Inez Booth (white) during the course of a sexual assault. The electric chair marked this case closed on July 1, 1958. Source: *Charleston (WV) Daily Mail*, 1/7/58 (2:5); *Charleston (WV) Gazette*, 7/2/58 (1:4).

1959

Elmer David Bruner (white, age 39). *Murder.* The crime was committed on 5/27/1957 in Cabell County. Electrocuted for the killing of 58-year-old Ruby H. Miller (white), whom he battered to death with a hammer. Motive: burglary gone awry. Bruner was executed at the state prison on April 3, 1959. Source: *Charleston (WV) Gazette*, 5/28/57 (1:1) and 4/4/59 (1:3); *Front Page Detective*, 9/57; *Master Detective*, 9/57 and 1/63.

Appendix: Preliminary Lists of Executions Before 1866

Delaware

Warning: These lists are incomplete and subject to revision.
(B) = Burned at the stake
(R) = Recidivist (had been sentenced to death on a previous conviction, obtained clemency and then gone on to offend anew)

Date of Execution	Name of Offender	Venue	Specific Felony
03/15/1688	Judith Rowe	Kent	Murder
05/09/1722	Eleanor Moore	New Castle	Murder
03/ /1730	Unidentified Man	New Castle	Arson
07/ /1731	Unidentified Negro	New Castle	Rape
09/10/1731	Catherine Bevan (B)	New Castle	Murder and Petty Treason
09/10/1731	Peter Murphy	New Castle	Murder and Petty Treason
05/ /1747	Terrence White	New Castle	Burglary
11/ /1748	Thomas White	New Castle	Bestiality
06/ /1749	John Gillespie	New Castle	Burglary
06/ /1749	John Roach	New Castle	Burglary
06/ /1749	John Slain	New Castle	Rape
09/ /1750	Negro Phil	Kent	Burglary
02/08/1752	Alice Cunningham (R)	Kent	Murder
02/08/1752	Archibald Cunningham	Kent	Murder
08/27/1754	James Duffy	Kent	Murder
06/ /1757	David Brown	New Castle	Burglary
06/ /1757	James Coughlin	New Castle	Burglary
06/ /1757	Margaret Sexton	New Castle	Murder
05/ /1761	Eleanor Evans	Kent	Murder
06/09/1770	Hugh Barclay	New Castle	Burglary
09/11/1770	Negro Charles	Kent	Rape
10/06/1773	Negro George	Kent	Murder
09/15/1783	Cheney Clow	Kent	Murder
05/ /1784	John Green	New Castle	Murder

Date of Execution	Name of Offender	Venue	Specific Felony
11/28/1786	Negro Ben	Kent	Rape
12/21/1787	Sarah Kirk	New Castle	Mariticide
09/14/1792	Negro Ben	New Castle	Rape
12/18/1792	John Morris	Kent	Rape
04/08/1806	Elihu Prettyman	Sussex	Murder
04/21/1807	George Parker	Kent	Rape
04/13/1813	Henry Brereton	Sussex	Murder
04/13/1813	John Griffith	Sussex	Murder
12/21/1815	John Smith	New Castle	Murder
04/18/1820	William Piper	Sussex	Murder
01/05/1822	Henry Douglass	Kent	Murder
12/31/1822	Jacob Elliott	New Castle	Murder
11/08/1825	Elisha Sharp	Sussex	Murder
11/08/1831	Robert Morris	Sussex	Murder
06/17/1839	Thomas Morgan	New Castle	Murder
02/08/1849	Perry Bailey	New Castle	Rape
07/31/1851	James Anderson	New Castle	Murder
07/31/1851	Empson Bayard	New Castle	Murder
09/08/1852	Samuel Ward	New Castle	Murder
02/10/1860	John Bowen	New Castle	Murder
12/14/1860	Sarah Bradley	Sussex	Murder
12/14/1860	John Cannon*	Sussex	Murder
12/14/1860	Levi Jenkins	Sussex	Rape
12/28/1860	John Cannon*	Kent	Rape
02/13/1863	Thomas Orskins	Kent	Murder

*John Cannon and John Cannon (1860) are two different people.

District of Columbia

Date of Execution	Name of Offender	Specific Felony
10/28/1802	James McGirk	Murder
03/11/1813	Negro Patrick	Attempted Rape
09/02/1853	Daniel Woodward	Murder
06/26/1858	Jesse Powers	Murder
12/13/1861	William Johnston	Army Desertion
01/06/1862	Michael Lanahan	Murder
12/05/1862	John Kessler	Murder
03/06/1863	Augustus Ford	Murder
07/08/1864	Cornelius Tuell	Murder
08/26/1864	Charles Fenton Beavers	Parole Violation
09/30/1864	William Lynch	Army Desertion
11/25/1864	Charles Williams	Murder
03/03/1865	Charles Sperry	Rape
07/07/1865	George Atzerodt	Conspiracy to Commit Murder
07/07/1865	David Herad	Conspiracy to Commit Murder
07/07/1865	Lewis Powell	Conspiracy to Commit Murder
07/07/1865	Mary Surratt	Conspiracy to Commit Murder
11/10/1865	Henry Wirz	Alleged War Crimes

Maryland

(B) = Burned at the stake (G) = Gibbeted after execution
(Q) = Drawn and quartered (R) = Recidivist (had been sentenced to death on a previous occasion, obtained clemency and then gone on to offend anew)

Date of Execution	Name of Offender	Venue	Specific Felony
06/20/1638	Thomas Smith	St. Mary's	Piracy
——1653	Counaweza (Indian)	St. Mary's	Murder
——1653	Skigtamongh (Indian)	St. Mary's	Murder
——1654	William Eltonhead	St. Mary's	Treason
——1654	William Leggatt	St. Mary's	Treason
——1654	John Lewis	St. Mary's	Treason
——1654	John Pedro	St. Mary's	Treason
07/ /1657	Mr. Parr's Servants	Ann Arundel	Petit Treason
10/03/1657	John Dandy (R)	St. Mary's	Murder
07/08/1664	Elizabeth Greene	St. Mary's	Murder
10/04/1664	Negro Jacob	St. Mary's	Rape
01/ /1665	Joseph Fincher	Ann Arundel	Murder
10/ /1665	Two or More Indians	Charles	Not Specified
11/ /1665	Negro Jacob	St. Mary's	Murder
11/ /1665	Two Indians	St. Mary's	Not Specified
01/07/1669	Walter Pake	St. Mary's	Murder
05/08/1669	Anatchom (Indian)	St. Mary's	Not Specified
10/18/1670	Joan Colledge	St. Mary's	Murder
04/14/1671	Negro John	St. Mary's	Murder
04/14/1671	James Sall	St. Mary's	Murder
04/14/1671	Robert Spear	St. Mary's	Murder
04/14/1671	Robert Warby	St. Mary's	Murder
04/17/1671	Isabella Yausley	St. Mary's	Murder
——1681	William Sewick	St. Mary's	Bestiality
10/09/1685	John Edwards	St. Mary's	Burglary
10/09/1685	Rebecca Fowler	St. Mary's	Witchcraft
10/09/1685	Joseph Tomlinson	St. Mary's	Rape
10/09/1685	Richard Vanson	St. Mary's	Murder
12/07/1685	Mary Axell	St. Mary's	Murder
09/20/1687	Joseph Emeritt	St. Mary's	Murder
09/20/1687	Thomas Leister	St. Mary's	Murder
04/28/1691	John Woodcock	St. Mary's	Murder
12/ /1692	Abigail Kimball (B)	St. Mary's	Petit Treason
12/ /1692	William Luffman	St. Mary's	Petit Treason
05/ /1693	Mary Lunt	St. Mary's	Murder
10/ /1693	Jenkin Powell	St. Mary's	Murder
07/ /1696	Unnamed Indian	Ann Arundel	Not Specified
04/ /1701	John Bracher	Ann Arundel	Murder
05/ /1701	Three Felons	Ann Arundel	Uncertain
10/ /1702	George Groves	Ann Arundel	Murder
05/ /1703	William Ward	Ann Arundel	Murder
05/ /1703	Margaret Ward	Ann Arundel	Murder
10/ /1705	Negro Tom	Ann Arundel	Rape
01/ /1706	David Blake	Ann Arundel	Uncertain

Date of Execution	Name of Offender	Venue	Specific Felony
01/ /1706	James Pride	Ann Arundel	Uncertain
08/ /1706	John Patterson	Ann Arundel	Murder
05/ /1707	George Adams	Ann Arundel	Burglary
05/ /1707	Margaret Caine	Ann Arundel	Murder
05/ /1707	Thomas Peacock	Ann Arundel	Burglary
10/ /1707	Griffin Morris	Ann Arundel	Burglary
04/ /1708	Richard Clark (Q)	Ann Arundel	Treason
04/ /1710	Elizabeth Williams	Ann Arundel	Burglary
——1711	Negro Will	Dorchester	Uncertain
07/ /1711	Negro Montillion	Baltimore	Murder
12/ /1711	Negro Boatswain	Baltimore	Murder
04/ /1712	Negro Hector	Ann Arundel	Murder
11/ /1713	Elizabeth Spurrier	Ann Arundel	Murder
11/ /1713	Sarah Tracy	Ann Arundel	Murder
08/ /1718	Negro Mingo	Ann Arundel	Storehouse Robbery
05/ /1719	John DuVall	Ann Arundel	Murder
05/ /1719	Negro Sambo	Ann Arundel	Burglary
11/ /1719	Hugh Marr	Ann Arundel	Rape
05/ /1720	Philip Long	Ann Arundel	Burglary
05/ /1720	William Perry	Ann Arundel	Murder
10/ /1720	John Hutchins	Ann Arundel	Burglary
10/ /1720	Thomas Wright	Ann Arundel	Burglary
05/ /1721	John Boswell	Ann Arundel	Burglary
05/ /1721	Edward Divine	Ann Arundel	Burglary
05/ /1721	John Holmstead	Ann Arundel	Burglary
05/ /1721	Frances Horne	Ann Arundel	Burglary
05/ /1721	Thomas Peign	Ann Arundel	Burglary
05/ /1721	Joseph Stiff	Ann Arundel	Arson
05/ /1721	Robert Strickland	Ann Arundel	Burglary
11/ /1721	Mulatto Daniel	Ann Arundel	Burglary
11/ /1721	John Ford	Ann Arundel	Burglary
11/ /1721	Elizabeth Jones	Ann Arundel	Burglary
11/ /1721	Richard Lee	Ann Arundel	Burglary
11/ /1721	Benjamin Moxon	Ann Arundel	Burglary
11/ /1721	John Plant	Ann Arundel	Burglary
11/ /1721	Isaac Ragg	Ann Arundel	Storehouse Robbery
11/ /1721	Thomas Sodman	Ann Arundel	Burglary
11/ /1721	John Woodworth	Ann Arundel	Burglary
05/ /1722	William Burston	Ann Arundel	Storehouse Robbery
05/ /1722	John Goodman	Ann Arundel	Burglary
05/ /1722	Thomas Lazenby	Ann Arundel	Storehouse Robbery
05/ /1722	George Rogers	Ann Arundel	Burglary
10/ /1722	John Butler	Ann Arundel	Murder
10/ /1722	Peter Fagan	Ann Arundel	Burglary
10/ /1722	Anne Robinson	Ann Arundel	Burglary
05/ /1723	Jasper Andrews (R)	Ann Arundel	Burglary
05/ /1723	Negro Bristoe	Ann Arundel	Burglary
05/ /1723	John Bruington	Ann Arundel	Burglary
05/ /1723	Eleanor Carrah	Ann Arundel	Burglary

Date of Execution	Name of Offender	Venue	Specific Felony
05/ /1723	William Gordon	Ann Arundel	Burglary
05/ /1723	Negress Hannah (G)	Ann Arundel	Murder
05/ /1723	James Jones	Ann Arundel	Burglary
05/ /1723	Mary Reed	Ann Arundel	Privately Stealing
05/ /1723	John Williams	Ann Arundel	Burglary
10/ /1723	Robert Abbott	Ann Arundel	Burglary
10/ /1723	Henry Bishop	Ann Arundel	Murder
10/ /1723	Mary Burrass	Ann Arundel	Privately Stealing
10/ /1723	Thomas Gibbon	Ann Arundel	Burglary
10/ /1723	Mary Mounting	Ann Arundel	Privately Stealing
06/19/1724	Robert Dutch	Cecil	Not Specified
11/27/1726	Patrick Dennison	Talbot	Burglary
11/27/1726	Thomas Jones	Talbot	Burglary
11/27/1726	John Martin	Prince George	Burglary
03/ /1727	Mary Jackson	Kent	Murder
05/08/1727	John Weldon	Ann Arundel	Not Specified
02/01/1728	Richard Lane	Calvert	Murder
11/15/1728	Negro Tom	Cecil	Murder
12/16/1728	Negro Jack	Charles	Burglary
12/16/1728	Negro Jupiter	Charles	Burglary
12/16/1728	Negro Pompey	Charles	Burglary
04/18/1729	Negro Parraway (G)	Prince George	Murder
05/16/1729	Negro Corra (G)	Baltimore	Murder
05/19/1729	Richard Dowman	Talbot	Horse Stealing
05/19/1729	Thomas Garnett	Talbot	Not Specified
05/19/1729	Charles Smith	Talbot	Not Specified
06/17/1729	Negro Babb	Kent	Burglary
11/25/1730	James Boardman	Prince George	Not Specified
11/25/1730	Negro Coacko	Prince George	Not Specified
06/23/1731	Richard Townsin	Baltimore	Murder
01/28/1732	Thomas Burke	Charles	Not Specified
01/28/1732	Henry Hall	Talbot	Not Specified
11/10/1732	Negro Ben	Prince George	Not Specified
11/10/1732	Tom Latter	Prince George	Not Specified
05/16/1733	Negro Stepney (G)	Charles	Rape
10/03/1733	Negro Tom	Ann Arundel	Not Specified
11/14/1733	John Bennett	Prince George	Not Specified
11/14/1733	Negro Harry	Prince George	Not Specified
11/08/1734	Thomas Collins	Ann Arundel	Burglary
11/08/1734	Thomas Johnson	Ann Arundel	Burglary
11/08/1734	Charles Lynch	Ann Arundel	Burglary
01/16/1735	Michael Aley	Queen Anne	Not Specified
08/01/1735	Daniel Sullivan	Cecil	Not Specified
11/10/1736	Negro Anthony	St. Mary's	Not Specified
11/10/1736	John Brewer	Prince George	Storehouse Robbery
11/10/1736	Negro Kildare	Ann Arundel	Not Specified
11/10/1736	Jeremiah Lillie	Somerset	Not Specified
11/10/1736	Negro Sam	Prince George	Not Specified
11/10/1736	Negro Tango	Prince George	Not Specified

Date of Execution	Name of Offender	Venue	Specific Felony
11/10/1736	Jacob Tinmore	Ann Arundel	Not Specified
05/27/1737	Negress Chloe	Ann Arundel	Not Specified
05/27/1737	Indian Jack	Prince George	Not Specified
05/27/1737	Negro Jack	Ann Arundel	Not Specified
05/27/1737	Negro Jago	Ann Arundel	Not Specified
05/27/1737	Richard Wright	Ann Arundel	Not Specified
06/01/1737	Mary Finmore	Queen Anne	Not Specified
06/01/1737	Negro Jack	Charles	Not Specified
11/16/1737	Henry Murphy	Charles	Not Specified
05/26/1738	John Mason	Baltimore	Burglary
06/07/1738	Negress Bess	Prince George	Poisoning
06/07/1738	Negro Lot	Prince George	Poisoning
11/15/1738	James Wood	Charles	Burglary
12/20/1738	Negro Charles	Calvert	Not Specified
02/23/1739	Negro Jack	Ann Arundel	Murder
02/23/1739	Ralph Jones (R)	Ann Arundel	Burglary
03/30/1739	Negress Judy	St. Mary's	Conspiracy to Poison
03/30/1739	Negro Pompey	St. Mary's	Conspiracy to Poison
05/31/1739	John Watson	St. Mary's	Burglary
06/22/1739	William Turner (R)	Ann Arundel	Horse Stealing
07/25/1739	Negro Jupiter	St. Mary's	Not Specified
08/17/1739	Richard Giant	Queen Anne	Murder
08/29/1739	Negro Robin (G)	Ann Arundel	Rape
08/29/1739	Negro Robin	Ann Arundel	Burglary
11/07/1739	James Cating	Kent	Not Specified
12/21/1739	Negro Caesar	Baltimore	Murder
03/26/1740	Negro Abraham	Ann Arundel	Burglary
04/04/1740	Jack Ransom (G)	Prince George	Insurrection
12/26/1740	Negro Hannibal	Charles	Rape
01/14/1741	Negro Davy	Prince George	Burglary
03/06/1741	Nicholas Broaly	Kent	Burglary
03/06/1741	Job Morgan	Kent	Burglary
03/06/1741	John Pinkstone	Kent	Burglary
03/13/1741	Negress Judith (Q)	Queen Anne	Murder
05/15/1741	John Jones	Ann Arundel	Privately Stealing
05/15/1741	Negro Sam	Ann Arundel	Storehouse Robbery
04/28/1742	Negro Ben (Q)	Calvert	Murder
04/28/1742	Negro Caesar (Q)	Calvert	Murder
04/28/1742	Negro Charles (Q)	Calvert	Murder
04/28/1742	Negro Cooper (Q)	Calvert	Murder
04/28/1742	Negro Marlborough (Q)	Calvert	Murder
04/28/1742	Negress Moll (Q)	Calvert	Murder
04/28/1742	Negro Seamore (Q)	Ann Arundel	Murder
05/15/1742	Peter Coleman	Dorchester	Not Specified
07/02/1742	Negro Nacy	Charles	Burglary
08/04/1742	George Roberts	Ann Arundel	Murder
12/06/1742	Negro Liverpool	Somerset	Rape
12/06/1742	Negro Tom	Somerset	Rape
02/02/1743	Negro Mingo	Kent	Not Specified

Date of Execution	Name of Offender	Venue	Specific Felony
06/15/1743	John Lilleston	Ann Arundel	Burglary
07/01/1743	Negro Harry	Prince George	Murder
07/01/1743	Negro Jack	Prince George	Murder
07/22/1743	Negro Frank	Ann Arundel	Burglary
07/22/1743	Negro Jack	Ann Arundel	Burglary
08/26/1743	William Hills	Prince George	Murder
11/22/1743	Negro Peter	St. Mary's	Burglary
12/23/1743	John Malcolm	Ann Arundel	Counterfeiting
12/23/1743	Alexander Taylor	Ann Arundel	Murder
06/06/1744	Negro James	Charles	Not Specified
08/17/1744	Negro Will	Prince George	Storehouse Robbery
10/31/1744	Roger Crooke	Ann Arundel	Horse Stealing
10/31/1744	Robert Davis	Ann Arundel	Storehouse Robbery
05/11/1745	James Barrett	Ann Arundel	Murder
07/26/1745	Negro Cato (Q)	Talbot	Murder
01/03/1746	Negro Jerry	Prince George	Storehouse Robbery
01/03/1746	Negro Quod	Prince George	Storehouse Robbery
05/13/1746	Esther Anderson (B)	Kent	Petit Treason
05/13/1746	Hector Grant	Kent	Petit Treason
05/13/1746	James Horney	Kent	Petit Treason
07/11/1746	Negro Ned	Somerset	Storehouse Robbery
05/13/1747	Thomas Lamb	Prince George	Murder
06/28/1747	Negro Tom	Ann Arundel	Burglary
11/27/1747	Negro Joe	Baltimore	Rape
12/09/1747	Negro York	Ann Arundel	Horse Stealing
08/19/1748	Thomas Hill	Prince George	Burglary
08/19/1748	Mulatto Jack	Prince George	Horse Stealing
09/21/1748	Joseph Humes	Ann Arundel	Burglary
09/21/1748	Matthew Lapear (R)	Ann Arundel	Storehouse Robbery
09/28/1748	Unnamed Negro	Cecil	Murder
10/28/1748	Mulatto James	Charles	Burglary
12/21/1748	William Diskins	Prince George	Horse Stealing
12/21/1748	Negro Tom (G)	Prince George	Murder
05/31/1749	William James	Baltimore	Storehouse Robbery
05/31/1749	George Simonette (R)	Baltimore	Storehouse Robbery
12/13/1749	Negro Jack (G)	Calvert	Rape
12/15/1749	John Murphy	Frederick	Burglary
12/22/1749	Negro Carolina (G)	Cecil	Arson
03/14/1750	Enos Carty	Cecil	Murder
05/25/1750	Negro Jack	Worcester	Burglary
06/20/1750	Thomas Richards	Prince George	Horse Stealing
08/30/1750	Negro Cuffee	Ann Arundel	Horse Stealing
12/13/1750	Negro James	Charles	Storehouse Robbery
12/13/1750	Robert Rustin	Charles	Storehouse Robbery
02/01/1751	Negro Joe (Q)	Cecil	Murder
04/10/1751	Negress Grace	Ann Arundel	Arson
04/10/1751	Negress Jenny	Ann Arundel	Arson
04/12/1751	Negro Tangio	Calvert	Burglary
04/17/1751	John Steadman (G)	Ann Arundel	Murder

Date of Execution	Name of Offender	Venue	Specific Felony
04/17/1751	David Sullivan (G)	Ann Arundel	Murder
04/22/1751	Negro Sharper (G)	Dorchester	Rape
04/29/1751	Jeremiah Swift (G)	Ann Arundel	Murder
06/10/1751	Jacob Windsor	Queen Anne	Horse Stealing
06/26/1751	Onesiphorus Lucas	Ann Arundel	Burglary
11/01/1751	Thomas Bevin	Ann Arundel	Residential Robbery
12/06/1751	Negro Ben	St. Mary's	Burglary
01/10/1752	Martha Bassett	Baltimore	Murder
01/10/1752	Mary Powell	Baltimore	Murder
01/15/1752	John Berry (G)	Baltimore	Murder
05/15/1752	Thomas Hornbrook (R)	Baltimore	Horse Stealing
05/15/1752	James Powell	Ann Arundel	Burglary
06/05/1752	George Wilson (G)	St. Mary's	Murder
08/28/1752	John Batter	Cecil	Burglary
10/19/1752	Terrence Connor	Ann Arundel	Murder
10/20/1752	Negro Joe	Talbot	Burglary
12/29/1752	William Rice	Cecil	Burglary
05/16/1753	John Brown	Ann Arundel	Burglary
05/16/1753	Charles Campbell	Ann Arundel	Storehouse Robbery
05/16/1753	Daniel Spinkse	Ann Arundel	Storehouse Robbery
06/13/1753	Negro Jack	Somerset	Insurrection
12/04/1753	John Barrett (G)	Baltimore	Murder
03/27/1754	Negro Phil	Ann Arundel	Horse Stealing
05/03/1754	Mulatto James (G)	St. Mary's	Murder
05/24/1754	Samuel Knowler	Charles	Burglary
05/24/1754	Yellow Dick	Charles	Burglary
07/03/1754	Negro Caesar	Ann Arundel	Personal Robbery
07/03/1754	Negro Tom	Ann Arundel	Personal Robbery
08/07/1754	Mulatto Toney (G)	Ann Arundel	Murder
08/07/1754	John Wright (G)	Ann Arundel	Murder
09/20/1754	Negro Pompey	Ann Arundel	Storehouse Robbery
11/22/1754	John Williams	Frederick	Horse Stealing
12/27/1754	Negro London	St. Mary's	Not Specified
03/26/1755	Negro Joe (G)	Ann Arundel	Murder
05/15/1755	Edward Brease	Kent	Storehouse Robbery
05/15/1755	John Roberts	Kent	Storehouse Robbery
07/04/1755	Negro Dick (R)	Charles	Burglary
07/04/1755	Negro Jack	Charles	Attempt to Poison
07/04/1755	Negress Jemmy (G)	Charles	Murder
07/04/1755	William Stratton (G)	Charles	Murder
07/04/1755	Negro Toney (G)	Charles	Murder
09/19/1755	Mulatto Bob	St. Mary's	Burglary
10/31/1755	Negro Harry (G)	St. Mary's	Conspiracy to Poison
11/12/1755	Negro Cork (G)	St. Mary's	Conspiracy to Poison
01/16/1756	Negro Joe	St. Mary's	Storehouse Robbery
05/14/1756	John Christopher	Queen Anne	Horse Stealing
05/14/1756	Negro Jack	Kent	Storehouse Robbery
09/03/1756	Negro Ben	Charles	Not Specified
01/28/1757	Negro Simon	Worcester	Burglary

Date of Execution	Name of Offender	Venue	Specific Felony
04/06/1757	Negress Tida	Ann Arundel	Attempt to Poison
04/13/1757	Negro Booz	Dorchester	Burglary
05/27/1757	John Grimshaw (R)	Prince George	Burglary
09/02/1757	Negro Caleb	Baltimore	Conspiracy to Poison
09/02/1757	Negro London	Calvert	Storehouse Robbery
09/02/1757	Negro Reuben	Calvert	Storehouse Robbery
11/09/1758	Maurice Mongall	Baltimore	Storehouse Robbery
08/25/1759	Negro Tomboy	Baltimore	Horse Stealing
10/07/1759	Matthew Dugan	Kent	Murder
11/14/1759	John Burke	Queen Anne	Murder
04/30/1760	James Horner	Dorchester	Rape
10/17/1760	John Harrison	Frederick	Horse Stealing
06/08/1761	Negro Peter (G)	St. Mary's	Murder
07/31/1761	Mulatto Roger	Calvert	Storehouse Robbery
10/07/1761	Negress Rachel	Calvert	Attempt to Poison
10/07/1761	Negro Samuel	Calvert	Attempt to Poison
10/23/1761	Negro Tony	Prince George	Storehouse Robbery
05/05/1762	Negro Cuffee	Ann Arundel	Murder
05/07/1762	Michael Oroonoko	Cecil	Murder
05/26/1762	Richard Crosby (R)	Frederick	Murder
09/03/1762	Negro Jonathan	Charles	Burglary
10/08/1762	Thomas Cooper	Ann Arundel	Storehouse Robbery
10/08/1762	Michael Peck	Frederick	Murder
04/08/1763	Negro Adam	St. Mary's	Conspiracy to Murder
09/28/1763	Negro Wapping	Prince George	Attempt to Poison
05/18/1764	Negro Jacob	Baltimore	Storehouse Robbery
06/20/1764	Negress Betty	Calvert	Attempt to Poison
06/20/1764	Negro Joe	Calvert	Attempt to Poison
06/20/1764	Negro Sambo	Calvert	Attempt to Poison
07/25/1764	Negro Davy	Queen Anne	Murder
07/27/1764	Negro Stephen	Baltimore	Burglary
10/04/1765	John Hubbert	Ann Arundel	Murder
10/04/1765	Edward Rudgeking	Ann Arundel	Murder
11/02/1765	Negro Tom	Prince George	Murder
12/27/1765	Negro Caesar	Baltimore	Arson
04/30/1766	Negro Jack	Charles	Murder
06/04/1766	Negress Beck	Calvert	Arson
09/24/1766	Negro George	Charles	Not Specified
09/24/1766	Negro Jonathan	Charles	Not Specified
10/15/1766	Patrick McKenzie	Baltimore	Horse Stealing
01/14/1767	Negro David	Talbot	Attempt to Poison
01/14/1767	Negro Nero	Talbot	Burglary
01/28/1767	Daniel Dunn	Frederick	Highway Robbery
05/06/1767	Negro Glasgow	Dorchester	Attempt to Poison
06/26/1767	Thomas Hulme	Dorchester	Burglary
06/26/1767	Negro Toby	Dorchester	Burglary
07/08/1767	Levi Thompson	Somerset	Murder
09/07/1768	Negro Sam	Ann Arundel	Burglary
09/09/1768	Negro Daniel	Dorchester	Burglary

Date of Execution	Name of Offender	Venue	Specific Felony
09/09/1768	Joseph Frampton	Frederick	Burglary
09/09/1768	Dennis Igoe (R)	Frederick	Burglary
09/09/1768	James Johnson	Frederick	Burglary
12/14/1768	Philip Fitzgerald	Dorchester	Not Specified
08/09/1769	Negro David	Charles	Rape
09/08/1769	Mulatto Jack	Prince George	Rape
10/06/1769	Negro Pompey	Charles	Attempt to Poison
10/22/1769	John Stinson	Baltimore	Burglary
05/02/1770	Negro Tom	Somerset	Murder
05/25/1770	Samuel Pelton	Frederick	Murder
07/04/1770	Jack Crain	Prince George	Murder
07/04/1770	Negro Davy	Prince George	Murder
07/04/1770	Jack Wood	Prince George	Murder
10/ /1770	John Jones	Kent	Slave Stealing
10/11/1770	John Boswell	Ann Arundel	Burglary
10/11/1770	Francis Chase	Ann Arundel	Burglary
10/19/1770	Negro David	Charles	Not Specified
01/23/1771	Negro Daniel	Ann Arundel	Burglary
01/23/1771	Morris McCoy (G)	Ann Arundel	Murder
02/01/1771	James Fitzpatrick	Frederick	Murder
02/01/1771	Roger Mockbee	Frederick	Burglary
03/15/1771	Negress Eve	Queen Anne	Not Specified
07/12/1771	Sam Banning	Queen Anne	Not Specified
10/16/1771	Negro Jacob	Baltimore	Not Specified
10/16/1771	Michael Woolden	Baltimore	Burglary
10/18/1771	Negro Vin	Dorchester	Not Specified
04/30/1773	Negro Ben	Baltimore	Aggravated Assault
04/30/1773	Negro Charles	Baltimore	Aggravated Assault
05/21/1773	Robert Cooper	Frederick	Murder
05/21/1773	John Thatcher	Frederick	Murder
10/22/1773	Christopher Chisholm	Frederick	Murder
10/22/1773	James Dennon	Frederick	Murder
10/22/1773	Cornelius Jacul	Frederick	Murder
10/22/1773	Abraham Wright	Frederick	Murder
09/01/1775	Negro Caesar	Prince George	Arson
09/01/1775	Joseph Long	Baltimore	Burglary
09/01/1775	Patrick Pearce	Baltimore	Burglary
11/17/1775	Negress Jenny	Calvert	Murder
11/17/1775	Negro Miall	Calvert	Rape
10/ /1776	Negro Kitt	Dorchester	Murder
10/ /1776	Negro Robin	Dorchester	Murder
10/ /1776	Negro Toby	Dorchester	Murder
08/ /1777	John Beard	Baltimore	Murder
08/ /1777	Michael Murphy	Frederick	Murder
01/ /1778	Negro Peter	Prince George	Rape
07/08/1778	William Clarke	Baltimore	Residential Robbery
07/08/1778	George Crow	Baltimore	Burglary
01/ /1779	Negro Matt	Talbot	Murder
04/ /1779	Negro Cato	Ann Arundel	Rape

Date of Execution	Name of Offender	Venue	Specific Felony
11/02/1780	Thomas Taylor (R)	Washington	Horse Stealing
03/02/1781	Thomas Locklan	Baltimore	Highway Robbery
03/02/1781	Joseph Lowe	Baltimore	Horse Stealing
08/17/1781	Caspar Fritchie	Frederick	Treason
08/17/1781	Yost Plecker	Frederick	Treason
08/17/1781	Peter Sueman	Frederick	Treason
10/24/1781	Negro George	Montgomery	Attempt to Poison
10/24/1781	Negro Peter	Montgomery	Attempt to Poison
05/15/1782	Negro Jacob	Montgomery	Horse Stealing
06/26/1782	Negro Jack	Charles	Burglary
06/26/1782	Negress Judith	Calvert	Arson
12/27/1782	Negro James	Worcester	Burglary
04/25/1783	Negro Joe	Somerset	Burglary
04/25/1783	Negro Paul	Somerset	Burglary
05/09/1783	John Bevan (R)	Worcester	Burglary
11/05/1783	Robert Conaway	Baltimore	Burglary
11/05/1783	John Lee	Baltimore	Burglary
01/09/1784	George Riggs	Worcester	Burglary
06/11/1784	Benjamin Furr	Frederick	Horse Stealing
07/14/1784	Edward Rock	Baltimore	Personal Robbery
07/23/1784	Bridget Martin	Baltimore	Murder
10/15/1784	William Marchmont	Dorchester	Burglary
10/15/1784	William Richards	Dorchester	Burglary
11/26/1784	Patrick McDonald	Baltimore	Burglary
04/06/1785	Negro Mingo	Baltimore	Murder
05/18/1785	John Brown (G)	Talbot	Murder
05/12/1786	Negro Leander	Harford	Murder
12/15/1786	Bartholomew Bannim	Worcester	Burglary
05/16/1787	Robert Collins	Baltimore	Murder
10/17/1787	Negro Stephen	Frederick	Murder
12/21/1787	John Thompson	Charles	Burglary
03/19/1788	Peter Donnelly	Baltimore	Personal Robbery
03/19/1788	Peter Mooney	Baltimore	Personal Robbery
02/11/1789	Patrick Cassidy (R)	Baltimore	Aggravated Burglary
02/11/1789	John Webb (R)	Baltimore	Aggravated Burglary
03/27/1789	Negro Isaac	Dorchester	Murder
04/24/1789	John Davenport	Queen Anne	Not Specified
05/01/1789	George Robinson	Queen Anne	Not Specified
08/26/1789	Negro George	Charles	Attempted Rape
09/04/1789	Negro Clem	Charles	Attempted Rape
03/03/1790	Negro George	St. Mary's	Rape
09/23/1791	Negro Charles	Calvert	Rape
10/12/1791	David Rathel	Talbot	Murder
11/16/1791	Negro Andrew	Dorchester	Rape
05/16/1792	Negro David	Montgomery	Murder
01/10/1794	Negro Andrew	Talbot	Rape
05/08/1795	Negro Ned	Ann Arundel	Murder
01/15/1796	Henry Wheeler	Dorchester	Murder
01/20/1797	Negro Charles	Baltimore	Murder

Date of Execution	Name of Offender	Venue	Specific Felony
07/28/1797	Negro Abram	Somerset	Murder
07/28/1797	Negro Draper	Somerset	Murder
12/29/1797	Negro Simon	Kent	Rape
09/07/1798	Peter Jennings	Prince George	Arson
12/01/1798	Negro Ben	Ann Arundel	Murder
12/17/1798	Negro Isaac	Worcester	Murder
04/12/1799	Negro Emanuel (R)	Washington	Murder
04/12/1799	Negro Jack	Washington	Murder
11/27/1801	Peter White	Caroline	Horse Stealing
09/07/1802	Domingo Lours	Baltimore	Murder
11/29/1802	Negro Quamus	Dorchester	Rape
03/30/1803	Negro Sam	Frederick	Murder
04/15/1803	John McDaniel	Washington	Burglary
05/18/1803	Negro Jack	Prince George	Murder
01/11/1804	Stephen Jay	Prince George	Murder
05/08/1805	Negro Dennis	Ann Arundel	Murder
05/08/1805	Negro George	Ann Arundel	Arson
05/08/1805	Negress Kate	Ann Arundel	Murder
05/08/1805	Negro Ned	Ann Arundel	Murder
08/09/1805	Negro Doss	Dorchester	Rape
04/22/1808	Caleb Dougherty	Baltimore	Murder
04/22/1808	Daniel Dougherty	Baltimore	Murder
04/22/1808	William Morris	Baltimore	Murder
04/22/1808	William Robinson	Baltimore	Murder
04/22/1808	John Worrilow	Worcester	Storehouse Robbery
11/25/1808	Frank Johnson	Washington	Murder
11/29/1809	Negro Cato	Queen Anne	Murder
11/29/1809	Negro Will	Queen Anne	Murder
01/12/1810	Negro Perry	Queen Anne	Murder
02/16/1810	Negro Ned	Prince George	Arson
07/13/1810	Stephen Hersey	Worcester	Murder
10/11/1811	Edward Brookes	Ann Arundel	Rape
11/06/1811	John Armstrong	Queen Anne	Murder
08/21/1812	Negro Aquilla	Baltimore	Murder
08/21/1812	Negro Ben	Baltimore	Murder
01/26/1816	Negro Harry	Frederick	Murder
01/26/1816	Negro Jonathan	Frederick	Murder
01/26/1816	Negro Nimrod	Frederick	Murder
01/26/1816	Negro Solomon	Frederick	Murder
10/11/1816	Matthew Chapman	Baltimore	Murder
10/10/1817	Negro Jacob	Montgomery	Murder
08/12/1818	Negro Dick	Ann Arundel	Rape
09/10/1818	John Alexander	Baltimore	Mail Robbery
09/10/1818	Joseph T. Hare	Baltimore	Mail Robbery
02/25/1820	John Cotterill	Washington	Murder
02/25/1820	William Cotterill, Sr.	Washington	Murder
02/25/1820	William Cotterill, Jr.	Washington	Murder
04/13/1820	Israel Denny	Baltimore	Piracy
04/13/1820	John Ferguson	Baltimore	Piracy

Date of Execution	Name of Offender	Venue	Specific Felony
07/14/1820	Morris Hull	Baltimore	Murder
07/14/1820	Peregrine Hutton	Baltimore	Murder
08/16/1820	Jesse Griffith	Dorchester	Murder
03/02/1821	Negress Kitty	Frederick	Murder
03/02/1821	Negro Peter	Frederick	Murder
10/05/1821	Negro Allen	St. Mary's	Rape
10/19/1821	Negress Jenny	Somerset	Murder
07/23/1824	Robert Johnson	Worcester	Murder
10/29/1824	Negro George	Baltimore	Rape
10/29/1824	Negro Henry	Baltimore	Rape
08/05/1825	William Turvey	Charles	Murder
06/15/1827	Negro Robert	Worcester	Rape
06/22/1827	Negro Frederick	Prince George	Rape
04/11/1828	Jim Truxton	Talbot	Murder
10/02/1829	George Swearington	Allegany	Murder
12/04/1829	Shelby Jump	Caroline	Murder
05/13/1831	Negress Henny	Dorchester	Murder
06/24/1831	John Markley	Frederick	Murder
11/20/1832	Isaiah Willin	Dorchester	Murder
12/20/1833	Aurelia Chase	Baltimore	Murder
12/20/1833	Nelson Wallis	Baltimore	Rape
01/16/1835	Negress Judah	Prince George	Murder
05/29/1835	William Adams	Baltimore	Murder
01/13/1837	Dave Thomas	Talbot	Murder
04/ /1839	John Brown	Montgomery	Rape
11/24/1843	William Chrise	Allegany	Murder
11/24/1843	Negro Daniel	Prince George	Murder
01/12/1844	Adam Horn	Baltimore	Murder
02/14/1844	George Rustin	St. Mary's	Murder
02/14/1844	James Williams	St. Mary's	Murder
06/27/1845	Henry McCurry	Baltimore	Murder
02/26/1847	Joseph Alexander	Baltimore	Murder
06/04/1847	Negro Charles	St. Mary's	Rape
06/02/1848	Negro Tom	Ann Arundel	Rape
07/21/1849	Conrad Vinter	Baltimore	Murder
06/28/1850	Edward Brown	Calvert	Murder
03/07/1851	Thomas McLaughlin	Allegany	Murder
08/08/1851	Amos Green	Howard	Rape
08/08/1851	Nicholas Murphy	Kent	Murder
08/08/1851	William Shelton	Kent	Murder
08/08/1851	Abraham Taylor	Kent	Murder
11/19/1852	David Green	Howard	Rape
01/07/1853	David Johnson	Ann Arundel	Murder
01/07/1853	White Slocum	Montgomery	Rape
08/05/1853	Thomas Connor	Baltimore City	Murder
04/20/1855	Robert Swift	Cecil	Murder
01/03/1856	Frederick Miller	Allegany	Murder
02/29/1856	Saul Brown	Queen Anne	Murder
07/08/1856	Jim Mills	Worcester	Rape

Date of Execution	Name of Offender	Venue	Specific Felony
07/08/1856	Littleton Stevens	Worcester	Rape
01/15/1858	John Gowings	Somerset	Murder
01/29/1858	Philip Hawkins	Frederick	Murder
07/02/1858	Alfred Dashiell	Somerset	Murder
04/08/1859	Peter Corrie	Baltimore City	Murder
04/08/1859	Marion Cropp	Baltimore City	Murder
04/08/1859	John Cyphus	Baltimore City	Murder
04/08/1859	Henry Gambrill	Baltimore City	Murder
06/24/1859	Rebecca McCormick	Carroll	Murder
10/04/1861	Mary Naylor	Ann Arundel	Murder
11/22/1861	Perry Kennard	Baltimore	Rape
12/23/1861	John Lanahan	Frederick	Murder
03/07/1862	William Kuhnes	Ft. McHenry	Murder
09/05/1862	Bill Ferguson	Calvert	Murder
04/10/1863	Frederick Smith	Washington	Murder
07/05/1863	William Richardson	Frederick	Espionage
07/17/1863	Ned Davis	Somerset	Murder
07/17/1863	Bob Jones	Somerset	Murder
07/17/1863	Negro Morris	Somerset	Murder
08/21/1863	George Coard	Worcester	Rape
05/09/1864	Henry Burnham	Pt. Lookout	Army Deserter
05/23/1864	Andrew Laypole	Baltimore City	Espionage
07/11/1864	Francis Gillespie	Allegany	Murder
07/22/1864	Granville Smeltzer	Frederick	Murder
09/27/1864	George McDonald	Baltimore City	Army Deserter
11/10/1864	John Provost	Allegany	Murder

Virginia

(B) = Burned at the stake
(G) = Gibbeted after execution
(F) = Federal jurisdiction
(Q) = Drawn and quartered
(R) = Recidivist (had been sentenced to death on a prior occasion, obtained clemency and then gone on to offend anew)
(*) = White for Murder of Negro

Date of Execution	Name of Offender	Venue	Specific Felony
——1608	George Kendall	Jamestown	Espionage
——1610	Unidentified Man	Jamestown	Murder and Cannibalism
03/01/1622	Daniel Frank	Jamestown	Grand Larceny
——1624	Richard Cornish	Jamestown	Sodomy
06/ /1626	Thomas Hayle	Jamestown	Rape
07/ /1630	William Matthews	Jamestown	Murder
——1632	Jane Champion	Jamestown	Not Specified
06/24/1633	Margaret Hatch	Jamestown	Murder
03/12/1658	Huntington Ayres	Yorktown	Not Specified
01/ /1677	Thomas Hansford (Q)	Jamestown	Treason

Date of Execution	Name of Offender	Venue	Specific Felony
01/ /1677	Capt. Wilford (Q)	Jamestown	Treason
01/19/1677	Thomas Hall (Q)	Jamestown	Treason
01/19/1677	Henry Page (Q)	Jamestown	Treason
01/19/1677	James Wilson (Q)	Jamestown	Treason
01/19/1677	Thomas Young (Q)	Jamestown	Treason
01/27/1677	John Baptista (Q)	Jamestown	Treason
01/27/1677	William Drummond (Q)	Jamestown	Treason
01/31/1677	William Cookson (Q)	Jamestown	Treason
01/31/1677	James Crewes (Q)	Jamestown	Treason
01/31/1677	John Digby (Q)	Jamestown	Treason
01/31/1677	William Rookings (Q)	Jamestown	Treason
01/31/1677	William West (Q)	Jamestown	Treason
03/15/1677	Anthony Arnold (Q)	Jamestown	Treason
03/15/1677	Giles Bland (Q)	Jamestown	Treason
03/15/1677	Richard Farmer (Q)	Jamestown	Treason
03/15/1677	John Isles (Q)	Jamestown	Treason
03/15/1677	Robert Jones (Q)	Jamestown	Treason
03/15/1677	Richard Pomeroy (Q)	Jamestown	Treason
03/15/1677	Robert Stoakes (Q)	Jamestown	Treason
03/23/1677	William Scarborough (Q)	Jamestown	Treason
03/23/1677	John Whitson (Q)	Jamestown	Treason
08/05/1678	Thomas Hellier (G)	Charles City	Murder
——1682	Two Unnamed Men	Jamestown	Crop Cutting
04/ /1683	Bartholomew Austin	Jamestown	Treason
04/ /1683	Somerset Davis	Jamestown	Treason
——1688	Negro Toby	Henrico	Not Specified
11/ /1692	Unnamed Woman	Jamestown	Murder
07/15/1693	Tom Cary	Northampton	Arson
10/30/1699	Indian Peter	Williamsburg	Murder
11/01/1699	Samuel Bray	Williamsburg	Murder
03/12/1700	Indian Jamey	Surry	Murder
05/08/1700	John Ide	Williamsburg	Murder
05/15/1700	John Hoogling	Princess Anne	Piracy
05/15/1700	Three Unnamed Men	Princess Anne	Piracy
11/ /1700	John Smith	Williamsburg	Murder
10/ /1701	Slave (Lownd)	Henrico	Rape
11/07/1701	Derby Collnon	King & Queen	Murder
10/ /1703	John Moore	Williamsburg	Murder
01/14/1704	Negro Tom	Westmoreland	Murder
07/05/1704	Negress Bridget	York	Arson
10/12/1704	Tom Anthony	Richmond Co.	Murder
10/12/1704	Indian George	Richmond Co.	Murder
10/12/1704	Bearded Jack	Richmond Co.	Murder
10/12/1704	Jack the Fiddler	Richmond Co.	Murder
10/12/1704	Old Master Thomas	Richmond Co.	Murder
06/16/1705	Negress Sarah	Northampton	Arson
09/09/1706	Negro Dick	Westmoreland	Burglary
09/09/1706	Negro Frank	Westmoreland	Burglary
09/09/1706	Negro George	Westmoreland	Burglary

Date of Execution	Name of Offender	Venue	Specific Felony
09/09/1706	Negro Jack	Westmoreland	Burglary
09/09/1706	Negro Robin	Westmoreland	Burglary
12/26/1706	Negro Frank	Surry	Murder
——1707	Negro Samson (G)	Essex	Not Specified
——1707	Negro Toney (G)	Essex	Not Specified
09/01/1707	Jack Rascow	Middlesex	Burglary
05/21/1708	Thomas Ashwell	Williamsburg	Murder
05/21/1708	James Pertnock	Williamsburg	Murder
01/31/1710	Indian Ned	Surry	Burglary
05/ /1710	Negro Salvatore	Surry	Insurrection
05/ /1710	Negro Scipio	Surry	Insurrection
——1712	Elizabeth Gordon	Williamsburg	Burglary
——1712	Negro Jack	Essex	Not Specified
10/15/1712	Negro Tom	Middlesex	Burglary
03/23/1713	Negro Jemmy	Henrico	Murder
03/23/1713	Negro Tony	Henrico	Murder
04/14/1713	Negro Jack	Northumberland	Burglary
05/21/1713	Indian Prince	Northumberland	Burglary
05/25/1713	Negro Jack	Middlesex	Burglary
07/14/1713	Negro Bass	Middlesex	Burglary
06/14/1714	Negro Tom	Lancaster	Burglary
09/24/1715	Negro Guy	York	Burglary
09/24/1715	Mulatto Harry	York	Burglary
09/24/1715	Negro Sam	York	Burglary
01/15/1717	Negro Roger	Middlesex	Burglary
01/15/1717	Negro Toney	Middlesex	Burglary
08/29/1717	Negro Charles	Middlesex	Hog Theft (3rd Time)
06/ /1718	Unnamed Slave	Nansemond	Not Specified
01/28/1719	Two Pirates	Hampton	Piracy
03/28/1719	James Blake	Williamsburg	Piracy
03/28/1719	Joseph Brooks	Williamsburg	Piracy
03/28/1719	Negro Caesar	Williamsburg	Piracy
03/28/1719	John Carnes	Williamsburg	Piracy
03/28/1719	Stephen Daniels	Williamsburg	Piracy
03/28/1719	Thomas Gates	Williamsburg	Piracy
03/28/1719	John Gills	Williamsburg	Piracy
03/28/1719	Richard Greensail	Williamsburg	Piracy
03/28/1719	John Martin	Williamsburg	Piracy
03/28/1719	Joseph Phillips	Williamsburg	Piracy
03/28/1719	James Robbins	Williamsburg	Piracy
03/28/1719	Edward Salter	Williamsburg	Piracy
03/28/1719	Richard Stiles	Williamsburg	Piracy
03/28/1719	James White	Williamsburg	Piracy
02/ /1720	Tobias Butler	Williamsburg	Piracy
02/ /1720	Daniel Daggett	Williamsburg	Piracy
02/ /1720	William Farrow	Williamsburg	Piracy
02/ /1720	William Williams	Williamsburg	Piracy
03/ /1720	Thomas Hall	Williamsburg	Piracy
03/ /1720	William Pomeroy	Williamsburg	Piracy

Date of Execution	Name of Offender	Venue	Specific Felony
07/26/1720	Negro Jack	Henrico	Murder
08/11/1720	Negro Terro	Henrico	Burglary
03/02/1721	Negro Stanto	Henrico	Murder
03/02/1722	Negro Peter	Henrico	Murder
06/02/1722	Negro Wapping	Lancaster	Murder
09/27/1723	Negro Dick	King George	Horse Stealing
01/29/1724	Negro Harry	Lancaster	Rape
06/02/1724	Hercules (Indian)	Henrico	Storehouse Robbery
10/07/1724	Negro Caesar	Northampton	Burglary
11/13/1724	Negro Robin	Lancaster	Burglary
03/17/1725	William Plummer	Richmond Co.	Burglary
11/20/1725	Negro James	Elizabeth City	Burglary
08/16/1726	Negro Ben	Richmond Co.	Murder
05/ /1727	John Hostock	Williamsburg	Murder
06/ /1727	Negress Hannah	Elizabeth City	Murder
10/ /1727	Edward Coleman	Williamsburg	Piracy
10/ /1727	Unnamed Pirate	Williamsburg	Piracy
——1728	Unnamed Indian	Pittsylvania	Murder
04/17/1728	Mulatto Sarah	York	Arson
09/28/1728	Negro Will	Elizabeth City	Storehouse Robbery
01/03/1729	Negro Gomery	Elizabeth City	Burglary
01/03/1729	Negro Mount	Elizabeth City	Burglary
09/ /1729	Two Unnamed Men	Williamsburg	Piracy
09/ /1729	Unnamed Mulatto	Williamsburg	Piracy
09/ /1729	Unnamed Woman	Williamsburg	Piracy
——1730	Two Sailors	Williamsburg	Sodomy
10/ /1730	Two Slaves	Princess Anne	Conspiracy to Rebel
10/ /1730	Two Slaves	Norfolk	Conspiracy to Rebel
10/17/1730	Negro Will	York	Murder
11/03/1730	Negro James (Q)	Richmond Co.	Murder
04/19/1731	Negro Tom	Westmoreland	Storehouse Robbery
05/03/1732	Negro Jack	Spotsylvania	Insurrection
08/29/1732	Negro Pompey	Spotsylvania	Murder
06/27/1733	Negro Champion	Goochland	Murder
06/27/1733	Negro Valentine	Goochland	Murder
09/13/1734	Negro Robin	Caroline	Burglary
06/04/1736	Negro Andrew	Caroline	Rape
07/17/1736	Negro Jeffrey	Westmoreland	Burglary
08/20/1736	Negro Anthony	Westmoreland	Storehouse Robbery
11/26/1736	Elizabeth Greenley (R)	Williamsburg	Murder
11/26/1736	James Matthews	Williamsburg	Horse Stealing
01/ /1737	Female Slave (Prudden) (B)	Nansemond	Petit Treason
01/29/1737	Negro Hazard	Goochland	Burglary
02/ /1737	Slave (Broadnax)	Charles City	Storehouse Robbery
02/ /1737	Slave (Moody)	Charles City	Storehouse Robbery
02/ /1737	Slave (Walker)	Charles City	Storehouse Robbery
02/11/1737	Negro Dick	Lancaster	Murder
02/17/1737	Negro George	Goochland	Burglary
05/27/1737	Francis Ford	Williamsburg	Burglary

Date of Execution	Name of Offender	Venue	Specific Felony
05/27/1737	John Plew	Williamsburg	Burglary
05/27/1737	Robert Thompson	Williamsburg	Burglary
05/30/1737	Negro Roger	Middlesex	Poisoning
06/23/1737	Negro Peter	Orange	Murder
07/01/1737	Benjamin Milwood	Williamsburg	Burglary
10/ /1737	Negro Tom	Elizabeth City	Burglary
11/ /1737	Mulatto Jacob	Richmond Co.	Burglary
11/18/1737	Bryan Connor	Williamsburg	Murder
11/18/1737	Peter Heckie	Williamsburg	Murder
11/25/1737	Daniel Handley	Williamsburg	Storehouse Robbery
01/13/1738	Andrew Thompson	Williamsburg	Burglary
04/29/1738	Negro Berwick	Elizabeth City	Burglary
07/ /1738	Negro Will	York	Burglary
07/18/1738	Negro Jemmy	Goochland	Rape
07/28/1738	Negro Saul	Westmoreland	Burglary
11/24/1738	Anthony F. Dittond	Williamsburg	Murder
——1739	Negro Phil	Caroline	Arson
11/09/1739	Negro Martin	Prince George	Murder
11/23/1739	John Cobbidge* (R)	Williamsburg	Murder
11/23/1739	Joseph Lightburn (R)	Williamsburg	Highway Robbery
11/23/1739	Constantine Matthews	Williamsburg	Storehouse Robbery
11/23/1739	Elizabeth Maze	Williamsburg	Murder
11/23/1739	Nathaniel Morgan	Williamsburg	Horse Stealing
11/23/1739	Charles Quinn*	Williamsburg	Murder
11/23/1739	David White*	Williamsburg	Murder
——1740	Negro Devonshire	Princess Anne	Not Specified
01/04/1740	Jonathan Faithful (R)	Williamsburg	Storehouse Robbery
01/31/1740	Negro George	Accomack	Storehouse Robbery
08/22/1740	Negro Matthew	Westmoreland	Burglary
09/30/1740	Negro Cutjoo	Accomack	Storehouse Robbery
03/20/1741	Negro Isaac	Goochland	Horse Stealing
08/07/1741	Negro Dick	Spotsylvania	Aggravated Burglary
12/22/1741	Negro Davy	Goochland	Murder
03/27/1742	Negro Philip	Northumberland	Burglary
06/04/1742	Henry Davis	Williamsburg	Not Specified
06/30/1742	Negro Jack	Goochland	Murder
06/30/1742	Negress Lucy	Goochland	Murder
06/30/1742	Negro Yorkshire	Goochland	Murder
11/26/1742	Anne Plunkett	Williamsburg	Murder
——1743	Negro Charles	Norfolk	Not Specified
——1743	Negro George	Princess Anne	Not Specified
——1743	Negro George	Princess Anne	Not Specified
04/11/1743	Negro Jack	Northampton	Storehouse Robbery
11/11/1743	Negro Frank	Norfolk	Burglary
12/ /1743	Negro Bradford	York	Horse Stealing
12/ /1743	Little Jack	Orange	Storehouse Robbery
12/26/1743	Negro Jack	Northumberland	Storehouse Robbery
01/20/1744	Negro Guy	Lancaster	Storehouse Robbery
03/ /1744	Negro Frank	Orange	Storehouse Robbery

Date of Execution	Name of Offender	Venue	Specific Felony
03/17/1744	Negro Tom	Norfolk	Rape
03/17/1744	Negro William	Norfolk	Rape
08/ /1744	Negro Sampson	York	Grand Larceny
08/20/1744	Negro Otho	Westmoreland	Aggravated Burglary
08/20/1744	Negro Tom	Westmoreland	Aggravated Burglary
09/ /1744	Negro Kirandy	York	Storehouse Robbery
10/05/1744	Negro Harry	Henrico	Storehouse Robbery
01/ /1745	Two Slaves (Beverley)	King & Queen	Murder
03/02/1745	Negro Frank	Orange	Horse Stealing
03/02/1745	Negro Jack	Orange	Horse Stealing
03/02/1745	Pappaw Frank	Orange	Horse Stealing
04/18/1745	Negro Stephen	Northumberland	Storehouse Robbery
10/21/1745	Negro Cuffy	Goochland	Burglary
11/29/1745	William Holloway	Williamsburg	Murder
01/20/1746	Tom Wood	Spotsylvania	Storehouse Robbery
01/23/1746	Negress Eve (B)	Orange	Petit Treason
02/05/1746	Negro Billy	Spotsylvania	Storehouse Robbery
03/20/1746	Negro Boatswain	Louisa	Murder
05/ /1746	John Smith	Williamsburg	Murder
08/22/1746	Negro George	Spotsylvania	Burglary
05/01/1747	Negro Caesar	Elizabeth City	Not Specified
06/22/1747	Negro Will	Amelia	Murder
06/30/1747	John Benton	Williamsburg	Horse Stealing
——1748	Negro James	Norfolk	Not Specified
——1748	Negro Tom	Norfolk	Not Specified
06/27/1748	Negro Peter	Louisa	Murder
08/02/1748	Negro Tom	Orange	Burglary
——1749	Negro Solomon	Princess Anne	Not Specified
04/21/1749	Negro Bob	York	Storehouse Robbery
05/02/1749	Negro Sam	Westmoreland	Storehouse Robbery
09/ /1749	Negro Norman	Richmond Co.	Burglary
09/ /1749	Negro Sam	Richmond Co.	Burglary
09/25/1749	Negro Abraham	Middlesex	Storehouse Robbery
09/25/1749	Negro Phil	Middlesex	Storehouse Robbery
07/ /1750	Negro Guy	Northumberland	Storehouse Robbery
06/ /1750	George Afflax	Williamsburg	Murder
06/11/1750	Negro Mark	Northumberland	Murder
08/15/1750	Negro Tom	Spotsylvania	Burglary
10/10/1750	Negro Harry	King George	Murder
10/29/1750	Negro Philip	Norfolk	Murder
11/05/1750	Negro Tom	Spotsylvania	Burglary
12/08/1750	Negro Caesar	Lancaster	Not Specified
12/26/1750	Negro Caesar	Amelia	Horse Stealing
12/26/1750	Negro Ned	Amelia	Horse Stealing
——1751	Negro Cuffey	Caroline	Murder
01/18/1751	James McGuire	Williamsburg	Murder
01/18/1751	William Simmons	Williamsburg	Armed Robbery
02/04/1751	Negro Peter	Middlesex	Storehouse Robbery
02/04/1751	Negro Robin	Middlesex	Storehouse Robbery

Date of Execution	Name of Offender	Venue	Specific Felony
03/06/1751	Negro Bristol	Accomack	Storehouse Robbery
04/05/1751	Negro Scotland	Norfolk	Not Specified
04/05/1751	Negro Vernon	Norfolk	Not Specified
04/08/1751	Negro Matt	York	Not Specified
04/08/1751	Negro Simon	York	Not Specified
07/12/1751	Negro Josiah	York	Jail Breaking
08/19/1751	Negro Harry	Caroline	Burglary
12/20/1751	George Kerr	Williamsburg	Murder
12/20/1751	Henry Stanworth	Williamsburg	Murder
12/24/1751	Negro Jemmie	Elizabeth City	Not Specified
01/10/1752	Peter Bateman	Williamsburg	Storehouse Robbery
01/10/1752	Day Thoroughgood	Williamsburg	Murder
03/06/1752	Negro James	Brunswick	Burglary
04/03/1752	Negro Bob	Isle of Wight	Storehouse Robbery
06/06/1752	Negro Davie	Lancaster	Not Specified
06/06/1752	Negress Moll	Lancaster	Not Specified
06/19/1752	Negro Jemmy	York Aggravated	Burglary
07/03/1752	John Sparks	Williamsburg	Murder
07/06/1752	Negro Peter	Brunswick	Insurrection
08/ /1752	Negro Will	Northumberland	Storehouse Robbery
10/01/1752	Unnamed Slave	James City	Not Specified
11/13/1752	Negro Robin	Middlesex	Storehouse Robbery
12/08/1752	Negro Andrew	Northumberland	Storehouse Robbery
01/12/1753	Thomas Aubrey	Williamsburg	Horse Stealing
01/12/1753	Alexander Gauling	Williamsburg	Highway Robbery
02/05/1753	Negress Sue	Norfolk	Murder
02/08/1753	Negro Sam	Lancaster	Burglary
04/05/1753	Negro Peter	Northampton	Burglary
04/13/1753	Lowe Jackson	Williamsburg	Coining
06/09/1753	Negro Dick	Lancaster	Not Specified
07/08/1753	Henry Bates (R)	Williamsburg	Grand Larceny
07/08/1753	Thomas Green	Williamsburg	Not Specified
09/14/1753	Negro Bristol	Northumberland	Murder
09/17/1753	Negro Cudjo	Cumberland	Murder
09/21/1753	Negro Daniel	Northumberland	Burglary
09/21/1753	Negro Will	Northumberland	Burglary
11/30/1753	Negro Daniel	Richmond Co.	Burglary
12/28/1753	Negro Charlton	Norfolk	Not Specified
12/28/1753	Negro Mark	Norfolk	Not Specified
12/29/1753	Negro Pliny	Accomack	Murder
12/29/1753	Negro Solomon	Accomack	Murder
——1754	Negro Ned	Princess Anne	Not Specified
01/ /1754	Negro Jemmy	Surry	Murder
01/25/1754	Negro Putney	York	Storehouse Robbery
01/25/1754	Negro Tom	York	Storehouse Robbery
03/01/1754	Negress Cate	Southampton	Murder
03/25/1754	Negro Hall	Amelia	Preparing Poison
05/04/1754	Negro Jack	Middlesex	Burglary
05/24/1754	Christopher Bettie	Williamsburg	Horse Stealing

Date of Execution	Name of Offender	Venue	Specific Felony
05/24/1754	Randall Gibson	Williamsburg	Privately Stealing
06/08/1754	Negro Toney	Middlesex	Burglary
07/05/1754	John Gowdie	Williamsburg	Not Specified
07/05/1754	Patrick Hoggan	Williamsburg	Horse Stealing
07/07/1754	Negro Hampton	Elizabeth City	Not Specified
07/07/1754	Negro Scipio	Elizabeth City	Not Specified
08/02/1754	Negro Charles	Henrico	Rape
08/02/1754	Negro Tom	Spotsylvania	Storehouse Robbery
09/ /1754	Negro Harry	Prince William	Not Specified
12/17/1754	Negro Gloster	King George	Murder
12/17/1754	Negress Pegg	King George	Murder
02/26/1755	Negro Tom (Q)	Amelia	Murder
03/07/1755	Negro Ambrose	Northumberland	Grand Larceny
05/23/1755	Mary Murray	Williamsburg	Privately Stealing
05/23/1755	John Turner	Williamsburg	Murder
10/18/1755	Negro Sambo	Lancaster	Storehouse Robbery
11/21/1755	John Nicholas	Williamsburg	Murder
01/30/1756	Negro Stephen	Norfolk	Not Specified
03/02/1756	Indian Jamie	Sussex	Not Specified
05/17/1756	Negress Dido	Cumberland	Preparing Poison
06/ /1756	Negro Hampton	Bedford	Poisoning
10/16/1756	Negro Toby	Henrico	Rape
12/ /1756	Negro Abraham	Prince William	Grand Larceny
01/17/1757	Negro Harry	Cumberland	Arson
05/06/1757	Negro Scias	Isle of Wight	Storehouse Robbery
09/30/1757	Negro Harry	Northumberland	Rape
11/ /1757	Robert Colclough	Williamsburg	Incestuous Rape
01/31/1758	Negro Sam	Westmoreland	Murder
04/03/1758	Negro Ralph	Westmoreland	Storehouse Robbery
04/03/1758	Negro Sampson	Westmoreland	Storehouse Robbery
07/12/1759	Negro Coy	Lunenburg	Murder
07/20/1759	Negro Pompey	Spotsylvania	Storehouse Robbery
10/12/1759	Negro Bolster	Sussex	Not Specified
11/30/1759	Caesar Valentine	Williamsburg	Not Specified
——1760	Negro Davy	Princess Anne	Not Specified
01/25/1760	Negro Dick	Accomack	Murder
01/25/1760	Negro George (G)	Accomack	Murder
01/25/1760	Negro Stepney (G)	Accomack	Murder
10/25/1760	Negress Jenny	King George	Murder
12/17/1760	Godfrey Titas	Prince Edward	Not Specified
05/08/1761	Negress Rachel	Spotsylvania	Attempt to Poison
05/19/1761	Negro Daniel	Cumberland	Burglary
07/ /1761	John Kay	Williamsburg	Murder
08/07/1761	Negro Daniel	Caroline	Murder
09/ /1761	Negro Stepney	Amelia	Poisoning
10/16/1761	Negro Nelson	Bedford	Grand Larceny
10/17/1761	Negro Sam	Princess Anne	Sheep Stealing
10/26/1761	Negro Bristol	Spotsylvania	Burglary
11/09/1761	Negro Davy	York	Storehouse Robbery

Date of Execution	Name of Offender	Venue	Specific Felony
11/13/1761	Negro Will	Elizabeth City	Poisoning
11/27/1761	Negro Charles	Isle of Wight	Burglary
12/04/1761	Negro James	York	Storehouse Robbery
04/06/1762	Negro Peter	Caroline	Conspiracy to Poison
05/27/1762	Negro Cupid	Caroline	Poisoning
06/22/1762	Negro Abel	Caroline	Poisoning
07/24/1762	Negro Will	Charles City	Burglary
11/09/1762	Negro Roger	Caroline	Storehouse Robbery
11/19/1762	Negro Scipio	Southampton	Horse Stealing
12/26/1762	Negro Mustapha	Cumberland	Murder
01/17/1763	Negro Matt	Chesterfield	Burglary
02/ /1763	Tom Bolling	Prince William	Storehouse Robbery
03/07/1763	Negro Peter	Cumberland	Conspiracy to Poison
04/28/1763	Negress Nan	Caroline	Not Specified
05/ /1763	Negro Bosun	Lunenburg	Arson
05/25/1763	Negro Peter	Caroline	Preparing Poison
06/17/1763	Negro Cuffy	York	Murder
11/19/1763	Negro Tom	Augusta	Murder
02/02/1764	Negro Aaron	Accomack	Rape
03/29/1764	Negro Tom	Caroline	Burglary
05/25/1764	William Abney	Williamsburg	Counterfeiting
05/25/1764	Robert Barnard	Williamsburg	Forgery
05/25/1764	Bartholomew Roberts	Williamsburg	Counterfeiting
05/25/1764	Littlebury Thompson	Williamsburg	Murder
02/15/1765	Negro Davy	Isle of Wight	Arson
04/12/1765	Negro Stepney	Princess Anne	Grand Larceny
05/31/1765	Negro Charles	York	Burglary
05/31/1765	Negro Sam	York	Burglary
05/31/1765	Negro Tom	York	Burglary
06/06/1765	Negro Peter	Cumberland	Conspiracy to Poison
06/18/1765	Negress Bellow	Cumberland	Conspiracy to Poison
07/05/1765	Negro Will	Northumberland	Poisoning
09/06/1765	Negro Peter	Henrico	Not Specified
10/04/1765	Negro Dick	Goochland	Poisoning
10/14/1765	Negro Taffy	Goochland	Poisoning
11/08/1765	Negro George	Princess Anne	Burglary
11/12/1765	Negro Aaron	Caroline	Burglary
11/30/1765	Negro Griffin	Princess Anne	Grand Larceny
——1766	Negro Pompey	Louisa	Not Specified
04/25/1766	Negro Jack	Northampton	Not Specified
05/16/1766	Negro Jack	Mecklenburg	Storehouse Robbery
05/31/1766	Negro Harry	Princess Anne	Grand Larceny
06/02/1766	Negro Pharoah	Northumberland	Burglary
06/02/1766	Negro Tom	Northumberland	Burglary
06/13/1766	Negro Ned	York	Storehouse Robbery
06/13/1766	Negro Will	York	Storehouse Robbery
07/04/1766	Negro Dan	York	Burglary
07/04/1766	Patrick O'Bryan	Williamsburg	Not Specified
07/04/1766	Negress Sukey	Chesterfield	Murder

Date of Execution	Name of Offender	Venue	Specific Felony
07/11/1766	Negro Harry	Isle of Wight	Storehouse Robbery
07/11/1766	Negro Mingo	Isle of Wight	Highway Robbery
08/30/1766	Negro Harry	Charlotte	Preparing Poison
09/09/1766	Negro Obadiah	Accomack	Grand Larceny
09/12/1766	Negro Dick	Princess Anne	Storehouse Robbery
11/17/1766	Negro Peter	York	Sheep Stealing
12/05/1766	John Coleman	Williamsburg	Not Specified
12/05/1766	Philip Hoffman	Williamsburg	Not Specified
12/19/1766	Negro James	Isle of Wight	Burglary
——1767	Negro Sam	Pittsylvania	Not Specified
01/17/1767	Mulatto Cooper	Essex	Grand Larceny
02/ /1767	Negro Garwin	Prince William	Conspiracy to Murder
02/ /1767	Negro Harry	Prince William	Conspiracy to Murder
02/28/1767	Negro Jupiter	Elizabeth City	Murder
03/02/1767	Negro Joe	Loudoun	Murder
03/02/1767	Negro Pendoe	Loudoun	Murder
03/02/1767	Negro Sam	Loudoun	Murder
03/19/1767	Negro Cupid	Cumberland	Burglary
05/12/1767	Negress Esther	Accomack	Murder
05/16/1767	Negro Peter	Middlesex	Burglary
06/10/1767	Martha Sharp	Williamsburg	Murder
09/19/1767	Negro Glasgow	Accomack	Aggravated Burglary
09/25/1767	Negro Tom	Elizabeth City	Rape
10/15/1767	Negro Tom	Orange	Burglary
12/ /1767	Four Slaves	Fairfax	Poisoning
——1768	Two Slaves	Westmoreland	Not Specified
01/08/1768	Alexander Heath	Williamsburg	Burglary
01/08/1768	Thomas Heath	Williamsburg	Burglary
02/ /1768	Negro Duke	Essex	Burglary
02/ /1768	Negro Peter	Essex	Burglary
03/30/1768	Mulatto Matthew	York	Burglary
06/ /1768	Unnamed Slave	York	Not Specified
07/ /1768	Negro Sam	Essex	Burglary
08/12/1768	Negro Mercer (Q)	Loudoun	Murder
02/24/1769	Negro Mingo	Mecklenburg	Grand Larceny
05/20/1769	Negro James	Princess Anne	Rape
05/26/1769	James Biggers	Williamsburg	Horse Stealing
05/26/1769	John Derby	Williamsburg	Pickpocketing
05/26/1769	William Jones	Williamsburg	Horse Stealing
05/26/1769	Robert McMachen	Williamsburg	Murder
06/10/1769	Negro Simon	Spotsylvania	Aggravated Burglary
06/20/1769	Male Slave (Ashley)	James City	Conspiracy to Rebel
07/11/1769	Negro Phil	Stafford	Murder
07/11/1769	Negress Winny	Stafford	Murder
07/14/1769	Negro Aaron	Southampton	Rape
09/16/1769	Negro Sam	Prince Edward	Not Specified
11/24/1769	Thomas Brown	Williamsburg	Not Specified
11/24/1769	John Garland	Williamsburg	Horse Stealing
11/24/1769	John Johnston	Williamsburg	Horse Stealing

Date of Execution	Name of Offender	Venue	Specific Felony
11/29/1769	Negro Harry	Essex	Burglary
12/21/1769	Negress Betty	Essex	Conspiracy to Murder
12/26/1769	Negro Caesar	Bedford	Rape
02/02/1770	Negro Isaac	York	Not Specified
04/28/1770	Negro Frank	Essex	Conspiracy to Poison
05/05/1770	Negro Will	Southampton	Burglary
05/18/1770	Negro Grigg	Prince Edward	Poisoning
05/25/1770	John Hamilton	Williamsburg	Murder
06/06/1770	Negro Lewis	Prince Edward	Poisoning
07/13/1770	Negro Phil	Essex	Horse Stealing
07/14/1770	Negro Mintus	Essex	Storehouse Robbery
10/24/1770	Negress Sarah	York	Burglary
11/12/1770	Negro Harry	Dinwiddie	Burglary
11/29/1770	Jesse Townsend	Williamsburg	Murder
01/11/1771	Negro Tom	Essex	Murder
01/24/1771	Negro Sam	Goochland	Murder
03/20/1771	Negro Peter	Sussex	Not Specified
04/15/1771	Negro Champion	Pittsylvania	Burglary
06/22/1771	Negro Jack	Mecklenburg	Grand Larceny
06/27/1771	William Robinson	Williamsburg	Storehouse Robbery
06/27/1771	Richard Sowerbutts	Williamsburg	Burglary
07/06/1771	Negro Paul	York	Burglary
08/ /1771	Negro Luke	Essex	Burglary
08/19/1771	Negro Anthony	Lancaster	Burglary
08/19/1771	Negro Daniel	Lancaster	Burglary
08/21/1771	Negro Jamaco	Princess Anne	Rape
09/12/1771	Negro David	Lunenburg	Storehouse Robbery
10/30/1771	Negro Abram	Middlesex	Murder
12/ /1771	Negro Jemmy	Chesterfield	Storehouse Robbery
12/ /1771	Negro Will	Chesterfield	Storehouse Robbery
01/24/1772	Negro Paddy	Norfolk	Not Specified
01/30/1772	Negro Abraham	Caroline	Burglary
04/13/1772	Negro Aaron	Augusta	Murder
04/13/1772	Negro Jacob	Augusta	Murder
05/09/1772	Negro Jem	Prince William	Not Specified
05/18/1772	Negro Davis	Lancaster	Burglary
05/29/1772	Negro Lewis	Middlesex	Murder
06/17/1772	Negro Charles	Northumberland	Burglary
06/22/1772	Negro Jack	Mecklenburg	Rape
06/26/1772	Negress Judith	Brunswick	Poisoning
07/03/1772	Negro Jack	Sussex	Burglary
07/20/1772	Negro Harry	Sussex	Burglary
08/03/1772	Negro Ned	Sussex	Rape
11/11/1772	Negro Bob	Charles City	Not Specified
11/19/1772	Negro Tom	Essex	Burglary
12/02/1772	Negro James	Norfolk	Not Specified
01/11/1773	Negress Sall	Brunswick	Murder
02/02/1773	Negro James	Lancaster	Burglary
02/05/1773	Negro Jack	York	Burglary

Date of Execution	Name of Offender	Venue	Specific Felony
06/03/1773	Eliphalet Musgrove	Williamsburg	Murder
06/28/1773	Negro Ned	Spotsylvania	Highway Robbery
07/08/1773	Joseph Berry	Williamsburg	Horse Stealing
07/08/1773	William Childrey	Williamsburg	Armed Robbery
07/08/1773	James Revell	Williamsburg	Burglary
08/18/1773	Negro Gruff	Prince George	Not Specified
09/08/1773	Negro George	Prince William	Rape
09/08/1773	Negro Jack	Prince George	Not Specified
09/20/1773	Negro Abraham	Accomack	Burglary
09/24/1773	Negro Jack	Sussex	Burglary
10/11/1773	Negro Dagon	Henrico	Not Specified
10/21/1773	Negro Caesar	Cumberland	Poisoning
11/19/1773	Negro Frank	Mecklenburg	Grand Larceny
12/03/1773	John Currie	Williamsburg	Horse Stealing
12/03/1773	John Elliott	Williamsburg	Burglary
12/03/1773	Adam Rutter	Williamsburg	Horse Stealing
12/08/1773	Negro Will	Prince George	Not Specified
01/21/1774	John Whitney	Spotsylvania	Burglary
02/11/1774	Negro Jack	Charles City	Not Specified
03/07/1774	Negro Will	Charlotte	Burglary
03/19/1774	Negro Elisha	Essex	Burglary
03/22/1774	Negro Hannibal	York	Grand Larceny
03/29/1774	Negro Ned	Cumberland	Storehouse Robbery
05/13/1774	Negro Dick	Brunswick	Not Specified
05/13/1774	Negro Seneca	Brunswick	Not Specified
06/03/1774	Catherine Peppers	Williamsburg	Murder
07/ /1774	Negro Simon	Dinwiddie	Burglary
08/05/1774	Negro Joshua	Northumberland	Storehouse Robbery
11/29/1774	Negro Ned	York	Burglary
12/10/1774	Negro Bennett	Essex	Burglary
12/10/1774	Negro Robin	Essex	Burglary
01/13/1775	Susannah Brazier	Williamsburg	Murder
01/13/1775	William Moore	Williamsburg	Burglary
01/13/1775	Edward Porter	Williamsburg	Horse Stealing
03/31/1775	Negro James	Norfolk	Grand Larceny
04/21/1775	Emanuel de Antonio	Norfolk	Rebellion
04/21/1775	Negro Emanuel	Norfolk	Rebellion
05/12/1775	William Gray	Williamsburg	Burglary
05/12/1775	William Pitman*	Williamsburg	Murder
05/12/1775	John Watkins	Williamsburg	Rape
05/12/1775	John Wood	Williamsburg	Burglary
06/30/1775	Negro Jack	Mecklenburg	Grand Larceny
07/24/1775	Negro Gloucester	Caroline	Storehouse Robbery
09/18/1775	Negro Nat	Lancaster	Rape
10/27/1775	Negro Charles	Middlesex	Burglary
10/27/1775	Negro Garvin	Middlesex	Burglary
12/29/1775	Negro David	Brunswick	Not Specified
01/20/1776	Negress Synor	Northumberland	Arson
03/17/1776	Negro Ned	Chesterfield	Not Specified

Date of Execution	Name of Offender	Venue	Specific Felony
05/14/1776	Negro Caesar	Isle of Wight	Burglary
09/03/1776	Negress Frances	Cumberland	Murder
10/18/1776	Negro Reuben	Middlesex	Not Specified
01/ /1777	Negress Jenny	Williamsburg	Not Specified
01/ /1777	Negro Tom	Amherst	Not Specified
02/11/1777	John Meachum*	Williamsburg	Murder
02/21/1777	Negro James	Williamsburg	Burglary
03/ /1777	Negro Ben	Essex	Not Specified
03/ /1777	Negro John	Essex	Not Specified
03/ /1777	Negro Simon	Chesterfield	Not Specified
03/ /1777	Negro Toney	Essex	Not Specified
03/07/1777	Negro Tom	Sussex	Burglary
03/09/1777	Negro John	Cumberland	Murder
04/ /1777	Negro Pritch	Hanover	Not Specified
04/04/1777	Negro March	Spotsylvania	Burglary
05/ /1777	Negro Jeffrey	Cumberland	Murder
05/09/1777	Thomas Green	Williamsburg	Murder
05/09/1777	William Wallace	Williamsburg	Murder
07/28/1777	Negro Caesar	Bedford	Not Specified
09/10/1777	Negro Daniel	Lancaster	Not Specified
11/ /1777	Negro Lewey	Hanover	Not Specified
12/ /1777	Negro Cain	Elizabeth City	Murder
12/ /1777	Negro Davy	Elizabeth City	Murder
12/ /1777	Negro Jack	Elizabeth City	Murder
12/ /1777	Negro Mingo	Elizabeth City	Murder
12/ /1777	Negress Rachel	Elizabeth City	Murder
01/03/1778	Old Bristol	Amelia	Murder
01/03/1778	Young Bristol	Amelia	Murder
01/03/1778	Negro Simon	Amelia	Murder
04/ /1778	Negro James	Williamsburg	Rape
04/06/1778	Negro Aaron	Northumberland	Not Specified
06/18/1778	Negro Will	Rockingham	Not Specified
08/07/1778	Negro Bob (G)	Norfolk	Murder
08/07/1778	Negro Sandy (G)	Norfolk	Murder
09/ /1778	Unnamed Slave (Voss)	Culpeper	Not Specified
12/ /1778	Negro Will	King William	Not Specified
12/04/1778	Josiah Blankenship	Williamsburg	Incorrigible
12/04/1778	Robert Hodges	Williamsburg	Armed Robbery
12/04/1778	Henry McClanen	Williamsburg	Armed Robbery
12/04/1778	Josiah Phillips	Williamsburg	Armed Robbery
12/04/1778	John Reizer	Williamsburg	Murder
01/01/1779	Negro Minora	Louisa	Rape
01/22/1779	Negro Fountain	Sussex	Murder
01/22/1779	Negro Gabe	Sussex	Murder
01/22/1779	Negro Kitt	Sussex	Murder
01/22/1779	Negress Polly	Sussex	Murder
04/30/1779	Gilbert Pearce	Williamsburg	Murder
04/30/1779	Wilston Pinkerton	Williamsburg	Murder
06/11/1779	Negro Frank	Charlotte	Burglary

Date of Execution	Name of Offender	Venue	Specific Felony
07/23/1779	Negro Tim	Loudoun	Burglary
09/16/1779	Negro Ben	Powhatan	Burglary
09/17/1779	Negro Charles	Brunswick	Not Specified
11/15/1779	Andrew Wilson	Williamsburg	Army Deserter
02/04/1780	Negro Hercules	Spotsylvania	Aggravated Assault
02/04/1780	Negro Spencer	Spotsylvania	Aggravated Assault
03/04/1780	Negress Violet	Augusta	Arson
03/31/1780	Negro Jack	Princess Anne	Storehouse Robbery
05/03/1780	John Hampton	Richmond	Horse Stealing
05/03/1780	Drewry Hodges	Richmond	Horse Stealing
05/03/1780	John Hudgins	Richmond	Horse Stealing
06/02/1780	Ben Bacon	York	Burglary
06/10/1780	Negro Jack	Essex	Burglary
08/03/1780	Randall Boush	Richmond	Incorrigible
10/17/1780	Negro Abram	Sussex	Not Specified
10/17/1780	Negro Charles	Sussex	Not Specified
10/17/1780	Negro Jim	Sussex	Not Specified
10/27/1780	Negro Ned	Princess Anne	Burglary
11/ /1780	Unnamed Slave (Wells)	Amelia	Not Specified
11/ /1780	Negro Will	Lancaster	Burglary
——1781	Unnamed Slave (Fitzhugh)	King George	Not Specified
——1781	Unnamed Slave (Howlett)	Gloucester	Not Specified
——1781	Slave (Mountcastle)	Charles City	Not Specified
03/02/1781	Negro Charles	Goochland	Burglary
04/04/1781	Negress Penelope	Charles City	Not Specified
05/ /1781	Four Soldiers	Yorktown	Mutiny
07/14/1781	Negro Pompey	Prince Edward	Not Specified
11/15/1781	Negro Dick	Chesterfield	Not Specified
——1782	Unnamed Slave (Holt)	James City	Not Specified
01/25/1782	John Chapman	Richmond	Horse Stealing
01/25/1782	James Robinson	Richmond	Burglary
02/16/1782	Negro Minas	Dinwiddie	Burglary
02/16/1782	Negro Will	Dinwiddie	Burglary
05/23/1782	Negro Cary	Orange	Rape
09/19/1782	Negro Tom	Powhatan	Burglary
11/29/1782	Maurice Wheeler	Richmond	Murder
——1783	Unnamed Slave	New Kent	Not Specified
04/16/1783	Negro Philip Augusta	Murder	
05/ /1783	Negro Jack	Dinwiddie	Not Specified
05/ /1783	Negress Moll	Dinwiddie	Not Specified
05/15/1783	Francis Nutter (?)	Richmond	Storehouse Robbery
07/18/1783	James Anderson	Richmond	Murder
07/18/1783	James Storrs	Richmond	Horse Stealing
08/28/1783	Negro Sailor	Bedford	Rape
12/05/1783	Michael Newman	Richmond	Armed Robbery
12/05/1783	John Raines	Richmond	Horse Stealing
——1784	Unnamed Slave	Dinwiddie	Not Specified
——1784	Unnamed Slave	Princess Anne	Not Specified
04/23/1784	Negro Jim	Norfolk	Murder

Date of Execution	Name of Offender	Venue	Specific Felony
10/08/1784	Negro James	Brunswick	Rape
11/02/1784	Negro Phil	Botetourt	Rape
12/03/1784	Stephen Yancey	Richmond	Murder
12/ /1784	Negro Bob	Prince George	Burglary
01/28/1785	John Tyler	Richmond	Murder
01/28/1785	Matthew Womble	Richmond	Murder
07/15/1785	Negro Sam	Chesterfield	Not Specified
07/29/1785	Reuben Jones	Richmond	Murder
08/20/1785	Negro Jonathan	Prince George	Burglary
02/04/1786	Negro Dollan	Lunenburg	Poisoning
04/22/1786	Negro Joseph	Culpeper	Not Specified
05/20/1786	Negro Isham	Campbell	Not Specified
06/01/1786	Negro Bob	Frederick	Burglary
08/04/1786	Thomas McAuley	Richmond	Rape
08/04/1786	Negro Toby	Richmond	Burglary
09/ /1786	Negro Billy	Prince William	Not Specified
09/01/1786	Negro Ben	Essex	Attempted Rape
09/09/1786	Negro Ben	Nansemond	Not Specified
09/15/1786	Negro Chelsea	York	Not Specified
10/21/1786	Negro Willis	Middlesex	Not Specified
11/29/1786	Negro Bob	Montgomery	Murder
11/29/1786	Negro Sam	Montgomery	Murder
12/ /1786	John Barnett	Richmond	Horse Stealing
12/08/1786	Negro York	Rockbridge	Murder
01/12/1787	Negro Mesico	Richmond	Not Specified
01/26/1787	Elisha Lassiter	Richmond	Murder
01/26/1787	Isaac Reade	Richmond	Murder
02/ /1787	Negro Whitt	Brunswick	Not Specified
05/11/1787	Negro Clem	Sussex	Murder
06/08/1787	George Abbott	Richmond	Murder
06/30/1787	Negro Tom	Henry	Arson
08/01/1787	Negro Dick	Richmond	Murder
08/01/1787	Richard Downs	Richmond	Burglary
08/01/1787	Joseph Taylor	Richmond	Horse Stealing
10/09/1787	Negro George	Norfolk	Not Specified
12/01/1787	James Phillips	Richmond	Burglary
12/01/1787	William Wilson	Richmond	Horse Stealing
01/25/1788	James McConnell Fox	Richmond	Murder
01/25/1788	John Price Posey	Richmond	Arson
03/28/1788	Negro Tom	Petersburg	Not Specified
06/06/1788	William Armstrong	Richmond	Burglary
06/06/1788	John Candy	Richmond	Burglary
06/06/1788	John Coody	Richmond	Murder
07/31/1788	Archibald Campbell	Richmond	Murder
09/20/1788	Harry Cutts	Nelson	Rape
12/05/1788	Negro Ben	Amherst	Not Specified
12/05/1788	James Scott	Richmond	Murder
12/05/1788	Levi Smith (R)	Richmond	Highway Robbery
12/05/1788	William Wallace	Richmond	Horse Stealing

Date of Execution	Name of Offender	Venue	Specific Felony
01/05/1789	Negro Dick	Spotsylvania	Murder
01/09/1789	Negro Primus	Spotsylvania	Not Specified
01/31/1789	Matthew Farley*	Richmond	Murder
01/31/1789	Thomas Williamson	Richmond	Murder
03/14/1789	Negress Creese	Northampton	Arson
04/13/1789	Negro Bristow	Mecklenburg	Burglary
06/05/1789	George Bird	Charlottesville	Horse Stealing
07/03/1789	Jett Roach	Dumfries	Horse Stealing
07/31/1789	Negro Phil	Nottoway	Not Specified
10/16/1789	Frederick Briggs	Farmville	Horse Stealing
10/16/1789	William McElheney	Farmville	Horse Stealing
01/04/1790	Negro Ned	Southampton	Burglary
03/26/1790	Negro Ben	Nottoway	Murder
03/26/1790	Negro Joe	Nottoway	Murder
06/11/1790	Solomon Watson	Winchester	Horse Stealing
06/19/1790	Negro Abraham	Chesterfield	Burglary
08/14/1790	Negro Moses	Chesterfield	Not Specified
10/01/1790	Negro Isaac	Nottoway	Poisoning
10/01/1790	Negro Mark	Nottoway	Poisoning
10/22/1790	James Medlicott	Winchester	Murder
04/01/1791	Negro Abraham	Nottoway	Attempted Murder
05/27/1791	Thomas Thomas	Charlottesville	Horse Stealing
07/08/1791	Negro George	Fauquier	Murder
07/08/1791	Negress Moll	Fauquier	Murder
09/02/1791	Negro Ben	Amelia	Rape
11/11/1791	Emanuel Driver	Williamsburg	Burglary
11/11/1791	John Driver	Williamsburg	Burglary
11/11/1791	Hugh Shavers (R)	Richmond	Storehouse Robbery
11/11/1791	William Smith	Williamsburg	Burglary
03/02/1792	Gumbo Billy	Halifax	Murder
03/02/1792	Negro Jerry	Gloucester	Burglary
05/25/1792	Ralph C. Anderson	Richmond	Murder
07/06/1792	Hugh Dowdall	Farmville	Coining
07/06/1792	John Crane, Jr.	Winchester	Murder
07/06/1792	William Johnson	Winchester	Murder
07/09/1792	Negro Daniel	Northampton	Attempted Murder
07/09/1792	Negro Jack	Northampton	Attempted Murder
07/09/1792	Negro Matthew	Northampton	Attempted Murder
07/23/1792	William Towe (R)	Suffolk	Horse Stealing
09/03/1792	Negro Isaac	Hanover	Burglary
09/17/1792	Negro Joe	Spotsylvania	Murder
09/17/1792	Negro Tom	Spotsylvania	Murder
10/19/1792	John Young	Winchester	Horse Stealing
11/15/1792	Joshua Knight (R)	Fredericksburg	Horse Stealing
11/21/1792	Negro Will	Cumberland	Murder
12/23/1792	Negro Allen	Charles City	Murder
01/11/1793	Negro Harry	Henrico	Poisoning
03/15/1793	Negro Daniel	Fauquier	Rape
04/29/1793	Negro George	Louisa	Murder

Date of Execution	Name of Offender	Venue	Specific Felony
05/10/1793	Negro Tony	Norfolk	Burglary
08/02/1793	Negress Daphne	James City	Murder
08/20/1793	Negro Roger	Warwick	Rebellion
09/27/1793	Negro Cromwell	Uncertain	Burglary
10/04/1793	Negress Nelly	James City	Murder
10/18/1793	John Bullitt	Staunton	Horse Stealing
10/25/1793	Negro Billy	Northumberland	Rape
10/25/1793	James Conway	Winchester	Murder
10/25/1793	James McCabe	Winchester	Murder
03/03/1794	Negro Charles	Orange	Murder
03/15/1794	Negro Jack	Chesterfield	Conspiracy to Poison
03/31/1794	Negro Nelson	King George	Murder
05/ /1794	Negress Lucy	Dinwiddie	Murder
05/ /1794	Negro George	Dinwiddie	Murder
05/30/1794	Negro Mingo	Middlesex	Poisoning
06/10/1794	Negro Essex	King & Queen	Preparing Poison
06/24/1794	Negro Joe	Powhatan	Murder
06/24/1794	Negro Pompey	Powhatan	Murder
07/18/1794	Negro James	Powhatan	Murder
08/11/1794	Negro Harry	Spotsylvania	Murder
08/11/1794	Negro Ned	Spotsylvania	Murder
08/22/1794	Negro Emanuel	Henrico	Murder
08/22/1794	Negress Polly	King William	Preparing Poison
08/29/1794	Negro Tom	Dinwiddie	Murder
09/ /1794	John Ford	Farmville	Murder
11/28/1794	Negro Jack	Franklin	Rape
04/06/1795	Negro Spencer	Pittsylvania	Rape
06/12/1795	Negro Sam	Chesterfield	Rape
08/01/1795	Negro Joe	Lunenburg	Poisoning
08/07/1795	Negro Ned	Dinwiddie	Burglary
08/14/1795	Negro Ned	Prince George	Murder
09/25/1795	Negro Ned	Lancaster	Murder
10/29/1795	Negro Moses	Cumberland	Burglary
10/30/1795	Negro Allen	Sussex	Poisoning
10/30/1795	Negro Reuben	Sussex	Poisoning
11/06/1795	Negro Peter	Middlesex	Murder
11/06/1795	Negro Tom	Nottoway	Murder
11/13/1795	Negro Joe	Elizabeth City	Rape
11/27/1795	Negress Chloe	Prince Edward	Murder
01/25/1796	Negro Jack	Fairfax	Murder
03/14/1796	Negro Stepney	Mecklenburg	Murder
04/29/1796	Negro Ben	Northumberland	Not Specified
07/29/1796	Negro George	Mathews	Burglary
07/29/1796	Negro Harry	Mathews	Burglary
07/30/1796	Negro Lewis	Greenville	Murder
08/12/1796	Negro Fortune	Shenandoah	Murder
08/19/1796	Billy Harris	Henrico	Storehouse Robbery
09/16/1796	Negro William	Frederick	Arson
10/28/1796	Archer Branch	Richmond	Horse Stealing

Date of Execution	Name of Offender	Venue	Specific Felony
10/28/1796	John Young	Richmond	Horse Stealing
11/12/1796	Negress Moll	Halifax	Murder
12/13/1796	Negro Daniel	Rockingham	Murder
02/17/1797	Negro Will	Chesterfield	Murder
04/22/1797	Negro Sam	King & Queen	Murder
06/20/1797	Negro Dick	Gloucester	Conspiracy to Poison
07/07/1797	Negress Jenny	Gloucester	Poisoning
07/14/1797	Moses Nimrod	Gloucester	Poisoning
08/11/1797	Negro Peter	Surry	Rape
09/22/1797	Negro Dick	New Kent	Grand Larceny
11/17/1797	Roz Norman	Winchester	Rape
11/17/1797	Jesse Scott	Winchester	Horse Stealing
12/10/1797	Negro Davy	Isle of Wight	Not Specified
02/13/1798	Negro Jack	Wythe	Horse Stealing
02/16/1798	Negro Claibourne (R)	Petersburg	Arson
03/09/1798	Negro Caesar	Petersburg	Burglary
03/09/1798	Negro Glasgow	Petersburg	Burglary
03/12/1798	Negro Abram	Greenville	Murder
03/23/1798	Negress Polly	York	Murder
06/15/1798	Negro Gabriel	James City	Burglary
06/16/1798	Negro Joshua	King George	Burglary
06/16/1798	Negro Robin	King George	Burglary
07/20/1798	Negro Ralph	Frederick	Poisoning
07/31/1798	Negro Jack	Prince William	Burglary
09/21/1798	Negro Daniel	Westmoreland	Murder
09/21/1798	Negro Willoughby	Westmoreland	Murder
11/02/1798	Negro Daniel	Petersburg	Highway Robbery
11/09/1798	Negro Lewis	Chesterfield	Highway Robbery
11/30/1798	Negro Nat	Northampton	Highway Robbery
12/14/1798	Negro Philip	Princess Anne	Rape
01/ /1799	Negro Ned	Southampton	Murder
01/11/1799	Negro Bob	Henrico	Attempted Murder
01/18/1799	Negro Simon	Nansemond	Storehouse Robbery
01/18/1799	Negro Zach	Shenandoah	Murder
01/22/1799	Negro Billy	Middlesex	Rebellion
01/22/1799	Negro Burgess	Middlesex	Rebellion
02/15/1799	Negro Nat	Mecklenburg	Murder
03/01/1799	Negro Horatio	Orange	Rape
03/15/1799	Negro Isaac	Henrico	Burglary
04/18/1799	Negro Beeks	Pittsylvania	Murder
04/18/1799	Negro Solomon	Pittsylvania	Murder
06/04/1799	Negro Isaac	Surry	Murder
06/15/1799	Negress Amy	King & Queen	Murder
10/18/1799	Negro Isaac	Hanover	Rape
04/11/1800	Negro Sam	Southampton	Murder
08/08/1800	Negro Ned	Sussex	Burglary
08/20/1800	Negro Tom	Henry	Murder
08/31/1800	Negro Abram	Buckingham	Murder
09/05/1800	Negro Harry	Hanover	Rape

Date of Execution	Name of Offender	Venue	Specific Felony
09/12/1800	Negro Isaac	Henrico	Conspiracy to Rebel
09/12/1800	Negro John	Henrico	Conspiracy to Rebel
09/12/1800	Negro Ned	Henrico	Conspiracy to Rebel
09/12/1800	Negro Solomon	Henrico	Conspiracy to Rebel
09/12/1800	Negro Will	Henrico	Conspiracy to Rebel
09/15/1800	Negro Billy	Henrico	Conspiracy to Rebel
09/15/1800	Negro Charles	Henrico	Conspiracy to Rebel
09/15/1800	Negro Frank	Henrico	Conspiracy to Rebel
09/15/1800	Negro Martin	Henrico	Conspiracy to Rebel
09/15/1800	Negro Michael	Henrico	Conspiracy to Rebel
09/18/1800	Negro Isham	Henrico	Conspiracy to Rebel
09/18/1800	Negro Jupiter	Henrico	Conspiracy to Rebel
09/18/1800	Negro Peter	Henrico	Conspiracy to Rebel
09/18/1800	Negro Sam	Henrico	Conspiracy to Rebel
09/18/1800	Negro Sawney	Henrico	Conspiracy to Rebel
10/03/1800	Negro Peter	Greensville	Rape
10/10/1800	Sam Byrd	Henrico	Conspiracy to Rebel
10/10/1800	Negro Gabriel	Henrico	Conspiracy to Rebel
10/10/1800	Negro George	Henrico	Conspiracy to Rebel
10/10/1800	Negro Gilbert	Henrico	Conspiracy to Rebel
10/10/1800	Negro Isaac	Henrico	Conspiracy to Rebel
10/10/1800	Negro Laddis	Henrico	Conspiracy to Rebel
10/10/1800	Negro Michael	Henrico	Conspiracy to Rebel
10/10/1800	Negro Sam	Henrico	Conspiracy to Rebel
10/10/1800	Negro Tom	Henrico	Conspiracy to Rebel
10/10/1800	Negro William	Henrico	Conspiracy to Rebel
10/24/1800	Negro Peter	Dinwiddie	Not Specified
02/13/1801	Negro Aaron	Albemarle	Burglary
03/06/1801	Negro Stephen	Henrico	Murder
04/10/1801	Negress Nan	King George	Not Specified
07/10/1801	George Poindexter	Rocky Mount	Murder
01/ /1802	Negro Ned	Amelia	Murder
01/10/1802	Negro Aaron	Amherst	Murder
01/16/1802	Negro Bob	Nottoway	Insurrection
01/16/1802	Negro Joe	Nottoway	Insurrection
02/12/1802	Negro Isaac	Brunswick	Insurrection
02/12/1802	Negro Phil	Brunswick	Insurrection
02/19/1802	Negro Hall	Mecklenburg	Murder
02/26/1802	Negro George	Southampton	Murder
02/26/1802	Negro Henry	Southampton	Murder
02/26/1802	Negro Hercules	Southampton	Murder
02/26/1802	Negro Punch	Prince Edward	Conspiracy to Poison
03/02/1802	Negro Bob	Lunenburg	Conspiracy to Poison
03/12/1802	Negro Cato	Caroline	Murder
05/01/1802	Negro Patrick	Caroline	Murder
05/15/1802	Negro Abram	Halifax	Insurrection
05/15/1802	Negro Absalom	Halifax	Insurrection
05/15/1802	Negro Frank	Halifax	Insurrection
05/15/1802	Negro Martin	Halifax	Insurrection

Date of Execution	Name of Offender	Venue	Specific Felony
05/15/1802	Negro Sancho	Halifax	Insurrection
05/28/1802	Negro Jeremiah	Norfolk	Insurrection
06/04/1802	Negro Jonas	Norfolk	Murder
06/05/1802	Negro Abraham	Loudoun	Poisoning
06/11/1802	Negro Dick	Mecklenburg	Attempt to Poison
07/29/1802	Negro John	Halifax	Poisoning
05/17/1803	John Semphill	Williamsburg	Murder
07/15/1803	Negress Sarah	Albemarle	Aggravated Assault
10/28/1803	Negress Charity	Princess Anne	Poisoning
10/28/1803	Negro George	Princess Anne	Poisoning
10/28/1803	Negro Ted	Mecklenburg	Murder
11/11/1803	James Scott	Winchester	Murder
11/25/1803	James Cherry	Suffolk	Murder
11/25/1803	Gabriel Reed*	Suffolk	Murder
11/28/1803	Lewis McWhaine	Charlottesville	Murder
05/04/1804	Negro Jack	Bedford	Murder
05/18/1804	George Bartlett	Richmond	Murder
06/01/1804	James Hennesey	Winchester	Murder
06/14/1804	Negro Daniel	Lancaster	Murder
09/07/1804	Mulatto Jesse	Winchester	Rape
11/16/1804	Reuben Howman	Fredericksburg	Murder
02/15/1805	Negro Abraham	Stafford	Insurrection
03/15/1805	Billy Scott	Henrico	Rape
05/14/1805	Negro Archie	Botetourt	Rape
07/09/1805	Negro Peter	Patrick	Rape
11/30/1805	Peter Twine	Fairfax	Rape
01/17/1806	Negro Moses	Williamsburg	Aggravated Assault
02/28/1806	Negress Fanny	Charlotte	Poisoning
03/15/1806	Negress Charlotte	Caroline	Murder
05/30/1806	Negress Crease	Chesterfield	Murder
07/11/1806	Negress Sall	Chesterfield	Murder
07/18/1806	Negro Harry	Frederick	Murder
09/19/1806	Negro Jack	Chesterfield	Burglary
09/19/1806	Negro Kitt	Chesterfield	Burglary
03/13/1807	Negro Isaac	Pittsylvania	Storehouse Robbery
05/29/1807	Negro Billy	Nottoway	Poisoning
11/02/1807	Negro Moses	Hanover	Highway Robbery
01/14/1808	Bill Williams	Norfolk	Murder
01/29/1808	Negro Tom	Albemarle	Conspiracy to Poison
03/04/1808	Negro Will	Norfolk	Highway Robbery
03/19/1808	Negro Jim	Campbell	Murder
04/18/1808	Negro Ben	Charles City	Murder
04/18/1808	Negro Lewis	Charles City	Murder
04/18/1808	Negro Spencer	Charles City	Murder
05/09/1808	John Blanks	Prince Edward	Murder
08/08/1808	Samuel Hill	Fredericksburg	Murder
09/28/1808	Negro Mooklar	Westmoreland	Rape
12/20/1808	Negro Dick	Southampton	Child Molestation
01/01/1809	Negro Jacob	Nelson	Insurrection

Date of Execution	Name of Offender	Venue	Specific Felony
05/05/1809	Negress Flora	Frederick	Murder
07/14/1809	Negro Edmund	Mathews	Murder
07/14/1809	Negro Frank	Mathews	Murder
07/14/1809	Negro Jack	Mathews	Murder
07/14/1809	Negro James	Mathews	Murder
10/27/1809	Negro Sam	Montgomery	Murder
03/16/1810	Negro Sutton	Gloucester	Highway Robbery
06/01/1810	Major Jackson	Goochland	Aggravated Assault
07/28/1810	Negro Glasgow	Culpeper	Arson
10/ /1810	Negro Ned	Chesterfield	Not Specified
12/14/1810	Negro Will	Prince Edward	Murder
12/27/1810	Negro Dick	Greensville	Aggravated Burglary
02/01/1811	Ben Burns	Botetourt	Murder
02/01/1811	Frank Bush	Botetourt	Murder
02/01/1811	John Darrell	Botetourt	Murder
02/01/1811	Negro Perry	Botetourt	Murder
02/01/1811	Bob Toogood	Botetourt	Murder
05/11/1811	Negro Stephen	Fauquier	Rape
03/13/1812	Negro Abram	Bedford	Murder
05/18/1812	Negro Tom	Henry	Murder
10/02/1812	Negro Isaac	Nansemond	Rape
12/11/1812	Negress Amy	Augusta	Murder
04/23/1813	Negro Harry	Mathews	Not Specified
04/23/1813	Negro Humphrey	Mathews	Not Specified
08/21/1813	Negro Phil	King & Queen	Murder
08/27/1813	Negro Mike	Amelia	Burglary
09/03/1813	Negro Isham	Prince Edward	Murder
09/05/1813	Negro Robin	Sussex	Burglary
10/08/1813	Negro Caesar	Prince William	Highway Robbery
11/13/1813	William Proctor	Norfolk	Army Deserter
12/10/1813	Cadet LaRue	Portsmouth	Murder
02/ /1814	Negro George	King George	Not Specified
05/03/1814	Negro Andrew	Dinwiddie	Murder
05/03/1814	Negro Hal	Dinwiddie	Murder
05/24/1814	Negro Matt	Bedford	Murder
05/28/1814	Jeremiah Lucas	Giles	Murder
07/01/1814	Negro Isaac	Bedford	Rape
08/05/1814	Negro Isaac	Fairfax	Rape
08/20/1814	Negro Ralph	Botetourt	Murder
11/11/1814	Negro Hercules	Shenandoah	Aggravated Burglary
05/19/1815	James Archibald	Halifax	Murder
07/14/1815	Negro Caesar	Norfolk	Murder
10/27/1815	Negro Archer	Chesterfield	Burglary
02/23/1816	Negress Jenny	Powhatan	Murder
03/29/1816	Negro Mack	Louisa	Insurrection
03/29/1816	Negro Matt	Louisa	Insurrection
03/29/1816	Negro Ned	Louisa	Insurrection
03/29/1816	Negro Tom	Louisa	Insurrection
04/05/1816	Negro Charles	Spotsylvania	Insurrection

Date of Execution	Name of Offender	Venue	Specific Felony
04/05/1816	Negro Emanuel	Spotsylvania	Insurrection
06/28/1816	John Fox	Gloucester	Arson
06/28/1816	Negro Nelson	Gloucester	Arson
07/12/1816	Negro Watt	Rockbridge	Murder
07/26/1816	Negress Delphy	Louisa	Poisoning
10/04/1816	Negress Clara	Spotsylvania	Murder
01/31/1817	Negro Daniel	Cumberland	Poisoning
04/17/1817	Negro Miles	Isle of Wight	Murder
08/17/1817	Negro Luke	Northampton	Murder
11/14/1817	Negro Anthony	Franklin	Rape
01/30/1818	Negress Caty	Brunswick	Murder
03/10/1818	Negro Jacob	Sussex	Burglary
03/10/1818	Negro John	Sussex	Burglary
05/22/1818	Sylvanus Brewer	Russell	Murder
07/10/1818	Negro Landon	Frederick	Murder
07/10/1818	Jeremiah Oldham	Northumberland	Murder
07/10/1818	Negro Randolph	Frederick	Murder
07/10/1818	Negress Sarah	Frederick	Murder
07/10/1818	Joseph Wildy	Northumberland	Arson
07/14/1818	Negro Manuel	King George	Murder
09/04/1818	Negro Lewis	Lunenburg	Rape
09/04/1818	Negro Tom	Norfolk	Highway Robbery
09/25/1818	Negro Joe	Pittsylvania	Murder
09/25/1818	Negro Squire	Pittsylvania	Murder
10/02/1818	Negro Jack	Orange	Rape
10/27/1818	Robert Gibson	Henrico	Murder
03/06/1819	Negro Henry	Botetourt	Murder
07/16/1819	Abner Vance	Washington	Murder
08/20/1819	Negro Reuben	Campbell	Rape
12/17/1819	James Vest	Chesterfield	Murder
12/24/1819	Negro Stephen	Charles City	Highway Robbery
01/21/1820	Negress Chaney	Madison	Poisoning
01/21/1820	Negro Moses	Madison	Poisoning
03/03/1820	Negro Robin	Amherst	Murder
03/24/1820	Negro Jordan	Henrico	Murder
04/07/1820	Negro Abram	James City	Murder
06/09/1820	Negro Ned	King William	Murder
08/12/1820	Negro Bob	Sussex	Murder
11/17/1820	Negro Jack	New Kent	Murder
11/24/1820	Negro Burrill	Surry	Burglary
11/24/1820	Negro Jeff	Surry	Burglary
05/04/1821	John Miller	Orange	Murder
06/01/1821	Jose Demas Garcia	Norfolk	Murder
06/01/1821	Manuel Felipe Garcia	Norfolk	Murder
06/09/1821	Jesse Carbell	Nansemond	Murder
06/11/1821	Negro Armistead	Charlotte	Murder
07/06/1821	Negro Winston	Orange	Rape
08/10/1821	Negro Patrick	Louisa	Murder
08/15/1821	Negro Abel	Southampton	Murder

Date of Execution	Name of Offender	Venue	Specific Felony
08/15/1821	Negress Celia	Southampton	Murder
09/25/1821	Negro Tom	Campbell	Murder
10/28/1821	Benjamin Hopkins	Rockingham	Murder
11/03/1821	Negress Pat	Charlotte	Murder
11/30/1821	John Gillman	Caroline	Murder
12/14/1821	William Reid	Caroline	Murder
03/01/1822	Negro Henry	Mecklenburg	Murder
03/29/1822	Negro Ned	Cumberland	Attempted Murder
06/21/1822	Michael Montgole	Montgomery	Murder
07/26/1822	Negro Ned	Norfolk	Rape
09/21/1822	Negro Plato	Bedford	Murder
11/15/1822	Negro Ralph	Bedford	Murder
06/06/1823	Negro Scott	Lunenburg	Murder
06/20/1823	Dempsey Carr	Isle of Wight	Murder
06/27/1823	Negro Lewis	Norfolk	Murder
07/11/1823	Negro Alexander	Orange	Rape
07/11/1823	Negro Jasper	Norfolk	Murder
07/12/1823	Negro Charles	Campbell	Rape
07/25/1823	Bob Ferebee	Norfolk	Murder
08/07/1823	Negro Bill	Augusta	Rape
11/21/1823	Negro John	Chesterfield	Rape
01/16/1824	Negro Mingo	Nansemond	Murder
03/26/1824	Negro Sam	New Kent	Murder
04/02/1824	Negro Humphrey	Hanover	Murder
04/02/1824	Negro Thornton	Hanover	Murder
06/25/1824	Reuben Wicks	Nottoway	Murder
09/03/1824	Negro Jack	Nansemond	Arson
10/26/1824	Negro Dick	Culpeper	Aggravated Burglary
10/26/1824	Negro Lawrence	Culpeper	Aggravated Burglary
12/10/1824	Hudson Sprouce	Rockingham	Murder
12/31/1824	Negro Reuben	Orange	Murder
12/31/1824	Negro Stephen	Brunswick	Murder
01/21/1825	Negro Sam	Nansemond	Murder
02/04/1825	Negro Ned	Dinwiddie	Arson
04/08/1825	Negro Jim	King William	Murder
04/08/1825	Negro Johnson	King William	Murder
06/ /1825	Negro Tom	Lancaster	Murder
07/08/1825	Joseph Burgess	Prince William	Murder
09/29/1825	Negro Moses	Hanover	Murder
10/21/1825	Negro Isaac	Albemarle	Attempted Rape
04/14/1826	Negro Bartlett	King & Queen	Murder
05/05/1826	Negro Bill	Madison	Murder
05/05/1826	Negro Henry	Madison	Murder
06/30/1826	William Hooe	Fairfax	Murder
07/28/1826	Negress Molly	Patrick	Murder
07/28/1826	Negro Stephen	King George	Not Specified
08/04/1826	Negro Solomon	Prince Edward	Murder
08/11/1826	Negro Dinwiddie	Sussex	Rape
08/25/1826	Negro Charles	Cumberland	Murder

Date of Execution	Name of Offender	Venue	Specific Felony
10/06/1826	Negro Jim	Accomack	Burglary
10/06/1826	Negro Leven	Accomack	Burglary
10/06/1826	Negro George	Princess Anne	Highway Robbery
11/10/1826	Negro David	Brunswick	Murder
04/27/1827	Negro Archer	Lunenburg	Murder
04/27/1827	Negro Billy	Lunenburg	Murder
04/27/1827	Negro David	Lunenburg	Murder
04/27/1827	Negro Nathan	Lunenburg	Murder
04/27/1827	Negro Sam	Lunenburg	Murder
04/27/1827	Big Stephen	Lunenburg	Murder
04/27/1827	Negro Tom	Lunenburg	Murder
05/ /1827	Negro Peter	Essex	Not Specified
05/11/1827	Negro Jack	Princess Anne	Highway Robbery
06/01/1827	Negro Edmund	Lunenburg	Attempted Murder
06/15/1827	Negro Jim	Northampton	Burglary
06/27/1827	Jonathan DeVaughn	Arlington	Murder
07/27/1827	Negro Lewis	Cumberland	Murder
08/17/1827	Felix Barbeito (F)	Henrico	Murder
08/17/1827	Jose Casares (F)	Henrico	Murder
08/17/1827	Jose Morando (F)	Henrico	Murder
09/07/1827	Negro Henry	Mathews	Aggravated Burglary
10/26/1827	Negress Judy	Fluvanna	Murder
11/01/1827	Negro Buck	Halifax	Rape
11/30/1827	Negro Allen	Washington	Murder
12/28/1827	Negro Frank	Dinwiddie	Not Specified
03/17/1828	Negress Nelly	Southampton	Murder
06/23/1828	Negro Sam	Lancaster	Murder
06/24/1828	Negro Robert	Petersburg	Murder
08/22/1828	Negro Jeffery	Louisa	Rape
11/21/1828	Negro Shadrach	Pittsylvania	Murder
12/19/1828	Joseph Whiteford	Chesterfield	Murder
01/09/1829	Negro Harry	Powhatan	Murder
06/26/1829	Negro Dick	York	Not Specified
07/24/1829	Negro Lewis	Mecklenburg	Rape
08/21/1829	Negro Gabriel	Patrick	Rape
08/26/1829	Negro Adam	Hanover	Murder
08/28/1829	Negro Davy	Hanover	Murder
08/28/1829	Negro Sandy	Hanover	Murder
10/16/1829	Negro Aleck	Bedford	Murder
10/21/1829	Negress Annis	Amelia	Attempt to Poison
11/22/1829	Negro Joseph	Shenandoah	Rape
03/05/1830	Negro Reuben	Henry	Murder
06/25/1830	Negro Henry	Franklin	Attempted Rape
07/16/1830	Pvt. Wheeler	Chesterfield	Murder
07/30/1830	Negro Daniel	Henrico	Murder
08/16/1830	John Jones	Lynchburg	Murder
11/26/1830	Charles Young	Caroline	Murder
07/29/1831	Negro Dick	Loudoun	Rape
09/05/1831	Negro Daniel	Southampton	Insurrection

Date of Execution	Name of Offender	Venue	Specific Felony
09/05/1831	Negro Moses	Southampton	Insurrection
09/09/1831	Negro Davy	Southampton	Insurrection
09/09/1831	Negro Nat	Southampton	Insurrection
09/09/1831	Negro Nelson	Southampton	Insurrection
09/12/1831	Negro Curtis	Southampton	Insurrection
09/12/1831	Negro Davey	Southampton	Insurrection
09/12/1831	Negro Dred	Southampton	Insurrection
09/12/1831	Negro Hark	Southampton	Insurrection
09/12/1831	Negro Jack	Southampton	Insurrection
09/12/1831	Negro Nathan	Southampton	Insurrection
09/12/1831	Negro Sam	Southampton	Insurrection
09/12/1831	Negro Stephen	Southampton	Insurrection
09/23/1831	Jack Niles	Nansemond	Insurrection
10/14/1831	Negro Jarrett	Spotsylvania	Murder
10/21/1831	Negro Booker	Sussex	Insurrection
10/21/1831	Negro Ned	Sussex	Insurrection
10/21/1831	Negro Nicholas	Sussex	Insurrection
10/21/1831	Negro Solomon	Sussex	Insurrection
10/24/1831	Negro Joe	Southampton	Insurrection
10/24/1831	Negress Lucy	Southampton	Insurrection
10/27/1831	Negro Dick	Westmoreland	Not Specified
11/04/1831	Negro Sam	Southampton	Insurrection
11/11/1831	Nat Turner	Southampton	Insurrection
11/16/1831	Negro Anthony	Prince George	Murder
11/16/1831	Negro Dennis	Prince George	Murder
11/16/1831	Negro Ellick	Prince George	Murder
11/16/1831	Negro Ephraim	Prince George	Murder
11/16/1831	Negro Preston	Prince George	Murder
12/20/1831	Negro Ben	Southampton	Insurrection
03/09/1832	Negress Elizabeth	Norfolk	Poisoning
05/04/1832	Negro John	Richmond Co.	Murder
05/11/1832	Barry Newsome	Southampton	Sedition
10/05/1832	Negress Fanny	Prince Edward	Poisoning
10/05/1832	Negress Renah	Prince Edward	Poisoning
11/02/1832	Negro Joshua	Prince Edward	Rape
11/09/1832	John Tumms	Scott	Murder
03/22/1833	Negro Sam	Northumberland	Highway Robbery
04/19/1833	Negro Bob	Chesterfield	Rape
06/14/1833	Negro John	King & Queen	Murder
06/21/1833	Negress Mary	Southampton	Attempted Murder
06/21/1833	Negro Ben	Frederick	Rape
10/18/1833	Negro Lee	Albemarle	Murder
10/18/1833	Negro Peter	Albemarle	Murder
11/08/1833	Negro Sim	Madison	Murder
07/11/1834	Negro Peter	Grayson	Rape
07/18/1834	Caleb Watts	Westmoreland	Attempted Rape
08/01/1834	Negress Nelly	Bedford	Murder
08/03/1834	Negro George	Prince Edward	Murder
08/03/1834	Negro Littleton	Prince Edward	Murder

Date of Execution	Name of Offender	Venue	Specific Felony
10/31/1834	Negro Nelson	Lynchburg	Murder
03/06/1835	Negro Ben	Fauquier	Murder
07/03/1835	Thomas Jones	Westmoreland	Murder
07/24/1835	Robert Hoy	Rockingham	Murder
07/31/1835	Pleasant Gillis	Petersburg	Murder
07/31/1835	Negro Ephraim	Accomack	Highway Robbery
07/31/1835	Negro Lewis	Accomack	Highway Robbery
07/31/1835	Negro Spencer	Accomack	Highway Robbery
04/15/1836	Negro Humphrey	Caroline	Murder
05/13/1836	Negress Phoebe	Essex	Murder
04/07/1837	Negro Simmons	Nottoway	Murder
12/01/1837	Negro Frank	Henrico	Murder
12/08/1837	Negro David	Pittsylvania	Rape
12/15/1837	Henry Jackson	Fairfax	Murder
12/15/1837	Negro Orange	Lunenburg	Attempted Murder
12/29/1837	Jacob Crabtree	Botetourt	Murder
01/19/1838	William Bennett	Pittsylvania	Murder
07/13/1838	Negro Randolph	Louisa	Murder
09/14/1838	Negro George	Powhatan	Murder
09/24/1838	Negro Andrew	Bath	Murder
09/24/1838	Negress Lucinda	Bath	Murder
10/12/1838	Negro Jim	Bedford	Murder
11/30/1838	Negro Mehegan	Nansemond	Murder
12/28/1838	Benjamin Puller	Frederick	Murder
03/13/1839	Negro Frank	Southampton	Rape
03/13/1839	Negro Jeff	Southampton	Rape
05/03/1839	Negro Bob	Cumberland	Arson
05/22/1839	Negro Henry	Wythe	Arson
09/06/1839	Negro Henry	Spotsylvania	Attempted Murder
11/08/1839	Negro Jacob	Madison	Arson
12/10/1839	Henry Morris	York	Attempted Murder
12/20/1839	Negro Henry	Uncertain	Murder
02/18/1840	Negro Henry	Orange	Attempted Rape
05/22/1840	Negro Spencer	Fairfax	Conspiracy to Rebel
07/14/1840	Negro Random	Nottoway	Murder
09/11/1840	Negro Lewis	Nottoway	Murder
10/16/1840	Negro Anthony	Lunenburg	Aggravated Assault
10/20/1840	Negro Nicholas	Southampton	Conspiracy to Rebel
10/23/1840	Negress Betsy	Fauquier	Murder
11/27/1840	Negro Ampey	Dinwiddie	Rape
03/01/1841	Negress Diana	Greensville	Attempt to Poison
03/12/1841	Negro Stephen	Chesterfield	Murder
10/01/1841	Negro John	Norfolk	Attempted Murder
04/08/1842	Negro Captain	Page	Murder
04/08/1842	Negro Martin	Page	Murder
06/24/1842	David Lucas	Giles	Murder
08/12/1842	Daniel Wright	Alleghany	Murder
09/16/1842	Negro Robin	Northampton	Attempted Murder
12/23/1842	Negro Ephraim	Dinwiddie	Arson

Date of Execution	Name of Offender	Venue	Specific Felony
12/23/1842	Negro Matthew	Dinwiddie	Arson
01/06/1843	Benjamin Stegall	Halifax	Murder
01/20/1843	Negro Fleming	Chesterfield	Murder
05/19/1843	Negro Beverly	Halifax	Rape
11/10/1843	Negro Arthur	Albemarle	Rape
11/24/1843	Negro George	King William	Rape
12/22/1843	Negro Jerry	Lunenburg	Rape
01/05/1844	Negro George	Fluvanna	Murder
02/03/1844	Negro Lewis	Cumberland	Rape
03/29/1844	Negro Robin	Pittsylvania	Murder
04/12/1844	Negro Willis	Pulaski	Attempted Rape
08/09/1844	Negro Andrew	Albemarle	Rape
09/27/1844	Negro John	Accomack	Rape
01/15/1845	Negro Frederick	Washington	Poisoning
03/28/1845	Negro Jack	Norfolk	Attempted Rape
06/20/1845	Negro Jerry	Campbell	Attempted Murder
12/19/1845	George Freeman	Augusta	Rape
12/19/1845	Negro George	Augusta	Rape
12/19/1845	Negro Jim	Augusta	Rape
12/19/1845	Moses Johnson	Henrico	Murder
01/31/1846	Negro John	Petersburg	Aggravated Assault
03/24/1846	Moses Henry	Henrico	Murder
05/07/1847	Negro Bob	Nottoway	Murder
05/21/1847	Negro Peter	Goochland	Murder
05/21/1847	Negro Posey	Goochland	Murder
06/04/1847	Everett Day	Chesterfield	Attempted Rape
07/30/1847	Negro Daniel	Halifax	Murder
07/30/1847	Negro Willis	Sussex	Murder
12/10/1847	Negro Giles	Henrico	Murder
04/28/1848	Negro Billy	Petersburg	Murder
05/12/1848	Negro King	Henrico	Murder
07/28/1848	Negro Jefferson	Wythe	Murder
09/16/1848	Negro William	Gloucester	Murder
10/06/1848	Negro Simon (1)	Prince Edward	Conspiracy to Murder
10/06/1848	Negro Simon (2)	Prince Edward	Conspiracy to Murder
11/10/1848	Negro Reuben	Albemarle	Attempted Murder
12/15/1848	Lewis Neal	Loudoun	Murder
12/22/1848	William Epes	Dinwiddie	Murder
09/28/1849	Jim Mays	Pittsylvania	Murder
10/12/1849	Negress Eliza	Brunswick	Poisoning
10/12/1849	Negress Roberta	Brunswick	Poisoning
10/19/1849	Negro Bob	Halifax	Attempted Murder
12/28/1849	Negro Wesley	Mecklenburg	Attempted Rape
02/08/1850	Negro Peter	Prince George	Arson
04/05/1850	Negro Henry	Southampton	Murder
06/28/1850	Henry Gunn	Henrico	Murder
07/19/1850	Negress Agnes	Prince William	Murder
08/16/1850	Negro Robert	Lancaster	Murder
11/29/1850	Negro Ben	Rockbridge	Rape

Date of Execution	Name of Offender	Venue	Specific Felony
03/07/1851	Negro Dick	Mecklenburg	Poisoning
10/31/1851	Negro Jack	Grayson	Murder
10/31/1851	Negro Lewis	Grayson	Murder
10/31/1851	Negro Simon	Grayson	Murder
12/19/1851	Negro Bickerton	Louisa	Murder
12/19/1851	Negro Frank	Louisa	Murder
12/26/1851	Negro Andrew	Middlesex	Attempted Rape
03/26/1852	Edmund Clore	Madison	Murder
04/23/1852	Edward Clements (F)	Henrico	Murder and Piracy
04/23/1852	Thomas Reed (F)	Henrico	Murder and Piracy
05/14/1852	Negress Mahalia	Giles	Murder
09/10/1852	Negress Jane	Powhatan	Murder
09/10/1852	Negress Molly	Sussex	Attempted Murder
09/10/1852	Jane Williams	Henrico	Murder
09/24/1852	Negro Jerry	Page	Aggravated Assault
10/22/1852	John Williams	Henrico	Murder
11/12/1852	Negro Miles	Princess Anne	Attempted Rape
01/07/1853	Negro Sydney	Nottoway	Murder
06/10/1853	Negro Andrew	Charlotte	Rape
06/24/1853	John Wormley	Chesterfield	Murder
07/01/1853	Negro Tom	Mecklenburg	Arson
08/12/1853	Margaret Buckner	Culpeper	Murder
08/12/1853	Joshua Goings	Albemarle	Murder
08/12/1853	Jim Phillips	Culpeper	Murder
09/09/1853	Negro Buck	Sussex	Attempted Murder
09/09/1853	Negro Harris	Sussex	Attempted Murder
09/09/1853	Negro John	Sussex	Attempted Murder
12/09/1853	Ben Smith	Washington	Rape
01/06/1854	Andrew H. Thayer	Augusta	Murder
02/17/1854	Negress Sally	Halifax	Not Specified
03/10/1854	Jim Gooch	Rockbridge	Murder
08/29/1854	Negro Jack	Henry	Murder
10/06/1854	Negro William	Surry	Rape
11/17/1854	Negro Washington	Henrico	Arson
04/27/1855	Negro Frank	Prince Edward	Murder
06/29/1855	Negro Henry	Buckingham	Murder
08/31/1855	Negro Ned	Dinwiddie	Murder
10/26/1855	Joe Jones	Chesterfield	Attempted Rape
11/ /1855	Jim Jones	Bedford	Murder
11/16/1855	Negro John	Dinwiddie	Murder
02/01/1856	Negro George	Wythe	Attempted Rape
04/11/1856	Negro Farris	Bedford	Murder
04/21/1856	Negro Jacob	Charles City	Murder
05/28/1856	Negro Julius	Charlotte	Murder
08/01/1856	Negro Henry	Goochland	Murder
08/01/1856	Negro Smith	Goochland	Murder
09/12/1856	Negress Amelia	Caroline	Murder
09/26/1856	Negro Sam	Highland	Murder
10/10/1856	Negro Jesse	Buckingham	Attempted Rape

Date of Execution	Name of Offender	Venue	Specific Felony
11/07/1856	Negro Anderson	Spotsylvania	Rape
11/09/1856	Negro James	Bedford	Murder
02/13/1857	Negress Betsy	Prince William	Murder
02/13/1857	Negro James	Prince William	Murder
02/13/1857	Negress Nelly	Prince William	Murder
06/05/1857	Negro Reuben	Caroline	Attempted Murder
08/21/1857	Negress Catherine	Louisa	Murder
10/23/1857	Negro Anthony	Amherst	Aggravated Assault
10/23/1857	Negro Reuben	Appomattox	Murder
11/06/1857	James Crowley	Caroline	Murder
11/20/1857	Negro Harvey	Nansemond	Attempted Murder
11/20/1857	Negro Jim	Nansemond	Attempted Murder
02/26/1858	Negress Jenny	Arlington	Murder
03/19/1858	Negro Dick	New Kent	Murder
03/19/1858	Negro Henry	New Kent	Murder
03/19/1858	Negro Major	New Kent	Murder
04/30/1858	Jesse Crockett	Stafford	Murder
06/25/1858	Baxter S. Pate	Scott	Murder
08/06/1858	James Catlett	Frederick	Murder
08/13/1858	Tom Long	Pittsylvania	Murder
09/03/1858	Negro Madison	Surry	Murder
09/10/1858	Negress Jane	Bedford	Murder
01/14/1859	Bray Sanders	Southampton	Murder
03/25/1859	William Brown	Alleghany	Murder
04/19/1859	Negro Richard	Henry	Poisoning
05/13/1859	James Johnson	Washington	Murder
05/17/1859	Negro Dow	Henry	Poisoning
05/17/1859	Negro Harry	Henry	Poisoning
07/01/1859	Patrick Murphy	Alleghany	Murder
07/22/1859	Negro David	Richmond Co.	Attempted Rape
09/30/1859	Negress Angelina	Culpeper	Arson
03/02/1860	Negro Henry	Goochland	Rape
03/02/1860	Negro Jim	Bedford	Murder
04/06/1860	Negress Ann	Essex	Murder
04/06/1860	Negress Eliza	Essex	Murder
05/11/1860	Negro Branch	Nottoway	Murder
05/11/1860	Negro Elisha	Nottoway	Murder
05/18/1860	Negro Jordan	Danville	Murder
05/18/1860	Negro Winston	Greene	Attempted Murder
08/03/1860	Negro Elisha	Louisa	Murder
08/31/1860	William Hendricks	Lynchburg	Murder
09/ /1860	Negro George	Halifax	Rape
11/09/1860	Negro Colin	Lunenburg	Attempt to Poison
11/09/1860	Negro Dick	Lunenburg	Attempt to Poison
11/09/1860	Negro John	Lunenburg	Attempt to Poison
11/16/1860	William Totty	Henrico	Murder
01/25/1861	Negro Nelson	Caroline	Murder
02/28/1861	Negro Andrew	Caroline	Arson
05/30/1861	Benjamin Lambert	Manassas	Espionage

Date of Execution	Name of Offender	Venue	Specific Felony
06/29/1861	Negro Charles	Louisa	Aggravated Burglary
08/02/1861	William Murray	Alexandria	Murder
09/ /1861	Negro Hiram	Rockingham	Rape
10/11/1861	Negro Mark	Nottoway	Arson
11/ /1861	Negress Harriet	Frederick	Murder
11/26/1861	James Miller (CSA)	Winchester	Insubordination
12/ /1861	Negro Nelson	Appomattox	Murder
12/11/1861	Dennis Corcoran (CSA)	Centreville	Insubordination
12/11/1861	Michael O'Brien (CSA)	Centreville	Insubordination
03/28/1862	Negro Isaac	Orange	Murder
04/18/1862	Negro Ben	Amherst	Rape
05/01/1862	Timothy Webster	Henrico	Espionage
05/23/1862	Negress Clara Ann	Henrico	Murder
06/13/1862	John McMahon (USA)	Fort Wool	Murder
06/20/1862	John Buck	Lunenburg	Aggravated Assault
07/15/1862	Negro John	Chesterfield	Rape
07/15/1862	Negro Martin	Chesterfield	Rape
07/26/1862	Negro Addison	Dinwiddie	Aggravated Assault
08/12/1862	Martin Hogan (CSA)	Henrico	Army Desertion
08/19/1862	John Layman (CSA)	Mt. Pisgah Ch.	Army Desertion
08/19/1862	James Riddell (CSA)	Mt. Pisgah Ch.	Army Desertion
08/19/1862	John Rogers (CSA)	Mt. Pisgah Ch.	Army Desertion
08/21/1862	John Richardson	Henrico	Counterfeiting
08/22/1862	Charles Mason	Gordonsville	Espionage
09/12/1862	Negro Bibb	Sussex	Attempted Rape
09/12/1862	Negro Oscar	Botetourt	Murder
10/04/1862	John Kelleher (CSA)	Henrico	Army Desertion
10/04/1862	Patrick McGowan (CSA)	Henrico	Army Desertion
10/10/1862	Negro Johnson	Nottoway	Murder
11/04/1862	John Bowers (CSA)	Petersburg	Army Desertion
11/04/1862	James Cain (CSA)	Petersburg	Army Desertion
01/02/1863	Negro John	Henrico	Attempted Murder
01/09/1863	Negress Margaret	Henrico	Murder
01/16/1863	Negro Emanuel	Lunenburg	Rape
01/16/1863	George Todd (CSA)	Fredericksburg	Army Desertion
01/23/1863	Negro Jerry	Washington	Murder
01/23/1863	Negro Jim	Washington	Murder
01/23/1863	Frederick Letz (USA)	Fort Wool	Army Desertion
01/30/1863	John Mulligan (CSA)	Henrico	Army Desertion
02/ /1863	Negress Mary Jane	Hanover	Aggravated Assault
02/21/1863	James Broderick (CSA)	Henrico	Army Desertion
02/23/1863	William Tomlin (CSA)	Fredericksburg	Army Desertion
02/28/1863	William Pace	Guinea Depot	Espionage
03/02/1863	Charles Clark (USA)	Yorktown	Murder
03/02/1863	William Dormady (USA)	Yorktown	Murder
04/ /1863	Negro Herod	Bedford	Murder
04/10/1863	Alfonso C. Webster	Henrico	Espionage
05/ /1863	Unnamed Soldier (CSA)	Petersburg	Army Desertion
05/15/1863	Orris Brown	Southampton	Arson

Date of Execution	Name of Offender	Venue	Specific Felony
05/22/1863	Negro Morgan	Petersburg	Arson
05/29/1863	Negro Richard	Henrico	Aggravated Assault
06/12/1863	John P. Woods (USA)	Falmouth	Army Desertion
06/15/1863	Negress Alsie	Craig	Attempted Murder
06/19/1863	William Grover (USA)	Leesburg	Army Desertion
06/19/1863	Christopher Krubert (USA)	Leesburg	Army Desertion
06/19/1863	William McKee (USA)	Leesburg	Army Desertion
06/20/1863	Charles Kelley (CSA)	Henrico	Army Desertion
06/26/1863	Negro Henry	Patrick	Burglary
07/01/1863	Negro Armistead	Amherst	Murder
07/01/1863	Negress Bet	Amherst	Murder
07/01/1863	Negro George	Amherst	Murder
07/01/1863	Negress Jane	Amherst	Murder
07/01/1863	Negress Sarah	Amherst	Murder
07/01/1863	Negro Seaton	Amherst	Murder
07/31/1863	Negro Miles	Amelia	Attempted Murder
08/01/1863	Bradford Butler (USA)	Warrenton	Army Desertion
08/14/1863	Thomas Jewett (USA)	New Baltimore	Army Desertion
08/14/1863	James Stover	Roanoke	Murder
08/21/1863	Jesse Mayberry (USA)	Morrisville	Army Desertion
08/28/1863	William Hill (USA)	Morrisville	Army Desertion
08/28/1863	John Smith (USA)	Morrisville	Army Desertion
08/29/1863	John Folancy (USA)	Beverly Ford	Army Desertion
08/29/1863	George Kuhne (USA)	Beverly Ford	Army Desertion
08/29/1863	Emil Lai (USA)	Beverly Ford	Army Desertion
08/29/1863	John Rionese (USA)	Beverly Ford	Army Desertion
08/29/1863	Charles Walter (USA)	Beverly Ford	Army Desertion
09/05/1863	William Barefoot (CSA)	Orange C.H.	Army Desertion
09/05/1863	Francis Benson (CSA)	Orange C.H.	Army Desertion
09/05/1863	John Bledsoe (CSA)	Orange C.H.	Army Desertion
09/05/1863	Benjamin Bunn (CSA)	Orange C.H.	Army Desertion
09/05/1863	Dorsey Bunn (CSA)	Orange C.H.	Army Desertion
09/05/1863	Duncan Clarke (CSA)	Orange C.H.	Army Desertion
09/05/1863	James Ellis (CSA)	Orange C.H.	Army Desertion
09/05/1863	John Futch (CSA)	Orange C.H.	Army Desertion
09/05/1863	William Kelly (CSA)	Orange C.H.	Army Desertion
09/05/1863	Kearney Privett (CSA)	Orange C.H.	Army Desertion
09/05/1863	John Rainer (CSA)	Orange C.H.	Army Desertion
09/11/1863	Negro Charles	Powhatan	Murder
09/11/1863	Negro Jacques	Powhatan	Murder
09/11/1863	Negro Joe	Powhatan	Murder
09/11/1863	Negro Landon	Powhatan	Murder
09/18/1863	John Barnett (USA)	Portsmouth	Highway Robbery
09/18/1863	Edward Elliott (USA)	Brandy Station	Army Desertion
09/18/1863	Albert Jones (USA)	Culpeper C.H.	Army Desertion
09/18/1863	George Layton (USA)	Brandy Station	Army Desertion
09/18/1863	William Smith (USA)	Culpeper C.H.	Army Desertion
09/18/1863	Cornelius Treece (USA)	Culpeper C.H.	Army Desertion
09/18/1863	George Vann (USA)	Culpeper C.H.	Army Desertion

Date of Execution	Name of Offender	Venue	Specific Felony
09/18/1863	Jacob Wierdain (USA)	Culpeper C.H.	Army Desertion
09/25/1863	Spencer Kellogg (CSA)	Henrico	Army Desertion
09/25/1863	Daniel Sullivan (USA)	Brandy Station	Army Desertion
09/25/1863	John Timlin (USA)	Brandy Station	Army Desertion
09/25/1863	Charles Williams (USA)	Brandy Station	Army Desertion
10/02/1863	Adam Smalz (USA)	Culpeper C.H.	Army Desertion
10/02/1863	William Smith (USA)	Culpeper C.H.	Army Desertion
10/09/1863	Joseph Connelly (USA)	Brandy Station	Army Desertion
10/16/1863	Henry Beardsley (USA)	Fairfax C.H.	Army Desertion
10/16/1863	James Haley (USA)	Fairfax C.H.	Army Desertion
10/23/1863	David Wright	Norfolk	Murder
10/30/1863	John Roberts (USA)	Bank's Ford	Army Desertion
11/09/1863	Mitchell Vandall (USA)	Portsmouth	Army Desertion
11/09/1863	Francis Wales (USA)	Portsmouth	Army Desertion
11/10/1863	Joseph Adams (CSA)	Spotsylvania	Army Desertion
12/04/1863	Cyrus Hunter (USA)	Brandy Station	Army Desertion
12/18/1863	Winslow Allen (USA)	Brandy Station	Army Desertion
12/18/1863	George Blowers (USA)	Brandy Station	Army Desertion
12/18/1863	John McMann (USA)	Brandy Station	Army Desertion
12/18/1863	John Tague (USA)	Brandy Station	Army Desertion
12/18/1863	William DeVoe (USA)	Stevensburg	Army Desertion
01/09/1864	J. B. Martin (CSA)	Louisa C.H.	Army Desertion
02/07/1864	William Ormsley (USA)	Lewensville	Army Desertion
02/19/1864	Spencer Deaton (CSA)	Henrico	Army Desertion
03/07/1864	William Abraham	Yorktown	Espionage
03/11/1864	Negress Emma	Botetourt	Poisoning
04/15/1864	John Eagan (USA)	Yorktown	Army Desertion
04/15/1864	Henry Holt (USA)	Yorktown	Army Desertion
04/25/1864	Thomas Dawson (USA)	Morrisville	Army Desertion
04/28/1864	Jacob Morgan (USA)	Norfolk	Army Desertion
04/29/1864	Owen McDonough (USA)	Williamsburg	Army Desertion
04/29/1864	James Scott (USA)	Williamsburg	Army Desertion
04/29/1864	John Thompson (USA)	Alexandria	Army Desertion
05/21/1864	John Starbird (USA)	Spotsylvania	Army Desertion
06/13/1864	David Creigh	Lexington	Espionage
06/20/1864	William Johnson (USA)	Near Petersburg	Rape
07/15/1864	Daniel Geary (USA)	Near Petersburg	Rape
07/15/1864	Ransom Gordon (USA)	Near Petersburg	Rape
08/05/1864	Isaac Whitlow (USA)	Monacacy	Army Desertion
08/08/1864	Frank McElhenny (USA)	Deep Bottom	Army Desertion
08/26/1864	Negro Fred	Mecklenburg	Conspiracy to Rebel
09/02/1864	Negro Bob	Nottoway	Conspiracy to Rebel
09/02/1864	Seldon Chandler (USA)	Near Petersburg	Army Desertion
09/16/1864	Samuel Downing (USA)	Alexandria	Army Desertion
09/20/1864	John Sweeney (USA)	Fort Hughes	Army Desertion
09/23/1864	Negress Agnes	Dinwiddie	Aggravated Burglary
10/07/1864	Negro Henry	Henrico	Arson and Conspiracy
10/14/1864	Charles Merling (USA)	Hancock Station	Army Desertion
10/21/1864	Negro Ben	Henrico	Burglary

Date of Execution	Name of Offender	Venue	Specific Felony
10/21/1864	Negro William	Henrico	Burglary
10/28/1864	John Velon (USA)	Near Petersburg	Army Desertion
10/31/1864	Henry Howell (CSA)	Henrico	Army Desertion
12/10/1864	Edward Rowe (USA)	Near Petersburg	Army Desertion
12/10/1864	Daniel Smith (USA)	Near Petersburg	Army Desertion
12/16/1864	William Kane (USA)	Near Petersburg	Army Desertion
12/16/1864	Christopher Suhr (USA)	Near Petersburg	Army Desertion
12/16/1864	John Thompson (USA)	Near Petersburg	Army Desertion
12/21/1864	Thomas Dix (USA)	City Point	Army Desertion
12/21/1864	John Hall (USA)	City Point	Murder
12/21/1864	Henry McCurdy (USA)	City Point	Army Desertion
12/21/1864	John Smith (USA)	City Point	Army Desertion
12/21/1864	James Thompson (USA)	City Point	Army Desertion
12/22/1864	William Smith (USA)	Portsmouth	Army Desertion
12/23/1864	George Bradley (USA)	Fort Wheaton	Army Desertion
12/23/1864	John Dixon (USA)	Near Petersburg	Army Desertion
12/23/1864	James Lynch (USA)	Fort Wheaton	Army Desertion
12/23/1864	William Miller (USA)	Fort Wheaton	Army Desertion
12/26/1864	James Brown (USA)	Near Richmond	Army Desertion
12/30/1864	Michael Genan (USA)	Near Petersburg	Army Desertion
12/30/1864	Negro Nat	Pittsylvania	Rape
01/03/1865	John Foster (USA)	City Point	Army Desertion
01/03/1865	William Johnson (USA)	City Point	Aiding Desertion
01/06/1865	John Benson (USA)	Near Petersburg	Army Desertion
01/06/1865	Peter Cox (USA)	Near Petersburg	Army Desertion
01/06/1865	Waterman Thornton (USA)	Near Petersburg	Army Desertion
01/06/1865	Michael Wert (USA)	Near Petersburg	Army Desertion
01/06/1865	Negro Tom	Bedford	Attempted Murder
01/06/1865	Charles King	Winchester	Espionage
01/06/1865	Henry Regley	Winchester	Espionage
01/07/1865	James Collins (USA)	Ft. Harrison	Army Desertion
01/07/1865	William Dix (USA)	Ft. Harrison	Army Desertion
01/24/1865	Bill Simms	Washington	Not Specified
01/27/1865	Newell Root (USA)	City Point	Army Desertion
02/09/1865	Joseph Sharp (USA)	City Point	Army Desertion
02/10/1865	Negro Bob	Nottoway	Conspiracy to Rebel
02/12/1865	James L. Hicks (USA)	City Point	Army Desertion
02/12/1865	Samuel Clement (USA)	City Point	Army Desertion and Cowardice
02/17/1865	John Hoeffer (USA)	Near Richmond	Army Desertion
02/17/1865	Michael Landy (USA)	Near Richmond	Army Desertion
02/18/1865	John Brown III (USA)	Near Richmond	Army Desertion
02/18/1865	Thomas Jones (USA)	Near Richmond	Army Desertion
02/25/1865	John Parker (USA)	Near Richmond	Army Desertion
03/10/1865	William Griffin (USA)	City Point	Army Desertion
03/10/1865	William Jackson (USA)	Near Richmond	Army Desertion
03/10/1865	James Kelly (USA)	Near Petersburg	Army Desertion
03/10/1865	John Mahoney (USA)	Near Richmond	Army Desertion
03/10/1865	John Nicholas (USA)	Near Petersburg	Army Desertion

Date of Execution	Name of Offender	Venue	Specific Felony
03/16/1865	William Cooper (USA)	Near Richmond	Army Desertion
03/17/1865	Negro Claiborne	Franklin	Rape
03/18/1865	Joseph Johnson (USA)	Alexandria	Army Desertion
03/18/1865	John Smith (USA)	Near Petersburg	Army Desertion
03/24/1865	Negro Gilley	Petersburg	Attempted Rape
03/26/1865	Frederick Brandt (USA)	Near Richmond	Army Desertion
03/26/1865	James Weaver (USA)	City Point	Army Desertion
03/27/1865	Jeremiah Roberts (USA)	City Point	Army Desertion
03/31/1865	Newell Jangrow (USA)	Near Petersburg	Army Desertion
03/31/1865	Anthony Raymond (USA)	Near Petersburg	Army Desertion
04/20/1865	Samuel Mapp (USA)	City Point	Mutiny
04/21/1865	Negro Marcellus	Lynchburg	Burglary
04/21/1865	Negro Sam	Lynchburg	Burglary
05/26/1865	William Cowell (USA)	City Point	Murder
07/28/1865	William Wilson (USA)	Alexandria	Army Desertion
10/13/1865	John Sheppard (USA)	Ft. Monroe	Murder

West Virginia

(R) = Recidivist (had been sentenced to death on a prior occasion, obtained clemency and then gone on to offend anew)

Date of Execution	Name of Offender	Venue	Specific Felony
08/02/1783	Negro Jem	Greenbrier	Murder
——1784	Slave (Hamilton)	Greenbrier	Not Specified
06/19/1797	Charles Donaldson	Monongalia	Murder
09/01/1798	Negress Milly	Monongalia	Arson
04/05/1799	Negro Aaron	Hampshire	Horse Stealing
07/12/1799	Jerry Hamilton (R)	Hardy	Rape
01/07/1803	Jack Neal	Kanawha	Murder
08/19/1803	Negro James	Jefferson	Rape
12/17/1803	Negro Abram	Kanawha	Murder
12/17/1803	Negro Isaac	Kanawha	Murder
07/05/1805	Negro Jerry	Berkeley	Armed Robbery
07/05/1805	Negro John	Berkeley	Armed Robbery
06/30/1806	Abel Clemmons	Monongalia	Murder
03/19/1811	Negro Moses	Monroe	Murder
06/11/1813	Thomas Queen	Harrison	Murder
11/18/1814	Jane Tygart	Monroe	Mariticide
02/12/1818	Negro Jim	Hampshire	Highway Robbery
11/17/1820	Negro Ellis	Tyler	Murder
01/05/1821	Negro Nathan	Tyler	Murder
12/26/1822	Negro Jack	Wood	Child Molestation
03/13/1824	Negro Tom	Greenbrier	Murder
05/02/1825	Negress Beck	Monroe	Murder
08/17/1827	Negro Joshua	Monongalia	Rape
08/27/1830	Ebenezer Cox	Kanawha	Murder

Date of Execution	Name of Offender	Venue	Specific Felony
09/28/1832	Negress Lucy	Tyler	Murder
07/22/1836	Thomas Wintringer	Ohio	Murder
09/09/1836	Negro Ned	Preston	Murder
09/23/1836	Boon Long	Ohio	Murder
01/12/1838	Negro Harry	Hampshire	Rape
02/26/1841	Negro John	Berkeley	Murder
12/18/1846	William Hudson	Pendleton	Murder
02/18/1848	Negro Bill	Logan	Murder
09/01/1848	Michael Whalen	Ohio	Murder
07/12/1850	Charles Cook Green	Jackson	Murder
08/30/1850	Lewis Uel	Kanawha	Rape
05/20/1853	Negro George	Jefferson	Attempted Murder
10/28/1853	Thomas Board	Barbour	Murder
11/25/1853	John McMahon	Mason	Murder
01/06/1854	Negro Charles	Jefferson	Attempted Rape
09/03/1858	John Burns	Ohio	Murder
09/17/1858	Preston Turley	Kanawha	Murder
10/01/1858	Negro William	Gilmer	Murder
12/02/1859	John Brown	Jefferson	Sedition
12/16/1859	John Cook	Jefferson	Sedition
12/16/1859	John Copeland	Jefferson	Sedition
12/16/1859	Edwin Coppie	Jefferson	Sedition
12/16/1859	Shields Green	Jefferson	Sedition
03/16/1860	Albert Hazlett	Jefferson	Sedition
03/16/1860	Aaron Stephens	Jefferson	Sedition
06/29/1860	Nathaniel Harten	Marshall	Murder
06/ /1861	Negro Reuben	Greenbrier	Conspiracy to Rebel
06/21/1861	Ezra Mason	Morgan	Murder
12/20/1861	Richard Gatewood (USA)	Charleston	Army Desertion
05/09/1862	Henry Kuhl	Braxton	Murder
03/13/1863	Richard Poole	Ohio	Murder
11/27/1863	Philip Raber (USA)	Fayetteville	Army Desertion
01/19/1864	John Marcum (USA)	Gauley Bridge	Murder
11/11/1864	Confederate Guerrilla	Charleston	Marauding
12/02/1864	William Loge (USA)	Harpers Ferry	Murder
03/03/1865	Frederick Murphy (USA)	Harpers Ferry	Army Desertion

Index

www.ingramcontent.com/pod-product-compliance
Ingram Content Group UK Ltd.
Pitfield, Milton Keynes, MK11 3LW, UK
UKHW041835100926
8556IPUK00018B/972

9 780786 495405